Praise for *Fan in Chief*

"No modern president has used sports as a political metaphor so effectively as Richard Nixon. And few moments match the Nixon presidency as a time when issues like race, players' rights, and feminism muscled their way onto the sports pages. Sarantakes breaks fresh ground in this intriguing study of how an awkward president employed his genuine love for sporting competition to demonstrate to his 'great silent majority' that he shared their values."

John A. Farrell, author of *Richard Nixon: The Life*

"Just when it appeared that the cottage industry that revolves around Richard Nixon and historians had run its course, Sarantakes has produced a remarkable and original book about one of our most controversial presidents. In his fair-minded and very well-researched study, the author not only skillfully explores the relationship between the president and sports but also demonstrates the powerful connection between sports and politics, a connection virtually invented by the Nixon administration."

Melvin Small, author of *The Presidency of Richard Nixon*

"In *Fan in Chief*, Nicholas Evan Sarantakes presents the Richard Nixon we never knew. Through his love of sports like baseball and football, we see how ordinary Nixon was—even as president of the United States. The book is packed with names fans will recognize, and Sarantakes shows us how a shared love of sports is a universal language that brings people together."

Luke A. Nichter, coauthor of *The Nixon Tapes: 1973*

"Sarantakes takes a serious look at President Richard Nixon's employment of sport for his political purposes and demonstrates that Nixon attempted to utilize the attributes of sport such as hard work, personal resiliency, and a commitment to following the rules and norms of society as a means to shape American core values and beliefs, epitomize democratic ideals, and promote a sense of community. Nixon believed that youthful voters primarily looked to the White House to define American identity rather than a set of particular policies."

Steven A. Riess, Bernard Brommel Distinguished Research Professor Emeritus, Northeastern Illinois University, and author of *City Games: The Evolution of American Urban Society and the Rise of Sports*

"Richard Nixon loved politics, and he loved sports. In this excellent book, Nicholas Sarantakes shows how the president fused these passions to win favorable publicity and promote his conception of traditional American values. Embedding his narrative in great events and forgotten games, Sarantakes shows us a Nixon we have never seen before."

Allen Matusow, author of *Nixon's Economy: Booms, Busts, Dollars, and Votes*

Fan in Chief

Fan in Chief

RICHARD NIXON AND AMERICAN SPORTS, 1969–1974

Nicholas Evan Sarantakes

University Press of Kansas

Published by the University Press of Kansas (Lawrence, Kansas 66045), which was organized by the Kansas Board of Regents and is operated and funded by Emporia State University, Fort Hays State University, Kansas State University, Pittsburg State University, the University of Kansas, and Wichita State University

Library of Congress Cataloging-in-Publication Data

Names: Sarantakes, Nicholas Evan, 1966– author.
Title: Fan in chief : Richard Nixon and American sports, 1969–1974 / Nicholas Evan Sarantakes.
Description: Lawrence, Kansas : University Press of Kansas, [2019] | Includes bibliographical references and index.
Identifiers: LCCN 2019006961
ISBN 9780700628520 (cloth : alk. paper)
ISBN 9780700628537 (pbk. : alk. paper)
ISBN 9780700628544 (ebook)
Subjects: LCSH: Nixon, Richard M. (Richard Milhous), 1913–1994—Political and social views. | Sports—Political aspects—United States—History—20th century. | Sports and state—United States—History—20th century. | Sports spectators—United States—Biography. | Presidents—United States—Biography. | United States—Politics and government—1969–1974.
Classification: LCC E856 .S27 2019 | DDC 973.924092—dc23
LC record available at https://lccn.loc.gov/2019006961.

British Library Cataloguing-in-Publication Data is available.

Printed in the United States of America
10 9 8 7 6 5 4 3 2 1

The paper used in this publication is recycled and contains 30 percent postconsumer waste. It is acid free and meets the minimum requirements of the American National Standard for Permanence of Paper for Printed Library Materials Z39.48-1992.

For my sister Katie

CONTENTS

Acknowledgments, *ix*

List of Abbreviations, *xiii*

Introduction, *1*

1 Welcome to Washington, *4*

2 The Second Centennial: The Texas-Arkansas Game and Other Football-Related Matters, *25*

3 The Olympics and the All-Star Game, *55*

4 The Midterm Elections of 1970, *75*

5 The Final Death of the Washington Senators, *109*

6 Of Redskins and Dolphins, *129*

7 The Election of 1972: The First Half, *148*

8 The Election of 1972: The Second Half, *165*

9 The Second Term, 1973–1974, *180*

Conclusion, *208*

Aftermath, *212*

Appendix A: Major League Baseball Centennial Greatest Players, *223*

Appendix B: US Supreme Court List of Greatest Players in Baseball History, *225*

Appendix C: Richard Nixon's 1972 Historic Baseball All-Star Selections, *227*

Appendix D: Richard Nixon's 1992 Historic Baseball All-Star Selections, *229*

Appendix E: Nixon and Sports Time Line, *231*

Notes, *251*

Bibliographic Essay, *317*

Sources, *323*

Index, *337*

A photo gallery follows page 96.

ACKNOWLEDGMENTS

This book has been a long time in the making. I started the research for this project in 1995, while I was doing the research for my dissertation. My plan was to put together an article on Nixon's list of the greatest baseball players of all time. I wrote that article, an early version of chapter 6, in 1996 before I started composition on my dissertation, and it was eventually published as "Richard Nixon, Sportswriter: The President, His Historical All-Star Baseball Team, and the Election of 1972" in the *Journal of Sport History* 24, no. 2 (Summer 1997): 192–202. In a favorable critique of my effort, one of the anonymous reviewers noted that Nixon had made other forays into the sporting world and that I should mention those in my article. Awarding the college football national championship in college football to the University of Texas was one of the incidents that this individual mentioned. Since I was living in Austin, Texas, at the time, that comment got me thinking about another article about Nixon and the Longhorns.

While I was doing my research, I realized there was enough material in the archives to sustain an entire monograph on Nixon and sports. I made the decision to move forward on that book during the summer of 1997. In the years since, I have been extremely busy: moving seven times, starting a new job six times, and trying to get my first book published and then writing four more.

I did the bulk of the research and writing for this book while I was at Texas A&M University–Commerce, where I had a heavy teaching load and was trying to adjust to being on faculty. But I always managed to get a little bit of work done on my Nixon project here and there when I had a free hour or two. I called it "sip research." Lyndon Johnson once said you could make Congress do a lot or a little if you make it sip or guzzle. Little by little, bit by bit, I moved forward on this project. When I was done with the research, I managed to find an hour or an hour and a half in between classes and committee assignments to write a page a day. After a month, I had a chapter and at the end of a semester I had the first draft finished. This approach was quite different than the process I took in writing my dissertation, where I just set aside ten months to organize my research and write. I enjoyed this project a lot. It was fun, no doubt because I took Nixon in moderate amounts.

A number of friends helped me in this project. Mike Burns and Mitch Lerner read earlier, smaller versions of this work. Mitch also took a critical look at my outline. In addition to providing a critical review of the text, Mike spent a lot of time helping me design and create a website about Nixon and sports. Both read an earlier draft of the entire book and gave me a good deal of constructive criticism in matters of not only prose, but also analysis. They caught many, many mistakes, and I am deeply grateful they took the time to evaluate the manuscript with evident care. Later, Mitch wrote a letter of recommendation in support of my application to take part in a National Endowment for the Humanities Summer Seminar on sport history.

During a research trip to the Lyndon Johnson Presidential Library on another project, archivist Mike Parrish, who remembered watching the 1969 Texas-Arkansas game on television, told me about J. Neal Blanton's *Game of the Century* (1970). I probably never would have found this informative book without his help. In 1998 when I was conducting my research at the National Archives, Marc Selverstone, then of Ohio University, convinced me to make some photocopies of Nixon's personal notes on his 1972 baseball team. I was planning to ignore these documents. I had already had an article published on this episode, and believed it could stand as it was. What need did I have for these documents? I listened to Marc and the documents became helpful as I converted my article into a chapter. At a National Endowment for the Humanities Summer Seminar on sport history, I met many scholars interested in sport, and many of them helped with this project. Stephen A. Riess and Patrick Miller ran the seminar in impressive fashion and gave me good feedback on early drafts of the manuscript. Mike Ezra, then of the University of Kansas, also gave me feedback. Kurt Kemper, now of Dakota State University, shared some of his research and directed me to an important book that helped explain much of the events surrounding the rise and fall of the Denver Winter Olympics. One of the major events of that seminar was a presentation about our research, and many of the social historians in the room did not really like my political approach and were a bit . . . well . . . hostile. This exchange was polite, but it tested me and I appreciated it, because it really helped me hone my arguments. Lori Cox Han, a political scientist specializing on the presidency, helped me significantly with pointers on the relevant literature on voter behavior. I also want to thank my research assistant Katerine Mary Hanna of the University of Memphis for finding material for me that I could not get to on my own.

While I was working on this book, a number of people expressed real interest in and fascination with this project, which went far beyond a polite "That's nice." I think that reaction says more about Nixon than about my skill as a storyteller. Three of these conversations were of particular importance in helping me sharpen my thinking about Richard Nixon and sports. In early 1999, I visited my sister in Dallas. At the time, she lived about a block and a half from Southern Methodist University. After seeing her, I made an unannounced visit to the history department and said hello to Tom Knock, the diplomatic historian at SMU. At the time, he was working on a biography of Nixon's opponent in the 1972 presidential election, Senator George McGovern. Over lunch we talked about diplomatic history, sports, and Nixon. Later that year at a diplomatic history conference at the University of California, Santa Barbara, I had two long conversations with retired television reporter Sander Vanocur, who was on the infamous enemies list, and historian Chester Patch, who was at work on *The Presidency of Ronald Reagan* for the University Press of Kansas presidency series. If memory serves me, both initiated our conversations and were quite supportive of my effort. I learned a lot about Nixon and presidential history that weekend. All three talks helped shape my thoughts as I wrote chapter 1. H. W. Brands, biographer of several presidents, gave me sound advice along the way about doing presidential history. My brother, Andy Sarantakes, made some useful comments that helped me return to this project and get it to a publisher after it had dormant for several years, and even then it took a long time. Meredith Hindley and Siva Vaidhyanathan listened to me tell stories about Nixon and offered encouragement along the way that really helped.

I also need to thank two scholars who invested a number of years in the Nixon tapes. Both Luke Nichter and Rick Moss have written interesting books that take full advantage of the tapes. Moss spent a year teaching with me in the Strategy & Policy Department at the US Naval War College. Both he and Nichter had spent several years working to create finding aids for the tapes as part of their work in the Office of the Historian at the Department of State for the documentary publication series *Foreign Relations of the United*

States. In addition to this work, they created the NixonTapes.org website, where all the tapes are available for anyone to listen to them. Moss convinced me that I should use the tapes before I published my book. I did not want to do that; I had tried to use them before and became quite frustrated, but something in the back of my head told me he was right. I knew of historians who had written on Lyndon Johnson and had ignored the recordings of his phone conversations to their disadvantage. Rick guided me through the use of the finding aid—which is rather complex—and showed me where to find the recordings on the websites of either NixonTapes.org or the Nixon Library. I spent about six weeks listening and transcribing. Because of Nichter and Moss I did all of this research from the confines of my office. No travel required. That was a major advantage for which I am grateful.

I had significant institutional support. A talk I gave to the Texas A&M University–Commerce honors colloquium in 1998 helped me sharpen my thinking on the issues I wanted to explore in this undertaking. The University Research Committee at A&M–Commerce provided me with an Organized Research Grant that underwrote three weeks of research in the summer of 1998 at the National Archives and the Library of Congress.

This last line might sound cliché, but it is also extremely accurate—the assistance that all these good people rendered to me helped make this a better book, but as the author I alone must take responsibility for any flaws that remain.

NEΣ
Winter 2019
Los Angeles, California
Austin, Texas
Commerce, Texas
Chicago, Illinois
Ann Arbor, Michigan
Newport, Rhode Island
Portsmouth, Rhode Island
Riverside, Rhode Island

ABBREVIATIONS

The following terms are used in the text and notes of this work.

1B	First Base
2B	Second Base
3B	Third Base
AAU	Amateur Athletic Union
ABA	American Basketball Association
ABC	American Broadcasting Company
AFC	American Football Conference
AFL	American Football League
AL	American League
AP	Associated Press
C	Catcher
CCF	Citizens for Colorado's Future
CIA	Central Intelligence Agency
DH	Designated Hitter
DNC	Democratic National Committee
DOC	Denver Olympic Committee
DOOC	Denver Olympic Organizing Committee
ed	Editor
ESPN	Entertainment Sports Programming Network
FBI	Federal Bureau of Investigations
GI	Government Issue (nickname for US soldiers)
GOP	Grand Old Party (Republicans)
IF	Infielder
IOC	International Olympic Committee
MC	Master of Ceremonies
MVP	Most Valuable Player
NACP	National Archives, College Park, Maryland
NALB	National Archives Los Angeles Branch, Laguna Niguel, California
NASA	National Aeronautics and Space Administration
NBA	National Basketball Association

NBC	National Broadcasting Company
NCAA	National Collegiate Athletic Association
NFC	National Football Conference
NFL	National Football League
NL	National League
NPP	Nixon Presidential Project
NU	University of Nebraska
OF	Outfielder
OSU	Oklahoma State University
P	Pitcher
P	President (when in Haldeman's diary)
POW	Prisoner of War
PPP	*Public Papers of the Presidents of the United States*
PR	Public Relations
RFK	Robert F. Kennedy
RN	Richard Nixon
R.P.M.	Rotations per Minute
SMU	Southern Methodist University
SS	Shortstop
T.V.	Television
UCLA	University of California, Los Angeles
UPI	United Press International
USC	University of Southern California
USOC	United States Olympic Committee
USS	United States Ship
USSR	Union of Soviet Socialist Republics
VIP	Very Important Person
vol.	Volume
vols.	Volumes

Fan in Chief

Introduction

Richard Nixon went home one last time.

April 27, 1994, was a temperate day in Yorba Linda, California, and the United States buried the thirty-seventh president a few feet from the house where he was born. Nixon had come full circle. The outpouring of sympathy from the American public the week before surprised both Nixon's friends and foes. Long lines of people waited outside his presidential museum to pay their respects while his body lay in state the day before the funeral. At 1 a.m., despite a rainstorm, the wait was between five and seven hours long.[1]

The next day, Nixon biographer Stephen E. Ambrose was sitting in an ABC News television booth as the network covered the first presidential funeral in over twenty years, and was simply dumbfounded at what he had seen and was seeing. "I'm struck by—I think every American over 30 years old is astonished at this outpouring of affection and emotion for Richard Nixon," Ambrose remarked during the telecast. "I just don't understand how this happened."[2]

Why did the American people despise and love Richard Milhous Nixon?

The answer to the first half of this question is so obvious that it deserves no serious exploration. Throughout the course of his career, Nixon used divisive, polarizing tactics that seemed to indicate that he had little regard for ethical considerations. While a resident of the White House he showed even less respect for the laws he had sworn to uphold, which led directly to his downfall. The purpose of this book, however, is not to make or repeat charges against Nixon. Others have already done so elsewhere.[3] Nixon's legacy will never escape the stain of Watergate. Suffice it to say that the American people, even those who had supported him, were outraged and offended when presented with evidence of his wrongdoing in his own voice. Such developments and reactions, however reasonable and understandable, give the second half of the initial question even more value. Why did the American people love Richard Nixon? It is the mission of this book to try and provide an answer.[4]

Why sports and Nixon? The answer to that question is simple. The only two areas of popular culture that Nixon really enjoyed were film and sports.[5] Nixon was not particularly interested in television. "The only thing I really like on television is sports," he explained.[6] Many historians have made note of Nixon's love of sport. In his Nixon biography, Ambrose observes, "Batting averages, yards gained per carry, earned run averages, pass completion percentage, the whole never-ending stream of numbers was to Nixon what the Western novels were to Eisenhower, the perfect relaxation." Ambrose is correct, but there is more to the story. Sports is central to understanding Nixon. He opened up when he was in the sports world. What follows is an in-depth exploration that tells much about the man and his times.[7] To be blunt, the main argument of this account is that Nixon used sport as a way for the American people to understand him through his values and theirs.

On the other hand, many observers have argued that the people loved Nixon because of his policies. The public reaction after his death certainly supports that view. In April of 1994 average citizens called talk shows and told reporters that he was a great man, paying tribute to his achievements mainly in the area of foreign affairs. There is, however, an impressive amount of political science literature that makes it clear that voting behavior is not based simply on policies. These assessments make sense. How many Americans could explain the revisions to copyright law that the Nixon administration sponsored, or its policies toward Native Americans, or its actions on wetlands? The answer: few. Voting has a lot to do with factors such as partisan affiliation and political identification.[8] This account will offer a different take. Voting and the love or hate of Nixon was a product of—in order of importance—policy, partisanship, and personality.

Sports is a helpful tool in this last category. Nixon exposed core elements of his personality, character, and values when he was in the world of sports.

Nixon and sports is the story of political theater, but the president was a real fan, and nothing about his interest was manufactured. He used various games as a recreational pastime and even occasionally provided leadership in social, cultural, and domestic policy through this venue. Put another way, Nixon and sports is the story of both personality and politics.

This story of Richard Milhous Nixon that follows will culminate with the destruction of Watergate, as it must, but before that disaster it will go places not normally associated with the thirty-seventh president: the Super Bowl, the World Series, and the Kentucky Derby. The account that follows is the story of politics and the American zest for athletic glory. This tale begins with the arrival in Washington of three men in three different professions: Vincent T. Lombardi, Ted Williams, and Richard M. Nixon.

1

Welcome to Washington

The early months of 1969 were a period of dramatic transition in Washington, DC. On January 20, Richard Milhous Nixon became the president of the United States, and a Republican administration replaced the Democrats after eight years out of office. Less than a month into the new administration, the two major Washington sports teams made major coaching changes designed to end their shared perennial status as cellar dwellers and made Washington an exciting sports town for the rest of the year.

The Redskins went first. On Thursday, February 6, Vince Lombardi, the former Green Bay Packers coach who had won five NFL titles while in Wisconsin, accepted an offer to become the new executive vice president and head coach. Edward Bennett Williams, the controlling partner of the Redskins and an extremely influential figure in the District, agreed to give Lombardi authority over all major aspects of team operations. *Washington Post* sports columnist Shirley Povich called the press conference to announce the selection of the new coach "Washington's greatest transfer of power since Jan. 20."[1]

Then, only a week later, the Washington Senators made their own dramatic move. On February 14, the team revealed that Ted Williams, the legendary Boston Red Sox outfielder, had agreed to end his retirement from professional baseball and become the manager of the club.[2]

Williams, who had once said "you couldn't pay me enough to manage," was quite direct at the time and later about why he accepted the job: "I took this flight from sanity for two reasons: the price was right (there's a price for everything, and I was handed a total package worth more than $1.5 million), and the man who offered it was the smartest guy I ever met." The new team owner, Bob Short, had a slightly different take. Although he was a Democrat—he had been the treasurer for Hubert Humphrey's campaign in 1968—he was willing to use Nixon to appeal to the ball player's conservative leanings. Williams said "no" initially. "So then I told him I thought he had a responsibility toward the game, toward the country, toward Nixon, and the whole bunch of bull you throw into a business presentation."[3]

Williams also admitted that he wanted a chance to put some of his baseball theories into practice and had tired of the outdoor life of hunting and fishing that he had led for the past eight years. What made the arrival of Williams in Washington all the more amazing was his well-known contempt for coaching. "Managing *is* essentially a loser's job, and managers are about the most expendable pieces of furniture on earth," he remarked. In his memoirs, though, he conceded that he enjoyed his new job. "I admit, too, at this late date, that my first year on the job was fun—and sometimes funny."[4]

Nixon himself was excited that Williams took the job. "You have my warmest congratulations on your appointment," he wrote. "It's good to know that we share the same goal: to make Washington a first place city."[5]

The dramatic arrival in the District over the course of a month of three men who admired and respected one another registered with one sports columnist. "This is a crazy, mixed up business for sports writers," Bob Addie of the *Washington Post* wrote. "You could have had a great parlay a year ago if you had bet that Richard Nixon, Vince Lombardi, and Ted Williams all would be trying to improve Washington (in their various capacities) by working here at the same time."[6]

These coaching changes came during a period of significant transformation in the world of sports. During the 1960s baseball had slipped from its position as the national pastime. The sport was suffering from a number of self-inflicted wounds, and football had profited from these miscues. The relocation of several baseball franchises to new cities, although profitable to the individual teams, hurt the entire sport and weakened its fan base. After the Braves moved from Boston to Milwaukee to Atlanta in a decade and a half, Eddie Mathews became the first player to compete for the same franchise in three different cities. Interleague trading also hurt support for the game. This new practice led to greater player movement, but made it difficult for fans to follow and see their favorite players. Rapid expansion also diluted the caliber of play on the diamond. Statistically, pitchers and better defensive play—due to the development of bigger and better gloves—dominated the sport. Offenses produced fewer and fewer hits and runs. In 1968, batting averages sank to record lows and pitching dominated in a way not seen since before World War I. As a result, attendance dropped at stadiums and television ratings declined. In 1968 baseball was drawing fewer people on a per-team basis than it had in 1948 despite a 25–30 percent increase in the population. The overall numbers looked quite good, but that was due mainly to the expansion into new cities that naturally resulted in a deceptively larger aggregate.[7]

The new popularity of professional football made these self-inflicted wounds even worse for baseball. The speed of the gridiron seemed to come across better on television than that of the diamond. Nixon understood that fact. "Baseball is great when you are there, but it's not worth a damn on TV. You sit around. It's slow," he observed. Taking advantage of the fact that football did better on television, a number of businessmen in 1960 created a new league, the American Football League (AFL), to challenge the National Football League (NFL). The AFL teams were located mainly in smaller, second-tier cities compared to the homes of NFL teams. Both the leagues had television contracts, and as a result, even teams in small municipalities had large followings across the country.[8]

During this difficult time, Major League Baseball (MLB) lacked strong leadership. Commissioner William Eckert, a former lieutenant general in the US Air Force, had no real authority in his job. Aware that weak leadership was a major problem, the team owners fired Eckert at the end of the 1968 season. Unable to agree on a new candidate, the owners asked Bowie Kuhn, a Wall Street lawyer who had done some legal work for the National League (NL), to serve as interim commissioner. Kuhn became commissioner in February 1969 and oversaw the institution of a number of reforms designed to help the sport recover some of its popularity. Both leagues agreed to establish divisions, creating more interest in pennant races and postseason play. The owners also agreed to decrease the size of the strike zone and lower the pitching mound, reducing the effectiveness of the curveball and slider. Even the construction of the ball itself changed. The purpose of these changes was to increase the scoring in games. "Hits, home runs, long smashes into the outfield are what the paying customers want," the editorial board of the *Washington Post* declared just before the start of the 1969 season.[9]

The centennial celebration of Major League Baseball was another reason for the revival of the sport. Since the Cincinnati Reds played their first games in 1869, Kuhn decided that this date was the official beginning of the major leagues and made 1969 the centennial season of professional baseball. Nixon, a real fan of the game, did his part to support this historical observation. In a statement on the one hundredth season, Nixon declared, "I know that professional baseball, with its unique combination of strategy and skill, power and speed, will continue to entertain millions as it goes into its second century."[10]

As the sport prepared to celebrate its anniversary, individuals associated with the sport suggested a role for Nixon. Every baseball season started with games in Cincinnati and Washington. This tradition honored the seniority of the Reds and allowed the president to perform his ceremonial function of throwing out the first pitch. Since 1969 was a unique year, the Cincinnati Reds suggested that Nixon toss out the first ball of the season in Ohio, rather than in Washington. While Nixon was receptive to this idea, his schedule prohibited such a trip.[11]

Instead of starting the centennial season where the professional version of the game started, Nixon performed the traditional role of the president in Washington. On April 8 a crowd of 45,113 filled Robert F. Kennedy Stadium to watch the Senators play the New York Yankees. As *New York Times* columnist Tom Wicker put it, "Stadium filled to capacity, which means rest of season will be downhill all the way." This gathering was the largest ever to assemble for an opening game in Washington, DC, but the people were there to see Williams, not Nixon. "For me," Kuhn stated, "Williams was the greatest personality in the game." In many ways, the Washington community saw him as a potential savior of the Senators. He received a loud ovation when he was introduced to the crowd. "It is joining hope with hallucination to expect the Senators to shift suddenly from losers to winners," the editors of the *Washington Post* declared, but "Ted Williams is here now. Though managers generally don't win ball games—base hits do—they are responsible for creating the mental conditions that make victory possible. Mr. Williams, despite his long sabbatical from the game, brings excitement back to Washington—as well as the baseball savvy that made him a great player."[12]

The president helped add to the sense that baseball was recovering, but there were some embarrassing mistakes that day. Nixon had little to do personally with the first presidential gaffe of the day. As he arrived at his box, reporters noticed that the seal of his office was misspelled. Nixon was the "Presidnt of the United States." Numerous press accounts insisted on mentioning this blunder. A bank of photographers and baseball officials assembled in front of the presidential box. "It's great to see you again," Williams remarked. The president made a "crisp" throw that easily cleared the bulk of photographers in front of him. A number of players chased after the ball. Several Yankees bobbled the play, even though one chased the ball with a butterfly net. Hank Allen of the Senators eventually ended up with ball. Then, just as Nixon was to throw out the second "first pitch," he dropped the ball. Williams could not help grinning, and the *New York Times* called the dropped ball "the first error of the 1969 season." The president recovered and threw two more balls, and Washington players caught both.[13]

During the game, Nixon was the subject of as much public attention as the players on the field. When not watching the game, he spent most of his time chatting with Kuhn, Senators' team owner Bob Short, and six Little League players who accompanied him to the stadium. "He talked easily about current and past players," the commissioner recalled. Fans tried to treat Nixon to hot dogs and sodas twice, but he turned these offers down. He avoided a public relations setback by giving the food to the youngsters sitting with him. The early innings went poorly for the Senators. The Yankees took an 8–0 lead, scoring four runs in the fourth inning. A reporter for the *Washington Post* noted that during this inning Nixon was absentmindedly pounding the glove that the Senators had presented to him, perhaps indicating a subconscious desire to get into the game. Wicker and many other fans, thinking the game was over, began leaving the stadium early. The Senators refused to give up, though, and began scoring runs in the eighth and ninth innings. Washington slugger Frank Howard hammered in a home run in the bottom of the ninth, and a roused president stood and applauded as the ball player rounded the bases. "Aren't you glad we stayed?" Nixon asked one of the boys sitting with him. The Senators rally faded and the Yankees hung on to win, 8–4.[14]

Nixon was a real baseball fan, and his refusal to leave proved that fact to many commentators. Of course, they politely failed to note that concerns about public perceptions made it difficult for him to leave the game early.

Wicker took an even larger lesson from the event: "Moral: the main things it takes to become President of the United States are physical stamina and spiritual strength (although it also helps if the management provides a cushion for you to sit on, the way they did for Mr. Nixon)."[15]

As the season progressed, the president stayed engaged, and he took a number of other actions to help baseball return to its role as the national pastime. When New York Yankees legend Mickey Mantle decided to retire, Nixon sent him a short letter wishing him well and congratulating him on an impressive career. "I saw you in action on many occasions and from the roar of approval you always received from your fans I knew I was fortunate that you were not in politics." He added his name to a baseball on display at the Hall of Fame that had the signatures of nine other chief executives. "This is the most famous autographed baseball," the president remarked at the time.[16]

Williams was a political supporter; he kept a portrait of Nixon in his office and in later years would say that Nixon was one of the five greatest Americans alive during his lifetime. Beyond their political affinity, Williams realized it was a major boost to the morale of his club to have the president of the United States in the stadium rooting for his team. "He's a real baseball fan. We've got to get him out to the ball park more often," he told the press. Nixon obliged. He attended a number of games; often arriving at RFK Stadium unannounced. Williams even arranged for him to visit the locker room, and Nixon stunned players when he was familiar with their statistics. "For the President, as busy as he had to be, to comment on that . . . ," pitcher Casey Cox said, shaking his head in astonishment, letting his sentence trail off.[17]

The Senators were starting to win under Williams, but Nixon did not attend a Washington victory until almost halfway through the season. Despite that fact, he generally saw games that had more hits, more home runs, and higher scores than in previous years. The excitement of these offense-oriented contests increased attendance in both leagues, particularly in Washington. An average of 2,700 more fans attended games in 1969 than the year before. Although the rule changes helped batters, the biggest reason for this increased production from offenses was that both leagues had undergone expansion in 1969, which had diluted pitching quality and endangered a few hitting records. On June 11, the president went to a Senators game against the Oakland A's. At the time, Oakland outfielder Reggie Jackson was hitting home runs on a pace to break Roger Maris's eight-year-old record for most home runs in a season. During the 6–4 Oakland victory, Jackson hit two home runs and a double.[18] The president was delighted and dictated a telegram of thanks to the player:

ALTHOUGH I ALWAYS ROOT FOR THE HOME TEAM, I HAVE NOTHING BUT THE HIGHEST ADMIRATION FOR YOUR PERFORMANCE ON THE NIGHT I SAW YOU.

Jackson was more than a little surprised at the attention. "I am most appreciative and thankful that the President would take the time to write me," he said. "It was a great honor for me to play in his presence."[19]

The fact that the president of the United States was in the stands was an attraction to the public as well. Nixon was receptive when young ball fans approached him and asked for his autograph or wanted to shake his hand. "It's hard to put into words the impression you made upon my son," one mother wrote. "I only know that you made him one happy boy. I can only add my thanks to you and close with the words of my son, 'Gee mom, President Nixon is a nice man.'"[20]

While Nixon enjoyed attending games, such trips unnerved his military staff. Colonel James Hughes had a conversation with Dwight Chapin, White House appointments secretary, about the matter and then sent him a memo. "I recognize fully and respect equally fully the President's wishes not to be accompanied by an Aide on certain occasions and to travel without a huge entourage," Hughes stated in his memorandum. "Having said that, there are fundamental services which must be available to the President whether or not he knows they are being provided." Hughes was particularly concerned that a medical doctor be available and that Nixon have ready communication access to the White House, including the codes necessary to launch US nuclear weapons.[21] This problem was soon rectified. Uniformed military officers are present in numerous photos of Nixon at later sporting events.

Baseball was not the only sport that interested the president in the spring of 1969. In May, Nixon became the first sitting chief executive to attend the Kentucky Derby. In fact, it was the first time a president was in the stands for a horse race since 1879. As with many of Nixon's actions in the world of sports, there was a political element to this visit. In 1968, he had made a promise to Kentucky governor Louie B. Nunn to attend the horse race as the president. More importantly, the Derby came at the end of the Republican Governors Association conference in Lexington, Kentucky. In 1969 over half of the governors in the United States were Republicans. Nixon had good reason to think that he might bring about a political realignment in the United States. Most of the governors attended the race as guests of Nunn after the meeting. The gathering gave Nixon an opportunity to talk with the governors, which he did in the VIP room at Churchill Downs. He worked the tables in the room like the seasoned politician that he was and talked with a number of congressional leaders who were also present.[22]

Nixon's presence at the race also allowed him to garner some useful publicity while presenting himself as an individual with interests similar to those of the average person. "I think it's a great idea," a horse-racing fan from California told the Louisville *Courier-Journal.* "It shows he's one of the people, and he has a feeling for the common man." A reporter from the paper observed, "At times it seemed almost as though Mr. Nixon's presence was at least as fascinating as the Derby itself." When he arrived at the track, all but a few hard-core spectators turned away from one of the preliminary races and greeted him with a thunderous ovation. "The crowd seemed to enjoy his presence as much as he enjoyed the Derby," another *Courier-Journal* writer noted.[23]

Celebrity watching was as much a part of the Kentucky Derby as the horse race, and Nixon dominated this element of the event. People, even those in the expensive boxes, shuffled forward to shake hands with the president and get his autograph on a race program. "I can see why people come the Kentucky Derby year after year," Nixon remarked to the press. "It doesn't matter whether you win or lose that counts—it's the people who make it a good time."[24]

Nixon knew little about horse racing and admitted as much. When asked which horse he was cheering for, the president quickly indicated he was for Majestic Prince. "I have to stick with the California horse. I don't follow racing closely, so I don't have a system." The Prince was born in Kentucky, but groomed and trained in California. As a result, confused reporters from the Louisville *Courier-Journal* took the president's comment to indicate that he was for Fleet Allied, the only horse native to the Golden State.[25]

Nixon, however, was even more explicit later. He told Senators Charles Percy and Everett Dirksen of Illinois and Mike Mansfield of Montana: "Majestic Prince. Put it on that. The California horse." The president turned out to be a decent prognosticator. Majestic Prince won the race in 2 minutes, 1⅘ seconds, just off the two-minute record that Northern Dancer set in 1965. "He won, he won," Nixon shouted at the end. Despite a story to the contrary in the Louisville paper, Nixon had no bet on the race and actually left Churchill Downs so quickly that many in his party who had wagers on the contest had to forgo collecting their winnings. In summing up the day, one journalist called Nixon's visit a "political coup."[26]

Sport was also a recreational activity for the new president. Bowling was the most prominent. He played either at Camp David or at some lanes in the basement of the Executive Office Building, located next to the White House. The White House press office, at his direction, promoted his interest in the sport and staged a couple of publicity events. He told members of the White House press corps he liked the game's double challenge: "Not only are you competing against another bowler but you're competing against yourself to improve your score." He, however, preferred to bowl alone. "Sometimes toward the end of the day, when I feel tired or stuffy, I just go over and bowl," he explained. "I usually bowl about 10 o'clock at night. When I'm here I bowl alone. I bowl seven to 12 games one after another. That gives you a tremendous workout." On some occasions, he played with members of his family, staff, guests, and a White House kitchen worker who had recently won a bowling tournament. When Edwin R. Luther and Aida Gonzalez visited after winning the men's and women's titles at the World International Tournament, he played a match while wearing a tie, with his shirt sleeves buttoned down. With such formality it is no wonder that he rolled a gutter ball. "I want you political writers to notice I did it in the right lane," he quipped.[27]

He also took up golf once he came into office. Although he once called the sport "a waste of time," he quickly developed a real liking for the game as vice president. This development was almost to be expected; playing golf is part of the image Americans have come to expect from their presidents. Almost every occupant of the White House in the twentieth century has played the links. Nixon was a solid, unspectacular golfer with a handicap between eighteen and twenty-two and scores in the low nineties. These numbers might be a little generous, but given his awkward physical nature and how little time he had devoted to developing skill at the game, they are better than what one might expect. "In golf, I would say, he maximized his potential. He got everything out of himself that he could get," George P. Shultz, who was in Nixon's cabinet as secretary of labor and then later as secretary of treasury, observed. Orville Moody was less generous. The winner of the 1969 US Open, Moody analyzed his swing. Nixon needed to rotate his shoulders more and use more leg thrust. "Mr. President," Moody wrote for a golf magazine, "your swing is like that of a great many other golfers who don't get to play much. You appear to be fighting the swing." As Don Van Natta Jr. argues, Nixon often resorted to mulligans and a little cheating to bolster his score. Professional golfer Sam Snead played a round with him and was less than impressed at his blatantly cheating. "What could I say? He was the President." He would cheat "when he didn't think nobody could see him," Snead remarked. "All hackers do that."[28]

Nixon cut corners when he was learning the game as vice president. During the 1960s, he started to develop more skill at the game. In office, Nixon played honestly—mostly—and often. He had sets of clubs stored for his use all over the country, including a set at the Burning Tree Country Club in Maryland, one at the White House, another in Key Biscayne, Florida, and four at his residence in San Clemente, California.[29]

"Are you a golfer?" he asked Gale Sayers, the Chicago Bears legend, during an Oval Office visit.

"No," the running back replied.

"Don't take it up," the president replied.[30]

Laughter greeted that comment, but, unlike many other sports, golf had a strong downside that worried many Nixon supporters. Many of the best golf courses in the United States were at country clubs that discriminated against minorities. Warren Adler, of the Republican National Committee, warned the White House staff that Nixon should avoid playing at these types of establishments . "It is, in my judgment, (aside from the political considerations) morally wrong for the President to avail himself of any facilities that are discriminatory." Adler acknowledged that there were tacit agreements between the Jewish and non-Jewish elements of the business communities in cities all over the nation that tolerated such arrangements, but the president of the United States should have nothing to do with such social understandings. "For a businessman to accept the idea of such clubs is one thing. It is quite another for national leaders to exacerbate a situation that could be easily and diplomatically avoided."[31]

Nixon also enjoyed water sports. He swam in the ocean on a regular basis when he stayed at his residence in San Clemente. The Secret Service installed shark nets for his protection in Key Biscayne, where sharks were often spotted. In an aside to the White House press corps, he urged them to visit the beach while they were in California, because swimming "proves you have vigor."[32]

Nixon also played table tennis. In a conversation with his press secretary, Ron Ziegler, that the White House tapes captured, he said, "I was a pretty good ping-pong player." He had played a lot in law school, but had not used the Ping-Pong table at Camp David. "Chou En-lai may challenge," Ziegler quipped.[33]

Being a fan in the baseball stands, though, was something special to Nixon, and his team, the Senators, were finally winning. During a visit to Montreal, he told his audience, "For 14 years in Washington, I rooted for the Washington Senators and they were in the cellar every year. And now they are out of the cellar, and so will the Expos be, if you just stick with them." In another speech, he observed, "I have always been for the Senators, and believe me, you have to be a baseball fan to have been for the Senators in those days." As far as Nixon was concerned, the fan was part of the team.[34]

While Nixon was tapping into sport, Kuhn was tapping into nationalism. As part of the centennial observations, he decided to hold the annual baseball All-Star Game in Washington, DC. That development gave Nixon an idea that soon became a political victory. During a cruise on the *Sequoia*, the presidential yacht, he decided to have an event at the White House for an assortment of current and former players, high-ranking officials of the sport, and the next of kin of deceased stars. "P came up with great idea for baseball dinner at time of All-Star Game, which is baseball's 100th anniversary," Haldeman noted. "Wish he'd do more of this kind of thing." Nixon later changed his mind and decided to have a reception that included retired players as well as the current All-Stars. Finding a time to hold the event proved difficult. The crew of Apollo 11 was scheduled to walk on the moon on Monday, July 21, and the game was set to be played the next evening. "Our options for a White House function seem to be quite limited," one staff member informed Haldeman.[35]

The White House reception was an unexpected addition to the All-Star celebrations. Kuhn decided that a number of banquets, parties, and community events would accompany the midsummer classic. He also had the game played at night in an effort to garner high television ratings. The evening before the game, Major League Baseball held a banquet at the Sheraton Park Hotel to honor two rosters: the greatest players of all time and the greatest living players. The recipients were announced to a drum roll from the United States Marine Band, on loan from the White House. Colonel Frank Borman, the astronaut, acted in the capacity of the president's personal representative, presenting each honoree or his next of kin with a gold trophy.[36] Babe Ruth was named the "Greatest Player of All Time." Joe DiMaggio officially became the Greatest Living Player and was also named the Greatest Centerfielder of All Time. He was the only postwar player to make the Greatest of All Time team, and Willie Mays was the only active player to make the Greatest Living Team.[37] "We originally had asked the President to present the award to the Greatest Player of All Time," Kuhn told *Sports Illustrated*, "but his aides explained that he would be too busy that night. Then one day Mr. Nixon's office called and said that the President wanted to throw a party for baseball. When was the last time that happened?"[38]

The White House staff and the commissioner's office eventually arranged to hold a short reception at the executive mansion a few hours before the game. On July 22 at 4:00 p.m., five chartered buses arrived at Pennsylvania Avenue from the Shoreham Hotel carrying roughly 450 guests. The visitors wandered through four rooms on the first floor, each equipped with a full-service bar. Many complained that the glasses, silverware, ashtrays, and such had no official markings. "No little souvenirs from the White House today," one remarked. After forty minutes the Marine Band played "Hail to the Chief." Nixon entered the East Room and delivered a few remarks to his guests. "I want you all to know that of the many receptions that have been held in this room, this is one of the most exciting of all; exciting because like so many who never made the team, I am always awed in the presence of people who have made the team and are champions."[39]

The first section of the president's remarks offered reminiscences about past glories of the sport and his love of the game. "Baseball is great because anything can happen through the ninth inning." Despite his well-known contempt and hostility toward the media, he harbored few grudges toward sports reporters. In fact, he recognized that in the early days of the sport, those journalists played a crucial role in helping foster the popularity of the professional game. "I just want you to know that I like the job I have, but if I had to live my life over again, I would have liked to have ended up as a sports writer," he said. "So I pay tribute today to those who have written baseball so well that those of us who never saw a game could learn to like it as well as we did." Sportscaster Joe Garagiola was in the audience and quipped, "I won't sleep any better tonight knowing Nixon wants to be a sportswriter."[40]

The president also addressed what he considered the proper social role of athletes as moral leaders to the rest of the country. "Those who are in baseball are people we can look up to, that our young people look up to. I think that is something we are all very proud of." He also made it clear that he would do his part to be a good supporter. "I am proud to be in your company. I am one of your fans, and even though I didn't make the team, I am with you in spirit and I am going to be delighted to meet each and every one of you here today."[41]

After Warren Giles, president of the National League, presented the president with a lifetime pass to all NL games, the commissioner spoke. "I don't think another word is necessary to demonstrate to all of us here in this room, indeed to all America, that I have standing at my left America's number one baseball fan." Kuhn then presented Nixon with a trophy identical to those given out the night before. Inscribed on the award was "Baseball's Number One Fan."[42] Nixon was touched. "Well, it took a lot of years, but I finally made it," he remarked, smiling. "I am most grateful, and this award will have a very proud place in the Presidential Library. Now, I know that we have got to get to the game on time, so let's get this reception going."[43]

Nixon then greeted every guest as they passed through the receiving line. Kuhn introduced each of them. Nixon had comments to make to almost every individual he met, which made the line move slowly. "He had memories to share with the old-timers, topical comments and advice for those now in the game and pertinent observations for many of the sportswriters and broadcasters," Kuhn recalled. When Lefty Grove, the former star pitcher for the Philadelphia A's whom Nixon had mentioned by name in his comments, came through, the president asked him why he had lost so many games. "It wasn't me; it was the other eight guys," he replied. According to press accounts, Nixon laughed "heartily" in response.[44]

When Joe DiMaggio passed in line, Nixon commented on the former Yankee player's role as a hitting coach for the Oakland A's and his star pupil,

Reggie Jackson. "You're doing a good job teaching that fellow how to hit," he stated. "No, I'm not," DiMaggio answered. "He's doing it all on his own."[45]

Mickey Mantle warned him he might yet get the opportunity to become a sportswriter. "Mr. President, if the stock market doesn't start doing better you might get your wish."[46]

Throughout the introductions, reporters found Nixon smiling and looking genuinely happy. Doug Brown, a sports columnist for the Baltimore *Evening Sun*, wrote, "It was instantly obvious that Nixon is a genuine fan. He talked easily and at length. He had an audience he could not fool. This was not a subject on which he could be briefed and then try to bring off a polished discourse before a knowledgeable group."[47]

The White House event was near-surreal to many of the participants, many of whom were longtime veterans of either politics or baseball. "The President practically turned over the White House to baseball," former commissioner Ford Frick said. "I don't believe anything like this has ever happened before." An individual asked White House communications director Herbert Klein if the reception was the largest in history. "I don't know about that," he replied, "but I think he [Nixon] had the most fun at this one." Morris Siegel, a sports columnist for the Washington *Evening Star*, wrote, "You had to see it to believe it. Mickey Mantle and Stan Musial in a corner of the Red Room discussing the stock market." Siegel then quoted Felix Millan of the Atlanta Braves: "You don't get to see people like this every day." A White House aide was equally ecstatic about the opportunity to meet so many celebrities. "This is the greatest. This is pure heaven. I've already got autographs from DiMaggio and Musial and I'm going to try for Stengel and Mrs. Ruth. I never dreamed I'd see so many famous people in the White House." Bing Devine, vice president of the St. Louis Cardinals, recounted to the *New York Times* his conversation with Nixon in the receiving line. "At the White House reception I said to the President—imagine that—I said to the President 'that after meeting all these dignitaries, the All-Star Game would be an anticlimax.' I never thought I would say an All-Star Game would be an anticlimax." Frank Cashen, vice president of the Baltimore Orioles, quickly realized how important this event was to the fate of the major leagues. "You know, it's great to have a President who really knows and likes baseball. Look what Ike did for golf."[48]

Siegel went all the way back to 1829 to find a precedent for such an odd gathering at the executive mansion. "Yesterday's invasion was a throw back to the Andrew Jackson times when the grooviest parties of all were held." The baseball reception, however, gave "the current rule the dubious honor of hosting the most unusual reception in White House history."[49] Siegel captured the atmosphere of the event best in a passage of his column that described a White House tour that a guide might give in the future:

> There is the East Room, where many formal dinners are held. It was here in this room, on July 22, 1969, that Ted Williams gave batting instructions, right there near the painting of Martha Washington.
>
> And now we are in the Red Room, a small after dinner gathering place for guests. It was here in this room, near the Thomas Jefferson portrait, that, on July 22, 1969, Dizzy Dean pointed to the toe he hurt in the 1937 All-Star Game in Washington.
>
> This is the foyer. Here on that same date in history, near those stairs leading to the presidential living quarters, is where Casey Stengel vividly recalled how Walter Johnson struck him out four times in an exhibition game in Coffeyville, Kan., during the Woodrow Wilson administration. This also is the place where the Marine band plays "Hail to the Chief" when the President arrives.[50]

Even the weather was on Nixon's side. Rain was pouring outside. At first, Kuhn and Nixon were put out with this development. The president was going to the Pacific to greet the astronauts of Apollo 11, just back from the moon, and was afraid he would miss the contest. "Try to get the game in, because I'd like to be there and can't make it tomorrow," he told the commissioner. Kuhn also wanted to go ahead according to schedule; if he postponed the game, he was looking at the loss of prime-time television ratings. Kuhn promised Nixon and his staff that he would wait until 8:00 p.m. before calling off the classic.[51]

A reporter noticed that the guests became more relaxed after the storm started, and tarried longer than they might have otherwise: it was obvious that there was going to be no game. The thunderstorm only grew in strength. Water began to weigh down on the three circus tents set up to the east of RFK Stadium, where the commissioner was holding a pregame party for four thousand Washington and baseball dignitaries. The waiters wore the hard, flat straw hats that were popular in 1869 and the mustache and sideburns styles of that day, but spent a good deal of their time using folding chairs to push against the top of the tent to get water to run off. "I know why it's raining so hard tonight," Congressman Clarence J. Brown of Ohio told an *Evening Star* reporter. "The gods are angry that the 100th anniversary game isn't being played in Cincinnati, where the first game was played in 1869." Kuhn waited until the last possible moment before making a decision about going ahead with the game, but he had little choice. Water had flooded the American League (AL) dugout, running over television cables, and even the press room on the second floor of the stadium was full of water. At 8:16 p.m., Kuhn postponed the All-Star Game for the first time in baseball history.[52]

What is truly important about that evening is that Nixon had cracked the code of professional journalists. He had gotten the type of publicity that a politician loves: it was positive, flattering, respectful. Nixon might have had a hostile relationship with the news media, but there are many professional divisions among reporters. He could depend on sports reporters to advance the story, which is exactly what they did. With no All-Star Game, the White House reception was the story of the day. Photos of Nixon greeting sports legends such as DiMaggio, Casey Stengel, and Roy Campanella appeared in the sports and lifestyle sections of many newspapers. Almost every sports columnist and reporter covering the All-Star Game felt obliged to mention the event. The result was that often more than one story about the reception appeared in newspapers.[53] The presence of the president of the United States at a sporting event was a unique feature, which gave the reporters leverage over their colleagues from the other sections of the newspapers, stations, and networks that covered news, politics, business, entertainment, and lifestyle and cultural issues. Airtime and page space is limited, and being at the White House, reporting on someone as well known as the president gave them an advantage in how much they could report and where their stories appeared. Nixon's presence on their beat enhanced their own professional standing. Nixon and sports reporters had a symbiotic relationship.

The president's comments about wanting to be a sportswriter resulted in some surprising dividends. The Baseball Writers' Association of America made him an honorary member the next day. They also asked the president to meet with Ted Williams and see if he could get the manager to change his policy of keeping his locker room closed for the first fifteen minutes after a game. Williams had never enjoyed a good relationship with the press, and in his comments Nixon had said he would have treated the baseball legend decently, if he had been a sportswriter. Despite that qualification, some journalists decided to give Washington's manager a hard time about their special status. The next day, as Williams playfully bantered with a throng of reporters, one reminded him about Nixon's comments. "I didn't hear him say anything about wanting to be a left fielder," one journalist told the former Red Sox star. Williams muttered something about everyone being entitled to a mistake, even Richard M. Nixon.[54]

On the afternoon of July 23, the fortieth annual All-Star Game went forward without the president of the United States. Nixon had left for the Pacific the evening before, but Vice President Spiro Agnew filled in for the absent chief executive, tossing a ball to the catcher of each team. According to a *New York Times* reporter, he "displayed good stuff and fine control with two strong, straight deliveries." Presidential son-in-law David Eisenhower and daughter Julie Nixon Eisenhower represented the Nixon family. Some ceremonies planned for the previous evening, like the introduction of the greatest players of all time, were canceled. Despite playing in an American League ball park, the National League team dominated. In the third inning, NL batters exploded for five runs to take an 8–1 lead. The visitors eventually won, 9–3. "The bat was back. The people were back. And baseball was back, too," a *Sports Illustrated* writer declared.[55]

Despite the complications, the All-Star Game was a success for both Nixon and Major League Baseball. Kuhn had lost the hoped for prime-time ratings, but that turned out to be a minor issue. "The whole thing went off so well, that I could not even get depressed by the rain and the postponement," he said at the time. "There were U.S. Senators standing there in two inches of rain talking about baseball. How could I get depressed?" Years later, he observed, "One way or another, it was a centennial celebration that no one would ever forget." The morning after the White House reception Kuhn received congratulatory calls from Pete Rozelle and Walter Kennedy, his counterparts in the NFL and NBA respectively. Jerome Holtzman, a sports reporter for the *Chicago Tribune*, speculated in his 1998 book on the baseball commissioners that the gathering at the Executive Mansion "may have been the most satisfying moment in Bowie Kuhn's reign."[56]

The sport owed a large debt to the president of the United States for the success of the midsummer classic. The editors of the *Sporting News* recognized as much. "Man's historic landing on the moon chased virtually every other piece of news off the nation's front pages," they wrote in an editorial. "Who could pay any heed to an All-Star Game at one of mankind's great moments?" The White House reception was responsible for helping baseball compete with the trek of the astronauts. "President Nixon was not alone in finding baseball an engrossing topic, but his interest certainly heightened the drama surrounding baseball's midsummer special." Even though some purists thought Cincinnati was a more appropriate choice for the centennial All-Star Game, the *Sporting News* editors thought the nation's capital turned out to be an extremely good venue. "Washington turned out to be a beautiful choice, thanks largely to President Nixon, the most knowledgeable and eager baseball fan in the White House since Warren Harding."[57]

The importance of the event and the broad publicity that Nixon had helped bring to the event became apparent aboard the USS *Hornet*, when Nixon welcomed back the crew of Apollo 11 after they returned from space. The president made a game effort to banter with the astronauts, but he was never very good at small talk. He mixed praise of them and their wives with jokes about the tolls for his phone conversations with the three while they were on their mission. As was often the case in these situations, he turned to sports as a way to reach out to individuals. "Did you know about the All-Star Game?"[58]

During the exchange that followed, Colonel Edwin "Buzz" Aldrin was direct in dealing with the commander in chief. Neil Armstrong also proved to be quite capable of bantering with Nixon, while Mike Collins, the third member of the crew, was silent during the exchange about baseball. Aldrin's answer to Nixon's question was direct "Yes, sir." The president followed up with another inquiry: "Were you American League or National League?" Again, Aldrin gave a clear answer: "National League." Armstrong, however, was more circumspect: "Neither one." Nixon had an opening. "There is the politician in the group," he remarked.[59]

"We are sorry you missed that," Armstrong continued.

That comment caught Nixon off guard. "You knew that, too?"

"We heard about the rain," Armstrong elaborated. "We haven't learned to control the weather yet, but that is something we can look forward to."[60]

There was more baseball to come in 1969. The second half of the season was exciting for many fans, including those who like Richard Nixon rooted for the Washington Senators. The team was never a threat to take the division title, finishing in fourth place in the AL Eastern Division, but the team closed the season with a 86–76 record, a twenty-one-game improvement over the year before. This mark was the first winning season in franchise history and the first winning season for a professional baseball team in Washington in seventeen years. The Washington community responded to the quality product the team offered. Attendance doubled and club revenue tripled.[61]

Much of the credit for this turnaround went to Ted Williams. At the time, he never made any claim to the credit for the modest success of the team. In a later decade, he stated, "The truth, of course is that I had little to do with it, except for maybe being a little more enthusiastic about certain things, including—*especially* including—hitting." At the time, the Washington skipper told reporters that he "always felt that Washington was a great baseball town. That was an enthusiastic 900,000 fans that showed up this year. Yes sir, like nowhere else in this league." He attributed most of the success to the attitude and effort of his players. "They hustled all year." The members of the Associated Press disagreed. On October 20, they named him American League Manager of the Year. He was on a safari in Africa when Bob Addie of the *Washington Post* contacted him with the news. "I thought it was a joke," he recalled. "I said, 'If that's true, Bob, it's one more example of how wrong the writers can be.'" In a column that appeared in the *Washington Post* the next day, Shirley Povich explained why Williams got the award. His presence was the only major change in a team that was "ninth-place seaweed" the year before. His tutelage was evident in the fact that the batting average of ten Senators increased. Still, Williams had a hard time accepting the success. "I was flabbergasted," he recalled later. He had not even voted for himself. Nixon quickly fired off a telegram of congratulations:

> There is a satisfaction that comes simply from accepting a challenge. But you have every reason to be especially proud of your decision to return to basebal1.[62]

The other big baseball success story was the rise of the "miracle" Mets of New York. An expansion team that joined the National League in 1962, the club had developed a reputation and strong following as lovable losers. Suddenly in 1969, this team that baseball historian Charles C. Alexander described as "a collection of perpetually platooned everyday mediocrities" stunned the nation. The Mets had an advantage that few other teams enjoyed in a year when expansion diluted pitching quality: a strong, young staff of future stars. The Mets trailed the Chicago Cubs for most of the season, but in August and September the team surged forward, capturing the division championship by eight games. The 1969 Mets' record of 100–62 was a twenty-seven-game improvement over their finish the year before.[63]

The Mets quickly made their way into the World Series, where they faced the Baltimore Orioles. The series started in Maryland and the Orioles won 4–1. The Mets then won the next three games, setting up a climatic Game Five in New York's Shea Stadium. The Orioles took an early 3–0 lead, but the home team charged back to score five runs in the sixth, seventh, and eighth innings. The Mets won the world championship one inning later, stunning baseball fans across the country.[64]

Shortly after the series ended, Nixon called the Mets locker room to offer his congratulations. The practice of the president talking with the victorious team after a major sporting event might have become routine in the years since, but in 1969 that was not the case. Establishing this tradition was another way in which Nixon merged his genuine interests in sports with the ceremonial and social roles the public expected from a president of the United States. Joan Payson, owner of the team, answered the phone when it rang. The aftermath of the victory was an emotionally charged moment, and Payson was half laughing, half crying. The impact of having the president call, added to the excitement and thrill of the win, but was a bit much for her. After a few moments, she handed the receiver to manger Gil Hodges. He mainly listened to Nixon offer his congratulations to the players and team, and reflect on Hodges's role in helping the Dodgers win their only title while in Brooklyn. "Thank you and God bless you" was the last comment he made to the president. Afterward, he summarized the conversation to reporters. Hodges said he "told him how much we appreciate his interest in our game."[65]

Nixon had essentially invented the practice of the president making post-game congratulatory telephone calls to locker rooms and dugouts. The call to the Mets was not the first one, though. After Orville Moody won the U.S. Open golf tournament in 1969, he got a phone call from the president. "I was astounded," Moody said. A former US Army sergeant, Moody was a professional golfer, but had to qualify for the Open through sectional qualifying events, making him something of an underdog. Nixon told domestic affairs advisor John Ehrlichman that he wanted the White House staff to keep a list of sports figures who supported him in 1968 so he could contact them when they did something of significance. "For example, today I called Arnold Palmer when he made a very good showing but failed to win the Open and also called Mooney [Moody] when he won the Open. I don't know where Mooney stands but it was probably a good idea in any event."[66]

As the 1969 baseball season came to an end, Nixon could look back on his tenure so far with satisfaction. He had, in a way few of his predecessors had even imagined, used sport to his political advantage. In doing so, he also helped the national pastime recover some of the popularity that the lords of baseball had foolishly squandered over the previous decade. As summer turned into autumn, football season came to the forefront of athletic endeavors in the country. Nixon was as much a fan of this game as he was of baseball, and he continued to find ways to serve his political interests with sporting events.

2

The Second Centennial

The Texas-Arkansas Game and Other Football-Related Matters

In the second half of 1969 Nixon turned to football to service his political needs. On December 6, he scored a major political victory with the collegiate game. On that date the undefeated football teams of the University of Arkansas and the University of Texas played for the national title in college football in what became known as the "Big Shootout." The hype of this much-promoted event increased when Nixon decided to attend the game in person. Although Nixon loved the sport, his trip was far from a recreational outing. He went to the game in an effort to win support in the South in general, and Texas and Arkansas in particular, using the informal powers of the presidency to his political advantage. As he had with baseball, Nixon used football to present himself both as a man of the people and as a social authority capable of shaping popular cultural. His effort—despite some regional backlash and a dispute with Coach Joe Paterno of Penn State—was a success. He gained a good deal of visibility and positive press attention that had little to do with politics, never bad for any elected official. Even the dispute with Paterno worked to Nixon's advantage.

The president genuinely loved football. He had played it in college and had an important role on his team despite his limited abilities. "Unable to succeed on the field, he nevertheless became a valued member of the squad," historian Herbert Parmet wrote. "Nixon, it turned out, contributed something more than cannon fodder. He became vital for the squad's morale." According to Parmet, "he was an asset on the bench, sitting there, waiting for the outcome to be decided one way or another so he could see some action, but mostly serving to bolster the others." Nixon's own assessment was a bit different: "I got to say it was good for me," he told Gale Sayers of the Chicago Bears. "It teaches you a little humility."[1]

Sporting venues changed the man a bit. Clumsy with little dexterity, the president underwent a physical transformation when he was around athletes. Videos and films show a near-graceful Nixon excitedly chatting with players who were equally thrilled at the opportunity to meet the chief executive. Reporters often noticed and commented on his animation. At a testimonial dinner in Anaheim, California, just before the inauguration, Nixon's old college football coach, Wallace "Chief" Newman, presented him with a varsity letter from Whittier College. Nixon had been a member of the school's football team, but never advanced beyond the practice squad or qualified for the award. After his old coach made his presentation, fifty of the president-elect's former teammates came out onto the stage and gave him the actual bench he sat on during games. A reporter for the *Orange County Register* wrote of this moment, "Plain folk Dick could hardly contain himself."[2]

As the mood in the country started to turn ugly, Nixon had a solid ally in the world of football. Vince Lombardi, the new Redskins' coach, was a man with cultural values similar to Nixon's. Even though he had voted Democratic, he ended up supporting Nixon on a number of foreign policy initiatives and in efforts to promote traditional American virtues, challenging the youth of the counterculture. Team owner Edward Bennett Williams, a major figure in the Democratic Party, would later comment on Lombardi, "He was rather naïve politically." Nixon reciprocated the admiration of the coach. "You have always demonstrated on the field and off the qualities of faith and determination which are at the heart of true patriotism," he wrote Lombardi.[3]

The coach wanted Nixon to attend Redskins games. "If the President is a pro football fan, he ought to be out to our games here in his home city," he declared at his first press conference in the nation's capital. Nixon was interested in attending a game, but the White House staff had reservations. The common practice was for VIPs, regardless of political affiliation, to attend as guests of Williams. Clark Mollenhoff, a Pulitzer Prize–winning reporter of the *Des Moines Register* who had joined the Nixon administration in 1969, warned John Ehrlichman that the White House might have a problem with aspects of Williams's legal career. He had represented a number of gamblers and members of organized crime. Williams also did not have firm control over the team, and there was a strong likelihood that this matter would be resolved through litigation. Mollenhoff, who had earned his Pulitzer for exposing corruption in organized labor, worried that news stories involving Williams might pull Nixon in as well. In particular, he thought these pieces might stress the unsavory characters on Williams's client list. If these articles suggested that these individuals were inappropriate associates for a figure in professional sports, then the president could end up in an embarrassing situation if he sat with Williams.[4]

This argument was an easy sell to Nixon. He believed because of their visibility and success athletes had a duty to do right. The failure to live up to this responsibility explains the special contempt he had for New York Jets quarterback Joe Namath. When the football player temporarily retired from the game earlier in the year rather than sell his one-third interest in a bar where known gamblers frequented, Nixon was ecstatic. "Good riddance," he scrawled on a news summary his staff had prepared. "These guys must set an example."[5] Such contempt goes a long way toward explaining the reason the quarterback was on the infamous "enemies list" that former counsel to the president John W. Dean III made public four years later. Namath was the only athlete on the roster. He was, however, misidentified as a New York Giant. The day after the list was made public, Namath—who had never been political at all—said he found his inclusion on the list "a little crazy."[6]

While the White House staff worried about the Williams problem, Nixon made a little history. On October 4, while in Florida, he went to the Orange Bowl and watched from the stands, like any other fan, as the Miami Dolphins and the Oakland Raiders played to a 20–20 tie. That game was the first and only time that a president of the United States attended an American Football League contest. Jim O'Brien of the *Miami News* observed that the crowd jumped to its feet three times following the kickoff returns of Mercury Morris and that the reception Nixon received when the public announcer introduced him to the crowd was of equal intensity. In fact, it "set a mood for the evening." The only sour note of the evening actually came two days later when the *News* printed a photograph showing a smiling Nixon autographing a Minnesota Vikings pennant. The problem: the Vikings were a NFL team, not an AFL one.[7]

In November, circumstances allowed Nixon to claim another first. Under Lombardi, the Redskins began to win. In the middle of November they had a 4-4-2 record. On November 12, Williams sent the president a handwritten note on team stationary, inviting him to the Redskins game on the sixteenth against their archrivals, the Dallas Cowboys.[8]

The letter arrived at a fortuitous time. In the early summer, the honeymoon, or grace period, that Nixon had enjoyed on the Vietnam War was coming to an end. On June 30, the Vietnam Moratorium Committee called for a national strike and demonstration against the war on October 15. Less than two weeks after that announcement, the Student Mobilization Committee announced that it would organize a massive antiwar protest in Washington on November 15.[9]

The fall of 1969 looked to be turning into a difficult time for the Nixon administration. Members of Congress were beginning to criticize Nixon's Vietnam policy openly. The presidents of seventy-nine colleges and universities signed an appeal, asking him to speed up the withdrawal from Southeast Asia. There was ugly unrest on college campuses across the country, and civil rights leaders were questioning Nixon's actions in implementing school desegregation. Of that time, one Nixon biographer writes: "The White House was, figuratively, under siege; literally, there were protesters carrying signs, sometimes in large number, sometimes only a few, but always there, surrounding the White House." Despite administration efforts to downplay the event, and despite coming in the middle of the week, the Moratorium became the largest antiwar protest in the history of the United States. A study that the White House staff itself conducted counted more than two hundred demonstrations across the country on October 15. The crowd in Boston numbered more than one hundred thousand. One national television reporter observed that the rallies "looked like a cross-section picked by the census bureau," including housewives, working-class laborers, and middle-class professionals of all ages. Melvin Small, in his book on the antiwar movement's impact on the Johnson and Nixon administrations, called the Moratorium the "single most important one-day demonstration of the entire war."[10]

With the Washington Mobilization looming, the administration decided to fight back. Six days after the Moratorium, Nixon began work on what would become his "Silent Majority" speech. The White House staff was charged with excitement about "the speech." On November 3, speaking from the Oval Office in a stern voice with a measured and calm bearing, the president took the high road. He announced that he would continue to pursue his policy of negotiations and withdrawing troops from Vietnam. "Any hope the world has for the survival of peace and freedom will be determined by whether the American people have the moral stamina and the courage to meet the challenge." He closed with the section that gave name to the speech: "And so tonight—to you, the great silent majority of my fellow Americans I ask for your support." Nothing less than the future of the nation was at stake. "North Vietnam cannot defeat or humiliate the United States. Only Americans can do that." Ambrose noted that those sentences indicated the real objective of the presidential address: "PR, not policy was his concern."[11]

Ten days later, a mere two days before the Washington Mobilization, Vice President Spiro Agnew took the low road. Speaking in Des Moines, Iowa, Agnew tore into the television news media. Using phrases such as "a small band of network commentators and self-appointed analysts" or "a small and unelected elite," he charged that the television media was trying to tell the public what to think and exercised influence that was out of proportion to its actual size.[12]

On November 15, a crowd of 250,000 gathered in Washington for the Mobilization, making it the largest single-city antiwar protest ever held in the United States, but Nixon used football to show the nation his contempt. The crowd was more radical than the Moratorium, and that hurt its own cause. Several protesters carried the flag of the enemy—the Viet Cong—and a splinter group broke off from the main section of the protest and rioted in front of the Department of Justice. During a photo session, Nixon told the White House press corps that he would spend the afternoon watching the Ohio State–Purdue football game. Ohio State won, 42–14.[13]

Such an investment of time was both recreational and political defiance. The next day, as a way of emphasizing the business-as-usual attitude of his administration, Nixon decided to go to the Washington-Dallas game. He solved his Williams problem by sitting in the stands with the rest of the people, just as he had done at baseball games. "In later years when historians assess the achievements of the Nixon administration, high among will be the ability to preempt 25 seats to a Redskin-Dallas Cowboys game on short notice," Povich joked in his *Washington Post* column the next day. In making this trip, Nixon claimed another first. He became the first US president to attend a regular-season National Football League game. He was largely welcome at the game. When the public announcer reported that Nixon was in attendance, the crowd responded with a big cheer and only a few boos. Despite the historic nature of the day, the home team lost to the Cowboys, 41–28.[14]

While he liked attending games in person, he thought the average fan did better watching at home. "I really believe that when you sit at home and see a football game on television, you can probably see it as well or even better than you can see it by being there, because the camera will watch that T formation or the quarterback and will be sure you're watching the ball rather than the fake," he explained.[15]

As useful as the professional game was to Nixon, the college version proved to be far more significant in that first year in office. Back in 1869 Princeton and Rutgers played the first college football game, and a hundred years later the NCAA was planning various events to celebrate the centennial of the sport. One of the key moments would be the game between those two New Jersey schools. As early as February, Senator Clifford Case requested that Nixon attend the game. Dwight Chapin responded, informing the senator that scheduling problems made it look unlikely that the president would be able to attend. He promised Case that Nixon and his staff would "take another look" as the game got closer on the calendar. Chapin was as good as his word. In June, with work on the baseball reception underway, he initiated another a look at the schedule. In July, Walter Byers, the executive secretary of the NCAA, also raised the subject with Charles "Bud" Wilkinson, the former head coach at the University of Oklahoma who was working in the White House with the title of Special Consultant to the President. Byers asked Wilkinson if Nixon might issue some type of statement about the collegiate football centennial. Wilkinson wrote a memo recommending that Nixon either make a statement that he provide to the ABC television network for use in a documentary on college football or make some remarks at the Rutgers-Princeton game, which he thought the president should attend. The former coach also suggested that Nixon provide some words for inclusion in every college football program. Nixon liked this idea, but decided against attending the game in New Jersey. Instead, he would make a short statement that would be in used in the preseason documentary. Despite the widespread perception that the Nixon White House staff under

H. R. "Bob" Haldeman was an efficient organization, it seems that no one followed through on either of these ideas. Although Chapin and Wilkinson sent each other a number of memos about filming a presidential statement for use during the Princeton-Rutgers halftime, there is no record in the obvious sources that this ever happened, either. The centennial celebrations, nevertheless, went on without the president in attendance. Princeton defeated Rutgers, 29–0 on September 27.[16]

A week before this game, Harry Dent, the White House staff member charged with acting as a liaison between the administration and Southern members of Congress, suggested another way that Nixon might associate himself with college football. On October 6, he had read an article in the *New York Times*, titled "In the South, Football is a Religio-Social Pastime," which stated, "Football has probably replaced church-going as the number one social function in the South." The article discussed the impact the sport had on local economies, and the important role teams played in regional identification even among those who had never attended college. "The university football team belongs to all the state, not just the students."[17]

This article gave Dent an idea: "If at any time during the remainder of this term the President wants to see and be seen by a tremendous crowd of enthusiastic Southerners, I suggest we consider sending him to one of the big football rivalry games." He suggested that the White House be on the lookout for a big game in a traditional interstate rivalry. "That would be a good way to get him into a key Southern state and get to see many good people from two states, without doing anything political."[18]

Dent's advice addressed an important issue for Richard Nixon. He needed to continue soliciting political backing in the states of the old Confederacy. The South was a critical base of political support for Nixon. Southern votes helped him win the 1968 presidential election, but this support, in the words of one biographer, was "soft" and "negative." Southerners backed Nixon, but not out of conviction, viewing him instead as simply the best available candidate. Support in the region could quickly dissipate and could never be taken for granted.[19]

Nixon and his staff had to wait only two months before events produced a game of the first magnitude. For most of the season the undefeated Ohio State Buckeyes, the defending national champions, were ranked first in the Associated Press and United Press International polls. The Tennessee Volunteers, also undefeated, were second. As the season neared an end, both teams faced opponents they regarded lightly—too lightly as things turned out. On November 15, Mississippi defeated Tennessee, and a week later, on November 22, Ohio State lost to Michigan. As a result, Texas and Arkansas replaced Ohio State and Tennessee as the top two teams in the polls.[20]

Using college football catered to Nixon's interests and inclinations well. Haldeman confided in his diary that Nixon had a difficult time late in the year, avoiding a scheduling conflict between a signing ceremony for a bill and several important football games. He wanted to watch them all. "He's really become a total addict," Haldeman observed.[21]

The suggestion that Dent had made on how to use Southern culture to Nixon's advantage was directly on point. In the 1960s the Texas Longhorns and the Arkansas Razorbacks were two of the most dominant powers in college football. In 1963 Texas had an undefeated season and won the national championship after defeating Navy in the Cotton Bowl. A year later Arkansas also went undefeated and won their own national championship. Even in the years when neither team won the title, the contests between the two had national implications. A Longhorn victory in 1962 and an Arkansas victory in 1965 cost the other school the national title.[22]

The 1969 matchup quickly took on the tone of an epic contest. With both schools undefeated, the game that had promised to be an important contest in determining the conference championship had suddenly become the national title game. Students, alumni, and fans of both schools eagerly and enthusiastically anticipated this matchup. Articles about "The Game" dominated the sports sections of the newspapers in major cities in Arkansas and Texas. Requests from media organizations for credentials were more than double the capacity of the press box. The mood in Arkansas was intense. A Little Rock bank gave away ten thousand "Beat Texas" lapel pins in two days, and a radio station in the city handed out fifteen thousand bumper stickers. The First Baptist Church in Fayetteville made national news when its outside marquee delivered notice upon the Texas head coach: "Attention, Darrell Royal. Do not cast your steers before swine." According to the estimate of a *Sports Illustrated* reporter, like-minded messages decorated about 80 percent of the marquees in Fayetteville. Clever managers of grocery stores announced sales of "Longhorn beef" and "Texas round steak." Winthrop Rockefeller, governor of Arkansas, proclaimed that first week of December "Beat Texas

Week." When John Mooney, the sports editor of the *Salt Lake Tribune* and president of the Football Writers Association of America, arrived in Arkansas, he was stunned at the widespread and intense following the Razorbacks enjoyed. Fayetteville is "absolutely nuts" he told his readers. "Here you are for Arkansas, or you are in trouble." The game between Rutgers and Princeton had a "relaxed air" compared to the sentiment in Arkansas.[23]

Similar passion for "The Game" existed in Texas. The mayor of Austin renamed Congress Avenue, which leads straight to the state capitol, Longhorn Avenue, and declared Saturday, December 6—the day of the game—"Texas Longhorn Day in Austin and Fayetteville." Reporters from the *Austin American* were unable to get any comment from Fayetteville city officials.[24] Not to be outdone, Preston Smith, governor of Texas, held a press conference and presented Royal with a commission, making the coach a "field general" for the "Battle of Fayetteville."[25] A pep rally in Austin held at the north end of Memorial Stadium drew a crowd of twenty-five thousand—a good showing for a school of thirty-five thousand. The mania began to worry the editorial board of the *Austin American*, and the paper printed an editorial titled "Keeping 'The Game' in Perspective," urging fans to remember that it was an amateur athletic event and not a professional football game.[26]

Even politicians added to the hoopla. In the hallowed halls of the US Congress, the staff of the House Ways and Means Committee picketed their own office with signs supporting the University of Arkansas. The committee chairman, Arkansas Democrat Wilbur Mills, did not join his staff, but Representative George Bush, a Houston Republican, and his staff organized a counterdemonstration. Bush left a committee hearing to carry a sign that said, "Beat Arkansas."[27]

Both coaches responded calmly to the hoopla. "God should be kept neutral," Royal said when informed of the marquee at the First Baptist Church in Fayetteville.[28] "The man who invented football, never intended of it to be this big," Arkansas head football coach Frank Broyles said. He also ruefully noted that he had lost six games his first year as head coach, and even asked his father if he could join the family insurance company. "I sure never envisioned anything like this." He also took steps to keep the pressure of the big game from getting to his players, prohibiting them from talking with reporters.[29]

The hype and attention of the Texas-Arkansas contest was everything

White House staffers could have wanted for a presidential trip. Although Nixon was interested in attending a game in the South, there was nothing preplanned about his attendance.[30] For months, though, there had been speculation that he would be in Arkansas. In March Roone Arledge, the president of ABC Sports, got Broyles to agree to reschedule the game for the last weekend of play in December. The network wanted a special game, and after plotting several scenarios, Arledge thought that there was a good chance that at least one team, and maybe both, would be undefeated. In order to convince Broyles to change the date of the game, he "guaranteed" the coach that Wilkinson would have Nixon in attendance. Starting in August there had been speculation in the Arkansas sports media that Nixon would come to the game. After both teams won their Thanksgiving Day games and were undefeated going into the showdown, stories to the effect that the nation's number-one football fan would be traveling to Fayetteville became rampant on the sports pages in both states. The thing is: these articles were gossip and speculation passing as journalism, a fact that Arledge tacitly confirms in his memoirs. Inquiries and efforts to line up tickets had started, but it was not until 12:45 p.m., Monday, December 1, that the trip became official. Chapin sent a memo stamped HIGH PRIORITY to several other staffers, informing them that the president had decided to attend the game. A number of newspapers carried reports in their December 2 issues that Nixon might attend the game, which the White House confirmed later in the day.[31]

The White House publicly attributed the trip to two telegrams Nixon received from Mooney of the *Salt Lake Tribune* and John Paul Hammerschmidt, the US congressman representing Fayetteville. Hammerschmidt's message read:

> YOUR ATTENDANCE WOULD BE ESPECIALLY APPROPRIATE IN THIS CENTENNIAL YEAR OF COLLEGE FOOTBALL.

Mooney made the same point and also hoped that the president could meet with sports reporters the evening before the game. Both invitations were gratuitous in practical purpose and effect. Neither Hammerschmidt nor Mooney had extra tickets to give the White House, nor could either provide the housing to accommodate a presidential visit. More importantly, Nixon had already decided to attend the game before the White House received the cables.[32] The invitations, however, were important politically as they enabled Nixon to avoid appearing as an uninvited guest.

Several points are worth making about Nixon's interest in attending the Texas-Arkansas game. First, Dent's suggestion on how to use Southern culture to Nixon's advantage was a good one. Two states were gearing up for this one game. Another point is that White House documents indicate that Wilkinson had little to do with giving the suggestion to Nixon. It was Nixon's idea and his alone. Finally, if Nixon had simply gone to Arkansas to watch a football game, there would have been little significance to this episode, but he also decided to award a plaque to the winner, and that changed the dynamics of the game. Nixon's award was a clever way to garner even more attention from the visit. "This presentation will be especially significant in that it will commemorate the One Hundredth Anniversary of College Football as well as recognize the nation's Number One Football Team," he explained. Although he never came out and explicitly asserted his authority to award the national title to the winner of the game, the president was for all practical purposes making that claim, since custom in college football held that the team ranked first in the polls at the end of the season received a trophy that represented a "national championship."[33] The fact that Nixon and his staff stopped short of actually claiming this authority was a fine distinction, but one that would be important a few days later.

Nixon's decision to attend the game and award a plaque only made the hype stronger—if that was possible. "We are highly elated and greatly honored that he has elected to come to the game," David Mullins, president of the University of Arkansas, said. Stories about Nixon's less-than-spectacular days as a college football player appeared in papers. The chief of the White House advance team was the subject of a front-page interview in the *Arkansas Democrat.* The Arkansas sports publicity department, which was struggling to find enough room for the surge of sports reporters covering the game, suddenly had to find more space for the White House press corps. There was also the issue of finding seating for the presidential party. "Somebody is going to have to give him tickets," Broyles wryly observed. "Right now, I'm worried about my own family and I don't think my wife will give up hers." The editorial boards of several newspapers gave Nixon some good-natured ribbing. "By now it is probably clear that President Nixon is not our candidate for the Top Ten presidents, or even the Top Twenty for that matter," observed the editorial board of the *Arkansas Gazette.* The board noted, however, "that any president who plans to fly to Fayetteville for the Arkansas-Texas game can't be all that bad." The rival *Arkansas Democrat* noted, "Mr. Nixon should sort of prepare himself for an unusual experience. This may well be the first time in history that the arrival of a President will NOT be the biggest event of the day."[34]

As far as security arrangements went, the *Arkansas Democrat* was wrong; Nixon's visit was the issue of the moment. The Fayetteville police and county sheriff departments had mobilized all their personnel. Combined with a hundred state police officers and the secret service agents who would accompany the president, this made for the largest law enforcement security force ever assembled in that small Arkansas town. "The big game, which is a great attraction in itself anytime, and the President's visit already have put more gray hairs into my head than all of the other football seasons combined," the police chief said.[35]

On December 6, Air Force One departed Washington just before 10 a.m. with a large, bipartisan contingent of Texas and Arkansas politicians, including Bush, Hammerschmidt, Senators John McClellan and J. William Fulbright of Arkansas, and Representatives J. J. "Jake" Pickle, George Mahon, Robert Price, and Jim Wright of Texas. Also on the plane were Attorney General John Mitchell, National Security Advisor Henry Kissinger, Haldeman, and University of Oklahoma running back Steve Owens, the winner of the Heisman Trophy. It is no surprise that these men discussed football, and Nixon impressed many of them with the depth of his knowledge of the game. Governor Rockefeller and Mills joined the presidential party in Arkansas.[36]

When Air Force One landed in Ft. Smith, Arkansas, the weather was chilly and overcast, but four thousand hog-calling fans waited to greet Nixon. "I have never heard a yell like that before," he later remarked. The reception also impressed him. "We flew over the airport and I saw the cars parked for, well, actually not just feet nor yards, but miles down the road," he told the crowd. The people of Arkansas, as far as Richard Nixon was concerned, understood well that it was their duty as fans to support their team. A reporter for the *Arkansas Democrat* observed that there were no protesters at the airport, just people carrying signs backing the Razorbacks and welcoming the president. "All that I know is that we are going to see today, in this 100th anniversary of football, one of the great football game of all time, and both of them I wish could be Number 1," the president remarked.[37]

The presidential party flew to Fayetteville aboard marine helicopters. Bad weather forced the pilot to fly on instruments and caused the group to arrive late. "Nixon was very impatient," Hammerschmidt recalled. "He never wanted to be late to anything." Only a small handful of people were present to greet Nixon when his helicopter landed outside Razorback Stadium. The president and his entourage made their way to their assigned seats on the thirty-five-yard line, sitting among other fans on the west side of the stadium. When the stadium announcer commented on his arrival, he stood and waved, and the crowd gave him an enthusiastic welcome.[38]

At this early point in the game, the home team dominated. Arkansas had won the coin toss and elected to play with the wind to their back, so they kicked the ball to the Longhorns. On the second play of the game a Texas player fumbled, and Arkansas recovered on the twenty-two-yard line. Nixon had not even arrived when the Razorbacks scored five plays later. The Razorbacks made it into the end zone again when quarterback Bill Montgomery threw a twenty-six-yard touchdown pass, but a penalty nullified the play. The score remained 7–0. Texas did little better. Mistakes and the Razorback defense stopped Longhorn drives just as they began to gain momentum.[39]

Texas made it across the fifty-yard line only twice in the first half. The first time the Longhorns were at the forty-four-yard line, when Texas quarterback James Street threw a long pass that sailed down the field, but a Razorback intercepted the ball at the eight-yard line. This play brought the people in the stands, including the president of the United States, to their feet. The second time Texas crossed midfield, the Longhorn drive sputtered out at the thirty-one-yard line. The Arkansas defense had done an effective job of shutting down the most productive offense in college football.[40]

The presence of protesters at a presidential appearance is a common phenomenon, and this football game was no different. The Justice Department warned the White House staff that a number of groups had planned several demonstrations for the game. Most of these involved local issues associated with the desegregation of the campus. The only protests that involved Nixon were those about the Vietnam War. On a hillside overlooking the north end zone, several students constructed a giant peace sign. There were several other banners about the massacre in the Vietnamese village of My Lai. A reporter noted that the president looked at the sign and briefly displayed a "grave expression." Sports columnist Jack Keady of the *Arkansas Democrat* later wrote, "Let's hope the people around the nation saw on TV what really happened at Fayetteville, and won't believe all they'll read about the game in their eastern and coast newspapers." The attention that other journalists paid to the protests irritated Keady. "The *New York Times* writer was more interested in the twelve students who paraded a 'Peace' sign on the far away hillside." Actually, Keady's paper had more coverage of the protests; the article in the *Times* included no mention at all of any demonstrations at the game, and the television broadcast never showed the display. The political signs, however, were a small minority of those on display in and around the stadium. Most were about the game, and at the moment the president was more interested in football than politics. He reacted strongly to certain plays and had lively conversations with his entourage. In other words, he was an average fan.[41]

During halftime, Nixon was the center of attention. He strengthened his sports credentials during an appearance on television with ABC sportscaster Chris Schenkel. Because of the president's interview, the bands from both schools were featured only briefly on television. As the president made his way into the press box, the Texas band honored the presence of the president by forming the word "Nixon" on the field and playing "Hail to the Chief." The president waved to the band in acknowledgment from the broadcast booth, and then the television screen faded into a picture of Nixon and Schenkel. The politician was wearing a gray wool overcoat and was smiling and upbeat throughout the interview. He was a bit stiff in front of the camera, but it was cold in the booth. His breath was visible in the air. The camera stayed focused on him throughout the interview in either solo shots or in duo portraits with Schenkel. "I must say I have never seen a football game where there is more excitement in the air than there is today," he said at the start of the interview.[42]

The fans, as far as Nixon was concerned, were doing their part in this contest. After Schenkel asked him what he expected in the second half, Nixon's demeanor changed. The tone of his voice dropped, giving him a touch of authority: "I think that Texas has enormous power that is really not unleashed yet, and that in the second half they are likely to be much better offensively." Nixon also explained how the Longhorns would score. "I think they are going to have to throw more. They have an excellent passer and they will have to throw to open up the Arkansas defense. I think under those circumstances they are likely to score once or twice."[43]

Nixon was extremely careful in his interview to adopt a neutral stance. Every sentence praising one school was followed by another praising the other. Nevertheless, a reporter from the *Washington Post* took this remark as an indication that the president was rooting for Texas. After leaving the television booth, Nixon had to walk through the press box, and he stopped to chat briefly with the sports reporters. No one from the White House press corps had a chance to ask him any questions. The only room for the political reporters was along the sidelines, where they spent the game standing in the rain and chill.[44] The sports reporters had the advantage in every way.

The Razorbacks continued their domination of the Longhorns when the second half started. Arkansas recovered a Texas fumble at their own forty-seven-yard line and marched the fifty-three yards to the end zone in only five plays. The Razorbacks led 14–0. Texas had turned over the ball five times in their first eight possessions. As the game went into the fourth quarter of play, Arkansas players were talking about the design of their conference championship rings.[45]

The last fifteen minutes were dramatically different from the previous forty-five. The Longhorns started on their own twenty-yard line and reached the Arkansas forty-two when the final period began. Street tried to throw, but found his receivers covered and decided to run. He broke through a tackle at the line of scrimmage and raced down along the sideline, outrunning an Arkansas player the last fifteen yards into the end zone.[46]

Reporters covering the game could sense a shift in the momentum. The next play was a two-point conversion, which Street ran into the end zone again, making the score 14–8. Arkansas responded with a drive of seventy-three yards, which stopped at the seven-yard line when Montgomery had a pass intercepted in the end zone. This play prevented Arkansas from scoring a third time, meaning Texas could still win if it could put together one touchdown drive. The Razorback defenders, however, stopped the Longhorns on the resulting possession. The next time the Longhorns got their hands on the ball again, only six minutes and ten seconds remained in the game.[47]

This possession seemed as futile as those of the first half. With 4:47 left in the game, Texas was stuck at its own forty-threeyard line on fourth down.

After consulting with Royal on the sideline, Street came back to the huddle and told his teammates they were going to throw the ball long.[48]

The players were flabbergasted. Texas was not a program known for deep passes. "You gotta be shittin' me" was a comment many in the huddle attributed to tackle Bob McKay. Several players, including McKay, dispute this version. "I don't remember Bob saying anything, but I guarantee you, *everybody* in the huddle was *thinking*, 'You gotta be shittin' me,'" fullback Steve Worster recalled. Street had his receivers run deep routes, and they encountered heavy defensive coverage. Tight end Randy Peschel made it to the thirteen-yard line, and Street threw a long bomb that sailed directly between two Arkansas defenders into Peschel's outstretched hands. Two plays later the Longhorns reached the end zone, and kicked the extra point to go ahead 15–14 with just under four minutes to play.[49]

The home team refused to concede defeat. Montgomery marched the Razorbacks down the field, gaining a new first down on all but one play. A light, cold rain began to fall during this drive, making it more difficult to throw and catch. (Reporters noticed that Nixon remained bareheaded.) Arkansas was at the Texas thirty-nine and only needed to get within the field goal range of their kicker to win the game. After a time-out and a sideline conference with Broyles, Montgomery took the snap and threw to a receiver at the twenty-yard line. He caught the ball in the air, but a Texas defender decided to contest the play and stole it out of his hands—interception. The Arkansas drive was over. Texas had won the game, 15–14.[50]

The "Big Shootout" had lived up to its billing. "This was one of the great games of all time," Nixon proclaimed afterward. The president had a tendency to make outrageous statements that exaggerated the importance of truly dramatic moments. This occasion was not one of them. Even experts agreed that the game was one for the ages. Beano Cook, a sportscaster for ABC at the game, told two historians of football at the University of Texas that the contest was at that time the "greatest game since the end of World War II." The sports editor of the *Austin American* explained why: "The ebb and flow of play was such that it emotionally wrung out the followers of both sides."[51]

Nixon dominated postgame events just as he had the halftime show. After Texas players and coaches arrived in their locker room, the Secret Service closed off access to the room. Thinking that the agent guarding the door was a University of Arkansas official, Texas assistant coaches Fred Akers and Emory Bellard pushed their way inside. "It was one of the neater runs of the afternoon," a sports columnist commented. The broadcasters waited for Nixon to arrive in the locker room. When he did, he had a very large grin on his face and his trademark awkwardness was gone. He shook hands as he worked his way toward a raised platform where the microphones waited. The room exploded in applause and cheers when he stepped up to his place. Nixon became visibly stiff as he stood in front of the cameras, but he was still clearly enjoying the moment. He wasted no time in giving his award to the coach. "In presenting this plaque, I want to say first that the AP and the UPI will name Texas Number 1, as we know, after this game." There was no question, as far as he was concerned, about the Longhorns deserving this honor: "Having seen this game, what convinced me that Texas deserves that [ranking] is the fact that you won a tough one. For a team to be behind 14 to 0 and then not to lose its cool and to go on to win, that proves that you deserve to be Number 1, and that is what you are." The room exploded in cheers and applause again.[52]

Coach Royal accepted the trophy and expressed what were, in all likelihood, the sentiments of every member of his coaching staff and team, "Mr. President, it is a great thrill for us to win the football game, but the big thrill, I know I speak for all our squad, is for the President of the United States to take time to endorse college football and to honor us with your presence in our locker room." Royal was indeed speaking for his team. There were many Horns who had no love for Nixon politically, but were glad to have the president of the United States with them. Guard Bobby Mitchell, who had lost a brother in Vietnam, would later remark, "You were so elated, on such a high, it's kind of like you're on equal footing with the president and Billy Graham and we're national champions. Your frame of mind is that the whole world is watching and cares about football and nothing else exists, you're king of the heap. So why *wouldn't* the president be here?" Another tackle, Greg Ploetz, "wasn't crazy" about Nixon, but realized the moment was unique. "I sensed that because the president was there and he had come down to see us, this was a special deal. So I shook his hand." As Nixon left the room, television announcer Bill Fleming called the event "unprecedented."[53]

Nixon was too a good politician to ignore the Razorbacks. After leaving the Longhorns to celebrate their victory, he made his way to the other side of the stadium to visit with the Arkansas dressing room, shaking hands with an occasional bystander. The television cameras followed him as Schenkel talked on the air about past presidents and their association with football. In the Arkansas locker room, Nixon stood on a raised platform next to Broyles and said, "I know how you feel. In my field of politics, I have lost some close ones and I have won some close ones. But I want you to know that in the 100th year of football, in the game to prove which was to be Number 1, we couldn't have had a greater game."[54]

The Razorback locker room was solemn. Broyles was clearly devastated at the loss. After Nixon made his remarks he slowly walked out of the locker room with Senator Fulbright. Individual Arkansas players came up to the president and introduced themselves. He gave each of them a few seconds as the television cameras watched. Terry Stewart, a defensive back with strong antiwar views, saw the moment in nonpolitical terms. "I wasn't a big fan of his in terms of politics and the Vietnam War, but I don't think that made his presence any less special. I think you separate the office and the man from his politics." Safety Dennis Berner, a team captain, shared similar views. "It was an honor that he recognized us that way. I was not a big fan of President Nixon, but I still was glad he was there and that his office and what it represented was at that game."[55]

Several players wanted little to do with their guest. These views had little to do with politics; they were in pain. They did have the good taste not to say anything to the president. Outside the locker room, Nixon told reporters, "They're a great team. They know how to win, and they know how to lose." One television producer later recalled, "It was extremely moving, since, as we all realized, he was actually taking about himself." Later that evening, Broyles had dinner with some reporters and said, "I think what everybody will remember about this day is that Arkansas and Texas played a great game and the President came."[56]

Media coverage of the president's visit to Arkansas was extremely positive. Nixon and his staff could not have asked for better coverage, as Haldeman noted at the time:

> He did a great job and TV covered it thoroughly: the arrival by helicopter; the half-time interview in the press box; the plaque presentation to Texas (15–14); the crowd scene outside the locker room; the consolation visit to the Arkansas locker room. Great stuff. Especially at half-time, when [the] P gave thorough

analysis of the game so far, and outlook for second half, which proved 100 percent accurate. And some really good stuff in the locker rooms, talking to the players. A real coup with the sports fans.[57]

Photos of Nixon either watching the game or presenting the plaque to Royal appeared on the front pages of newspapers across the country. The *Arkansas Democrat* and *Arkansas Gazette* were exceptions. The *Democrat* ran a photo of the president in the Razorbacks' dressing room, while the *Gazette* had a photo of Nixon in the stands with Governor Rockefeller. In addition, the sports sections of many papers ran stories on Nixon that quoted heavily from his halftime interview and his comments to the two teams afterward.[58]

There was a sad note in the aftermath of the game. Freddie Steinmark, a starter all season for the Longhorns as a safety, had a bruised leg that would not heal. He had hidden the injury from the coaches all season out of fear that they might not let him play. After the game, he found the pain too much to bear and reported to the team trainer. After learning the details, the team doctor suspected a cancerous tumor and ordered X-rays, which supported his diagnosis. Steinmark and the doctor flew to Houston the next day to have the athlete admitted to M. D. Anderson Hospital for more testing. Royal broke off a visit to New York when he heard the news. "Suddenly that trophy didn't seem as important as it had just before that phone call," the coach reflected later. He was with his player when doctors said the leg would have to be amputated at the hip. The University of Texas established a trust for him and decided to pay for all Steinmark's medical bills.[59]

The fate of this Longhorn was national news. Nixon learned of it from a report on CBS. "A note to him," the president wrote on the side of his press summaries. The president, despite his image as an unprincipled politician, was capable of generous acts of kindness, particularly to individuals who were not particularly powerful and could do little to help him politically. This case was one example. Darrell Royal contacted his old college coach Bud Wilkinson and asked if Nixon would call Steinmark while he was in the hospital. The president agreed and rang the day after the surgery, but failed to reach him, talking instead with his father. The next day he tried again, and this time talked with Steinmark. "Honestly, I don't remember much of what was said; I was excited, of course, and they were still giving me sedation," the ball player would later recall. His father was deeply grateful. "The call sure picked my boy up a bit."[60]

Nixon also wrote the Longhorn, "It takes a special kind of man to be a great football player and it takes a special courage to face the difficult test of a serious operation. You were always a man to be reckoned with on the playing field and we know that the same hearty spirit will sustain and encourage you during this time you must spend in the hospital." Nixon also sent him an autographed photo that read, "To Freddie Steinmark, with admiration for his courage against great odds, from one of his fans."[61]

Steinmark appeared to a make rapid recovery and was on the sidelines for the Cotton Bowl, which his teammates and coaches dedicated to him. After their victory, the team presented him with a game ball. In 1970 he and Royal went to the White House for the start of the American Cancer Crusade. He presented Nixon with a ball that the entire 1969 team signed. "You had a lot of faith in us," Steinmark remarked, "so we'd like you to have this as a token of our appreciation." He also thanked the president for calling him in the hospital. "Well, you needed a lift then," Nixon replied. After presenting Steinmark with a framed certificate, he added, "We've all admired your courage and we are appreciative of the work you're doing for the American Cancer Society."[62]

The disease, however, was persistent. Steinmark fought the cancer for another year and a half, but died in June of 1971. His death was national news. Haldeman, in one last tribute, sent one of his assistants, Jay G. Wilkinson, an ordained minister in the Episcopalian Church and the son of Bud Wilkinson, to the funeral as a special White House envoy. Wilkinson spent an hour with the family and later told Haldeman that Steinmark had framed his letter from Nixon and had it hanging on the wall.[63]

A more immediate aftermath of the game was the regional dispute over the process of awarding the national championship in college football, which pushed Nixon into the role of Southern patron and turned Southerners into Nixon defenders. These developments ultimately helped the president in his efforts to keep support in the region. This controversy was the work of two Pennsylvanians: Governor Raymond Shafer and Joe Paterno, head football coach of the Pennsylvania State University Nittany Lions football team. Despite its success on the field, 1969 was a year without joy for Penn State. The Nittany Lions had completed their second consecutive undefeated season and had a twenty-nine-game winning streak that went back to 1967, yet the team believed they had not received due credit. Ohio State had overshadowed Penn State during most of the Nittany Lions' long undefeated streak. The Buckeyes had also gone undefeated in 1968 and had won the national title, and had almost done the same in 1969. The Nittany Lions were never ranked first in either poll that year, and they watched Texas and Arkansas start the 1969 season with higher rankings, even though both had enjoyed less success in 1968 than Penn State. "Who," Paterno demanded in obvious frustration when his season ended a week before the game in Fayetteville, "has Texas or Arkansas played? How many intersectional games has the Southwest Conference won? Five? Six?"[64]

The slights to the Penn State football team that so infuriated Paterno were byproducts of the informal system used to determine the national title. The National Collegiate Athletic Association (NCAA), which regulated intercollegiate athletics, had a playoff system to award a national championship in every sport it governed, except division I-A football. The "national championship" in this sport was basically a myth. Several different organizations awarded a trophy at the end of the year to the team that they claimed to have "won" the national title. In the culture of college football, the Associated Press and United Press International polls had the most influence. Whichever school occupied the top position at the end of the season was regarded as the national champion. Despite its appearance of objectivity, with numerical rankings and point scores, the polls were actually quite subjective, and a number of factors other than play on the field shaped the final outcome. Regional favoritism was a significant factor. In the 1960s, Southern schools placed well in the polls while schools from the East fared poorly. Even though college football started in New Jersey and the early powers in the sport were Eastern schools, most sportswriters, coaches, and fans in the 1960s thought the quality of the game was inferior in the East. A stronger influence on the polls was tradition. When ranking teams with comparable numbers, poll voters favored teams from established football powers over those from less well regarded programs. In 1969, Penn State was an Eastern school with a modest legacy of success in college football. The Nittany Lions were just beginning to develop into a national power, and they received less respect in the world of college football than either Texas or Arkansas, which were two of the most dominant powers in college football during the 1960s.[65]

Nixon's announcement that he would present a plaque to the winner of the Texas-Arkansas game was too much for the Penn State faithful to bear, but their protests turned the dispute into a regional issue and made Nixon a Southern patron. George Paterno, in his book on his brother, observed that "all hell broke loose in the State of Pennsylvania" that December. One Penn State student understood what the president was doing: "The only reason President Nixon agreed to go south with his trophy was to build Republican party strength there." A few alumni picketed the White House. "We looked it up and found he has no such powers in the Constitution," one remarked. Most of the expressions of outrage found their expression in writing. By the time Nixon left Washington for Arkansas, the White House had received ninety thousand letters and telegrams from angry Penn State students and alumni. The Republican members of the Pennsylvania House of Representatives also sent notes of protest.[66]

Shafer and Paterno made the same argument: it was premature to determine the national title before the bowl games even started. Shafer made this point in a telegram to Nixon and reminded the president that he had already invited him to the Orange Bowl in which Penn State would play. The governor also went public at a press conference the day before the Texas-Arkansas clash, where he posed with a Penn State pennant and a sign that read: "Numero Uno." He made his feelings clear: "I sincerely hope the President will reconsider and will wait until after the bowl games before attempting to designate the finest football team in the nation." Paterno said much the same thing: "Let's wait until all the evidence is in before picking a No. 1 team. After all, seven of the top 10 teams are in bowl games. We're still playing the season."[67]

The criticism forced a concession from Nixon and his White House staff. The day before the Texas-Arkansas game, at a morning press conference reporters peppered White House press secretary Ron Ziegler with questions about the Penn State protests. Ziegler, in the words of a *Washington Post* reporter, "airily" dismissed the Nittany Lions' complaints, noting that the winner of the press association polls was considered the national champion. This response satisfied no one, including Ziegler. He went to the Oval Office, consulted with the president, returned to the press room, and announced that Nixon would give Penn State an "appropriate" tribute for their accomplishments. Reporters asked the obvious question: what kind of tribute? Ziegler had no idea, and left the press room to consult again with Nixon. He returned a few minutes later, and announced that the president would present a plaque to Penn State for having the longest undefeated, untied record in college football. Reporters started asking other questions: what if Texas-Arkansas tied, would Penn State not deserve the title more since it would have a perfect record? "Gentlemen, I have done all I can," Ziegler said, ending discussion on the matter.[68]

Nixon felt obligated to mention the controversy while presenting his award to Royal. "We are going to present a plaque to Penn State as the team in the 100th year with the longest undefeated, untied record. Is that fair enough?" Royal responded quickly, "That is fair enough." When reporters later asked him about Nixon's remarks about Penn State, Royal remarked, "What else could he say."[69]

Paterno, however, rejected the award. "The blood-curdling nerve!," the coach wrote twenty years later. "In his Solomon-like presidential wisdom, Nixon *favored* us with an honor that any idiot consulting a record book could see that we had taken for ourselves, thank you, without his help." He also questioned the president's credentials, calling him "America's leading self-appointed athletic authority." Paterno was livid, but after his wife calmed him down, he issued a more temperate press release. "It would seem a waste of his very valuable time to present a plaque for something we already have undisputed possession of—the nation's longest winning streak," he declared after the Texas-Arkansas game. "To accept any other plaque prior to the bowl games, which will determine the final number one team would be a disservice to our squad, to Pennsylvania, to the East which we represent, and perhaps most important, to Missouri, which may be the best team in the country." Penn State was scheduled to play Missouri in the Orange Bowl on January 1, 1970.[70]

The Penn State protest had some influence. The new AP and UPI polls were released Monday, and Texas, as expected, retained its number-one ranking. Penn State had moved into second place. Arkansas fell to third. Ohio State, ranked first for most of the season, and undefeated but once-tied Southern California placed fourth in one poll and fifth in the other.[71] The UPI poll stopped with the end of the regular season, and according to this news service, Texas became the national champions of college football for 1969.[72] The UPI was the second organization to award Texas a national championship trophy, since the National Football Foundation and Hall of Fame announced on Sunday, December 7, that it was awarding the Mac-

Arthur Bowl, a trophy in the shape of a football stadium named after General of the Army Douglas MacArthur, to the University of Texas.[73] The Associated Press, however, recognized that the Penn State protesters had a point, and announced it would delay its final poll until after the bowl games. None of the top five teams was playing another, and it was altogether possible that any one of them might have a stronger claim than the others to the national title, depending on the outcome of the bowl contests. Paterno said he could live with second, for the time being: "I don't think Texas will be No. 1 at the end of the season."[74]

The announcement that the Associated Press would delay awarding its title put more emphasis on the Cotton Bowl, where Texas would play Notre Dame in Dallas on January 1. The Fighting Irish were ending a self-imposed prohibition against playing in postseason games. The fact that Notre Dame was one of the few football powers with a national following, because of its religious affiliation, only added to the attention directed at this game. Nixon's plaque would have less meaning if Texas lost the Cotton Bowl and its claim to the AP poll title, even though the Longhorns already had the awards of two major organizations.[75]

Southerners quickly took up the defense of the Longhorns, and many suggested that the Texas and Arkansas game had already resolved the matter about the national title. The Nittany Lions had actually been the Cotton Bowl selection committee's first choice as the at-large representative to play the Southwest Conference champion. The Penn State players, however, had voted to go to Miami to play in the Orange Bowl, since Ohio State was still in first place in the polls at the time and seemed unlikely to lose. When the Nittany Lions made their decision, it appeared that the Cotton Bowl would have little impact on the outcome of the national title, and Miami offered better amenities in a warmer climate. What went without mention at the time was that Texas was still a segregated, all-white team and that the black Penn State players had no interest in a contest where the Longhorns would essentially be playing a home game in a city that would not be particularly welcoming. Southerners focused on the Penn State decline of a Cotton Bowl bid in response to the Shafer-Paterno criticisms. A letter writer to the *Philadelphia Inquirer* called Paterno the "No. 1 Cry-Baby of the Year. Penn State could have played Number One—but it ran away!" Jack Keady, a sports columnist for the *Arkansas Democrat*, saw the dispute as a "ridicule" of the Texas-

Arkansas game. He vented his anger at his press colleagues from the East Coast, noting that "all the eastern invaders were trying to run down the 'Presidential Plaque' given Texas, instead of Penn State." The sports columnists of other Southern newspapers blasted Paterno, arguing that Penn State did not deserve the national title since it refused the Cotton Bowl invitation. These columnists failed to realize that Penn State made its decision long before the Cotton Bowl could offer a matchup with the top-ranked team. During this dispute Darrell Royal remained quiet. He could do little else. He had been the quarterback of the 1949 University of Oklahoma team that had gone undefeated, but placed second in the polls to Notre Dame.[76]

Nixon's reaction to the dispute was contradictory. He expected that the football dispute would be an issue that might come up during a presidential press conference, scheduled for Monday, December 8, and Haldeman's notes of conversation indicate that Nixon was not too concerned about the issue. "If comes up as gag—AP + UPI polls," Haldeman wrote. Haldeman, however, was far more concerned than he let on. After helping the president prepare, he recorded in his diary, "Big crisis at Penn State." Nixon brought up the issue as a joke in response to the last question posed to him. Nancy Dickerson, a reporter for NBC, asked him if he had any plans to reach out to the youth of the country. After giving a thoughtful answer about treating young people as adults, he added, "I know a way not to reach them, and that is to try to pick number one as far as the football teams are concerned." And with that comment the press conference came to an end.[77]

The next day the president contradicted himself. When Penn State won the Lambert Trophy as the best team in the East for a third consecutive year, tying the record set by West Point, Nixon sent Paterno a congratulatory telegram:

> ANY TEAM THAT CAN TIE THE RECORD OF THE ARMY JUGGERNAUT OF 1944-45-46 HAS CARVED FOR ITSELF AN ENDURING PLACE IN THE ANNALS OF FOOTBALL GREATNESS.[78]

That evening Nixon was the keynote speaker at the National Football Foundation and Hall of Fame banquet. The president was in his element throughout this black-tie gathering. One reporter noted he had a "relaxed, almost casual gait that seemed so unlike the tensely stiff figure of news conferences and speeches," and as he delivered his speech, he "became warmer and more animated than Washington observers ever could remember." He addressed the controversy with Penn State directly. "I understand that Penn State certainly is among those that should be considered for Number 1 in the United States of America." This comment received considerable press attention.[79]

He also repeated a comment he had made on the air with Schenkel. He was fully aware that having journalists vote one team over another as the champion of college football was a horrible way to award a title. He joked that he wanted to propose a playoff system for college football. "Maybe we ought to have a super college bowl after this," he told the sportscaster. If he had actually pushed that he might have actually succeeded. In his study of college football, Michael Oriard shows that the sport was undergoing massive changes in the late 1960s. Media outlets were making it a commercialized endeavor that had very little to do with the main educational missions of colleges and universities. The lack of a playoff system was only one of the many issues facing the sport, but both Oriard and Ronald A. Smith, in his history of reform efforts in college sport, come to similar conclusions: because of vested interests, real reform always requires outside intervention, be it from the courts, Congress, or the White House. Theodore Roosevelt had once intervened, forcing some fundamental changes that reduced the violence of the sport. If Nixon wanted to push a playoff system, the timing was right. As Smith shows, there was an opening. Sports for Nixon, though, was not about domestic affairs, policy, or legislation. It was political theater, and he was not going to push any agenda. He admitted as much that evening: "I was going to suggest that we have a super college bowl after the November or the January 1 games and then I thought I was in deep enough already."[80]

His other comments received less attention, even in Texas. He got roars of laughter when he remarked that his old college coach had played on a USC team that played and defeated Penn State in the Rose Bowl. In his closing remarks, he completed another reversal. "I think Texas deserved to be Number 1." As far as he was concerned, the gutsy play calling and refusal to give up when they trailed Arkansas 14–0 earned the Longhorns the right to be the top-ranked team in the country. The Longhorns had the spirit that represented football at its best, and the team refused to quit, earning his respect. "Texas demonstrated that day that they were playing to win, they set an example worthy of being Number 1 in the 100th year of college football."[81]

He also explained that he viewed football as being a key factor to American society. In a passage that exposed much of his own character, he explained that the sport developed strength. "Our great assets are not our military strength or our economic wealth, but the character of our young people, and I am glad that America's young people produce the kind of men that we have in American football today." The sport fostered a competitive spirit, the ability and determination to "come back and try again," pride, teamwork and the "feeling of being in a case bigger than yourself." These values and traits of the American people were the greatest national assets that the country enjoyed. The esprit and emotional charge of the team and the crowd that the sport instilled were more important than athletic ability and play calling. "What we need in the spirit of this country and the spirit of our young people is not playing it safe always, not being afraid of defeat—being ready to get into the battle and playing to win, not with the idea of destroying or defeating or hurting anybody else, but with the idea of achieving excellence."[82]

While Nixon explained the role of football in society, his staff retreated on the Texas versus Penn State issue. Ziegler sent out letters arguing that the president had not awarded any team the national championship. "The significance of the plaque was a presentation to the winner of a particular game which, in effect, commemorated an important contest between two major football teams on the 100th anniversary of collegiate football."[83]

Nixon remained in an embarrassing position until January 1, when Texas defeated Notre Dame in the Cotton Bowl. Darrell Royal was fully aware that the president was in an awkward situation. He was at the same National Football Foundation and Hall of Fame dinner with his team captains to accept the MacArthur Bowl, and he gave Nixon a Cotton Bowl watch and a promise that the Longhorns would not let him down.[84]

Even after the bowl games, Paterno kept agitating on the issue. Both Texas and Penn State won their bowl games. Penn State beat Missouri in the Orange Bowl. After his team threw him and Governor Shafer into the shower, a dripping Paterno addressed reporters about the national championship:

I don't like to keep pushing this thing but I still think we have as much right to be number one as Texas or anybody else. Why should I sit back and let the President of the United States say that so-and-so is number one when I got fifty kids who've worked their tails off for me for three years. People can say it is sour grapes, but I'd be a lousy coach if I didn't argue for my own team.[85]

That argument, while understandable, carried little weight with the poll voters. Texas defeated the Fighting Irish 21–17 and remained in first place in the AP poll. Penn State had to settle for the second spot. Nixon called Darrell Royal after the game to offer his congratulations. The dispute was on Royal's mind when he remarked, "I'm glad we didn't cause you to be embarrassed by your selection as number one." In an action that was a personal trademark, the president denied the obvious: "I wouldn't have been embarrassed even had you lost, because it was a great, hard-fought game by both teams and you played like champions."[86]

The dispute about the 1969 national title would irritate Paterno for years to come. On June 16, 1973, as the Watergate crisis exploded, he gave the commencement speech at Penn State. "I'd like to know, how could the President know so little about Watergate in 1973, and so much about college football in 1969." The audience roared. He later explained, "I was just trying to get a laugh, but some people took me seriously." Paterno had the grace, however, not to raise the issue in person with Nixon when he visited the White House a few weeks after the end of the 1969 season.[87]

Nixon loved football, but his trip to Arkansas had been about politics. Americans want a president to whom they can relate, but they also want one they feel is capable of serving in such a demanding position of authority. Even though these views are contradictory, Nixon presented himself successfully in both roles at both the Redskins-Cowboys game and "The Game." He gained a good deal of visibility and complimentary press coverage at both contests. Even the feud with Joe Paterno worked to his advantage. He had gotten extensive media coverage, using the professional norms of journalists to his advantage. His presence in the world of sports boosted the status of sports reporters, and these journalists had different issues, questions, and storylines from those of their colleagues who covered politics in the news departments. Those different concerns had resulted in a good deal of flattering press coverage for Nixon, because his very presence elevated the status of sports journalism even though the reporters made no effort to push the president on matters of policy.

Despite this success, it was difficult for Nixon to let go of old grudges.

On January 2, 1970, the *New York Times* ran a feature story about Nixon's involvement with sports in 1969. The story recounted his appearances at certain games and his phone calls to various players and coaches, which was a fairly new practice at that time. The article contained a few factual errors, but nothing that reflected poorly on the president. In fact, Nixon and his staff would have had difficulty generating press coverage as flattering. "The point is not so much that he is interested in sports, but that he has given the passions of others White House endorsement, which helps them psychologically and him politically," Robert Semple wrote in the story.[88]

Nixon quickly objected to the article. Haldeman recorded in his diary, "P was somewhat disturbed with the Bob Semple piece in the New York Times on describing his day yesterday because it concentrates on his seeing Boy Scouts, football players and Republican governors. Makes it appear that he does nothing of substance, and he thinks we've overreacted in trying to get out the personal interest stuff. I think basically he's right."[89]

The article mentioned nothing about Boy Scouts or Republican governors and might be easily dismissed as an example of Nixon's viewpoint that the major outlets of the national media were so hostile toward him that he refused to believe they would print anything flattering about him were it not for another incident involving the *Greenville News* of Greenville, South Carolina. An article in this small paper suggested that he set some type of record for number of hours spent in front of the television watching football, putting "him on comfortable common ground with most males as a staunch sports fan." Even though this paper was a minor regional media outlet with a limited audience, Nixon became livid when he learned about this article. "Get out fast I missed both games on (Jan. 2)," he noted on the margin of a document. "I never allow T.V. to interfere with state business." A day later a memo to that effect was sent out, instructing the White House staff to spread that message.[90]

The only problem was this statement was wrong. Haldeman made several entries in his diary showing that Nixon rearranged his schedule many times so that he could watch football games on television. Events were also scheduled to avoid competing with major sporting events for public attention. "I was thinking of Sunday night, but that is the day of the Super Bowl and I don't think we want to try and compete with that," Nixon told Kissinger about an announcement the administration planned to make about the Vietnam War. With that point made, official business always got done in a timely fashion even if sports affected timing of some matters.[91]

Nixon had done an impressive job in using sport as political theater. He had manipulated the media, using the divisions between various branches of journalism to his advantage. He had, however, shown something of his own views and values. He would continue to do the same in 1970, but his efforts in the midterm elections were far less successful.

3

The Olympics and the All-Star Game

After the college football bowls ended the dispute about the national championship—everywhere that is except in the dwellings of the Penn State faithful—Nixon spent the new year trying to build on the success he had enjoyed in 1969 in the world of sport. He scored some more attention-getting victories, but the defeats he suffered were more significant.

At the beginning of the year it looked like 1970 would be more of 1969. Early indicators, however, offered a deceptively positive forecast. Nixon was quite popular with the American people at the beginning of the year, and the Washington Senators entered the 1970 season trying to build on the foundation of their first winning season. In what was something of a minor political windfall, team owner Robert Short put Nixon on the cover of the team's program for the year.[1] Just before Super Bowl IV, the president called Hank Stram, head coach of the Kansas City Chiefs football team. Kansas City was about to play the Minnesota Vikings in the last AFL versus NFL Super Bowl. Nixon assured Stram that there was nothing to the rumors that quarterback Len Dawson would be indicted in a Justice Department probe into gambling and professional football. Nixon asked Stram to pass the word on to Dawson so the he could play the game without any worries. "I have long felt that a boost at the right time, particularly for an underdog, falls into the category of things we ought to do more often," he wrote, explaining the action. As far as Nixon was concerned, the fan was part of the team.[2]

Overall, though, this time was a difficult one for the administration. The president suffered a humiliating setback in the spring that was a disaster of his own making. In August 1969, Nixon nominated Clement F. Haynsworth, chief judge of the Fourth Circuit Court of Appeals, to a vacant position on the Supreme Court. The nomination of the South Carolina native was part of his effort to court Southern support. As retribution for the rejection of Associate Justice Abe Fortas as a nominee for the position of chief justice in 1968, and then for the way in which he was driven off the high court under the threat of impeachment for corruption, liberal Northern Democrats quickly went after the nominee, even though he was a Democrat. It was apparent in September that the Haynsworth nomination was dead, but Nixon stuck with his nominee in an act of defiance. On November 21, the Senate voted 45–44 against the judge. Many observers thought Nixon strengthened his political support in the South—after all he had tried to advance the agenda of the region. He tried to get his next nominee through quickly, since the liberals had spent their political capital. On January 19, 1970, Nixon put forward the name of Judge G. Harrold Carswell. In a reflection of his contempt for the Senate, the president nominated an individual woefully underqualified for service on the high court. To make matters worse, Carswell had a long, clear record as a segregationist. As the beginning of the baseball season neared, so did the final vote on this second nomination. In fact, both were scheduled to take place on April 6. "I would imagine that the President has some strong personal beliefs about whether or not to open the baseball season," Dwight Chapin wrote his boss, Haldeman. He suggested that there was another way Nixon could show his disdain for the political games the legislators were playing with judicial nominations. "Since it has already been reported that the President is not going since he will be waiting at the White House for the outcome of the Carswell vote, it might be a good stroke for him to go on out to the ball park." Chapin wanted Nixon to throw the first pitch and then leave after an inning or two. Nixon, however, never left games early and decided that son-in-law David Eisenhower should perform the ceremonial duty. Eisenhower was a bit reluctant, but Short's direct request and his father-in-law's preference carried the day.[3]

On April 6, Eisenhower threw out the first ball for a game between Washington and the Detroit Tigers after a fifty-five-minute rain delay threatened to cancel the event. The official attendance figure was 45,012, representing the number of tickets sold, but the chilly, gloomy forty-two-degree weather resulted in several thousand no-shows. The Senators left twenty-nine runners stranded on base, one shy of the major league record, making this statistic a harbinger of the year to come for the team. When the game ended after dark with another Senators' loss, there were only 2,500 fans in the stands, but one of them was the president of the United States. After the Senate rejected Carswell 51–45, he left for Robert F. Kennedy Memorial Stadium, arriving in the fifth inning and staying with his family until the end of the game.[4]

Nixon's participation in the opening-day festivities was a symbolic function expected of him in his capacity as the head of state and allowed him on that particular date to minimize—to a small degree—the political defeat he had suffered in his role as chief executive. The interaction of most presidents with the athletic world rarely moves beyond these traditional functions, but at that very moment, Nixon had his administration and the US government involved in a secret campaign that would have had a major impact on sport if it had been successful. A few weeks before the start of the 1970 baseball season Nixon committed his administration to bring the Olympic Games of 1976 to Los Angeles. The last time the United States had hosted the summer games was 1932. Adding a nice bit of irony to the story, the host city that year was Los Angeles. The United States Olympic Committee (USOC) was interested in hosting the games again. Since the 1940s, Detroit had been the designated bid city for the United States. In 1960, the United States hosted the winter games in Squaw Valley, California. Repeated efforts to bring the sports festival to Michigan were unsuccessful. In 1968, the USOC replaced Detroit with Los Angeles as the official American nominee for the summer games, and named Denver for the winter ones in 1976. The International Olympic Committee (IOC) would make its decision in May 1970.[5]

These events might have passed without notice in Washington had people representing the Los Angeles effort not injected the Nixon administration into the bid process. In early January, members of the Los Angeles committee made several efforts to get administration support. The Los Angeles 1976 Olympic Committee tried and failed to make a presentation to President Nixon, so Bill Nicholas, a committee member, made a direct appeal during an Oval Office visit as part of a delegation from the Tournament of Roses Association. Another committeeman, Rodney Rood, contacted an old acquaintance of his, H. R. Haldeman. John Kilroy, committee president, also sent a letter to Nixon, but it appears that it was the Rood and Nicholas efforts that initiated action. Detroit had never enjoyed much support from the US government in its attempt to host the Olympics, but Los Angeles representatives used the fear that the games might go to Moscow to good advantage in obtaining federal assistance.[6]

The Soviet Union had decided to make a bid to host the 1976 games, and the selection process soon became a contest of prestige with Cold War overtones. Rood made this point quite clear with Haldeman: "We are now in direct confrontation with the Soviet Union on the level of international politics—a confrontation to determine international public appeal under the guise of non-politics—the award of the Summer Olympic Games of 1976." The Denver bid was a complicating factor. The Californians wanted help for Los Angeles and knew that the US government might feel obliged to provide equal assistance to Denver, which would dilute their effort. In the history of the modern Olympics only two nations, the United States in 1932 and Germany in 1936, had hosted both the winter and summer games. "The first objective of the United States should be to obtain the 1976 Summer Games, a far greater victory than the obtaining of the Winter Games in view of the magnitude of the athletic and cultural events associated with the Summer program, and the competition with Moscow and the Soviet Union," Rood stated. He also suggested that the fact that the United States had hosted the 1960 winter games would work against Denver and that Los Angeles had, as a result, a much better chance of winning the summer games. "Should Los Angeles fail, after an all-out effort, there may be a possibility for Denver on the Winter Games vote."[7]

The Los Angeles committee basically wanted the US government to provide service in support of their private effort. In January, Rood vaguely asked for the "support and endorsement of our program by the President." Three weeks later, he contacted the Haldeman and made four specific requests. First, that the president send a personal representative, preferably an astronaut, to the Caribbean Games to be held in Panama. The success of this gathering was extremely important to Virgilio de Leon, the Panamanian representative on the IOC. The Los Angeles committee had offered these games considerable support, expecting to win de Leon's vote. The Californians also hoped that he would persuade other Latin American IOC delegates to support the US bid. Rood also wanted the administration to get the National Aeronautics and Space Administration to provide a supply of moon rock that the committee could incorporate into pins to give to members of the IOC. The California businessman made an additional request; the US Information Agency should provide the committee with a one hundred thousand dollar grant to finance its operations. Until then, county and municipal governments and private business had funded the committee, putting it a competitive disadvantage. "We need financial assistance from the Federal Government because of our greatly accelerated visitation program necessitated by the aggressive competition of the Soviet Union." The one hundred thousand dollar request was a reduction from the quarter of a million dollars that Kilroy had asked Nixon to provide a month before. Finally, Rood wanted the administration to provide a waiver from the Civil Aeronautics Board so that Los Angeles committee members could fly the private, but regulated, US airlines for free, reducing their operating costs. Kilroy later requested that a presidential representative attend the Caribbean Games and that Nixon attend a black tie premiere party in Los Angeles for a documentary film on the 1968 Mexico City Olympics. Many members of the IOC were expected to attend.[8]

There was a brief exchange about these requests inside the White House and the Old Executive Office Building. Bud Wilkinson noted that in previous years the US government had clearly honored the ideals of this international sports movement by not using national resources to support a municipality's bid to host an Olympiad. "I do not believe the President should be personally involved in this campaign, and I am definitely opposed to giving Los Angeles any money."[9] Richard Nixon, however, thought differently, and the administration moved forward.

The Olympics issue quickly became involved in multiple bureaucratic efforts and attempts to delegate responsibility to others. Individuals from the State Department, the National Security Council, and the White House all worked on this project. White House aide Larry Higby realized this was counterproductive and thought that one individual should be responsible for the matter. Since the Olympics were an international movement, he thought the staff of the National Security Council was best equipped to coordinate administration efforts. The problem with this idea was that the people working for the NSC were trained as political scientists, historians, lawyers, military officers, and economists, and knew little about sports management. "I don't mind at all your throwing the ball back at me, because that allows me to engage in the same sport," NSC staff member Helmut Sonnenfeldt told Higby. "Seriously, we share your unfamiliarity with this problem, and as a result I'll offer you all the NSC type guidance I can; but I'm afraid it doesn't cover some of the points."[10]

Thwarted but still determined, Higby gave Haldeman a memo on administration efforts and suggested that one individual be tasked with overall responsibility. "I feel that this whole operation should be housed in Kissinger's office and would recommend that you sign Tab B, a memorandum to Kissinger asking him to assign a staff man for all Olympic matters." Haldeman scrawled a large "No" over the paragraph. The chief of staff agreed with advice about making one individual responsible, but he wanted to retain control over the White House effort rather than give it to Kissinger. Haldeman thought about the idea over the weekend, and when he returned to work on Monday, he made Charles Stuart the project manager. Haldeman called Stuart into the Oval Office for an unscheduled meeting. Nixon and Haldeman informed him he was going to be in charge of the White House effort. "This is a matter that is of the highest priority and you should act to do everything that is reasonably necessary to get the 1976 Olympics here in the U.S," the chief of staff informed Stuart in the memo assigning him the job. Nixon went further. He wanted both Denver and Los Angeles to host the Winter and Summer Games. Haldeman was blunt in a handwritten notation on another memo, "Do *everything* necessary to get 1976 Olympics in U.S." In fact, Stuart's work started that weekend. He went on a trip to the Scandinavian countries with the members of the Los Angeles committee.[11]

Despite this appointment, the conflicting bureaucratic interests continued to shape the actions of the administration. Haldeman had positioned himself and his staff to take credit for the achievement of helping bring the Olympics to the United States, but he also made it clear that others shared responsibility for the effort, if not day-to-day administration. At the bottom of a routine memo to Kissinger announcing Stuart's appointment, the White House chief of staff had added a sharp, handwritten note. "Henry—we've <u>got</u> to win this one—don't let it get away from us."[12]

The administration initially worked to honor most of the requests that Rood and Kilroy had made on behalf of the Los Angeles committee, but soon began advancing its own ideas. Nixon himself initiated this change. "He was captivated by the thought of having the summer games in California, his home state, as he would undoubtedly be invited to participate in some way or could better control events," Stuart recalled. The president sent a letter to all members of the International Olympic Committee supporting the city's bid. Nixon mentioned the "splendid climate" and "renowned hospitality" of the region. In a subtle dig at the Soviet Union, he also stated that the "freedom of movement and expression" that Southern California was known for would make Los Angeles "a particularly suitable and exceptionally attractive site for the Olympic competitions."[13]

Nixon also wanted to send a personal letter to the US ambassador in each country with a representative on the IOC "putting a personal responsibility on him to deliver that country's vote." He specifically wanted each ambassador to meet with their host foreign ministry and insist that officials in these agencies pressure their Olympic delegate to vote for Los Angeles. As Haldeman noted the ambassadors were to "sell like hell + deliver the vote." The chief of staff told Stuart to provide a list of the undecided delegates and warned, "Don't let this delay any longer than you have to because the President will keep pushing on it." Stuart recommended against this action, suggesting instead that the Department of State contact the ambassadors representing these nations in the United States and apply the pressure in Washington. This view prevailed. Brigadier General Alexander Haig, Kissinger's deputy, informed the State Department that the administration wanted to target twelve countries: Belgium, Chile, West Germany, Great Britain, Greece, France, Indonesia, Iran, Italy, Pakistan, Switzerland, and Yugoslavia.[14]

This idea of Nixon's was an exceptionally bad one, and it reflected a superficial understanding of the administrative structure of international sport. The International Olympic Committee was a private, self-selecting organization similar to a social or country club. The members were there because they knew other members. There was no federal structure to the organization. There were no delegates representing national Olympic committees of member nations. The IOC members liked to think they were ambassadors of the Olympic movement to their home nations rather than delegates representing a national prospective. As a result, there were many nations that had no voice on the committee. All the members were on the IOC as private individuals, even if they held important positions in government. Factors such as personal relationships and the strength/popularity of certain sports drove the internal politics of the IOC rather than issues of world affairs. With only two years left in his tenure as IOC president, Avery Brundage had no intention of violating or repudiating values he had held dear for his entire adult life, which included a stringent instance on maintaining the amateur status of athletes and a determined effort to keep politics out of the games. He was, however, a good American, and would love to see the Olympics back in the United States. He made himself available to members of the Los Angeles group and gave them advice—but that in no way means he was about to become the agent of the Californians. He constantly warned Los Angeles officials that they could not assume that appreciation for the achievements of US foreign policy would automatically garner them votes in the IOC. Brundage tried to explain these facts to the Californians, but they apparently did not believe him and clearly never shared these views with the Nixon administration.[15]

This transformation from general support to active lobbying also took place as part of the efforts to obtain a waiver from the Civil Aeronautics Board (CAB). Two airlines, Pan Am and TWA, were willing to provide free international transportation but were prohibited from doing so under federal regulations. The board could make exemptions if it was deemed of "paramount national interest." Denver had obtained such an exception in 1969, and the White House began pushing for exemptions for both cities in 1970. Historical precedent worked against this effort. In the past, the board had made exemptions only at the request of either the State or the Commerce Department, and only for foreign journalists traveling to the United States. The rationale for this policy was that it was a subtle way to assure the nation of favorable coverage in the media outlets of a number of other countries. In the middle of February, John Ehrlichman, believing the State Department had the power to waive CAB regulations, asked Kissinger to take the matter up with Acting Secretary of State Elliot Richardson.[16]

When Ehrlichman's memo arrived at the offices of the NSC, Haig recommended that they take no action. He had talked to members of Richardson's staff, and they told him they were concerned that requesting such a waiver would set a dangerous precedent—every other equally deserving group would expect assistance. "I am inclined," he told Kissinger, "to think that it would be dangerous to push this one too hard and suggest that you talk to Elliot Richardson about it and that we hold with whatever hard-nosed judgment State comes up with." Kissinger accepted this advice. He noted the "paramount national interest" requirement and observed, "This is a most difficult judgment for State to make in this case, and we should not be overly optimistic that the Secretary will be able to arrive at such a judgment."[17]

Since getting a waiver for members of the two committees was proving problematic, Stuart tried to obtain free travel for all the Olympic teams. This effort was sound and changed the focus of administration efforts. Such a measure would have made it much easier for some of the poorer national Olympic committees around the world to send their athletes and coaches to Los Angeles. Stuart found the CAB willing to make this type of waiver, but the International Air Transport Association of America, an aviation industry organization, was unwilling to go along with this effort. Stuart later learned that the two airlines that showed the most resistance were Pan Am and TWA. His idea was far more expensive than what these two corporations had originally volunteered to do for the Los Angeles committee.[18]

Under Stuart's direction the Nixon White House took a number of other actions to win support for the Los Angeles bid, many of which were done without any request from the committee. Some of these actions were nothing more than good lobbying efforts, but others were underhanded and suspect. Stuart continually wrote progress reports for Haldeman, establishing a strong documentary record of White House efforts. He sent presidential tie clasps to every member of the IOC. He traveled overseas with Los Angeles committee members as a "White House representative," showing that the city had high-level support. Stuart also arranged to have promotional brochures and other paperwork for both Denver and Los Angeles sent overseas via diplomatic pouch, saving the two committees a considerable amount of money in postage. Officials from the US embassy presented the publicity material to the individual IOC representatives. These deliveries helped give the Los Angeles and Denver efforts the cast of official US sanction. The State Department also provided Stuart with a number of support services that ranged from the mundane—tracking down addresses—to the critical—providing information that Foreign Service officers gained on the Olympics.[19]

Stuart failed in his efforts to influence Brundage on behalf of Los Angeles. The Los Angeles committee repeatedly suggested to Stuart that Nixon honor the IOC president in some way. "The Los Angeles Olympic Committee people feel that if Brundage were to receive some indication of Presidential recognition prior to his leaving for Amsterdam on May 1st, he would likely be so euphoric as to violate his established principles and really push for Los Angeles," Stuart explained to Haldeman. "I tend to believe this evaluation." Some of the honors that Stuart suggested included awarding Brundage the Presidential Medal of Freedom, holding a dinner or luncheon in his honor, staging the premiere of the film on the 1968 Mexico City Olympics at the White House, or just having Nixon meet with him in the Oval Office. "None of the above proposals were acceptable," Stuart noted vaguely. He urged Haldeman to have the president contact Brundage before the IOC vote and inform him that he would be receiving the Medal of Freedom later in the year. There is, however, no indication that Haldeman ever took the matter up with Nixon, which is probably just as well.[20]

Stuart also oversaw the use of subtle bribes to acquire IOC votes. According to John Kilroy, president of the Los Angeles 1976 Olympic Committee, the Latin American delegates were the key bloc in determining the outcome. General Jose Clark Flores, the representative from Mexico, wanted to become president after Brundage and was attempting to deliver votes for Moscow in return for the support of communist Eastern Europe in his personal campaign. "Although General Clark has called for solidarity in the Latin American bloc, we do not believe he controls this vote," Kilroy observed. He suggested that Virgilio de Leon of Panama, Eduardo Dibos of Peru, and Jose Beracasa of Venezuela had as much prestige and influence as Clark. "Mr. De Leon should be given significant support as he appears to be well accepted and friendly with all the Latin American members." Stuart did as suggested. The US government provided a grant to a Panamanian sports official to take a course in the United States in athletic stadium management. Another grant went to a Peruvian track coach in order to help him prepare for the Pan American games. What exactly was done with that money remains unclear. In both cases, Stuart reported to Haldeman that de Leon and Dibos initiated the contact and solicited the funds from the United States.[21]

White House efforts ended on May 12, when the International Olympic Committee met in Amsterdam, Holland. Los Angeles was never a strong contender. After the first round of balloting, Moscow led with twenty-eight votes, Montreal had twenty-five, and Los Angeles seventeen. According to IOC procedures the last-place contender dropped from consideration in the next round. After the second ballot, Montreal won over Moscow, 41–28, with one abstention. The Olympians cast their ballots secretly, but several things are clear from the final outcome. Moscow failed to gain any support in the second round, and since the twenty-eight votes the Russian city received matched the number of communist nations with representation in this international organization, Clark of Mexico never delivered.[22]

A number of factors contributed to the final outcome. The White House became involved in the process at an extremely late date. Stuart noted as much only two weeks after his appointment: "It is unfortunate that we were not asked to aid Los Angeles earlier for the game is now pretty much played out." A number of commentators remarked that the US-Soviet political confrontation that brought the Nixon administration into the effort eventually worked to Montreal's advantage. The committee wanted to avoid the political issues associated with having to choose between Moscow and Los Angeles. There was also concern about the reception awaiting tourists in the Russian capital that went beyond its hotel housing capacity. Many individuals wondered if a police state would really welcome, or even be prepared for, the massive influx of foreign tourists that come with the summer games. *New York Times* sports columnist Arthur Daley noted, "Moscow is dull. The I.O.C. prefers 'fun cities' for its games. Montreal qualifies." Stuart made a similar argument in his memoirs. In a State Department report, the US consul general in Amsterdam observed that a desire to avoid making a decision in favor of the United States or the USSR was clearly a factor, but other considerations were far more important. Montreal had an established history with the IOC, having barely lost the bidding process for the 1972 games to Munich, Germany, and Canada had never hosted an Olympic gathering, winter or summer.[23]

All of that is true, but the IOC records make it clear that the Los Angeles delegation showed an impressive level of incompetence in their presentation. Their session started poorly when Kilroy stumbled and fell down, knocking over a table. Members of the committee asked the Los Angeles group more questions than they did the Montreal or Moscow delegation. Most of the issues put to the Californians were rather fundamental in nature, suggesting that committee members had serious reservations about their administrative and organizational abilities. The delegation from Moscow was asked a series of substantive questions, Montreal only one. Lord Killanin, a citizen of the Irish Republic who had a British title, observed of the American effort: "Los Angeles made a flamboyant bid which did not impress the IOC." The Americans were passing out baseball caps, although baseball was not an Olympic sport. The Los Angeles group also had young women in short, skimpy clothing operating an orange juice dispenser for committee members. In 1970, the International Olympic Committee was an all-male organization, but the blunt sexuality of the Americans struck these refined gentlemen as crude.[24]

Although disappointed, the Americans could live with the decision. Los Angeles mayor Sam Yorty publicly said he was glad the games were staying in the "free world." On another level, since the Olympics would take place on the same continent, Americans would have little problem traveling to the games, and US television networks would be spared the difficulties of working across more than one or two time zones.[25]

The Amsterdam meeting of the IOC was not an entirely negative experience for the United States. Denver benefited from Montreal's success. The committee awarded the winter games to Denver on the third ballot; the unexpected success of Montreal undercut the campaign Vancouver was staging to host the winter festival, because the IOC was reluctant to award both the summer and winter games to the same nation.[26]

Despite this victory, the climate in the United States in the middle of 1970 was horrible. Divisions threatened to rip the country asunder in a way unknown since the end of Reconstruction. The issue: US foreign policy in general, and more specifically, the war in Vietnam. On some campuses, radicals blew up buildings over fairly trivial issues, such as the disbursements of mandatory student fees. This ugly atmosphere kept Nixon from attending the graduation ceremonies of his daughter Julie at Smith College and son-in-law David at Amherst College. The situation worsened after the president announced the incursion into Cambodia. He also made divisive remarks, calling protesting college students "bums." The shooting of twelve students at Kent State University and an indifferent White House statement about the incident that offered no words of sympathy to the families of the dead and wounded, many of whom were just on their way to class, only increased the trauma the nation faced. Campuses were in such turmoil that Governor Ronald Reagan of California shut down the entire state university and college system. The National Student Association began organizing a huge protest rally in Washington to be held on Saturday, May 9.[27]

In an effort to diffuse the situation, Nixon held a press conference on Friday evening and promised to have all American troops out of Cambodia by the end of June. After the press conference, Nixon was too tense and excited to sleep. At 4 a.m., he decided to visit the Lincoln Memorial, where many students were sleeping in expectation of the rally the next day. At the monument, he introduced himself to one group. The crowd slowly grew in size as he talked. At one point, he started to discuss the technical issues of arms control until he saw their attention wander. "They were not unfriendly," he wrote in a report he made of the visit. "As a matter of fact, they seemed overawed and, of course, quite surprised." The president of the United States was earnestly attempting to talk to a group of exhausted and disheveled students about matters of importance, which led one White House aide to call the scene "surrealistic." He addressed their concerns about the war and expressed the hope that their opposition to the conflict would not disillusion them with the system of government in the United States. He also offered some advice, recommending that they travel while they were young and had the opportunity. In an effort to make some connection across the political divide, he made a couple of remarks about surfing and the football teams of the students' schools. Despite the variety of topics addressed in the conversation, press accounts focused on his surfing and football comments. In this instance, his reliance on sports had failed him.[28]

Despite this setback, the president still had the moral authority of his office to shape public sentiment in a different direction. Polling data convinced Haldeman that the president was his own best weapon. "I've done an analysis, and we are just not getting any Presidential exposure, and haven't for some months," Haldeman observed. "Sure looks as if what the people really want is to see P on TV so they know he's in charge of things, even if he doesn't do it the way they want."[29]

With the midterm elections in November, Nixon decided he could use public interest in sports to help convince traditional-minded Americans that they should use their vote to express their disgust with the direction in which the country seemed to be moving. Such ballots were more against Democrats than for Republicans, but they would strengthen the president's political position nevertheless. Nixon informed his key subordinates, "We must get turned around on this before it is too late—Emphasize—anti-crime—anti-Demonstrations—anti-Drug—anti-Obscenity—Get in touch with the mood of the country which is fed up with the Liberals. This stuff is dynamite politically."[30]

His largest tactical success in 1970 came in Cincinnati, at the Major League Baseball All-Star Game. At first, a successful tie-in to the interleague contest seemed unlikely. Kuhn had implemented another new measure to rebuild popular interest in the game: fan voting for the All-Star teams. In early June, he sent a number of All-Star ballots to the White House and asked the president to take part. A quick survey of the appropriate White House staff members found no interest in seeing Nixon participate. His ballot would in all likelihood become public and could easily become counterproductive, since he would have to exclude many players.[31]

A month later, however, David Eisenhower suggested that Nixon attend the midsummer classic, making up for his absence the year before. The president liked the idea. The next day, Dwight Chapin wrote a memorandum for the file. "We should look for a possible afternoon activity," he noted. "It need not be a 'black' deal. Maybe a crime and or urban development type event." No announcement of the president's trip would be made until the day before the game. "There is a question whether we will take any Congressmen or Senators. Probably not—but maybe we would take Taft and two of the Congressmen from Cincinnati."[32]

On July 13 the White House announced that the president would go to Louisville, Kentucky, to attend the meeting of the Appalachian Regional Commission, an organization of state governors, and then make it to Cincinnati in time for the All-Star Game. The trip to Louisville was a facade, but it turned out to be a successful undertaking in its own right. A crowd that the police chief estimated at 7,500 greeted Nixon at the airport. Another crowd, estimated between 50,000 and 200,000 people, lined the route the president took to the Federal Building. Governor Louie B. Nunn, a Republican, had given state employees the day off with pay to come out and greet their president. At some points, the crowd was ten deep as the motorcade neared the meeting place. Handmade signs welcoming and praising Nixon littered the gathering and were on display in store fronts along the route. Nixon and Nunn stood standing through the sunroof so that the hood came to about chest level. Twice Nixon got out of the limousine, shaking hands with the assembled gathering. These gestures energized the cheering throng of people, and they surged forward. The president struggled to get back into the car the first time, so the second time he stood on the hood of the limousine and flashed his trademark victory sign.[33]

Wearing a rumpled blue suit and perspiring from the muggy, ninety-degree weather, Nixon spoke to another crowd assembled at the Federal Building. "I want to tell you how very grateful I am for this wonderful reception," he said, clearly winded from pushing through the crowd. "The President meeting with the governors is not unusual. It is not unusual for the Cabinet to meet with the governors. What is unusual is Washington coming to Kentucky, the government coming to Kentucky."[34]

Inside, he met with eleven governors for four hours.[35] In the first half of the meeting, he pushed his "New Federalism" program, which included revenue sharing that promised to return federal tax money to the states without restrictions. He also laid out his Family Assistance Plan, which was designed to offer welfare to the public across the board without economic qualification but required "workfare" from the recipients. Since the governors had already endorsed this idea, he was preaching to the choir. His main effort was to get these leaders to apply political pressure on congressional holdouts from their states. During the second half of the meeting, the governors urged Nixon to create other groups similar to their own for other parts of the country. Established in 1965, the Appalachian Regional Commission was an organization that allowed state governors to approve or reject federal programs designed for their poor Appalachian counties. Nunn said after the meeting that Nixon "asked a lot of questions" and seemed "interested."[36]

When Nixon arrived in Cincinnati he got another warm welcome. A small crowd greeted him at the airport and another, larger one waited for him at the hotel where he was to have dinner before the All-Star Game. He got out of his limousine and began working the crowd, shaking hands. Then, he got on top of his car again and pulled Congressman Robert Taft Jr., the Republican candidate for the US Senate race in Ohio, up along with him. The people cheered.[37]

When he arrived at Riverfront Stadium, the television cameras followed Nixon as he appeared on the diamond, and polite applause greeted him as he made his way to his seat behind home plate. The managers for both teams, Earl Weaver of the American League and Gil Hodges of the National League, approached him to talk for a few minutes before the president tossed out the first ball. Nixon actually threw out two "first pitches," one going to the catcher for each team. His short tosses were awkward and clumsy-looking, but Johnny Bench of the hometown Reds and Bill Freehan of the Detroit Tigers caught them without problem. After shaking hands with the two catchers, Nixon got the balls back, then tossed them into the upper level of the stands with good, clean throws. The crowd roared with approval. A third throw bounced off the upper deck, down into the seats in the lower section.[38]

Nixon was content to watch the game intensely, but scored several public relations successes as the night wore on. As Tom Seaver of the Mets and Jim Palmer of the Orioles battled one another in a pitching duel, Lindsey Nelson, a sportscaster for NBC, did a brief , on-air interview with Nixon between the third and fourth innings. Nelson was wearing a portable transmitter pack on his back and as he approached the commissioner's box, Kuhn got up to let him sit next to Nixon. As Nelson waited for his cue to begin the interview, Nixon chatted amiably: "Lindsey, how many All-Star Games for you? It think I read where Willie Mays has been in something like twenty-three." Nelson was more than a little nervous. He was about to interview the president of the United States and wanted to avoid botching the job. "I was listening for the cue that would be coming at any time, and I preferred that we had a little silence around here so I could hear it," he reflected in his memoirs. The cue came just as Nixon finished his question. Nelson ignored it and started the interview.[39] He first asked the president what he thought of the game. "Well, I think that it's a pitching game and that there are such powerful hitters on both teams that I don't think that it can stand up," Nixon replied, dropping the tone of his voice, giving it a professional tone that bolstered his authority. "I figure this to be a game where there'd be an awful lot of hitting. You know, but these—but they've had three great pitchers here—two great pitchers so far, wouldn't you say?"

"Yes," Nelson replied quickly.

"Both Palmer and, of course, Seaver have been," Nixon said, and then changed the structure of his sentence in mid-thought, "nobody could hit them."

Nelson also asked him what he thought of the new stadium. "I've never seen a more beautiful park and it's the first time I've seen the Astroturf. And I can see it may be more dependable and predictable but it's a lot faster. It really—the ball really moves in the infield here. I've, I've—really I imagine it is going to be the ball park of the future, don't—is what I would think." In the *Washington Post*, Shirley Povich called the manufacturers of Astroturf winners for this inadvertent endorsement. "A few other companies manufacturing synthetic grass for sale to stadium people may have winced at the use of the brand name."[40]

Nelson had time for one last question before the cameras had to cut back to the play on the diamond. On instructions from the commissioner's staff, the home plate umpire was killing time between the innings, dusting dirt off the plate several times. Despite being in the middle of an interview with the president, Nelson kept looking down at the charade taking place on the diamond in amazement. "There has never been a cleaner home plate in the history of this grand old game of baseball." He asked Nixon if he had played the game growing up. "I tried," the president replied in a relaxed voice. "They always put me in the field and where they didn't expect it to be hit. I wasn't very good at it."[41]

The NBC television crew cut back to Nixon two other times during the game, giving him even more exposure. First, some young girls approached his seats and asked for his autograph. The national television audience watched him perform this simple request. The girls were clearly a little embarrassed to be the focus of so much attention, but were grateful about having a chance to meet the president and wrote him a quick note of thanks that was handed to a White House staff member. "We are your true fans and we are very proud to have your signature. I will always treasure your hand shake." The television cameras focused on Nixon again in the fifth inning when Eddie Roush, a member of the Baseball Hall of Fame and the player voted the greatest Red of all time, came over to talk with him. Nixon had requested a chance to meet the former baseball star, and as the two talked, the television broadcasters mentioned that he had been scheduled to throw out the first pitch of the game until the president decided to attend.[42]

The game Nixon watched was a hard-fought contest that eventually went much the way he had predicted. Povich wrote that Nixon's remarks to Nelson "reinforced his reputation as a genuine follower of the game." Despite the strong pitching, hitters began to score runs. The American League took a 4–1 lead into the ninth inning. The National League responded in kind with three runs to take the game into extra innings. In the twelfth the Nationals had two hits that put local hero Pete Rose in a position to score the winning run. On a third hit, he turned the corner on third base and barreled into home plate. Rookie catcher Ray Fosse of Cleveland was blocking the plate. Years later, Fosse explained, "I was playing with guys like Brooks and

Frank Robinson and Harmon Killebrew. I wanted the respect of my peers. I wasn't going to look like a fool and get out of the way." Rose charged into him, knocking the defender back to score the winning run. "All I saw was the mask flying," Rose joked about the collision. "Did it land in President Nixon's box?" Fosse, however, suffered a severely bruised left shoulder and had X-rays taken. "I hope he's not hurt too bad, I like him," Rose said later.[43]

The injury Fosse suffered, however, had long lasting impact. He had sixteen home runs in the first half of the season. In the second half, he was unable to lift his arm over his head and had only two homers. With permanent damage to his shoulder, he developed a swing with less power, and he never hit more than twelve in the nine other seasons he played. He was part of two World Series Championships, but suffered from arthritis for the rest of his life. "I still feel it," he said in 1999. "From time to time, I wake up and it's killing me."[44]

The dramatic end to the interleague contest made every interested party happy. "NBC got more than its money's worth, and the viewers were sticking to the finish, not a captive audience, but an entirely captivated one," Povich declared. "No All-Star Game ever made as many friends for baseball."[45]

The presidential trip to the All-Star Game was an unqualified success. A huge photo of Nixon throwing the first pitch took up half the front page of the Cincinnati *Enquirer.* Mention of his presence at the game was almost mandatory in sports sections the next day. Many of them ran photos of him watching the game or meeting with the young girls.[46] A few days later in the chambers of the House, Taft said, "Yaz and Pete Rose may have starred on the field, but Dick Nixon had the nod with the fans in the stands." He went on to praise the city of Cincinnati for the "universally warm reception given to him as our Chief Executive who is uniting the country by the fact that, despite the overpowering and isolating nature of his responsibilities, he remains one of us." He said the trip performed an important social function. "In these difficult times of ever-arriving crises, it restores confidence to see the Nation and its leader able to relax in and thrill to the best baseball ever. The tremendous reception Dick Nixon received on arrival in the city and at the stadium were overwhelming testimony to the admiration of Americans for . . . their warm affinity with, the man they have chosen as their President."[47] Haldeman could not have agreed more. In his diary, he commented:

Louisville great success. Good airport crowd, great street crowds in town. P up on hood, stopped car, into crowd, etc. good for him, and especially good to stick it to press. Long meeting with Appalachian Governors. Then on to Cincinnati. Not much crowd there. Too late in day. Great reception at All-Star Game. P pleased crowd by throwing three balls into stands after throwing out first ball. Real late because of extra innings.[48]

The "Yaz" that Taft referred to was Carl Yastrzemski of the Boston Red Sox, winner of the All-Star Game Most Valuable Player award. On the plane ride back to Boston, he was sitting next to Major Jack Brennan, the Marine Corps aide to the president. During their conversation Yastrzemski indicated he wanted to give the trophy to Nixon as a gesture of his personal respect and admiration. The White House staff was willing to arrange an appointment between the ball player and the president, but scheduling conflicts prevented any such meeting during the 1970 season.[49]

Despite the positive results of the trip, Nixon focused on one of the few negative developments. Because the game started late and went into extra innings, the *Washington Post*, a morning paper, had to run an incomplete story about the event. Newspapers in other time zones did not face this problem, and there was a good deal of coverage of Nixon at the games in these accounts. Bob Addie, a sportswriter for the *Post*, wrote a column and a news story about the midsummer classic. In both he stressed events that tended to mitigate and explain the reasons the paper had failed to give complete coverage of the All-Star Game. His column focused on the scheduling and planning complications that the president's visit imposed on Major League Baseball. His news story stated that many people arrived early, but became impatient while they waited for the president and his party to arrive. Nixon took this as another example of media bias against him despite the generous reporting of the paper's sports department to date and vented his rage with Haldeman. The episode was the first thing the chief of staff noted in his diary: "Big flap about story in Post sport section that P delayed the game last night. He didn't and is mad at charges he did." Nixon had a point. Some of this criticism was sour journalistic grapes. Given the lateness of the game, the *Post* had to run an incomplete story. Coverage in papers in other time zones was more complete, but Nixon did himself a disservice with such sensitivity and micromanagement. Presidents need to worry about larger and more important issues, leaving these small details to others.[50]

Nixon had won and lost in using sports. The defeat in trying to help bring the Olympics to Los Angeles was hidden from the public for the most part. The public relations spectacle of Nixon's presence at the All-Star Game showed that he had a found a new, novel way to use the prestige of his office to engage with the average American. That success, though, did not last.

4

The Midterm Elections of 1970

Nixon had used America's interest in sports to his political advantage and decided to continue this effort. Nixon spent the second half of 1970 working to manipulate sports for the benefit of himself and his supporters in the midterm election. These efforts dominated all his other interests in the athletic world that year. Nixon scored small, tactical victories, but strategically this political campaign went against him. The partisan advantage the president gained did not exclude his interaction on other aspects of sport. The fan in him came out once again as he tried to play a part in determining the national title in college football, and at other times, he used the symbolic power of his position to provide emotional comfort when tragedy hit the athletic world.

Before the president could use sport in another political context, a sad duty pushed him back into the athletic world in a nonpolitical context. In June Vince Lombardi began a short, painful battle with cancer, which ended on September 3. He underwent surgery and spent a month in the hospital. Out for a week, he was readmitted for more surgery, never to leave. Nixon admired the coach and sent him a telegram and floral arrangement wishing him well. The president also called Lombardi. The conversation reportedly perked up the spirits of the dying football legend. In a sign of Nixon's sincerity, it was the coach rather than the White House staff that told the press about this exchange. Nixon was capable of amazingly gracious gestures like this one and would not leak them to the media, but wanted others to do it so he would look magnanimous. "I had called him to give him a lift but his attitude raised my spirits," Nixon remarked after the coach's death. "It was a great inspiration to talk with him."[1]

When Lombardi died it was a national event, and many Americans used it as an opportunity to examine society. "Many people remembered him not so much for his coaching genius but for his many other activities," Bob Addie wrote in his *Washington Post* column. The ABC television network aired a thirty-minute special on the coach the day after he died, entitled "Vince Lombardi—What His Life Was All About." The editorial board of the *Post* praised his coaching ability and the impact of his brief stay had on the District. "Vincent Lombardi was the best football coach of his time—and the year he spent among us was the best thing that has happened to this town in a long time." For the first time in a long time, Washington, a town full of transients, based on the industry of politics and compromise, had a civil leader committed without reservation to winning. In a social sense, this was quite new to the town. "We had the evidence in Lombardi—and still have it—that this town *can* travel first-class." His winning season was "a shot of adrenalin for a whole community and that is Vince Lombardi's particular legacy to all of us."[2]

Nixon took the lead in this moment of national mourning, even though there was no political upside to such an effort. When he learned of Lombardi's death, he stopped a state dinner in California and spoke about a coach who embodied the values he expected and admired in athletic figures. The coach, he said, was a "man who in a time when so many seem to be turning away from religion was devoutly religious and devoted to his Church; at a time when the moral fabric of the country seems to be coming apart, he was a man who was deeply devoted to his family; at a time when it seems rather square to be patriotic, he was deeply and unashamedly patriotic; at a time when permissiveness is the order of the day in many circles, he was a man who insisted on discipline . . . discipline and strength." Nixon also had the White House press office release another statement: "Vince Lombardi believed in fundamentals. On the football field this meant blocking and tackling and running to daylight. Off the field it meant his church, his home, his friends, and his family. He built his life—as he built his teams—around basic values and that is why his greatness as a coach was more than matched by his greatness as a human being." These comments were included in news stories along with other eulogies from figures in the football world. Memorial services were held for Lombardi in Green Bay, Washington, and New York. Nixon returned to the nation's capital in time to attend the services at St. Matthew's Cathedral. He also sent General Donald Hughes, his military aide, and Robert Finch, a long-time political associate and former secretary of health, education, and welfare, to Lombardi's funeral as his official representatives.[3]

While the nation mourned, the White House staff planned Nixon's participation in the midterm election. A major interest in the deliberations on strategy was the use of sport during campaign stops. The Nixon administration had decided to provide presidential assistance to the Republican candidates in Senate races in seventeen states.[4] In late August, appointments secretary Dwight Chapin asked Hugh Sloan and Bud Wilkinson to provide him with a list of major football games in those states that the president might attend with some of the candidates before the November election. "Most of the states that have target Senate races will not have nationally televised games," Wilkinson responded. Texas was the only one of these states that would have one of its universities on national television. "Any home game against a respectable opponent that the President wishes to attend would be satisfactory." He did note, however, that the telecasts of the California–Southern California, Minnesota-Missouri, Tennessee-Vanderbilt, and Notre Dame–Missouri games were going to reach about 70 percent of the country and recommended that Nixon consider attending one of these contests.[5]

Harry Dent also wanted the president to attend a college football game, but specifically one in Florida. Even though it would not be televised, he suggested the Florida–Florida State game. (At the time, neither school was a dominant power in the college game.) Dent worried about divisions forming in the state Republican party and recommended that Nixon attend the athletic contest with leading figures in the state party in an effort to "bring about some harmony." Nixon did eventually met with the Florida politicians, but not at a football game.[6]

Despite Nixon's success with sport, or perhaps because of the Penn State backlash, some members of the White House staff worried about the image he was projecting to the American people. The president's men were afraid that he might end up stereotyped as a man obsessed with sports in general, and football in particular, the way Eisenhower was with golf.[7]

Herb Klein disagreed with this thinking. "I think it helps many relate to the President. I think the American public wants very much to look at the President as a very strong leader, which it does, but I think it also enjoys a feeling of warmth toward the President such as comes from sharing a mutual hobby such as football or other sports."[8]

Nixon never attended any of the games his staff suggested, but athletics remained a constant subject in his speeches on the campaign trail. He used sports as a way to reach out to people, giving them a way to relate to him. His stump efforts started at Kansas State University in the school's basketball field house. The president's future biographer Stephen Ambrose was one of the fifteen thousand gathered to hear him deliver the Alf Landon Lecture. Ambrose later wrote, "The setting *was* ideal for Nixon and he played it like a master." The television networks carried his speech live. He began by noting that he was wearing a purple tie, even though it clashed with his blue suit. The tie was a gift from the Kansas congressional delegation and purple was one of the school's colors. "All I can say is I am proud to wear the purple at Kansas State." The crowd responded with what Ambrose called a "mighty roar." Waves and waves of cheering followed as he displayed the tie. He then told the crowd that he had waited in the basketball locker room. Kansas State had a successful program, which Nixon noted, "It is nice to be in a room with a winner, believe me." The school was a perennial loser in football, but the president found a way to turn that into a positive. "I think of the fans of Wildcat football here today who have known what it is to lose—and then who have known what it is to win." He compared the dogged determination of the football team to Landon's life after his defeat in the 1936 presidential election and his own after 1960. "Whether in a campaign, or a football game, or in debate on the great issues of the day, the answer to 'losing one' is not a rush to the barricades but a study of why, and then a careful rebuilding—or perhaps even a careful reexamination of whether the other fellow may have been right after all." More roars of approval followed. He worked his way into his give-'em-hell, law-and-order rhetoric that brought the audience to their feet with a roar that was "truly deafening." The speech was an impressive political victory, at least in an immediate sense, and the White House staff quickly acquired the funds to have the speech broadcast again on prime-time television.[9]

Nixon stayed with these proven themes. A month later he made his only appearance of the campaign at an athletic-related event. October 18 was Bart

Starr Day in Green Bay, Wisconsin. The smallest home of a NFL franchise was honoring the quarterback who had taken the Packers to five NFL titles and two Super Bowl championships, while setting the record for most years in the team's uniform. Starr was a Republican. He had campaigned for Nixon in 1968 and had given speeches at the state party convention. He was also the type of moral leader that the president expected athletes to be and deserved recognition for this attitude. An editorial in the *Green Bay Press-Gazette* agreed: "We believe Bart Starr deserves all the honors he is receiving because he exemplifies all the attributes of a good citizen, first, and as one of the all-time great professional football players, second. It has been Green Bay's fortune to have a Bart Starr to set a high standard of active citizenship as an example for others."[10]

Nixon's decision to attend a testimonial rally for Starr and deliver a speech was an easy one; he was in Green Bay to honor Starr, first, and to campaign, second. Many journalists thought that the trip was about politics as much as it was football. "As an avid football fan, President Nixon will be responding genuinely to a nonpolitical lure when he sets foot briefly in Wisconsin Saturday, to appear at the festivities honoring Bart Starr in Green Bay," the editors of the *Milwaukee Journal* commented. "He will be politicking nevertheless, for it is no coincidence that this trip comes at the height of nationwide campaigning to elect governors and congressmen." The editorial page editor of the Green Bay paper made a similar observation, noting that the presidency could not be divided into partisan and nonpartisan compartments. In fact, the *Milwaukee Sentinel* reported that various political squabbles over the visit were in danger of overshadowing Starr.[11]

None of that mattered after Air Force One arrived at Austin Straubel Field in Green Bay just before 7 p.m. on October 17. The president made a brief appearance at the bottom of the steps with the various GOP candidates for governor, the US Senate, and the US House of Representatives, then quickly ushered them into the plane. After a ten-minute meeting, the group reemerged and Nixon gave a short speech to the one thousand people gathered to greet him, endorsing the slate. About a hundred of the people at the airfield were antiwar protestors who began shouting obscenities at him. Their actions gave Nixon an opportunity to score some political points that he quickly took. "Let me say that I respect their right to be heard even if they do not respect my right to be heard. And let me say also, ladies and gentlemen,

I can assure them that they are a very loud minority in this country, but they are a minority, and it is time for the majority to stand up and be counted." A reporter present called the duel between the highly vocal group and the president, armed with a loudspeaker, a draw. Maybe, but reporters devoted more space in their stories to Nixon's remarks and ignored the protestors, other than their chants.[12]

After shaking hands with some people waiting behind a fence to see him, Nixon left for the Brown County Veterans Memorial Arena for the event. His introduction in the arena led to a lengthy standing ovation as a local high school band played "Hail to the Chief." Nixon waved to the crowd and flashed his trademark double victory signs above his head. "One thing about the president," the master of ceremonies joked. "He's a Ram fan." Nixon played along, pretending to leave the stage at that comment. When he started his speech, he drew attention to the obvious. "As some of you may have heard, we're in the midst of another political campaign in this country, but if there is one thing that is nonpolitical, it's being for Bart Starr tonight." He then spent several minutes praising the incumbent governor and repeating his airfield endorsement of the three candidates. All four men were sharing the stage with Nixon and the Starr family.[13]

After making these political remarks, Nixon turned his attention to the man of the hour. He focused not on Starr's athletic accomplishments, but on his will and determination. Nixon noted that Starr had been a brilliant college quarterback at the University of Alabama, but injuries in his last two seasons in school made him a questionable professional prospect. He had ended up a lowly sixteenth-round draft pick and spent his first few seasons as a backup. "And instead of whining about it, instead of saying that the coach was at fault or the system was at fault, and quitting or, for that matter, sulking—which seems to be rather a fashionable and common thing to do these days when everything doesn't go your own way—he just kept going along and trying harder, and eventually he came up. And that's what he stands for," Nixon said with admiration.[14]

His speech then moved on to the Vietnam War. Secretary of Defense Melvin Laird, a former Wisconsin congressman, was on the stage, and Nixon used his presence to compare the great Packer defenses of the 1960s to the national need for a strong military.[15]

After spending several minutes on this subject, he abruptly returned to the topic of Bart Starr. The Green Bay quarterback understood the proper role of the athlete in society. Starr had provided the moral leadership that was the obligation of any athlete, and Nixon wanted the audience to know it. "We honor him not for his technical skill, but as I've indicated, also for something that is just as important: his leadership qualities, his character, his moral fiber. It is this that will be his legacy to the Packers. It will be this that will be his legacy to the sport and his legacy to America."[16]

Starr was touched at having so many people come to honor him, and his own remarks were humble. "Today I'm the luckiest man in the world," he said, quoting New York Yankees legend Lou Gehrig. "Now I know what that man felt like." He corrected Nixon; he was a seventeenth- rather than a sixteenth-round pick. Overall though, he was speechless at this public demonstration of gratitude. "I've thought of a jillion things to say," he continued. "I just literally don't know where to begin." After Starr finished his remarks and sat down, the master of ceremonies joked, "Look out, Mr. Nixon, Bart's after your job." According to press accounts, the president laughed hard at that remark.[17]

With the event over, Starr and Nixon stepped off the stage, and the quarterback introduced the president to many of his current and former teammates. The crowd surged forward to meet the president of the United States and perhaps shake his hand. Nixon obliged many, to the clear consternation of his Secret Service detachment.[18]

The trip to Wisconsin was another successful political undertaking for the president. A page-one editorial and editorial cartoon directly under the masthead of the *Green Bay Press-Gazette* welcomed him. Local press coverage, including the Milwaukee papers, was positive and flattering. As was the case when the president visited smaller cities where the local media rarely had a chance to cover stories of national importance, journalists reported even the smallest details of the trip. A writer for the Green Bay paper even published a humorous article describing how he lost his pen after getting an autograph from Nixon. "I mean what do you do, when the President walks off with your pen, especially if it's the only one you have?" Nixon smiled when told he still had the ballpoint. "Take one of mine," he said with a jovial smile. The writer decided that he got the better of the exchange. "By the way, the pen writes fine. Much better than the one he ended up with."[19]

People in the audience were glad to see Nixon in person under positive circumstances, addressing a topic they understood. “It was a welcome relief to hear the President talking about Bart Starr instead of worrisome news like Vietnam,” one audience member said. “It was good to see him so relaxed and to laugh with him.”[20]

Nixon returned to Washington that evening, but began making more and more trips out to key states that month. Sport was a constant subject in his speeches. In fact, on October 19, when he arrived in Columbus, Ohio, to speak before the Ohio State House, Woody Hayes, head football coach of the Ohio State Buckeyes, delivered a few remarks to a crowd of twenty-five thousand waiting to greet the president. Hayes and Nixon had known each other for over a decade, and each deeply respected the other. The coach said the president was a good-luck omen for his team. Ohio State had won the national championship the two previous times that Nixon had come to visit Columbus, and Hayes obviously hoped the pattern would hold. After addressing the crowd and endorsing the Republican slate, Nixon followed up on these comments before the assembly, referring to his visit two years before. “There was a feel of victory in the air then. Ohio State was on the way to the Rose Bowl and I was on the way to the White House.” He made several comments that were a political windfall and made it possible for Buckeyes’ fans to connect with the president of the United States as another sports fan. “I have a complaint to the ABC national network, why they didn’t have the foresight and the judgement to make Ohio State and Michigan the game of the week so I could see it on TV.” He also talked about wanting to attend the Rose Bowl and related a conversation he had with Hayes about getting a pass. “I can’t even get a ticket,” he quoted the coach as saying. “I can’t get you one, even though you are President of the United States.” After the speech, Nixon decided to make a surprise visit to the Ohio State campus. The Secret Service refused to allow the unscheduled stop, but Nixon personally overruled the agents. The president thought the spontaneity of the trip would prevent any protests or violence, and it did. He showed up at the school unannounced and began talking with nearby students. The crowd grew as word spread. The campus visit was the success that Nixon had hoped the trip to the Lincoln Memorial might have been.[21]

Nixon’s interest in the Ohio State football program was genuine. He continued to follow the fate of the Buckeyes even after the election. On November 14, he watched the nationally televised game between Ohio State and Purdue

University. The 3-5 Boilermakers fought hard in a defensive game against the third-ranked team in the country. Ohio State emerged with a 10–7 win in the last three minutes of the game as Fred Schram, a little-used place kicker, delivered the winning field goal despite strong winds. After the game, Nixon called the Buckeye locker room and congratulated Hayes, and then spoke to Schram and quarterback Ron Maciejowski. "It's a thrill for a 20-year-old kid to talk with the President," Hayes told reporters. Ever the careful politician, Nixon also called the Purdue dressing room and talked with head coach Bob DeMoss: "Tell your kids they played a magnificent football game. I know how you feel, I've had a couple of tough losses myself."[22]

After leaving Ohio, Nixon went to Kansas City and continued with his sporting references. In a speech before a crowd of thirteen thousand, he said, "As you know, I am somewhat of a football fan. And I am always honored to be in the city of the champions of the world, the Kansas City Chiefs. I didn't make any votes in Minnesota with that one, did I?" The crowd roared with laughter.[23]

In Minnesota, he simply said, "It is good to be in Viking country." In Maryland he praised the Baltimore Orioles, champions of the World Series, and predicted that the Colts might equal the feat in football with a win in the Super Bowl. In Phoenix, he tried to win the support of Sun Devil voters. "When I am in Arizona, Arizona State is number one." He had apparently conceded the University of Arizona Wildcat vote to the Democrats.[24]

Occasionally, Nixon got his facts wrong, which always received wide notice. One such incident occurred in Dallas, Texas, in front of an overflow crowd of nearly twenty thousand people at Market Hall. The Southern Methodist University band played "Hail to the Chief" as he entered with George Bush, Republican candidate for the Senate, and Paul Eggers, the GOP gubernatorial nominee. Nixon warmed up with a few carefully chosen remarks about football in the Lone Star State. "First, I find that, and I must be very careful what I say here, that the AP poll puts Texas as number one. Second, I find that the Dallas Cowboys, after a slow start, are now tied for number one in their division." He also made a few comments about how the SMU band stole the show at the 1934 Rose Bowl when Southern Methodist beat Stanford, 7–0. "That was not something that was particularly new, because other teams from the East or the West or the South had won in the Rose Bowl. But what really made the news was the SMU band. It was the greatest they ever had." The only problem was the Mustangs were not in the 1934 game; they lost the 1936 contest, 0–7. Reporters from both the *Dallas Morning News* and the *Fort Worth Star-Telegram* noticed this mistake and wrote short articles focusing on this particular error. Some of the SMU fans in the audience cared not. "It's a lot better for him to credit us with winning a game we lost than to say we lost a game which we won," one remarked to the *Morning News.* Overall, the Texas trip went well despite this gaffe. "Rolled pretty easily through the day," Haldeman noted.[25]

The next day was one of the most difficult and controversial of the campaign. Nixon made appearances in Illinois, Minnesota, Nebraska, and California. His trip to Nebraska was to help two candidates for the House of Representatives, but the Cornhusker state was not on the original list of target races. In Omaha Nixon spoke for twenty-nine minutes in front of an overflow crowd of nine thousand, with another seven thousand waiting outside the auditorium. As some audience members held up a banner that said, "NU No. 1—Who's Texas," he made a few comments about sports to rouse the crowd. "Some of you are aware of the fact that I am somewhat of a football nut. I understand I have a lot of company here in this State." His speech was interrupted twenty-three times, with applause with one of the biggest ovations coming when he mentioned the University of Nebraska Cornhuskers football team. "I am in Nebraska now. You think you are going to be number one. All that I can say is: While I am in Nebraska, Nebraska is number one. That is for sure." Of the trip, Haldeman observed, "Omaha a waste of time, but nice to do."[26]

The controversy came later in the day during a campaign stop in San Jose, California. Governor Ronald Reagan and Senator George Murphy, both Republicans, were seeking reelection. Murphy was the priority, but he was running behind in statewide opinion polls, and his future looked doubtful. Nixon made a joint appearance in the San Francisco Bay area with the two at the San Jose Civic Auditorium. Security was tight because two distinctly different groups of protestors greeted the president as he arrived. Democrats had organized unemployed engineers, scientists, and union members to carry signs in front of the arena in an effort to make the economy a campaign issue. The other group was a collection of young left-wing antiwar protestors, numbering between one and two thousand, that had marched from eight blocks away after attending a rally at San Jose State College. Inside the auditorium an extremely energetic, partisan crowd waited to greet Murphy, Reagan, and Nixon. The crowd responded well to another one of his sports references. The Stanford University Indians were on their way to a conference title and a berth in the Rose Bowl. No matter what he heard in Ohio about the Buckeyes, or in Indiana about the Fighting Irish, or in Texas about the Longhorns, Nixon said he was certain about one thing: "When I am in California, Stanford is number one." He went on to give one of his standard 1970-style give-'em-hell campaign speeches. The partisan crowd interrupted him frequently with "fierce applause," and he left to a standing ovation.[27]

While he spoke, loudspeakers carried his words outside the building to the crowd. A number of protesters pounded on the walls and tried to break into the arena. The San Jose police drove them back with mace and kept them out. Nixon, however, wanted a confrontation with the hecklers to work up his supporters. Since there were no hecklers in the building, he waited inside for a few minutes to give the demonstrators time to focus on him. The police plowed a path through the crowd, and Nixon, whom some reporters said looked a little nervous, made his way to his car. Before he got in he decided to taunt the protestors. He later explained that he "could not resist showing them how little respect I had for their juvenile and mindless ranting." He climbed up on the hood and waved his hands above his head, flashing the double V-for-victory sign. "That's what they hate to see," he gloated.[28]

The mob's reaction was far more intense than anyone in Nixon's party expected. The crowd began throwing a variety of rocks, bottles, and eggs. There was little doubt of their target—a small rock whizzed past Nixon's head as he hurried into his armored car. Reagan and Murphy were inside with him as a barrage hit the automobile. "Eggs rained like hail," Reagan later said. Murphy told reporters that rocks "half the size of bricks" pounded the limousine. The mob also smashed the windows of buses carrying reporters. The San Jose police used mace and a two-men-deep flying wedge to break up the crowd so the motorcade could get out. "We probably would not have gotten him (Nixon) out of there without them," a Secret Service agent later remarked. As the motorcade sped away, a rock hit the car carrying Haldeman. The driver hit the brakes abruptly, stalling the vehicle, and causing a rear-end collision with the auto following it in the caravan. "Rather scary," the chief of staff commented in a massive understatement.[29]

Nixon had the affront he wanted. "Made a huge incident and we worked hard to crank it up, should make really major story and might be effective," Haldeman recorded later that day. The next day he ordered his staff to stress the event over the weekend. Shortly after the incident, the White House press office issued a statement from Air Force One denouncing the attack. Press secretary Ron Ziegler took a skeptical press on a tour of the battered presidential limousine the next day. On October 31, the White House staff made public correspondence between Nixon and two San Jose residents, the president of the student body at the college and Joseph Ridder, the publisher of the *San Jose Mercury* and *San Jose News*. In both exchanges, Nixon reassured the recipients that he held no grudge against the school or the city. On November 3, Ziegler released yet another statement on the incident.[30]

The outrage and backlash that Nixon wanted never quite materialized, except in San Jose itself. The San Jose *Sunday Mercury News* published the letter between Nixon and Ridder on the front page directly under the masthead. A page-one editorial praised Nixon for his generous comments about San Jose. The piece concluded with the thanks of the city, "Please visit us again. Your reception will not be marred a second time." John H. Bunzel, president of San Jose State College, quickly repudiated the actions of a mob. "This type of protest, whatever its motivation, is unpardonable and in some ways obscene in itself." He estimated that less than half the protestors were San Jose State students and that the vast bulk of the twenty-four thousand studying at the college had nothing to do with the episode.[31]

Nixon and supporters blamed the indifferent reaction on a hostile national media, but Haldeman believed that the fault was as much the president's as anyone else's. Nixon, despite saying he would, failed to hammer on the issue in a speech he gave the next night in Anaheim, California. Jeb Stuart Magruder and William Safire also believed the limited response was self-inflicted. They observed that many reporters resented the hard-sell efforts of the administration and thought they were being used. There was also a political consideration at work. Haldeman found that the administration had a difficult time following up on the stoning because various White House staff members believed they needed to give Murphy and Reagan political cover.[32]

Whatever concerns Nixon and his staff had about protecting those two were misplaced. Both candidates used strong, uninhibited rhetoric in an effort to use the episode to their advantage. Reagan called the protestors "a disgrace to the human race. They want a victory for the enemy. I express my contempt on behalf of the citizens of California." Murphy's language was more coarse. "I'm goddamned mad," he growled. "This was as vicious a crowd as I've ever seen in my life." He then lashed out at his opponents for failing to denounce the attack. The problem with this statement was that it was not true. Newspapers, even those that were in Murphy's camp and had endorsed his reelection, reported that Representative John Tunney had made comments deploring the threat to the president's safety.[33]

Nixon finally went on the offensive in Phoenix, Arizona. In a brief appearance at an airport hangar that lasted less than an hour, he gave a rousing twenty-six-minute speech to a partisan crowd that interrupted him with applause twenty-five times. The loudest response, according to a reporter for the *Arizona Republic*, came when he denounced the San Jose crowd. The White House staff then made a disastrous decision to broadcast the speech on television. A thirteen-minute version of the address made it on the air, but the technical quality of the film was poor and the editing made Nixon seem incoherent. Observers also could see that Nixon was clearly exhausted at the scene. The partisan address played poorly on television, especially in contrast to the Democratic response that Senator Edmund Muskie gave in a dignified manner from his home. Executives with CBS warned the Nixon staff about the poor quality of their tape, but these warnings were ignored. According to political advertising specialist Kathleen Hall Jamieson, the Republicans learned from this disaster. In 1972, campaign workers were more diligent and less complacent about the quality of the product they used to promote their candidate.[34]

Not all Nixon's interests and actions in matters related to sport had to do with the midterm elections. A number of sad developments befell the athletic world that fall, and Nixon responded to these tragedies by using the symbolic power of his office to offer the appropriate gestures of sympathy. These actions had little to do with politics or partisan gain and attest to the many roles that the president of United States is expected to play in American society. On October 2, a plane carrying forty people, including members of the Wichita State University football team, coaching staff, and athletic department officials, slammed into the side of a Colorado mountain. A total of thirty-one died in the crash. Another plane carrying the rest of the team landed safely in Logan, Utah, where Wichita State was to play Utah State. The game was canceled. Nixon took time off from the campaign to send a message of sympathy to the Wichita State community. On behalf of his entire traveling party he sent a telegram to university president Clark Ahlberg stating:

> WE KNOW THAT THE SPIRIT THAT CHARACTERIZED YOUR TEAM WILL LIVE ON IN YOUR LIVES AND YOUR MEMORIES. OUR THOUGHTS AND PRAYERS ARE WITH ALL OF YOU AT THIS SAD HOUR.

In December, after the school established a fund to help survivors of the crash pay for emergency expenses, Nixon sent a personal check for five hundred dollars.[35]

Six weeks later, another plane crash annihilated the football program at Marshall University. A mile and a half from the Tri-State Airport in Huntington, West Virginia, a Southern Airlines plane failed to clear the tree line of a ridge and crashed. Seventy-five people died in this accident, including thirty-seven Marshall players, coaches, and athletic department personnel. In a telegram to Donald Dedmon, president of the university, Nixon wrote:

> THERE IS BUT LITTLE COMFORT IN WORDS AT A TIME LIKE THIS. BUT OUR THOUGHTS ARE WITH THOSE WHO GRIEVE THE LOSS OF THEIR LOVED ONES. WE PRAY THAT GOD MAY ARM THEM WITH THE STRENGTH AND COURAGE TO BEAR THE ANGUISH OF A MISFORTUNE THAT TOUCHES THE HEARTS OF ALL THEIR FELLOW CITIZENS.[36]

Although paling in comparison to the misfortune that befell these two schools, November was a difficult month for Nixon. The midterm election was a setback for the Republican Party as the Democrats gained nine seats in the US House of Representatives and eleven governorships, giving them control over a majority of the state executive mansions. In the Senate, the Republicans gained two seats, and the independent candidate that won in New York said he would vote with the Republicans, but the Democrats still held the majority. The outcome was an even larger personal disaster for Richard Nixon. His preference that fall was to speak primarily on behalf of candidates running for either the Senate or the governor's mansion. In many instances, he added the names of candidates running for seats in the House of Representatives as a token gesture of party loyalty that often came at the last minute if that individual happened to be part of the group welcoming him when he arrived or onstage with him at his various speaking engagements. Overall, he mentioned the names of sixty-one candidates, implicitly or explicitly. Only twenty-four won. The results are even more meager when one considers that fourteen of the winners, many of them incumbents, were running for seats in the House. Of the twenty-one Senate candidates he made appearances with, only seven won. His results were even worse in gubernatorial races. Only three of the fifteen that he spoke for won.[37]

The enthusiastic crowds, the tough rhetoric, and the shrewd references to shared interests in sports had not been enough. In fact, the cheers might have been deceptive. "I've always mostly voted for Democrats," a Texas woman told the *Dallas Times Herald* after a Nixon campaign stop in East Texas. "I just brought the kids out to see him." Nixon realized as much and knew that the weak economy had hurt him and his party. "A Republican administration with any kind of economic slowdown is a disaster," Haldeman recorded him as saying two days later. "Without economic drag, [we] would have carried both House and Senate." Soon, however, Nixon slipped into a defensive mindset and wrote a self-serving analysis of the campaign, claiming the basic tactics and strategy were sound.[38]

Sports offered something of a distraction. He watched the college bowl games, but was unhappy with Stanford, despite his public comments in support of them. The team had failed in their moral obligations as Haldeman recorded:

> The P was very upset by a report in the sports section of today that the Stanford football team was running around their hotel in sandals and shorts, and that their quarterback had enjoyed posing for pictures with the topless dancers from San Francisco. The story was trying to make them out as being good guys because of this, and sneering at Ohio State as squares because they were wearing neckties and blazers. The P said for the first time he was going to root for the Midwest team in the Rose Bowl.[39]

Nixon was misleading his main subordinate. He had, in fact, rooted for Ohio State in previous Rose Bowls. He also did made no mention—he might not have known—that the quarterback in question was Jim Plunkett. The Stanford quarterback had beaten cancer as a teenager and was an inspiration in his own right. That Nixon was looking for a reason to root for Ohio State, however, takes nothing away from the president's perception that the squad from California had failed to do their duty.

That football game—and the others he watched on January 1—gave him an idea. He knew that the 1970 campaign had been a defeat and that he was politically weaker as a result. He also knew that the new circumstances would require a change in tactics. It was time for him to make conciliatory gestures toward the young, rather than defiant ones who only antagonized and divided the country. Shortly after the election, speechwriter Raymond Price suggested that Nixon talk about "something that would speak to the homes, to the goodness, to the elemental decency of the American people." It would be far more productive if the administration committed itself to reassuring the public, rather than playing to its fears. The widespread desire for an end to the rancor of the times was the one strong theme the Democrats had, so it was vital that the GOP stress this idea first. "Looking to the future," Price continued, "my recommendations would all center on developing and maintaining a climate of confidence in the Presidency as an institution, and in RN as President. We can go seriously astray if we think too much of 'issues' and not enough about the Presidency itself—its aura, its mystique, the almost religious way in which Americans respond to it."[40]

Nixon agreed and decided to make his move in Nebraska. The only major college team to finish the 1970 season undefeated was the University of Nebraska after it defeated Louisiana State University in the Orange Bowl. The other undefeated teams at the end of the regular season, Texas and Ohio State, had both lost their bowl games, and their claim to the "national championship" was rather weak. Nixon's habit of calling locker rooms after championship games had become so routine that the Cornhuskers waited for his call and were disappointed when the it never came. (Nixon had tried, but the phone system at the Orange Bowl was unable to handle the postgame traffic. He never got through.) Four days later, he told Haldeman he wanted to stop in Lincoln and present the Cornhuskers with a presidential plaque like the one he gave the Longhorns the year before. The chief of staff later summarized their conversation:

> He feels it's a good chance to give a speech playing on the theme of the 18 year old vote and their new participation in politics. He wants not to give a speech on dissent but, rather, one bringing the challenge to them of playing the game to win, playing hard, learning to lose and to win, that Nebraska was this kind of team. They'd never been number one before but they'd never quit, and that this is the kind of spirit that keeps the country going.[41]

This idea was not a popular one with some members of the White House staff. "I strongly recommend that the President not get involved at all in declaring one football team Number One this year," Pat Buchanan argued. "The reasons are many." Giving out the award would not help Nixon in Nebraska. Buchanan also recalled that the president's comments at his news conference after his trip to Arkansas implied that this undertaking had been a one-time event. The presidential advisor warned that getting involved in the determination of the mythical national championship in the centennial year of college football was one thing, but if the president continued awarding plaques, expectations would develop and this would become an annual event, getting Nixon involved in yearly disputes. Buchanan added that there were several claimants to the 1970 title. Nebraska might have finished the season with an unblemished record and the first spot in the final AP poll, but UPI and the National College Football Foundation and Hall of Fame had awarded their national championship trophies to Texas after the end of the regular season. Many Fighting Irish fans thought their team deserved the title after defeating the defending champion. "Admittedly, the other polls were taken before the Bowl games—but still they have validity for those schools—which are surely calling themselves Number 1 in their claims." Buchanan included a copy of the Shirley Povich column from the year before about the Nixon-Paterno dispute, which he noted was "just one mark of the crap we call in on ourselves—if we go ahead with this."[42]

Whatever merit Buchanan's reservations had—and he had some good points—Nixon ignored them. He was personally committed to the undertaking. He made his interest clear when he arrived on campus. Standing in the school's basketball arena behind the standard square podium with the presidential seal, he declared, "To come here to the only major college team that was undefeated, and to make an award is something that I am very proud to do, proud to recognize this university, to recognize its coach, to recognize its co-captains, to recognize its fine members of the team, and in so doing to present the plaque from the President of the United States." Nebraska head football coach Bob Devaney walked forward, and the crowd greeted him with applause even stronger than that which they had given to Nixon. "You ought to run for something in this State," the president joked.[43]

"Well, that's not what I'm going to do. I have no aspirations," the coach responded.[44]

Team cocaptains Jerry Murtaugh and Dan Schneiss joined Devaney on stage. The three of them accepted the award on behalf of the entire team. "This is the greatest honor that has ever been bestowed on any athletic team at the University of Nebraska," Devaney said. "To think the President of the United States would take time to make this presentation. It means a tremendous lot to the team and the university. Thank you." Governor J. J. Exon stood and led the audience in a standing ovation. Nixon took advantage of the moment and raised his arms, but instead of giving the crowd the double victory sign, he gave them a double version of the number-one sign. He also wore a huge grin.[45]

After the applause died down, Nixon explained that sport was a great metaphor for life and for issues the nation now faced. "It is a splendid thing to be champions. But a more splendid thing, I believe is the process by which a team becomes champion, the long struggle through defeat, through doubt, and then on to victory." It was important for what the individual took from the experience.

As vital as the understanding we gain in the classroom is the deeper understanding of ourselves that comes from competing against others and competing against ourselves. In these endeavors, we go beyond awareness of what we are and we discover a higher understanding of what we can be if we know and have the courage and if we have the will. It is in this way that we learn to believe in our dreams.[46]

The president knew that many in the crowd had strong views about the war in Vietnam. A small section of the crowd tried to shout antiwar slogans as he started speaking, but the rest of the audience booed them down. The White House staff had also taken the precaution of breaking up and diluting hostile-looking groups, making them sit in different parts of the arena. Nixon spoke of the weekly burden he faced of signing letters to the next of kin of American servicemen killed in action, and the loss that each message represented. "They were precious human lives and what they might have brought to America in peace no one will ever know. But there would have been poets among them and doctors and teachers and farmers; there would have been builders of America. I want nothing in the world so much as to be able to stop writing those letters."[47]

Nixon predicted that when the war came to an end—which was close at hand—the American people would have to face a whole new set of problems. "We must have great goals—goals that are worthy of us, worthy of our resources, our capacities, worthy of the courage and wisdom and will of our people." Divisions along lines of age were foolish. The country was a collective whole, and the problems it faced, such as poverty and ecological destruction, were ones that affected all the people. "I believe one of America's most priceless assets is the idealism which motivates the young people of America. My generation has invested all that it has, not only its love but its hope and its faith, in yours." He therefore proposed the consolidation of all the volunteer service organizations within the US government to offer young people an expanded opportunity to address these problems, either at home or abroad. He closed with a word on the burdens of duty that his college-student audience would soon face. In doing so, he drew on the similarities between these responsibilities and sports. "In the hard logic of life, for anyone to win, someone else has to lose. For some to know victory, others have to know defeat. That is part of democracy. For it is in the very nature of a free society that no one can win all the time, no one can have his own way all the time, and no one is right all the time."[48]

Reaction to the speech was mixed, but generally more positive than negative. "The P did a very good job at the University with a serious, uplifting speech preceded by his football presentation, which went over very well. He got a good reception by the students," Haldeman recorded. This greeting was far more significant than is normally the case in most presidential appearances. Nixon had put his opponents in a difficult position. Any protest, picketing, or jeering would come across as an insult to the football team. The *Nebraskan*, the school paper, had called on students to welcome Nixon with silence. This approach, the editors claimed, was a far more effective way to express opposition to the president's policies without becoming his foil or offering an affront to the team. In this context, the warm response Nixon got in the auditorium was a sign of real support. Devaney later told reporters, "More than anything else, I was pleased with the way the student body received the President. That meant a lot to me. There would have been some institutions and universities in this country where it might not have been this way."[49]

Several Nebraska students in the audience liked some of the programs and ideas Nixon proposed. Many of those on the team or closely associated with it appreciated the presidential recognition. "It was the Orange Bowl all over again," quarterback Jerry Tagge said. Others, however, were a little offended that their moment was sullied with politics. Guy Ingles, a spilt end, said it was obvious the president "has to mean well," but the plaque added nothing. "We were No. 1 the minute we walked off the field in the Orange Bowl." Pat Morell, a Cornhusker linebacker, said he "would rather had him [Nixon] meet us and congratulate us in private. It would have been more meaningful to us. I don't believe the President would have come here if we weren't the No. 1 team in the nation. His speech was obviously political but that is his prerogative." Annette Hudson, a Nebraska cheerleader and the homecoming queen, added, "I think he came to make amends for what he should have done before—like call and congratulate the team. This was definitely was a political move by the President."[50]

The reaction of the *Washington Post* editorial board was equally reserved. Much of the address was old clichés about the role of youth in society. "What made this—the unexceptional—exceptional, of course was the fact that Mr. Nixon made the speech." The journalists were a little wary of the conciliatory rhetoric, given previous attitudes within the administration, but the editorial closed on a hopeful note. "For all its commonplaces, we so ardently prefer Mr. Nixon's Nebraska speech to what has gone before that we hope the change is real."[51]

National security advisor Henry Kissinger thought the president had gone too far in the opposite direction and told him so. Nixon and Kissinger had a complex relationship, but the president knew enough to pay heed to his advisor's opinions. He phoned Haldeman to ask him if he had indeed overcompensated. Again, Haldeman summarized the conversation in his journal: "He called me after getting home to explore whether the speech today in Nebraska was too soft-line on the students. Apparently, Henry had told him that he had been too apologetic and backed down too much. I don't think that's the case, but there obviously is a fine line to be drawn in this regard."[52]

Nixon would continue along these lines long after Nebraska. In a series of notes to himself, he explained his vision: "The primary contribution a President can make is on Spiritual lift—not material solutions." He was more specific later: "I have decided my major role is moral leadership. I cannot exercise this adequately unless I speak out more often and more eloquently."

In these brief essays, written on yellow legal pads, he described the tactics he would use:

Add element of lift to each appearance . . . Hard work—Imagination—Compassion—Leadership—Understanding of young—Intellectual expansion . . .

Cool—Strong—Organized—Temperate—Exciting . . . Excitement—Joy in Life—Sharing. Lift spirit of people—Pithy, memorable phrases.[53]

Occasionally, the White House planted stories in the media that were intended to highlight specific themes or values, but these played a supporting, secondary role to the actual remarks and actions of the president. Sometimes, it was easy to misread his message. James Reston of the *New York Times* was off the mark when he suggested that sport interested Nixon because it had "more unity, more certainty at the end than most things—so he watches the games, not only because it is good politics, but because it is an escape from his normal problems that have no rules and no end." This comment tells us more about Reston than Nixon, since it is almost identical to comments he made to *Times* sports columnist Red Smith. A 1973 editorial in the *Nation* erred equally when it proclaimed that the president had a win-at-all-costs mentality like his friends Woody Hayes and George Allen, the head coaches of the Ohio State Buckeyes and the Washington Redskins, respectively. "The President's recent political behavior is that he exhibits the values and outlook of a successful head coach; he admires winners and scorns losers."[54]

Not really. In 1972, he quoted his old college football coach in remarks he made to a group of high school students: "'The way to be a good loser is to commit yourself that you are going to try again and try harder.'" His coach said losing was not wrong. "'What is wrong is not trying. What is wrong is not playing the game. What is wrong is when you lose, not getting up off that floor and coming back and fighting again.'" His advice to them was simple: "Don't quit. Don't ever quit. Keep trying, because this country needs the very best that you, the young generation of American, can give to it."[55] Nixon believed that people displayed their character in full only in the difficult moments of life. "What really proves that a person or a team or a country has it," he told another audience a year later, "is not when it is winning and everybody is cheering it on, but when it has lost one and it does not lose its spirit, it comes back, it comes back and goes on to win."[56]

As Richard Nixon's second year in the White House came to an end, he found himself politically weaker than he had been twelve months before. Affiliating himself with sport was a good way to win over crowds, gain electoral support, and garner positive publicity through venues that rarely covered politicians, but it was no magic wand. This approach had limitations, and the president realized as much. Yet, Nixon's interaction with the athletic world was more than just another politician seeking votes and support. As the president of the United States, Richard M. Nixon was more than a Republican politician. When the times demanded it, he could and did offer the informal leadership that the country expected of his office. Despite the setbacks of 1970, sport remained one of Nixon's most effective tools at reaching the nation. With that point made, it would be local Washington issues, not national ones, that would dominate most of Nixon's interaction with athletics in 1971.

First Ball: In the United States, the president preforms both the ceremonial duties of a head of state and the tasks related to politics and policy associated with a head of government. (In the United Kingdom two individuals, the monarch and the prime minister, perform these functions.) One of the ceremonial functions of the president is to throw out the first baseball of the season. Nixon loved this part of his job, and was often asked to throw out the first ball of regular games that he attended.

Nixon at the Ballpark: Nixon used sports in ways that gave voters a way to relate to the president of the United States. When he attended ball games, Nixon normally watched the games from the stands like the average fan, rather than from a luxury box or from the dugout or sidelines. The Secret Service was quite worried about the first couple of trips Nixon took to the ballpark because he went without access to the nuclear command codes and there was no doctor standing by in case of an emergency. Here he is attending a Washington Senators baseball game in 1969 with Attorney General John Mitchell. Secret Service agents and the US Army officer carrying the nuclear codes are visible sitting around the president.

The First Centennial: Major League Baseball celebrated its centennial in 1969. The night before the All-Star Game, which Washington, DC, hosted, professional baseball held a banquet where an assortment of players were recognized as the greatest individuals at their respective positions. Golden trophies were presented to these players or the next of kin of the deceased. The afternoon of the game, Nixon held a reception at the White House for these players and their wives. At this gathering, Baseball Commissioner Bowie Kuhn gave the president a trophy, similar to the type presented the night before, that read: "Baseball's Number One Fan."

There Is Something You Do Not See Every Day: Many reporters at the time found the reception almost surreal, watching baseball legends traipse about the executive mansion. More than one journalist called the event the strangest moment at the White House since a crowd barged into a reception held during the administration of Andrew Jackson. Nixon greeted the ballplayers, and one of the most widely circulated images was this one of him and Casey Stengel, former manager of the New York Yankees.

The Second Centennial: The centennial of college football was in 1969. At the end of the year, the University of Texas and the University of Arkansas were ranked first and second in the news service polls. As a result, their game, which came at the end of the season, would be for both the Southwest Conference Championship and the national championship that the wire services claimed to bestow on the team that finished first in their polls. Nixon attended the game in an effort to get media attention without taking any political or policy-related actions. Texas defeated Arkansas, 15–14, and Nixon visited the Longhorn locker room afterward. He presented Texas head football coach Darrell Royal with his presidential plaque live on national television. This image of Nixon and Royal appeared on the front pages of newspapers all over Texas and across the country. H. R. Haldeman, Nixon's chief of staff, thought the White House had achieved a major public relations victory for the president.

Nixon at the All-Star Game: During the 1970 midterm elections, Nixon made a number of appearances on the campaign trail and often mentioned local sports teams in his speeches. At the suggestion of son-in-law David Eisenhower, Nixon attended the Major League Baseball All-Star Game in Cincinnati after making an appearance at a governors' conference in Louisville, Kentucky. The president sat in the stands with Baseball Commissioner Bowie Kuhn (*on Nixon's left*) and Congressman Robert Taft Jr. (*on Nixon's right*), who was running for his father's old seat in the Senate.

The POTUS and the MVP: The Most Valuable Player of the 1970 All-Star Game was Carl Yastrzemski, an outfielder for the Boston Red Sox. Yastrzemski, an admirer of the president, decided to give him his MVP trophy. A meeting between the two was arranged on April 13, 1971, and the athlete presented the award to Nixon.

Nixon on Football: In 1971, Nixon gave a speech at the dinner the National Football League held in honor of the new inductees into the Hall of Fame. He expressed his belief that the sport helped shape "a spirit of competition, a spirit of trying to do our very best," which to Nixon was the thing that made America great.

Nixon and the Redskins: In 1971, the Redskins, a perennial loser in the National Football League, were winning and looked like they might make the playoffs for the first time since World War II. On November 21, the team lost a home game to the Dallas Cowboys, 13–0. Redskins' fans booed the players during the game. Two days later, Nixon took head coach George Allen up on a long-standing offer to visit with the team to give them a pep talk. He told the players to ignore those who booed. "A great majority of people in this town back the team," he remarked. "You have been good for this city." Many of the players were stunned and elated to have the president show his support.

The President and "the Dancing Bear": Nixon and Ron "the Dancing Bear" McDole, a defensive end on the Washington Redskins, talk football. Washington coach George Allen, who is standing next to the president, is clearly enjoying the moment and the effect it is having on his team.

A Great Fortune Befell Them All: The success of the trip is evident on the face of George Allen as Nixon talks to quarterback Billy Kilmer, who was for some reason wearing the number 88. He wore number 17 on game days. Nixon is clearly enjoying the moment. He later posed for pictures with the team and threw the ball. Even the sports reporters covering the event seem to be enjoying the moment.

The Sport of Presidents: Golf was another sport that Nixon took up while in office. His feelings for the game were less than enthusiastic at first, but it was an interest that Americans expected in their presidents. Nixon eventually developed a strong liking for the sport. He had sets of clubs at the White House, Camp David, San Clemente, and Key Biscayne so he could play whenever he wanted. His scores were decent given his physical awkwardness and a job that kept him from playing on a regular basis.

5

The Final Death of the Washington Senators

Entering his third year in the White House, Nixon and sports was still primarily a political story. His actions as a fan and inaction as a civic power earned him a good deal of publicity, and most of it had no hard, negative edge. As far as political theater goes, it was an impressive year for Nixon.

The Washington Redskins and the Washington Senators were two unifying forces in an extremely divided city, and sources of civic pride among a transient population. The Redskins had sold out their home games for years despite posting losing seasons on a regular basis.[1] Nixon realized these facts and commented on them directly with Redskins' team owner Edward Bennett Williams. "I suppose that the profound political commentators would scoff at any suggestion that the success of a football team could raise the morale of a whole city. But that is exactly what the Redskins have done over the past two years. People in this highly partisan town forget their feuds with each other in joining together to root for the Redskins."[2] Both District teams lost on a regular basis, and Nixon often used comments about their plight as friendly banter when talking with other powerful individuals in the city. In his formal comments at the swearing in of Walter E. Washington as the new mayor of the District of Columbia, Nixon charged him to see to it that the Redskins won the Super Bowl in or before 1976. "I am charging them up," Washington replied in kind.[3]

Basketball lacked this social function—it was not that popular among the American people in the early 1970s—and Nixon had little interest in the sport. Despite the dominance of the University of California, Los Angeles in college basketball and the presence of many Bruin Bear alumni in his administration, he had made no effort to attend any of their games, even when the NCAA championship game was played in College Park, Maryland, a suburb of Washington. He did surprise UCLA head coach John Wooden with a phone call after his team won the national title in 1970, their sixth in seven years. Wooden was fighting tears in the conversation, and considered that conversation one of the greatest honors in his career. For the most part, though, Nixon's congratulatory letters to basketball players and coaches were full of factual errors that did not appear in messages to athletes in other sports, and basketball letters were often misfiled, showing that the White House staff shared his lack of interest in the game. Another problem that minimized his participation with the sport was the rivalry between the National Basketball Association and the American Basketball Association, the two professional leagues in the United States at the time. Both circuits wanted to win his support, presenting him with passes to their games. Bud Wilkinson saw the problem after the ABA franchise in Washington proposed to give him a season pass. "If the President accepts the pass from the ABA, it would be necessary for him to do the same for the NBA. Consequently, I recommend that he not accept the pass." Turned out he was right. A year later, the NBA wanted Commissioner Walter Kennedy and Milwaukee Bucks star Lew Alcindor to present him with an honorary lifetime pass. Pat Buchanan of the White House communications objected, noting the reverse side of the issue, "Problem with A.B.A. would crop up—RN not that great a B-Ball fan."[4]

Nixon eventually overcame this lack of interest. A year later in 1972, he watched a Los Angeles Lakers–Milwaukee Bucks game on television. Wilt Chamberlain, a prominent Nixon supporter, was playing for Los Angeles. Nixon was impressed with what he saw. "You would never think a man that tall, seven feet, could be so graceful," he said with a bit of wonder in his voice. Despite that impression, he waited until 1992 to attend his first professional basketball game, when he watched the New York Knicks beat the Minnesota Timberwolves, 103–87. "I can see why this game draws so well," he said afterward. "So exciting. It's more than just the shooting and all. It's a ballet. And the way coaches . . . they've really got to be great psychologists. They call the timeouts just when they need them. It's something to see."[5]

Despite Nixon's strong love of sport, it would be wrong to overemphasize the importance of the Redskins and Senators. Common support for either team was in no way a venue for overcoming sharp political differences. Williams was a power in the Democratic party and the lawyer for the *Washington Post*, a major Nixon nemesis. According to Haldeman, Nixon wanted to enact some revenge when the 1972 election was over. The president intended to "cut Williams completely, and the Redskins and everything else, then build up our own lawyers in this kind of area." The administration eventually followed up on this threat, hitting Williams where it hurt most—in the pocketbook. The Nixon White House convinced the Teamsters Union, which did its legal business with Williams's firm, to find new representation. At the time, a fifth of the lawyers in this small, twenty-five-man firm worked on that one account.[6]

In 1971, though, these attacks lay in the future. Despite the promise of the 1969 season, both teams had returned to their losing ways in 1970. The Senators had been cellar-dwellers since they joined the major leagues in 1961 as an expansion team, after the original Washington Senators moved to Minneapolis and became the Minnesota Twins. (The nation's capital never went a season without a team because the powers behind Major League Baseball feared that Congress might revoke the exemption the sport enjoyed from antitrust laws.) In addition to being rather poor on the diamond, the original Senators were never a strong moneymaker, and the second Senators followed in both these traditions.

Bob Short bought the team in 1968 primarily with credit and soon found it difficult to pay his bills due to low attendance. Estimates of his debt ranged from $3 to 5 million. He made the situation worse after the 1969 season when he increased ticket prices so much that tickets to Senator games were the most expensive in either baseball league. In 1969 the people of Washington showed that they would come to the ball park to root for a winning team, even a modest one. Short, however, gutted the team of talent with disastrous personnel moves that on an individual basis seemed simply unwise, but collectively were self-destructive. He traded his support players for star athletes, but each big name had problems of equal size. Pitcher Denny McLain had won thirty games in a season for the Detroit Tigers, but his association with members of organized crime had gotten him suspended for half a season. He also had financial problems and filed for bankruptcy. As a Senator in 1971, he lost twenty-two games. Instead of becoming a baseball legend, he ended up in federal prison before the end of the decade.

A month after signing McLain, Short negotiated a trade with Philadelphia for Curt Flood, which was actually an even more disastrous acquisition than McLain when his salary is measured against the number of games he played in Washington. Flood sat out the entire 1970 season as part of his legal challenge to the reserve system in baseball, which prevented the development of free agency and kept player salaries at artificially low levels. After losing at trial, he returned to the game as his case worked its way on appeal to the US Supreme Court. Flood, however, found that he had been gone too long. He had failed to stay in condition, his skills had been fading even before St. Louis traded him to Philadelphia, and his heart was not in the effort; he was drinking a lot during spring training, becoming an alcoholic. After only five games, Williams benched him. During a road trip to New York, he retired for good, informing the team with a telegram and taking with him the half of his $110,000 salary that the team paid him in advance. When the cost of the contracts of the players that Short had traded to Philadelphia are included, Flood had cost the Senators $115,000 for the thirteen games he played.[7]

Despite these problems, the Washington club still had Nixon's support. The 1970 signing of relief pitcher Pedro Ramos, a player for the original Senators, was one move that excited him. Ramos's arm strength, though, had faded since his earlier days in Washington, and he had difficulty making the team. When Ramos survived the final cut, Nixon called to congratulate him. *Washington Post* sportswriter William Gildea wrote a column about the call and the president's support for the average athlete as well as the superstar favorites of the media. The next morning, a White House phone call woke the journalist. "I read your column today and enjoyed it," a familiar voice announced. "If Pete Ramos can come through, I think they can win the pennant." Surprised as he was at the call, Gildea disagreed. Ramos no longer had the power and ability he had earlier in his career. "It was before your time, but Lefty Grove still won games after losing his fast ball in his last few years," Nixon replied. Before hanging up, he complimented Gildea again on his article. "Thank you, sir," the reporter said, fumbling even this basic response.[8]

Such high-powered support did little to help the team. In order to pay these high salaries, Short traded a number of players with middle-income salaries for others with cheaper contracts and cash, stripping the team of its supporting cast. He increased promotional efforts, giving away pantyhose with tickets in the hope that this gimmick would attract female fans. Nixon still attended games, but his presence was the exception rather than the rule. Fans could easily travel to Baltimore or set their televisions to Maryland stations and watch the Orioles, a team that had won three of the last five AL titles.[9]

Even Nixon's faith in the Senators began to fade. In an Oval Office conversation that took place during the middle of the season, Nixon and Haldeman discussed his attending a game. "Frankly, it's too much of a pain in the ass to go much," the president grumbled. He believed he would get more publicity at the All-Star Game. Haldeman disagreed. Going to a Senators game was the right move. "You come through as a fan on this thing." He explained, "It gets you on the sports page which is good; it's good to be on there."[10]

In 1971 the ceremonial throwing of the first pitch was a metaphor for the decline of the team. Despite Nixon's strong interest in throwing out the first ball of the season, he was unable to arrange his schedule to permit his appearance. He still wanted to use the event for political purposes, specifically as a way to bolster support for the war effort. As a result, the White House staff made arrangements for Master Sergeant Daniel Pitzer to perform the ceremonial duty. Pitzer was a US Army Green Beret who had been a prisoner of war of the Viet Cong for four years. Given the brutality of their treatment at the hands of the enemy, prisoners of war were the only group to emerge as unquestioned heroes of the Vietnam War. As a result, the presidential party also included the families of five other POWs in Southeast Asia. Secretary of Defense Melvin Laird read a statement at the stadium during the throw: "As he [Pitzer] performs this American ritual of throwing out the first ball, he does so as a reminder that there are still a great many of our men in uniform—some sixteen hundred of them—who have not seen a ball game in a long time, much less seen their homes or families."[11]

Another baseball ceremony took place on April 13. Carl Yastrzemski finally met with Nixon in a short Oval Office meeting and gave him the trophy Yastrzemski had received as Most Valuable Player of the 1970 All-Star Game. The two talked about baseball and the ballplayer's work in drug education programs. Later that day, Nixon met with Haldeman in the Oval Office. "I don't know who thought it, thought it up," Nixon told Haldeman, "but that

Yastrzemski thing was about the best thing I've done for some time, because he said . . . "

Haldeman cut him off in midsentence, which was something he usually did not do: "You know who brought it up was Yastrzemski."

The astonished disbelief is clearly evident in Nixon's voice, "I can't understand why. I've never met the man!"

Haldeman replied in a manner of fact tone, "But he just got carried away and said, you know, he wanted to give you the award. He said it a long time ago, and we've been trying to work out, you know, jiggling . . . "

Nixon simply could not believe what he was hearing and cut him off: "He was all by himself?"

"Apparently so."

Nixon was flabbergasted. "Oh, my gosh. It's his award!"

"It was his idea," the White House chief of staff replied.

The president of the United States had no reply, and he paused for several moments. "Absolutely, great," he said, clearly dumbfounded.

Haldeman explained in clipped words and a now humble tone what Yastrzemski had done. "Had an amazing night. The guy wanted to do it."[12] The President never forgot this gesture. Years later when the Nixon Library opened the MVP trophy was on prominent display.[13]

Whatever goodwill such events developed, Nixon needed it that spring. The United States had initiated Lam Son 719 as a test of its Vietnamization policy. On February 18, the Army of the Republic of Vietnam sent 16,000 of its best troops into the Laotian panhandle to interdict North Vietnamese supply efforts along the Ho Chi Minh Trail. The South Vietnamese went in with aerial and artillery support from their American allies. The North Vietnamese responded with a force that was twice the size of the one that their southern cousins sent into Laos. Although the South Vietnamese inflicted 2.5 deaths for every solider they lost, they had fewer lives to give. "Lam Son destroyed the cream of the South Vietnam army and was far more serious and detrimental than was believed at the time. Our handling of that was very bad," General Alexander Haig admitted. Public support seemed to be collapsing. "Laos is one more straw—and a substantial one—on the camel's back," one member of the House of Representatives informed Nixon. "Most Americans—myself included—have come to feel that this war has gone on too long."[14]

As if to add insult to injury, the future of the Washington Senators was collapsing as well. The team's lease at Robert F. Kennedy Memorial Stadium expired at the end of the year, and Short was interested in moving to another city. He and Kuhn had a late-night phone conversation in April that the commissioner characterized as "long, rambling," and "emotional." In his memoirs, Kuhn quoted Short at length:

> No one can keep me in Washington, not Nixon, not Cronin, not Kuhn. I will cannibalize the club if necessary. I own it and I will take it to St. Paul if I want. I have lawyers too. I will move wherever I want. Congress will not help me because of your position. I don't give a goddamn if they stick you with the antitrust laws. I'll go to St. Paul, Dallas or Toronto. Goldberg is my lawyer and I'll go the whole goddamn distance with you. Hoffberger is a genius. Let him figure it out. Or let Walter O'Malley and his National League friends help out. No place in Washington is safe at night and Nixon can't do anything about it. I may sell Ted Williams to Boston or Knowles, or Howard or Epstein. Ted says Washington is a horseshit town and I've gotta get out. I'll go elsewhere before I'm forced into bankruptcy like Seattle. I know I had my eyes wide open when I went to Washington, but I told the American League I wouldn't keep it there forever. If we're to save Washington, everybody has to give something: me, the players, TV and the federal government. Even the Humphrey Democrats are now hitting me. Maybe things will work out in a Cinderella way, but that's not likely.

While it is doubtful that Kuhn's account is an accurate, verbatim rendering of this conversation, it is no doubt representative of the general tenor of the discussion. The commissioner noted that the talk convinced him that Short had no interest in staying in Washington. He now knew that Short wanted to relocate to a new market, where he could sell to a local ownership group for much more than he could get if the club stayed in the nation's capital. This move was hardly surprising. Short had done the same thing when he took the Minnesota Lakers of the NBA to Los Angeles.[15]

Kuhn was determined to keep professional baseball in the District of Columbia. "If baseball was going to repair its wounded image, the time had come to stop moving franchises," he observed. "Nor did it make any sense to leave a major growth area like Washington and the surrounding Maryland-Virginia suburbs. The area had not failed; management had failed to provide attractive baseball." The numbers supported Kuhn. When the team was winning in 1969, offering local fans an attractive entertainment venue for their dollars, ticket sales tripled. When the Senators returned to their traditional ways in the standings, ticket sales slumped. "Finally," Kuhn noted, "it made no sense to leave the nation's capital and to run the risk of antagonizing the government establishment to which we looked for legislative and administrative support."[16]

Due to baseball's special legal status, Kuhn had considerable powers invested in his office. He actually had the power to veto the relocation of a franchise. At a meeting of American League owners in Detroit on June 30, the commissioner made his position clear. The owners agreed with him that the team should stay if they could find a buyer for Short, and they established a special three-man committee of Kuhn, Short, and American League president Joe Cronin, an All-Star shortstop for the original Washington Senators, to find possible candidates. Kuhn ended up doing all the work. Short had no interest in selling to a local buyer; he stood to make more selling in a new market. Cronin was torn. He wanted to keep a team in the District, but the Senators were most likely going to move to Texas, and he wanted an AL presence in the Lone Star State to compete with the Houston Astros of the National League. "Thus began a miserable summer," Kuhn recalled years later. He spent the next few months working the city, looking for an individual or corporation interested in keeping the team in Washington. Marriott Hotels, the *Washington Post,* and the *Washington Evening Star* expressed no interest in the team when the commissioner approached them. Kuhn tried national corporations that might like a prize property, but met with the same luck. He talked with comedian Bob Hope, who had lost to Short in 1968 in an effort to buy the team, but the entertainer no longer wanted to get into the baseball business. Other sports entrepreneurs responded in a similar fashion.[17]

The plight of the Senators was well known, and several individuals suggested that Nixon might want to intervene in the matter. On July 1, Republican campaign strategist Roger Ailes suggested that it might make for good politics if Nixon tried to keep the team in Washington. It would give Nixon a "down-to-earth look" if he met with team management and expressed his concerns about their future not as the president, but as a sports fan. Senator William B. Spong Jr., the Virginia Democrat, was also concerned and wrote Nixon: "I wanted to alert you to the very real possibility that the Washington franchise may be moved in the future." Reporters, columnists, and editors from the sports department of the *Washington Post* also began working to try to keep the team in the District. Apparently unaware that the Washington Post Company had passed on an opportunity to buy the team, Martie Zad, executive sports editor for the paper, wrote Nixon: "It is my hope that Shirley Povich and I might be allowed to visit with you on this matter. And from this, maybe, Shirley can do a piece that would, I'm sure, take effect in the Senators' office, the commissioner's office and around the American League." Zad reminded the president that there was a historical precedent for such intervention. President Eisenhower had used his influence to pressure the original Senators to stay in Washington until the league was ready to replace them with an expansion team. Del Webb, coowner of the New York Yankees in the early 1960s and chair of the league expansion committee at that time, had been particularly susceptible to White House pressure. His construction company did a good deal of business building military bases, and Eisenhower got what he wanted. Zad also added, "Granting this wish will be a great service to baseball, Washington's long suffering fans, who now have some bright young talent and a future, and to the operation of Washington's stadium."[18]

Nixon was facing an opportunity, even if only on a local basis, to use the prestige of his office to provide some domestic social leadership in the world of sports. He chose, instead, to pass on the chance. Each letter writer received a pro forma response. Herbert Klein replied to Zad, offering the best explanation for the president's reluctance. While Nixon wanted the team to stay, "it would be inappropriate for him to intercede in this business/finance matter."[19]

Nixon had legitimate reasons for taking a neutral position, but administration officials undercut his efforts and forced him to take a public stand, albeit a weak one. Kuhn had found a local businessman interested in buying the Senators: Joe Danzansky, president of the Giant supermarket chain. "At last, it seemed, we had found the right answer," the commissioner recalled. Then two developments soon undid his work and doomed the Senators. The first one was the doing of the White House staff. Just before the American League meeting in Boston on September 21, where the league would approve a sale or transfer, Kuhn picked up the *Washington Post* and saw a White House statement that Nixon "had spoken with Short, and while dismayed about the prospects of losing the franchise, fully understood the circumstances and supported him." This statement, the work of Ron Zeigler, implied that the federal government had consented to the departure of the Washington franchise, and it weakened the cause of those fighting to keep the team in Washington.[20]

The president wanted the Senators to remain in Washington, but was hoping to stay out of the fray. Now he had to fix the mistake his press secretary had made. On the White House tapes, Ziegler warned him this "trivial thing" would come up later. Nixon agreed. "I think this being for your hometown isn't a bad idea, but I could give a shit about Short and the rest," he told Haldeman and Ziegler. What the Senators really needed was for the Baltimore Orioles to relocate, or a stadium with a better location. "To be perfectly candid with you, Washington is going to have to lose it due to the reason—due to the fact that they will go down in there for those football games but they will not go down there because it is too God-damned dangerous, you know, at night. I really think that is part of the problem."[21]

On September 20, Nixon had a photo session with Laurie Lea Schaefer, the 1972 Miss America, and her immediate predecessor, Phyllis George. As the reporters and photographers left the Oval Office, he called them back in to talk about the Washington club. "I know you've been asking what I thought about this," Nixon said. "I think it would be sad if the nation's capital would lose its baseball team." Ever the politician, he hedged his statement. "I don't want to deny Dallas a baseball team, but I do hope something can be worked out to keep baseball here." The two Miss Americas continued to smile, even though George was from the Dallas area. "Well, that's my plug for the Senators," the president said, and his audience laughed. These comments made the front page of both the *Evening Star* and the *Post.* Despite these comments, Shelby Coffey, the reporter writing the article on Nixon's views for the *Post*, noted that this statement had less force than the one he had made back in 1958 when the original Senators were threatening to leave town. "Washington without a major league baseball team would be unthinkable," the then vice president had declared.[22]

As bad as the White House miscue was, Danzansky's problems in securing the financing to buy the club were far more critical in destroying any chance of keeping professional baseball in Washington. The American League owners were meeting in Boston on September 21, and Short was going to ask for league permission to transfer his team to the Lone Star State unless he had a buyer. Danzansky lacked the personal financial resources to purchase the team and was arranging loans to secure the purchase, but because of the Rosh Hashanah holiday he did not have all the arrangements finalized by the meeting. In Massachusetts, he told the assembled team representatives that he needed a little more time. "As he left the room," Kuhn wrote after his tenure as commissioner ended, "I knew we were doomed. I had worked all summer and had unearthed only one group. And they needed more time."[23]

In contrast, Short and Mayor Tom Vandergriff of Arlington, Texas, the city where the team hoped to play, made a presentation that Kuhn admitted was "skillful." The Texans were offering an annual rent of $1 and a $7.5 million refinancing of Short's loans at taxpayer's expense. The only blemish was the small size of the stadium, but the Texas contingent promised to expand the stadium from its twenty-two-thousand-person seating capacity to thirty-five thousand by the start of the 1972 season and forty-five thousand in 1973.[24]

The AL meeting lasted thirteen and a half hours. Danzansky told a reporter for the *Washington Evening Star* that he was confident until the last ninety minutes that the league would accept his proposal. His expectations were misplaced. Accounts vary on the exact circumstances, but it is clear that the main issue was getting the three-fourths majority required under league rules to relocate a franchise, rather than a serious consideration of Danzansky's offer. The ballot was 10–2, with Baltimore and Chicago voting against. (Press accounts had California and Oakland abstaining before they switched their votes and the league approved the transfer. The minutes of the league meeting do not reflect this type of vote). Shirley Povich of the *Washington Post* had good reason for his bitter commentary that Kuhn's and Danzansky's efforts were a "pure waste of time." The reason was simple. "Short was always committed to go to Dallas where the money was." His counterpart at the *Star*, Merrell Whittlesey, agreed. He claimed that the move was a done deal as early as a week before the Boston gathering.[25]

Perhaps, but it was a decision that baseball officials would have preferred to avoid. Kuhn's notes show that he had reservations about the situation. The stadium in Texas was a minor league park that was substantially smaller than Robert F. Kennedy Memorial Stadium. A study that the commissioner had a consulting firm conduct made it clear that Washington was a better venue for baseball than Dallas–Fort Worth. Washington had a larger population than these two Texas cities; it was also a bigger television market, and the three Washington newspapers had more subscribers than the three papers in Dallas and Fort Worth. The study also rejected arguments that many had offered that Washington was a bad market for the national pastime. The expansion Senators had not offered much of an on-field product. "The club's record provides little basis for evaluating Washington as a baseball town," the report stated. The team had seen a sharp increase in attendance in 1969, the only season in which the team had more wins than losses. "This record does not justify a conclusion that Washington is a bad baseball town."[26]

These considerations were weighing on Kuhn. Under Major League Baseball's bylaws, the commissioner had to approve the sale and move of any franchise. After the vote, Cronin turned toward Kuhn and, with the room silent, asked, "Commissioner, will you now approve or disapprove of this action?" Kuhn asked for a recess to consider his decision. "I had no decent basis for a delay or veto." The civic and business comminutes in Washington had done nothing to help save the team, and he realized he had "no damned alternative." The meeting reconvened in a heavy silence. The old scoreboard boy at Griffith Stadium had tears in his eyes as he announced the death of the team that wore the heraldry of his former heroes. "I wish the American League well in Texas." And it was done. Washington, a founding member city of the American League, was out of the baseball business. Cronin, the former Senator All-Star, was on the verge of tears when he made the public announcement.[27]

The reaction in the Dallas–Fort Worth metroplex was one of sheer joy. Despite its name, the *Dallas Morning News* printed a special afternoon edition with a banner headline on the front page: "Washington's on the Trinity Now." Several news stories and a *Morning News* editorial gave all the credit to Mayor Vandergriff: "The successful quest is a tribute to the tenaciousness of the suburban mayor as well as the many qualities of the Dallas–Fort Worth area, which attracted attention of the major league owners." The *Times Herald* was more ecstatic in both its news coverage and its editorial commentary. "Dallas–Fort Worth is big league today" was the first line in its story announcing the move. An editorial in the paper called the move "another major advancement for this area" noting that "it will enhance the prestige of Dallas–Fort Worth." Vandergriff could not help but gloat in this moment of triumph. When his plane arrived at Love Field in Dallas, a small throng of supporters greeted him. He held up above his head a copy of the *Evening Star* with the headline: "Nation's Capital Loses to Arlington, Texas." He had circled the words "Arlington, Texas." Statements of congratulations were immediately forthcoming from the two Texas senators and the members of the House of Representatives from the Dallas–Fort Worth area. Galyn Wilkins, a sports columnist for the *Fort Worth Star-Telegram*, focused on the political aspects of the development and exaggerated the opposition from the Oval Office. "President Nixon had expressed the opinion that a move of the Washington Senators would be the worst thing to happen to the capital since the British set it afire. Some congressmen expressed tougher opinions, hinting that the probes into baseball's antitrust involvement would intensify." This resistance made Vandergriff's success that much more impressive. "A suburb mayor from Texas doesn't knock off Capitol Hill every day," Wilkins commented with glee.[28]

Despite the success of bringing baseball to Dallas–Fort Worth, some Texans expressed reservations about the team. Congressman Olin Teague wanted new management: "I don't have a lot of faith in Bob Short. These trades he made last year were fatal to the Senators. If he does the same thing in Texas, we're going to have problems." Sam Blair, a sports columnist for the *Dallas Morning News*, agreed. He called Short an "owner whose past activities make it important that he be greeted here with reservations." Blair noted that many of the problems Short encountered were of his own making. "Until he proves he will shape up and give this area a good organization and a sound program for building a contending team, no one should rush out and strew roses in his path."[29]

The response in the District of Columbia was quite different. "We're all disappointed," Mayor Washington said that evening. "We think that it's really a great blow to the city and all the sports fans and all the people." For his part, Nixon was resigned to the loss of his team and had White House press secretary Ron Ziegler announce that the president would now consider the California Angels his home team. A reporter for the *Washington Post* went to a number of Washington area bars and found that the attitudes of local fans generally mirrored those of Nixon in accepting the loss of their team as another disappointment at the end of a long, hard day. In his syndicated column, Red Smith of the *New York Times* saw anger as the more likely response from Capitol Hill: "Politicians have a tendency to rise in righteous wrath when one of their own oxen is gored." Kuhn expected as much and told the *Dallas Times Herald* that he expected a congressional inquiry into the legal status of the sport. His concerns were well placed. Members of Congress were far less accepting than Nixon or the local fans. "I think it (the Senators' teeter-totter) has created a tremendous amount of new interest in the baseball exemption," Senator John Tunney of California declared during hearings of the Senate Antitrust and Monopoly Subcommittee about the merger of the NBA and ABA. "It has focused attention on the cavalier way owners move franchises around the country. There's a fans be damned attitude on the part of some owners." The next day the chairman of the subcommittee, Senator Sam Ervin of North Carolina, made another forceful statement: "When people have the attitude toward the Nation's Capital that the public be damned, they have the brass to come to Congress to ask for exemption from antitrust laws." Senator Spong of Virginia appeared before the panel and asked that it expand its inquiry into professional baseball. The political pressure on the sport was strong. In December a delegation of civic, business, and congressional leaders from Washington flew to a meeting of Major League Baseball in Phoenix and obtained a pledge from the executive council that "there would be no further expansion or franchise movement without Washington being accommodated." Baseball would make an honest effort to live up to this pledge, at least initially. But such moves would come in the later years of the Nixon presidency.[30]

In Arlington, Texas, Mayor Vandergriff attempted to reduce some of the political pressure. Baseball traditionalists were asking what would happen to the custom of having the president throw out the first pitch of the season. Until then, the president had always performed this task in Washington. When he returned to Texas, Vandergriff said the tradition could continue in revised form. He would invite the president to perform the ceremony in Arlington. Nixon was not interested. Ziegler stated that the president intended to throw the first ball out in Anaheim, California, with his new team, the Angels. Vandergriff's offer was finally accepted in 1976, when President Gerald R. Ford did the honors.[31]

Nixon also suffered a bit for his refusal to act. Shirley Povich blasted him in a column later in the year for making no effort to save the Senators:

Mr. Nixon was the one resident of this city who by the power of his office might have persuaded the twelve AL club owners to call off their dirty game. All the evidence is that the President, instead, sat on his hands and was unmoved by the villainy being visited on Washington fans who were being voted out of baseball by the same owners who voted Robert E. Short in.

After noting that the league had made the original mistake of letting Short take control of the team with a shaky financial foundation, he redirected his contempt back to Nixon and his new support for the Angels. "The fan at 1600 Pennsylvania Avenue is more favored by the logistics than other Washington baseball fans, who don't happen to have an Air Force One handy for a hop to a summer White House at San Clemente, hard by Anaheim."[32]

What Povich did not know was that Nixon had already had meetings with Mayor Washington about bringing another team to the nation's capitol. Early talk suggested that the San Diego Padres were a possibility. Nixon dismissed that idea. "I don't think they will move. I don't think they will move." Team owner C. A. Smith was a Californian and was too committed to Southern California. "The White Sox are a possibility," Nixon remarked. Chicago did not need two teams. After listening to Washington explain the efforts the city was making to recruit a new team, Nixon told him these initiatives would fail to get the attention of Major League Baseball:

The way to really get that club is to do what Kansas City did. You recall they got a club back. And the way they done it is by season tickets. Now, you sell enough season tickets, you see, getting the club back, just giving them the money ain't, but if you sell 20,000, 25,000 season tickets they're going to come. Find out what Kansas City did and let's try to do that in Washington.

The city should have a drive to sell season tickets, which would basically be a financial commitment by people in the region to the next team sight unseen. "Twenty thousand season tickets for baseball should be easy, *easy*," Nixon said repeating himself with emphasis.[33]

With or without the Senators, Nixon remained a fan of the game. In fact, his enthusiasm had little to do with the fortunes of any one specific team. The month before the Senators left town, he met the Oakland A's at a special

White House reception for the team. The A's were a powerful team in the early 1970s, but pitcher Vida Blue was the phenomenon of the moment on the talented team. After less than a year in the major leagues, he had become a star. Jeb Magruder at the Nixon reelection committee suggested that Nixon call Blue when he earned his twentieth victory, and attend a game when he went for his thirtieth. Such a move "would strike a very positive note, particularly, among young Blacks." The president sent a letter to Blue when he won his twentieth, and directed his attention toward Blue when the team visited with him. Reflecting his prolabor orientation when it came to baseball, Nixon told the pitcher—who made $13,000—"You must be the most underpaid player in the game." He bantered with the rest of the team, which gave him a green and yellow A's cap. "He's a real sports fan and he knows his baseball," team manger Dick Williams remarked to a reporter. The A's made it into postseason play but lost in the American League championship series to the defending world champion Baltimore Orioles.[34]

In the World Series, Baltimore faced the Pirates of Pittsburgh. Three people—Kuhn, the governor of Maryland, and the mayor of Baltimore—sent individual invitations to Nixon to attend the fall classic. Joe Garagiola, the former St. Louis Cardinals star turned sportscaster, also contacted the White House and asked that Nixon do a piece with him for use in one of the pregame shows. Ziegler and John Scali, the former reporter for ABC News, opposed the idea. "The President is in danger of over doing the sports fan bit at this time," Scali argued. Ziegler thought the idea was beneath the man and office, "President Nixon is a statesman and leader of the free world, not a sportscaster." Herb Klein and Dick Moore thought a presidential appearance was a good idea, but both believed it should be a drop-in interview like the one he had done with Lindsey Nelson at the 1970 All-Star Game. The issue soon became moot, because Nixon was not able to arrange his schedule to attend any of the games, and he believed it was for the best. "I think my identification with baseball is so clear, I don't have to go to the Series."[35]

Nixon followed the contest closely, and after announcing his itinerary for his summit meeting in Moscow, he turned his attention toward game three. The Orioles had won the first two games in Baltimore, but the president suspected different results in Pennsylvania. "Pittsburgh should take this one today with their fast infield," he told the White House press corps. He was right; the Pirates won, 5–1. The champions of the National League went on to win all three games in Three Rivers Stadium, taking a 3–2 lead in the contest. Nixon, however, predicted the Orioles would win again when the series returned to Baltimore, and again he was on the mark. The Orioles won a ten-inning game six. Nixon called Haldeman afterward: "I think I'll give up this business and start predicting baseball games." Despite the home field advantage that had seemed to determine the outcomes of the previous games, the Pirates won game seven in Baltimore on October 17. A pitching duel between Mike Cuellar of Baltimore and Steve Blass of Pittsburgh ended when Pirates outfielder Roberto Clemente hit a home run off Cuellar in the fourth inning. A Willie Stargell run in the eighth inning gave Pittsburgh enough to win, 2–1. Nixon called both clubhouses and talked to the manager of each team. He congratulated Danny Murtaugh of Pittsburgh and offered his condolences to Earl Weaver of Baltimore and wished the Orioles luck on their pending tour of Japan.[36]

Haldeman realized that the president was striking political gold with his interest in sports, and he wanted to build on that success. He supported the idea of having Nixon go to one of the games in Baltimore. He also suggested that Nixon have a special meeting with sports reporters. As a professional group, they did not interact much with the president of the United States, and they were likely to be complimentary and deferential. "I have mixed emotions about it, mixed emotions," Nixon replied. He did not want to end up just doing a sports press conference. He also made it clear to Haldeman that if he went forward with this idea it would be an event with sportswriters, and only sportswriters. He did not want any television or radio journalists in the room. Although he was more favorably inclined toward sports reporters than those who covered politics, they were still journalists, and that made them the enemy. It was only a question of degree. He explained his views to George Allen, the new head coach of the Washington Redskins, in an easy conversation that was not marked with anger or bitterness: "Well look, a press guy—and it serves you in politics and it is true of some sports writers—they'd shoot their grandmother for a story. *Really!*"[37]

That fall Haldeman had his staff stage a publicity event to associate Nixon with auto racing. It had been something that Nixon had been wanting. He liked the idea of meeting race car drivers. They were competitive, they worked hard to succeed, they were "good men and they're good Americans." Haldeman noted that they were the type of men who had been fighter pilots in World War II. Nixon liked this idea. "My God, let's have our kind of people in here. What in the—we have these—hell horse's ass, God-damn college professors in here. I don't know." He also wanted a car at the event. "Let me look at it."[38]

The president got what he wanted. In September he welcomed 125 drivers, crew chiefs, promoters, car owners, sponsors, and race officials to the White House lawn. Nixon also had a reception for them in the mansion afterward. Jackie Stewart, the Scottish driver, told his host: "You are the first head of state in any country to honor motor racing officially. It's a fine thing. We are tremendously grateful." Not only were the guests thankful, they were impressed. "I was surprised how much he seemed to know about our cars," Mario Andretti said afterward. "He asked a lot of sharp questions, about the tires and horsepower and things like that. He was really impressed when we warmed up my [Indy] car at 5,500 r.p.m. He knew that the max on a passenger car is 3,000 or 3,500."[39]

"Imagine this, me walking through the White House," Johnny Rutherford, a race car driver, marveled afterward.[40]

Haldeman was not done with this sport. Race car fans were a demographic that Haldeman believed Nixon needed to attract in 1972. Ideas that White House staffers suggested included having Nixon attend one of the more important races, sending letters and making congratulatory phone calls to the winning drivers, getting major names in the various circuits to join a special White House task force promoting safe driving, inserting references to auto racing in presidential statements, involving leading drivers in the President's Council on Physical Fitness, and inviting people in the sport to White House social events. The chief of staff approved all these ideas. After the reception, Haldeman kept the pressure on his staff to follow through on the other ideas. In a memo, which represented his administrative style, he told Dwight Chapin: "Lest you think you have fulfilled your commitment with regard to a plan to identify the President with auto racing as a result of the event . . . let me assure you that is not the case."[41]

Bowlers were another demographic community that Nixon would try to woo. Bowling, according to Nixon, was a middle-American sport. "You know who [are] the lowest class of people in sports—bowlers!" the president declared. In a mocking, high-pitched voice, he explained that high-society types do not bowl. Tennis players do not bowl. No one from the sailing community nor homosexuals went bowling.[42]

He wanted the White House staff to promote his skill at the game. Ron Zeigler did as instructed. He managed to get reporters to do a story on Nixon's bowling. During the photo opportunity, which included television cameras, the president managed to make a strike without any warm-up. "It was a lucky shot," he admitted afterward. With that point made, Nixon still knew what he was doing in a bowling alley. While in office he set his personal record with a score of 229. "Which is pretty high," he explained. He had seven strikes, including four in a row. His previous record was 219, and he doubted he would go higher, given how little time he had to practice. "I say the President feels pretty happy today about his own athletic achievement," he boasted to his press secretary and chief of staff.[43]

There was also debate within the administration of attending a bowling event. One administration official wrote during discussions on the feasibility of having Nixon attend a bowling tournament, "There are obvious benefits to the President associating himself with bowling, the most obvious being the contact with that segment of the population that we consider to be part of the President's constituency." Another individual was even more blunt: "52 million U.S. bowlers make up a nice sports constituency that deserves attention." Nixon agreed: "More people bowl than anything else." Haldeman was less than enamored with this idea. He warned the president that if he attended a bowling event, he would have to bowl a few frames. "Wouldn't bother me a bit," Nixon replied.[44]

One of the ways the White House staff thought Nixon could attract support with minority communities was to meet with black and Hispanic athletes. The comments in staff memos were often explicit on these matters. When the idea of having Nixon play golf with Lee Trevino was being considered, one administration official wrote, "This may be an attractive thought, in view of our efforts to court the Spanish-Speaking vote." As a result, athletes had access to Nixon that few others enjoyed. Maury Wills, a star for the Los Angeles Dodgers, once arrived at Nixon's residence in San Clemente and was let through the gate and met the president even though he had no appointment.[45]

The president also used sport as a way to reach out to others. Despite his success in a profession that required contact with a vast number of people, Nixon had little skill in light conversation and was awkward in social settings. Hugh Sidey, a reporter for Time-Life, Inc., recognized as much. "Sports is Nixon's chief reservoir of small talk, a necessary link of this uncomfortable man to almost any informal audience. In Vietnam he summoned up a player or a game or a team to break the ice with the GIs he walked among. At airport fences and impromptu stops when the heavier matters of state are inappropriate he tells people about Southern California's defensive line or how Arnold Palmer was worrying about his game."[46]

There were limits to this approach to politics. Most recreational sports held little appeal for him. He also had little interest in spectator sports other than football and baseball. "I never watch basketball or anything else," he said in an Oval Office conversation. "I can't stand basketball. It's too boring. You just know it's going to be a big score, and track, I gave up on that years ago." Having lost his two front teeth in a game of hoops during his college years, he can be forgiven if he never really wanted to associate with the sport again.[47] There is little mention of sports such as boxing, hockey, tennis, and soccer in White House files beyond an occasional brief meeting and a photo with a visiting athlete. Nixon had no interest whatsoever in Olympic sports such as cycling, gymnastics, or any women's sports.[48]

In the time that remained in 1971, Nixon's interest would be focused on one of the sports he loved—football. His geographic flexibility and fan support, though, would put him in a little bit of a difficult situation when two of his teams met in the Super Bowl.

6

Of Redskins and Dolphins

Nixon was a fan. That was the only role he really wanted to play in the world of sports, but being president of the United States came with certain perks. Even if Nixon was a fan, he was a bit more than your average fan. There was a certain amount of wish fulfillment that he could indulge in. That was never more evident than during the 1971 football season.

His main interest that autumn in regard to sports was Washington Redskins football. With the departure of the Senators, the Redskins became all the more important to Washington. In 1970, following the death of Vince Lombardi, the team stumbled and returned to their traditional losing ways. In 1971, the Redskins hired a new coach, George Allen, a development that delighted Nixon. Allen had been the head coach of Nixon's alma mater, Whittier College, and the president had followed Allen's career with interest ever since. When the Allens moved to Washington, Nixon had none other than his two main subordinates, Haldeman and Ehrlichman, meet with the coach's wife to help her find a place to live in Washington. The coach liked the politician. Allen had a photograph of himself with Nixon prominently on display at his house. The two men shared a taste for rhubarb pie and thought much alike. "The President thinks football is a way of life," Allen said. The coach soon had special access to the president. White House staff member Charles Colson put Allen on a list of people that Nixon could call and chat with when he needed a diversion from the stress of his job. The president was also a good fan, supporting his team in the good times and the bad.

"I saw Nixon as a loyal and compassionate fan, especially after Redskins defeats," Jennifer Allen, the coach's daughter, recalled. "No one could lift Dad out of a losing slump like President Nixon." Using an extra extension on the family phone, she once listened in on one of their conversations that followed a Redskins loss. "The president spoke to my father like a son, 'Now George,' he would say, 'you have a lot to be proud of . . . ' "[1]

Allen had a saying, "The future is now," but in 1971 the legacy of the Lombardi name was still powerful in Washington and the country in general. Nixon was more than willing to help honor the late coach when asked. Lombardi had been the good moral leader that Nixon expected of athletes, and the president was willing to help foster the man's legacy. Before his death, the coach had agreed to chair a campaign to raise funds to build a new field house at Fordham University, his alma mater. With his death, the university decided to name the new building the Vincent T. Lombardi Memorial Athletic Center. The group that agreed to raise money for the project included a number of his old friends who otherwise had no attachment to Fordham. Nixon agreed to help the committee launch its fund-raising campaign with a photo session in the Oval Office. He met with Marie Lombardi, the coach's widow, and three others. Felix Larkin, president of W. R. Grace and Company and chair of the fundraising group, showed Nixon drawings and plans of the proposed building. The gathering in the White House received notice across the country, which is exactly what the group hoped would happen. [2]

Nixon, however, intended to be part of an even larger honor. Lombardi was being inducted into the Professional Football Hall of Fame in Canton, Ohio, that summer, and the president had decided to attend the ceremonies. The idea came from Congressman Frank Bow of Ohio. Bow had several reasons for making the suggestion. He knew of Nixon's interest in the game and in Lombardi, but equally important, he believed in the "need for the President to do something in Ohio" as one White House staff member put it succinctly.[3]

Bow's recommendation turned out to be right on the mark. The trip to Ohio was a huge success. On July 30 a crowd between twelve and twenty thousand greeted Nixon at the Akron-Canton Airport despite a drizzling rain that stopped just an hour before he arrived. After making a few remarks to the gathered crowd, the president had his limousine drive around the airport, and he waved out of the sunroof to the people who stood around the tarmac, waiting for a chance to see him. So many people had arrived that it took three hours for the airport parking lot to empty, and traffic was snarled along the twelve miles leading into the downtown area. Crowds also assembled along Interstate 77 as the Nixon entourage drove first to Canton and then back into Akron, where Nixon spent the night at the Downtown Holiday Inn. A writer for the *Columbus Evening Dispatch* reported seeing no negative signs in the crowd, although later that night Nixon saw a Viet Cong flag flying across the street and had the Secret Service take it down. "Unbelievable crowds," Haldeman told his diary. "There is obviously a strong ground swell of support there, because this was not a generated crowd by any means; it was people who were out to see the P on their own initiative. The P was very pleased with it and feels we've really got something going in the heartland as a result of it."[4]

There were a number of reasons for the reception Nixon got in Ohio. His daughter Tricia had married in the Rose Garden a month before, and the ceremony proved to be wonderful political pageantry. It was only the eighth wedding of a presidential daughter and was the first in the garden. Over sixteen hundred reporters requested credentials to cover the service. Far more important, though, was Nixon's announcement two weeks earlier that he would visit the People's Republic of China. This move represented an important turning point in the Cold War, taking advantage of the breach between China and the Soviet Union. The public was impressed by the boldness Nixon showed on the matter and his ability to alter world affairs on a grand scale, turning China into a de facto ally. His popularity was moving steadily upward.[5]

In Canton, before his speech, Nixon took time to indulge the fan in himself. National Football League commissioner Peter Rozelle and Hall of Fame director Dick Gallagher took him on a personal tour of the museum. He reminisced about his favorite player, Gene Brito of the Washington Redskins. "As a defensive end he was the best," the president stated. Gallagher said under the rules for election anyone can nominate a player, and Nixon had essentially made Brito a candidate. These comments led the press to rediscover the former MVP of the NFL who died from Lou Gehrig's disease at age thirty-nine. A month later, Arthur Daley of the *New York Times* wrote that Brito "stirred up a depth of hero worship such as Washingtonians had not experienced since the saintly Walter Johnson pitched for the Senators almost half a century earlier." Daley also believed Nixon was on the mark: Brito deserved membership in the Hall of Fame. Brito's cause, however, required more than Nixon's nomination. There was no effort to induct him into the Hall.[6]

Nixon also recorded an interview with ABC sportscaster Frank Gifford, which was aired the next day during halftime of the Hall of Fame preseason game between the Los Angeles Rams and the Houston Oilers. This interview has led to a popular story about the president that is most likely untrue. The telling of the story and the construction of a remark attributed to Nixon vary widely. According to Roone Arledge, president of ABC Sports, Nixon and Gifford took a break during the filming and the president came over to him and said, "I know Frank Gifford." Then, Nixon proudly added, "He remembers me." According to Gifford, the conversation took place during a confirmation telephone conversation, and the chief executive said, "Frank should remember me because I used to attend parties at his apartment." Gifford had, indeed, known Nixon for a while. He had campaigned for him in 1960, and the former vice president had been a guest at cocktail parties that Gifford and a teammate had hosted when he played for the Giants. Gifford was stunned when he heard the comment. "Can you believe that? Who the hell's not going to remember Richard Nixon?" While it is probable that Nixon made some remark about knowing the broadcaster, it is unlikely it was in the context that either Arledge or Gifford suggests. Arledge clearly misread the president. Nixon's interest in sport was genuine, and it was a topic he often used to make small talk. It is also unlikely that he was personally involved in confirming the interview, as Gifford states. The president had a staff to do that type of work.[7]

Gifford's account of his interview of Nixon is equally suspect. He recalls that he was nervous, but claims to have found Nixon even more so before the interview started. Again, this is unlikely. Nixon had far more experience in talking with the media than Gifford had in interviewing sitting US presidents. It is also important to note that the former Giants legend was about to begin play-by-play duty on ABC's premiere sports show, *Monday Night Football*. He was under a considerable amount of pressure. Gifford most likely projected his own feelings on Nixon and misremembered the whole episode.[8]

During the interview, the president said, "I think if you were to pick one man who has more caught the attention of sports it is probably Vince Lombardi because of his character." He also went on to talk about the fun he had at Gifford's apartment talking football with Y. A. Tittle and Andy Robustelli, both of whom were being inducted into the Hall of Fame with Lombardi. "If I had my life to live over again and did not go into politics I would like to have your job—you know, be a sportscaster or writer." Gifford was taken aback. "I thought Nixon was joking," he recalled. "Can you imagine Richard Nixon and Howard Cosell in the same booth? Just think about it." At the time, he recovered nicely and said, "We do have a good seat." After a moment, Gifford also got Nixon to explain how he could constantly back different teams. "I like to be for a team, for a man or for a team. I don't mean being so much against the other team, but for somebody I know. But what I have now decided is the best rule is to be for the team in the city I happen to be living."[9]

That evening at the dinner honoring the inductees, the president spoke at a podium that stood in front of massive pictures of each new member of the Hall. Nixon's talk was about football, the welfare of the nation, and the relationship of both to international affairs. Nixon saw the values he associated with football as being the key factor in preserving the central role the United States had in the world affairs, especially as international power became more diffuse. In this talk, he reminisced about the glories of football seasons past, and then observed that Lombardi was a disciplinarian just like Chief Newman, his old college coach. They had both believed that "when you lose you don't quit, that when you lose you fight harder the next time. That is what all of us need to know at this time in this country." These men had left their mark on the society through their tutelage of their players, and by infusing that spirit into the fans who watched their charges compete on the playing field.[10]

The president noted that there was a good deal of similarity between football and politics, but he was basically offering his personal philosophy of life. "Unless you try to do your best, unless you give everything that you have to your life and in the service of your country, then you have not been the man or the woman that you can be." The nation needed such vitalizing sentiment, Nixon argued as he turned the speech toward international affairs. The United States was still the strongest and most influential nation in the world, but Western Europe and Japan had recovered from the devastation of World War II. With that point made, these countries were in a position to contest the US role as a world leader. In challenging moments such as these, much more than in times of war, the nation needed the spirit that football fostered in its fans and participants. "In the spirit of American football at its best, let's always try to be number one, because we owe it to ourselves, we owe it to our country."[11]

Those words reflected one of Nixon's bedrock convictions. Sport served as a model for the nation. The American people had to keep faith with the government. This support was the only way to improve life in the country and fix problems; it was also the only way the United States could sustain itself in world affairs:

> It sometimes is said these days that it doesn't make any difference whether you are number one or not. Let me tell you, it makes a great deal of difference, not simply because we want to be number one so that somebody else can be number two in the world, but because unless you try to do your best, unless you give everything that you have to your life and in the service of your country, then you have not been the man or the woman that you can be. And for America at this time, when we are still the first nation in the world, to rest on our laurels and to let other nations that are competing with us pass us by, this is something that we cannot let happen and that we should not let happen.[12]

Nixon did not allow these important topics to overshadow the honorees. As each new member of the Hall was introduced, Nixon led a standing ovation and gave each one or his next of kin a congratulatory handshake. He joked with former Cleveland Browns running back Jim Brown about his red and blue knit suit, which was the style of the day. When it came time to honor Lombardi, his son Vince stood up to accept the recognition on his father's behalf. Nixon leaned over and told the younger Lombardi to tell his mother that he had remembered that the next day would have been her thirty-first wedding anniversary.[13]

Nixon had again hit the right tone with football and sport. "He did a superb job, as we would have expected he would, because of his unbelievable knowledge of football," Haldeman recounted. "He really dazzled them at the Hall of Fame and did a darn good job in his remarks at the dinner." Much of the press coverage that followed focused on his comments about global politics and the importance of the United States remaining a power in world affairs.[14]

As is almost always the case with Nixon, there was a political element to this trip. The Republican Party was badly split in Ohio. Senator Robert Taft Jr. was using a favorite-son presidential nomination as a way to gain control of the state party. This move had angered former governor James A. Rhodes, who had lost the primary race for the Senate nomination to Taft a year earlier, and State Republican Chairman John Andrews. The problem for Nixon was that Taft's candidacy, although not targeted against him directly, still ended up working against his own reelection campaign.[15] The morning after his speech at the Hall of Fame, the president met and had breakfast with Andrews, two local country Republican chairmen, and John S. Knight, president and editor of the *Akron Beacon Journal*, to talk about Ohio politics. Taft got the message. Soon after Nixon's trip, Taft announced that, in light of the massive showing of public support for Nixon, he would end his favorite-son campaign if the president so asked.[16]

Football was much harsher to another resident of the Buckeye state. In October in a game in Green Bay, Wisconsin, Cincinnati Bengals defensive back Ken Dyer attempted to tackle a runner. His neck hit the runner at a bad angle. Dyer instantly slumped to the ground. His neck was broken and he had suffered significant nerve damage. When Nixon learned of his injury, he decided to call him. Dyer took the phone call in his hospital room, and the president asked about his recovery. Dyer told Nixon he had feeling in his legs. The president told him to keep up his spirit and morale. The call was brief and Dyer spoke weakly, but it is clear he appreciated Nixon's attention. Dyer made a modest recovery. He never played football again, and while mobile in the years afterward, he never had great dexterity.[17]

That type of generosity was something that Nixon often did off the record without trying to get publicity, but he was still a politician and wanted as much positive media coverage as possible. Nixon knew there were limits as to how far he would go. He declined a request from Mike McGee, head football coach at Duke University, to help recruit for his alma mater. Nixon also had a self-deprecating sense of humor, at least in the area of sports. He often stressed that he had little athletic talent. When the cocaptains of the Whitman College football team presented him with a team jersey displaying the number one and lettered with his name, he joked with a grin, "It's the closest I ever came to making the team."[18] He would repeat this line with slightly different constructions over and over and over again. Of course, there was a bit of truth in the statement as well.

The majority of Nixon's football focus in 1971, though, was on the events in Robert F. Kennedy Memorial Stadium, where the Washington Redskins played their home games. George Allen began turning the team into a winner. He made the 1970 season, rather the 1969 one, the aberration. He began a series of stunning trades, acquiring many of his former Ram players. People soon began jokingly referring to the team as the "Ramskins." He also got the franchise to build a state-of-the-art practice facility in northern Virginia.

The new Redskins started off on a tear, winning their first five games. In November, the team began to falter. A tie and two losses made the November 21 contest in Washington with Dallas a contest for control of first place in the East Division of the NFC. The Cowboys took the lead with the first score and never looked back. Dallas controlled the game and kept the Redskins from scoring. The final score was 13–0. Frustrated with the play of their team, the crowd in RFK Memorial Stadium began booing the Redskins late in the first quarter and continued after halftime, until former starting quarterback Sonny Jurgensen came out on the field to replace Billy Kilmer. Jurgensen had missed the first nine games of the season with an arm injury, and it quickly showed when he threw an interception on his first play. The Dallas victory gave the Cowboys the lead in the division and suddenly made the Redskins' playoff chances seem suspect. As if to add insult to the injury of the Dallas victory, Bob Short announced two days later that the Senators had changed their name to the Texas Rangers. Like the Senators of old, their successors had left Washington and now played in the name of an entire state; the same state whose premier sports team had just humiliated the nation's capital in football.[19]

Nixon believed it was the duty of the fan to support the players on the field in the good times as well as the bad, and thought a show of support might help his team. He had his staff check to see where and when the Redskins practiced. Stephen Bull, one of Haldeman's assistants, told him that in light of the injuries to key players it was unlikely the franchise would hold practice on Tuesday. That next morning, Allen determined that it was in the best interests of the Redskins to have a practice session after all. Around one in the afternoon, after being informed of this development, Nixon decided to take the coach up on a standing offer to visit and sketched some notes for a pep talk he wanted to make to the team. "This is what I just want to do without seeking the publicity," he informed Haldeman. "There may or may not be any press out there. I will go out there. I don't think this is one where I want to haul out television cameras and all the rest to take pictures of me meeting football players. Just doesn't feel that right." He changed his mind as he spoke, twice: "If you got some people you want—I don't think so." Haldeman agreed with his original inclination: "No, I don't think you want to do . . . " Nixon cut him off: "It looks like a hell of a stunt!" Haldeman agreed. At the last minute, he told his chief of staff to join him. Allen and the front office got an advance warning of the pending arrival, but the players knew nothing about the visit. The Redskins first learned about the presidential excursion when they saw a pack of reporters and photographers approaching them from across their practice field. The players cheered when they realized who they were following. Haldeman followed behind the entourage with a home-movie camera. The film shows the awkward Nixon of old, but the cold, windy November weather was a contributing factor to this stiffness. The film also shows that Nixon was clearly enjoying the moment.[20]

The surprise of the visit visibly energized the Redskins, and Nixon bantered with individual players as they introduced themselves to him. "Old Red, from Duke," he remarked when he saw Jurgensen. "Of course, you're a little after my time but just a little." Reporters said the veteran began to blush. As the team assembled around him, he directed another remark toward his "unsung heroes," the offensive line. "I think they should be given a little more credit," and after a pause, he added, "and a little more money." A loud roar from the players followed.[21]

After assembling for a group photo and a few more introductions with individual players, Nixon addressed the team. "I just want you to know this whole city is very proud of you." He told the players that he knew something about being booed, and told them to put the incident behind them. "The great majority of people of this town . . . back this team. You have been good for this city. The city needed to have a team that was winning." He then predicted that Washington would make it into the playoffs by winning three of its last four games. "Let me say the sincerity of my remarks is proved by the fact that there are no votes in Washington, there are a lot in Texas." In spite of the two consecutive losses, the Redskins had spirit and determination that would sustain them and allow them to recover. After recounting a story about an episode from World War I in which General John J. Pershing had to remove an old friend from command of a unit on the western front because of low morale, he told the team that it had no problem in this area. "I just want to say this: that there is no question as far as this group is concerned. I could tell at the end of the game against Dallas, and the one against Kansas City. Oh, you might have been a bit tired, but there was nothing wrong with your morale, nothing wrong with your spirit."[22]

When Nixon finished, Allen led the players in a "hip hip hooray" cheer for the president. Photographers took several more photos of Nixon with the players, and then Allen had Kilmer throw a pass in honor of the team's guest. Nixon called the play, suggesting the quarterback try to connect with running back Charley Harraway. The pass was a successful completion. His work as the good fan completed, Nixon took some time to talk with the reporters accompanying him. One remarked that a positive mental outlook could do wonders for the Senators, forgetting that the team no longer existed. This comment lead Nixon to elaborate a little bit more about the importance of positive thinking in football. "The Senators? It would not help," he said in a matter-of-fact fashion. "In football, spirit, morale, is half the game—in baseball it doesn't make all that much difference." He went on to add, "In baseball, spirit and morale is important, but not decisive." Nixon believed that fan support was also important in football. "It is a very contagious thing. It is a team effort, and if the team has a feeling of being up, then it has got, I would say a 50 percent better chance today to win." The president had prepared written comments beforehand, but he spoke the entire time without notes. His presentation was extemporaneous, but in a sign of his intellectual power, he made every remark he had wanted to make.[23]

Excitement crackled in the air. Haldeman told his diary that the president "did a great job and really jazzed them up. It should be good for some excellent coverage and great photos. They gave him a big cheer as he came out on the field. He completely befuddled them with his tremendous knowledge of football as he went through all the comments he had to make about each of the individual guys, etc." Allen told a reporter from the *Washington Post* that the visit was "the lift we needed." The trip was page-one news in the sports sections of both Washington dailies.[24]

Praise for this visit was strong. White House press secretary Ron Ziegler told the president after he returned to the executive mansion, "As a former football player, that was great out there today." In an example of the team's importance to the community, Nixon foes like the editorial board of the *Washington Post* supported his effort on behalf of the Redskins. "He did the right thing for America and threw his weight behind the local club," an editorial stated. "It was a nice gesture." The official position of the paper was also close to the president's way of thinking about the role of the fan. In fact, the *Post* editors argued, the problem might be that Washingtonians had kept the faith with bad, inept teams for too long. They discussed a recent study of season ticket holders: "What the statistics reveal is that more or less the same people have been sitting up there watching Redskin teams lose football games year after year after year, so that now they can no longer recognize success." The journalists agreed with Allen and Nixon on the role of positive thinking; in this case, on the part of the fans. "Those are emotionally scarred people up there; some of them have been through too much. With a new coach and fresh playing talent, what is needed now to complete the Redskins rebuilding is a little more positive thinking, up there in the stands."[25]

That evening Allen called Nixon to thank him for the visit. "I thought it went very, very well," he observed. His players were stunned that the president of the United States was a fan of theirs. "A lot of them remarked to me that they were, they were amazed that you knew so much about them." Nixon had helped the team. "Being there today was a heck of a lift."[26]

Nixon was proud of what he had done. "Well, I had a great time yesterday," he told Secretary of State William Rogers. "I hadn't been to a game; I thought it would give them a lift."[27]

Shirley Povich used his column to sound one of the few negative notes. He disputed the contention that spirit and momentum had no role in the game of baseball. He pointed to the comeback of the Pittsburgh Pirates in the World Series as an example and then spent the rest of his column blasting Nixon for doing nothing to stop the relocation of the Senators.[28]

The most important response was that of the Redskins. "The visit was a shot of vitamin B-12 to the team now struggling to maintain second place in its division," Jennifer Allen noted. "The Redskins won the following week, and the President was deemed the Redskins' good-luck token." The team beat the Philadelphia Eagles in a contest that saw Jurgensen go down with an arm injury and the return of Kilmer behind the center. The next week the Redskins defeated the New York Giants, setting up an important game with the Los Angeles Rams. If the Redskins won, they would make the playoffs for the first time since 1945, when they lost the NFL Championship Game to the then Cleveland Rams. To make the showdown even more interesting, Allen was returning to the Los Angeles Coliseum for the first time since the Rams fired him.[29]

The game was wildly entertaining. In a contest televised on *Monday Night Football*, Washington decisively defeated Los Angeles, 38–24. The Rams scored first and never followed the Redskins during the first quarter, but Washington responded with a seventeen-point run in the second quarter. Both teams scored two touchdowns in the second half as the Redskins went on to victory. "It's our biggest win ever to date," Allen said. Nixon agreed. He listened to the game on Armed Forces Radio while in France to meet with President Georges Pompidou about monetary policies. He tried to call Allen after the game via satellite telephone, but was unable to get through. "He was all excited about the whole thing," Haldeman commented. "I guess it was a big victory." When he returned to Washington, Nixon watched a taped replay of the game, entering the White House through the underground entrance from the Treasury Building to avoid an ongoing reception for members of Congress.[30]

The Redskins lost their final regular-season game against the Cleveland Browns, finishing with a 9-4-1 record. Nixon believed he deserved some credit for the team's success. He wanted Haldeman to have a news story planted about the visit that would be "about the turning point in the Redskins season. They all say that privately, you know what I mean." It would be a "cute story." The success of the team filled with modest talent was quite impressive. "It's really a dramatic story as to what that team has done. Just, just what Allen has done; he's the greatest. He's coach of the year without a question. God, God damn, to beat the Rams! Shit, they're a good team. They got more, they got more, more, more, more horsepower than the Redskins. They got more stars."[31]

That lack of talent might be why the team's twenty-six-year absence from postseason play showed when the team returned to California for the playoffs against the San Francisco 49ers. Washington took an early lead, but failed to score on a drive late in the second quarter. The Redskins lost thirteen yards on a second down at the eight-yard line on a failed reverse play. Kilmer faked a handoff to running back Larry Brown and then gave the ball to receiver Roy Jefferson. The receiver was running down from the right side of the field when San Francisco defensive end Cedrick Hardman caught him from behind. Then center George Burman fumbled a snap that cost the team a field goal. The Redskins took a 10–3 lead into halftime, but fumbled the game away in the rain and mud of Candlestick Park. In the third quarter, Washington stalled on a drive again, this time on the San Francisco eleven-yard line. The 49ers then took the lead with a scoring streak of two touchdowns and a field goal. In the fourth quarter, San Francisco scored what turned out to be the margin of victory on a Washington mistake when Bob Hoskins recovered another bad Burman snap in the end zone for a touchdown. The 49ers won with a final score of 24–20.[32]

After the game, Nixon did what he thought a good fan should do. The Washington players were sitting in their dressing room, silent and dejected, when the president called George Allen. Nixon offered his support, telling the coach that the Redskins had played a fine game and that the entire city was proud of its team. He later told Haldeman that of all the phone calls he made over the Christmas holidays he enjoyed making this one the most, because it was unexpected.[33]

The person taking the loss the hardest was Burman. He sat in the locker room after the game in what a sports reporter for the *Washington Post* called "a literal state of shock." He made no excuses. There was nothing wrong with the texture of the ball in the rain. He had simply made a mistake. Nixon tried to call Burman to offer his support, but failed to get through and wrote a letter instead. "The purpose of this note is to tell you I know how disappointed you must feel after the loss. I think you should bear in mind, however, that one bad pass from center in six years of pro ball is a record to be proud of—and not in the least ashamed of. You must keep in mind that you still have a legion of friends among Redskin fans."[34]

A few days later, Nixon gained a little unwanted notoriety from this game. On December 27, the contest was replayed on local Washington television, and during the telecast, defensive lineman Bill Brundige remarked that Nixon had called Allen the night before and suggested the Roy Jefferson play that lost thirteen yards. Shirley Povich joked that the Redskins used the presidential suggestion because "for Allen it came down to whether or not his name would stay on the White House guest list."[35]

The only problem with this story is that it never happened. Allen wanted to inspire his team, so he told his players that the president had designed a play for them. "So, listen when we open that ball game with a screen pass, it's going to be your play," he told the president at the tail end of one of their phone conversations. He did not ask permission to invoke Nixon's name. The president chuckled and then said, "Oh, boy. Well, okay." If it had worked, everyone concerned would have looked good, but the play failed. Nixon, being the good fan that he was, kept quiet on the matter and never made any effort to correct the view that he had designed a bad play.[36]

After the Redskins lost, Nixon turned his attention to the Miami Dolphins. The Florida team had won the AFC title and were going to meet the Dallas Cowboys in Super Bowl VI. At 1:30 a.m. on January 3, the phone rang in the house of Miami head coach Don Shula. Normally asleep at that hour, Shula was watching a television rerun of the Dolphins' AFC Championship Game victory. "When the phone rang at that hour," Shula said, "I thought it must be some nut calling." Even after the operator announced the call, the coach remained skeptical. "At first I thought somebody was pulling my leg," he remarked. "I started scrutinizing the voice, but in only a few seconds I knew it was the President." (Nixon was in California where it was only 10:30 p.m.) It was the second conversation between the two in as many weeks. Nixon had phoned Shula while the coach was filming his television show the day after Miami's 27–24 playoff victory over Kansas City. This second time they talked about what the coach described as "technical football." The president warned Shula that the Dallas Cowboys had a really talented team. "But he told me, 'I still think you can hit Warfield on that down-and-in pattern against them.'" The conversation lasted ten minutes, and Nixon told Shula that he was going to be cheering for the Dolphins, even though he was a Redskins' fan, because he was a part-time Florida resident.[37]

This incident quickly got distorted. Nixon had done nothing other than take advantage of his high office to chat with a sports celebrity. The talk about using Warfield was nothing more than a suggestion; Nixon never designed or diagrammed a play with receiver routes and line-blocking patterns exclusively for Shula's use. Yet, in the days that followed, several stories appeared in reputable news outlets such as the *New York Times*, the *Christian Science Monitor*, and *Newsweek* with an illustration of the play the president had supposedly created. Shula tried to clarify matters in a talk with a *Miami*

Herald reporter. "The President wasn't that specific on a particular play," he said laughing about the matter. "He just said it would be a good idea to throw to Warfield."[38]

Despite Shula's effort to correct misperceptions, the idea of Nixon giving technical advice to such a talented and accomplished coach was too inviting a topic for commentators to pass up. "Beware of amateur coaches bearing gifts," an article in the *Washington Post* warned the head Dolphin. "Apparently, people who live in White Houses never learn to stop coaching on the phone." Shirley Povich started a column about the president and sport with the line: "After three years in office, Richard M. Nixon has yet to learn that football games are too important to be entrusted to presidents of the United States."[39]

A popular theme of many lampoons was the merger of football and politics. The *Post* and the *Evening Star* ran political cartoons of Nixon adopting this approach despite his lack of success with the Redskins.[40] James Reston, a columnist for the *New York Times*, imagined a conversation between the coach and the president if such an approach to politics were used:

SHULA: How's your running game?

NIXON: Not bad. We're using Connally and Mitchell on the power plays, though Mitchell fumbles a lot, and we've got a good shifty open field runner in Agnew, though he can't go to his left.

SHULA: Tell me about your offense.

NIXON: Well, our front four—Rogers, Romney, Volpe and Stans—are a little light. I may have to trade them next year, if I can. They don't penetrate much.

SHULA: How did you get into the play-offs with an outfit like that?

NIXON: You know, sometimes I wonder myself. For one thing, our opposition hasn't been much. All quarterbacks, no teamwork, and no real game plan. Once we junked that old conservative stuff and tried a little razzle-dazzle, they never managed to adjust.[41]

Down in Texas, the reaction had a slightly sharper edge. The *Dallas Morning News* ran a before-and-after diagram of the play above the masthead on its sports section. The after version, which according to the caption was "more realistic," had the Cowboys intercepting the Dolphins' pass and advancing to the two-yard line. In Austin, Governor Preston Smith of Texas diagramed a double reverse play that had running back Dan Reeves throwing a long pass to split end Bob Hayes. Smith showed a drawing of his design to reporters and then mailed it to Dallas head coach Tom Landry. In a telegram to the coach, former president Lyndon Johnson announced he was supporting the Cowboys:

MY PRAYERS AND MY PRESENCE WILL BE WITH YOU IN NEW ORLEANS ALTHOUGH I HAVE NO PLANS TO SEND IN PLAYS.

For his part, Landry, a well-known Republican, said he was not sure if he was going to vote for Nixon again, "I'm going to wait and see this time. I'm going to worry him a little." The coach also joked that Nixon was proving to be a good politician. "I think the president hedged a little on Coach Shula. He gave them a play they've been running all year."[42]

Sports columnist Blackie Sherrod was clearly jesting when he announced that Nixon had decided to serve only one term. He noted that even when combined, the District of Columbia and Florida had fewer electoral college votes than Texas, and yet the president had sided first with Washington and then Miami against Dallas. "Do those seem like the actions of a guy running for another term in office? Not to a political expert like ole buster here and let me make that perfectly clear."[43]

Even Shula was the brunt of jokes. Jack Faulkner, a scout for the Los Angeles Rams, and Upton Bell, general manager of the New England Patriots, pulled a prank on him. "He'd already had two telephone calls from the President," Bell explained later, "so we decided to bring in the Vice President." With Faulkner playing Agnew and Bell a Secret Service agent announcing the call, they tracked the coach down at the Dolphins' training facilities. Shula, who had once coached the Baltimore Colts, thought the former governor of Maryland was calling to congratulate him. Bell and Faulkner broke out into laughter after Shula fell for their deception. His reply, according to the two, was unprintable.[44]

Others warned Shula against using the play. Abe Zaidan, a sports columnist for the Knight newspaper syndicate that owned the *Miami Herald*, imagined another late-night conversation that might occur if Shula took Nixon's advice:

SHULA: Mr. President, this is Don Shula.
NIXON: What the devil are you doing; calling me at 3 a.m.?
SHULA I'm sorry, Mr. President. I couldn't get any sleep. The loss is hard to take.

NIXON: This is a cruel world, coach. You're going to have to learn to accept defeat with the same dignity that you accept victory.

SHULA: I guess you saw Mel Renfro intercept the down-and-in and run for the winning touchdown.

NIXON: Wasn't that something? I warned you, of course, that Renfro was a real good player on a real good team.

SHULA: But you suggested that the down-and-in would work.

NIXON: You're quoting me out of context.[45]

Lost in all this satire was the fact that the presidential football advice had some merit. Those journalists who paid attention to Shula's clarification and followed the sport closely realized Nixon was on to something. Writing about the play, Povich noted, "This was not quite as original a stratagem by the President as his Roy Jefferson flanker reverse inspiration." He explained that Miami had scored twelve touchdowns that season using down-and-in passes to Warfield. The Dolphin receiver noted that the president's suggestion was a pretty standard element in their offense. Others agreed in varying degrees and tones that Nixon's observation had merit. In a survey of sports reporters in town to cover the game, the New Orleans *Times-Picayune* found that several thought the Dolphins would be wise to use a game plan utilizing the type of plays the president favored. Dave Anderson of the *New York Times* predicted, "The Dolphins will find a way to win, quite possibly on President Nixon's suggested down-and-in pattern involving a pass from Bob Griese to Paul Warfield, while the Cowboys will find a way to lose." Bill Guthrie of the *New Haven Journal-Courier* predicted both that it would be a Dallas victory and that the Dolphins would score only in the manner that Nixon had favored. Guthrie joked, "Cowboys 24, Dolphins 7 is a probable score, because someone in Washington has given Federal aid to the underdog and ordered a Dolphin touchdown."[46]

Such predictions about the outcome were on the mark. Super Bowl VI was a one-sided affair. After years of losing championships in close games, the Cowboys dominated the Dolphins, allowing them into their half of the field only twice. The Dallas defense shut down the Miami running game and severely limited the effectiveness of their passing attack. The final score was not even close: 24–3. Three times the Dolphins tried to use the type of pass that Nixon had suggested, with little to show for the effort. On the fourth try Warfield gained five yards and helped set up the sole Miami score. After the game, Povich commented, "In all accuracy it must be reported that otherwise the Dolphins paid scant heed to the Nixon recipe for beating the Cowboys."[47]

Nixon was in a slightly embarrassing position after the game, but handled the situation with appropriate tact. He called Tom Landry in the locker room and offered him congratulations. The two talked for a few minutes, and Nixon praised every element of the Cowboys' game, comparing the team to the Green Bay Packers dynasty of the 1960s. "The President said our game today was the kind of game Vince Lombardi would like to watch," Landry said afterward with a smile. (Lombardi and Landry had been the offensive and defensive coordinators for the New York Giants between 1956 and 1959 when the team made three NFL Championship Game appearances.) "He congratulated everyone but singled out the offensive line." Someone in the crowd asked if Nixon had mentioned the down-and-in pattern he had suggested to Shula. The coach grinned. "No," he replied again with another smile. "When your down-and-ins aren't working, you don't talk about them." Nixon also wrote Super Bowl MVP Roger Staubach: "I think your performance Sunday was one of the greatest individual efforts in football history." He also sent letters to Shula and his wife, Dorothy, offering his condolences on the loss but reminding the Shulas that the Dolphins had a fine season despite the disappointing ending.[48]

Nixon was impressed with what he had seen from the Dallas Cowboys. In phone conversations he had with Representatives Hale Boggs, Gerald R. Ford, and Thomas "Tip" O'Neill two days later, he said they had real power. "The Cowboys—nobody is going to beat them for two or three years."[49]

That comment, though, was private, and in public, the people of Dallas insisted on gloating at the president's expense. The city council passed a special resolution naming Nixon "assistant coach of the year" for his assistance to Cowboy fans " through the giving of advice to that 'other team.'" The *Dallas Times Herald* printed an editorial cartoon showing a sulking Nixon with a broken Dolphins pennant in his hands. The *Dallas Morning News* ran a photo of Warfield dropping the down-and-in pass from Griese while taking a hit from Mel Renfro and Cliff Harris with the caption: "Sorry Mr. President. The only thing you overlooked Mr. Nixon, sir, was how Renfro and Harris would sandwich Warfield all day." After the game, in the dressing room Renfro vented his frustration. "That's all I heard all week from the writers; Warfield, Warfield, Warfield. That was supposed to be the key to the whole game, whether I could cover him or not." A reporter asked him if he would call Nixon, since his play suggestion was designed to beat him. The question was a clumsy effort to get a comment about the president, but Renfro took the bait. "No, I think I'll let him call me." Harris was even more blunt: "That Nixon, he's a great strategist, isn't he?"[50]

The Dallas Bonehead Club, a social organization, gave its annual "Bonehead of the Year" award to Nixon for backing not one but two teams that lost to the Cowboys. The trophy was presented each year to a "person or institution that has endeared themselves to the sports-minded public by their desire to participate and lose." In a telegram inviting him to attend their annual banquet in person, the club declared:

> THE AWARD WHICH WE BESTOW UPON YOU AT THIS TIME IS NOT TO LAUGH AT YOU, BUT TO LET THE WORLD KNOWN THAT YOU HAVE LEARNED TO LAUGH WITH US. MAY YOU ALWAYS HAVE THE ABILITY TO STIR THE SPORTING PUBLIC'S EMOTIONS, AND WE WILL ALWAYS RECOGNIZE YOU AS AMERICA'S NO. 1 SPORTS FAN.

Nixon had no interest in traveling to Dallas for this occasion, but sent a telegram back that responded to this distinction with a grace for which the president had little reputation:

> THIS IS AN HONOR I WOULD TRULY LIKE TO SHARE—WITH ANYONE ELSE, AND I AM ESPECIALLY GRATEFUL IT IS PRESENTED ONLY ONCE A YEAR. NEVERTHELESS, I ACCEPT THIS AWARD IN THE SPIRIT IN WHICH IT IS GIVEN . . . IN GOOD HUMOR.[51]

Such comments were hardly damaging politically and were part of being a fan. In 1971 fan and spectator were basically the only roles Nixon chose to play in the world of sport. A good fan, a faithful fan, in the view of the president, supported his or her team in times good and bad. Nixon did just that with the Redskins, offering his support at a time when he thought it might do some good. The team did indeed appreciate his effort and found it helpful. If he suffered a bit for such support, so be it. As Richard Nixon prepared for the last political campaign of his life, he again found a way to use sport to his political advantage. This time, with impressive results and with few, if any, negative consequences.

7

The Election of 1972: The First Half

Whatever Richard Nixon's faults were, being a bad campaigner was not one. He had undeniable strengths when election seasons rolled around. When 1972 started it was clear that, win or lose, it would be the last time that Nixon would be a candidate for public office. His campaign effort was a success, at least, in the immediate sense of getting him a second term. At the same time, though, showing that he was a one-man Greek tragedy, he sowed the seeds of his ultimate political destruction. But before his fall from grace, his clever use of baseball helped him, in part, to put together a huge, landslide victory.

In early 1972 victory in November seemed less than certain. The trip to China was a political success of the first order, and then came the announcement that Nixon would travel to the Soviet Union to sign a nuclear arms control treaty. While these developments stunned the public, conservatives were less than happy with them and Nixon. Representative John Ashbrook of Ohio offered a right-wing challenge to him in the Republican primaries. The other side of the Republican party was no more happy with him either. Representative Pete McCloskey of California also entered the race, on an antiwar platform. Neither effort ended up amounting to much of a challenge, and McCloskey's campaign basically ended on Easter Sunday when North Vietnam launched its largest operation of the war. The North had always attacked during the dry season of the spring, but what made this time different was that the North Vietnamese Army had launched a conventional assault that would last six months. By early May the North had seized major provincial cities, and General Creighton Abrams warned that the South Vietnamese Army might have lost its will to fight. If so, then the conflict was essentially over. Nixon briefly considered resigning, but like Lyndon Johnson before him, he said he was not going to be the first president to lose a war, and he ordered a massive bombing campaign to support the ground troops.

Nixon announced his decision in a televised speech. He also told the leadership in Hanoi that he would end the campaign in return for an armistice for all of Southeast Asia that included the freeing of all American POWs. As part of this agreement, the United States would remove its armed forces within four months. The air effort worked. Northern supply lines were vulnerable. The ground units were spread too thin, and the North eventually lost over half the troops it sent south. The North Vietnamese Army suffered a major defeat, losing control of the cities that it had briefly captured. These air operations forced Hanoi to realize that it could not defeat the United States militarily and accept a diplomatic solution.[1]

In addition to these developments, the 1972 baseball season started on a poor note and seemed to offer Nixon little chance to use the national pastime to his advantage. On April 1, professional baseball players walked out of their spring training camps. This strike was the first in baseball history and the first work stoppage in any US professional sport. At thirteen days, the strike was a relatively short and minor compared to those that befell the sport in later years, much less the work stoppages that have hit other industries. At the time, though, it was a horrible new development. For the first time since William Howard Taft started the tradition, the president of the United States did not throw out the first pitch on opening day. An editorial in the *Sporting News* called the players' action "the darkest day in sports history." Marvin Miller, director of the Major League Baseball Players Association, stated later, "The last thing I expected in 1972 was a strike; it really caught me unawares." The labor dispute was over what both Miller and Kuhn considered two relatively minor issues: owner contributions to the health care insurance plan and the use of surplus income from the pension fund to increase retirement benefits. Both men thought the strike was really a show of force, although they had vastly different interpretations of the motivation behind this test.[2]

Kuhn thought Miller was trying to precipitate a strike in an effort to intimidate the owners before the basic agreement between the players and the leagues came up for renewal in 1973, which was a far more important issue. Miller, on the other hand, thought the owners were trying to break the Players Association. "The owner's effort to bust the union made a bit more sense when you considered the strides the Association had made during the previous six years," he observed. "Before 1966, the owners had a unilateral right to do, literally, anything they pleased."[3] Specialists on the labor disputes in baseball have found more merit in Miller's observation than Kuhn's.[4]

Nixon contributed, in a small way, to the speedy resolution. The players showed far more solidarity than the owners had expected. Many of the less stringent owners, on the other hand, began rethinking their position when they saw how much they were losing on a relatively minor issue. "The owners, proud and opinionated, have always come asunder under pressure," Kuhn observed.[5]

Before the strike, Miller had suggested that Nixon or former chief justice Earl Warren select an arbitrator who would resolve the health care and retirement disputes. The proprietors of the sport rejected this proposal, but Nixon was thinking along similar lines as the union head. On April 8, Nixon had Haldeman call Kuhn to suggest that he and Agnew offer their services as arbitrators. "Kuhn said," Haldeman recorded, "that there's a lot under the surface and appreciated the P's offer but that he didn't think they should do anything about it now." The commissioner was stalling. He hinted that an agreement might be reached over the weekend, but told Haldeman that a presidential initiative would work against the interests of the owners. "Feels players assn put P's name in for pressure" the chief of staff wrote in his notes he made of their conversation. Nixon really did not care. Even though Francis Dale, owner of the Cincinnati Reds, was treasurer of the Committee to Re-elect the President, Nixon was inclined to favor the players in the labor dispute. The day after the Haldeman-Kuhn conversation, the White House Press Office announced that the president was willing to select an intermediary to broker a settlement to the dispute. Nixon needed to score some political points with the public and he did. Under pressure from all sides, including the White House, the owners reached an agreement with the players the next day.[6]

This brief episode makes one thing starkly clear: the focus of Nixon's attention in 1972 was on his reelection above all else. Things began to move in the right direction for him. The challenge from the fringes of his party faded, and the Democrats self-destructed when they nominated Senator George McGovern of South Dakota. As the nominee, McGovern represented the extreme left wing of his party and alienated many Democrats with his policy ideas.[7] In her history of presidential campaign advertising, Kathleen Hall Jamieson notes: "In 1972 Nixon would run not as a candidate but as The President." Nixon and his campaign staff saw this strategy as the best way to reach out to voters who normally voted for Democrats. The reelection campaign largely succeeded in its efforts to win over these voters. A deliberate effort was made to "humanize" the president, showing a side of Nixon that the public rarely saw. Campaign admen worked to make sure that advertising subtly presented his sense of humor, compassion, and other positive traits. This effort started in 1971 when Nixon family members and staffers began talking to reporters from media outlets that did feature stories rather than breaking news, such as the *Today Show* and *McCall's* magazine. An editorial in the *Wall Street Journal* dismissed the effort as being blatant fakery and irrelevant. What really mattered was a president's policies, not his personality. Nixon and his staff at both the White House and the reelection campaign disagreed and made efforts to present a more relaxed image of Nixon a major campaign strategy. As a result, attacks were left to either administration or campaign officials and were always launched against "McGovernites," not Democrats. A campaign organization called Democrats for Nixon ran more television ads than the Committee to Re-elect the President.[8]

Although it became part of the general effort to "humanize" Richard Nixon, the historical all-star team was not planned as such. On June 22, Nixon held a news conference in the White House. It was the first time he had met with the media since the arrest of four men breaking and entering into the offices of the Democratic National Committee (DNC) in an effort to plant listening devices on some phones. Lawrence O'Brien, chairman of the DNC, accused the burglars of having ties to the White House. The first question Nixon faced concerned this accusation, and he sidestepped it nicely. The seventh question he took concerned the recent rulings of US Supreme Court, including *Flood v. Kuhn.* Again, Nixon dodged the issue. "On the baseball matter, I must say I cannot even tell you who is in first place at the present time." After the laughter died down, he added, "In any event, as an old baseball fan, and the rest, I have no present thoughts on that. I would like, perhaps, to talk to Bowie Kuhn who is a good lawyer and also interested in baseball."[9]

Flood v. Kuhn was a dispute about labor relations in professional baseball. In 1969 the St. Louis Cardinals traded Curt Flood to the Philadelphia Phillies. Flood had no interest in relocating to Philadelphia. He wanted the right to determine where he worked and lived. The problem was the reserve clause. Since 1887 the uniform Major League Baseball player contract allowed clubs to renew their agreement with the on-field talent unilaterally for one year subject to a minimum salary. A team could also assign the contract to another franchise. As a practical matter, this provision limited the bargaining power of individual players in perpetuity. In 1922 in *Federal Baseball Club v. National League,* the Supreme Court ratified this practice, granting Major League Baseball an exemption from US antitrust laws. With the help of the Major League Players Association, Flood made a legal challenge to the reserve system and filed suit in federal court. He lost, and the Second Circuit affirmed this decision on appeal. The Supreme Court, however, decided to hear the case. "The decision to review meant that at least four justices had some question about the lower court decision—hardly a good sign," Kuhn observed. Flood's short, disastrous stint with the Senators had come during appeals.[10]

The Supreme Court ended up ruling against Flood with a decision that embarrassed many of its members. Justice Harry A. Blackmun wanted to write an opinion that he hoped would have as much literary and sociological merit as it did legal significance. In the body of the opinion he recounted the history of the game, and then listed the eighty-seven greatest players to play the game.[11] He included poems about baseball, such as "Tinker to Evers to Chance." In the portions of the opinion that dealt with the legal issues at hand, the court ate away at the special legal status that the sport enjoyed. Blackmun stated that professional baseball was engaged in interstate commerce (something the court did not find in 1922) and that the previous rulings on baseball made the sport an aberration, but that it was an exception the high court should allow to stand. "If there is any inconsistency or illogic in all this," Blackmun wrote, "it is an inconsistency and illogic of long standing that is to be remedied by the Congress and not by this Court." In a concurring opinion, Warren Burger called on the legislature to act.[12]

Although a victory for the owners, this ruling kept heavy pressure on professional baseball. Since the departure of the Washington Senators, many in Congress had used questions about the merit of the antitrust exemption of the sport as leverage to get a new Major League franchise for the nation's capital.[13] Kuhn was working to keep Congress from taking legal action against baseball and realized what had happened. "All we had was breathing time," he observed about the Flood case.[14]

Nixon dodged the question, which was understandable, but that only made the pressure on the owners stronger. Nixon could have taken some of the pressure off, but he chose to take no stand. His silence—part of his reluctance to provide social leadership in the athletic arena—indicated there was no turning to the executive branch for comfort on this matter.

The silence on the issue was also a mistake on Nixon's part. He was trying to use the election to build the Republican Party, and he could easily have stressed that Flood was fighting the good fight for an open market for labor. Such a stand could have shown voters that there were politicians on the right who valued personal liberties and blended two different strands of political philosophy together. It was a stand that would have cut across political divides and helped him win votes, but Nixon did not see the opportunity or did not believe it large enough to be worth the risk.

White House reporters unwittingly acquiesced in this endeavor at the June 22 press conference, asking no follow-up questions, but the subject of baseball intrigued Cliff Evans, a reporter for RKO General Broadcasting. He started the whole idea of a presidential all-star team after the formal end of the conference. Evans asked the president to name his favorite ballplayers. Nixon responded quickly. He named New York Yankees legend Lou Gehrig as his first baseman and put Jackie Robinson, the Brooklyn Dodgers hero, at second base. Then an idea flashed into his head, and he began to meander. Instead of naming his shortstop, he said "You must include Mickey Mantle." Then he added Ted Williams to the list, saying, "If not for the Korean War his record would have been greater. He was the only one to hit .400 since Ty Cobb." The president also included Stan Musial of the St. Louis Cardinals. "If he had played in New York he would have been the greatest," he commented. But there Nixon had a problem: Musial, like Gehrig, was a first baseman. The president quickly realized the difficulty inherent in picking and choosing between legendary players extemporaneously and stopped.[15]

Evans continued to press the issue. He followed up and asked, "Mr. President, as the Nation's Number One baseball fan, would you be willing to name your all-time baseball team?" Nixon found the temptation too strong to pass up. "I readily replied, 'Yes,'" Nixon later wrote.[16]

Nixon started work on the project the next day, quickly bringing others in on the effort. This project was a win-win opportunity. He would get to make a contribution to baseball, and the publicity associated with the sport would help "humanize" his image with potential Nixon voters. With that point made, he had juggled this undertaking with other—far more serious—concerns. He started the next morning, June 23, with a meeting where he and Haldeman plotted how to thwart the investigation into the break-in at the DNC offices. Nixon told his chief of staff to call the deputy director of the Central Intelligence Agency to have him warn the Federal Bureau of Investigations not to go deeper into the matter. "The CIA should call in the FBI and say, 'Don't go further into this case, period'!" They ended their conversation with a discussion of baseball. The Oval Office recording system captured their entire talk. The resulting record of their discussion became known as the "smoking gun" tape when it was released in July 1974 and showed that the president of the United States had actively participated in an obstruction of justice.[17]

Later in the day, he signed the 1972 Education Amendments Act. Title IX of this law involved sports, and it prohibited discrimination on the basis of sex or gender. This provision lead to the rapid development of women's team sports in the 1970s and 1980s. A myth associated with this amendment is that there were no women's sports in the United States before it was enacted. That view is simply not true. Babe Didrikson, Helen Willis Moody, Tenley Albright, Carol Heiss, Jill Kinmont, Wilma Rudolph, Althea Gibson, Cathy Rigby, and Billie Jean King were all well-known athletes before the passage of this legislation. All of them, though, earned fame in individual sports such as golf, tennis, skiing, track and field, figure skating, and gymnastics. Player development in these sports had little to do with schools and other educational institutions, which was what Title IX set out to address. Another point worth making is that college and universities had women's sports teams before Nixon signed this bill into law. In fact, Stanford and the University of California, Berkeley, played the first women's intercollegiate basketball game in 1896. Stanford won, 2–1.[18]

The major differences between men and women's sports in education was in resources and participation. In 1972 women's sports at colleges and universities had 30,000 participants. The men's sports, in contrast, had 248,000. There was also a major discrepancy in funding. At its peak in 1979, the Association for Intercollegiate Athletics for Women generated only about 4 percent of the profits of the National Collegiate Athletic Association (NCAA). Women's sports and men's sports were administered differently. Athletic departments ran the men's sports programs, and they embraced a commercial focus. They generated a good deal of publicity and—sometimes—profit for their schools.[19] The primary emphasis was on winning, which required athletes with better skills than those of their rivals. This focus often led players, coaches, and administrators to cheat in ways large and small. The administrators of women's sports had intentionally rejected this approach. "The field of men's athletes is full of sorry instances of this mad worship at the shrine of technique. Now that women's athletics are developing so rapidly all over our land, let us caution our leaders to hold fast to the ideals of worthy citizenship even at the expense of fine technique," Mabel Lee, one of the early pioneers in women's sports, remarked in the 1920s. Women's sports had basically taken this approach. The sports were administered usually out of physical education departments and emphasized values such as teamwork, good character, leadership, fair play, and perseverance. These were the values Nixon liked to attribute to sport.[20]

Another myth of Title IX is that it slipped past Congress, because no one paid attention to the antidiscrimination provisions on the basis of sex. "If those of us close to Title IX did not fully realize its impact, especially on sports, how could others have known what it would be?" Bernice "Bunny" Sandler, a civil rights activist who pushed for the legislation, remarked. Perhaps. It is correct that the hearings on the legislation had only briefly discussed sports and that the discussion on the Senate floor was short and focused on a literal reading of the legislation that women would be allowed to compete for places on the football team.[21]

The truth is a little more complicated than that simple version. The *Chronicle of Higher Education*, the main news publication on and for colleges and universities, began reporting on these features in 1970. In 1971 the *New York Times* actually published an editorial calling the bill unsound, because demographics rather than merit would play a major role in the college admissions process.[22]

These issues focused on the academic ramifications of the bill, but Richard Nixon understood the long-term ramifications to college sports. He called the bill a "monstrosity" when one aide advised that it could end the practice of colleges offering athletic scholarships. As part of its emphasis on values and education, the Association for Intercollegiate Athletics for Women prohibited the use of scholarships. Nixon liked the emphasis on values that women's sports fostered, but that was not what the bill was about. It was a civil rights bill for women in the world of education. Sport has always been a noisy, attention getting, but relatively minor aspect of higher education in the United States. The time for the legislation had come, and Nixon understood that fact. He signed the bill into law despite his genuine fondness for college football. He had an election to win, and he was not about to veto civil rights legislation.[23]

Although Nixon liked the values of women's sports, intangibles are difficult for lawyers and bureaucrats to measure. The policy community that had pushed for the 1972 Education Amendments Act had been made up primarily of Democrats, but it would be the Republicans of the Nixon administration who would do the implementation work. A direct and literal reading of the legislation would require that females be integrated into the existing teams, something that almost no one wanted to see happen. Women's rights activists knew it would be virtually impossible for women to compete against men for spots on the football and basketball teams. The Republicans in Nixon's administration wanted to limit the change coming to sport as much as possible. As a result, the two groups found common ground, and the regulations that Nixon/Ford Department of Health, Education and Welfare issued in 1975 required similar facilities and funding—which was a "separate but equal" approach. Some of Nixon's fears about scholarships have come to pass. Many colleges and universities have obeyed the letter of the law and cut men's athletic programs rather than spend the money to expand women's programs.[24]

All of these issues were for a later day. While Nixon contemplated the future of women's sports, White House press secretary Ron Ziegler sent him two memos on his baseball project. With the first, he included the roster of the 1969 Baseball Writers' Association historical all-star team and the selections that the editors and writers of *Sport* magazine made in 1955 for a similar list. In the second memo, Ziegler gave him a roster of Hall of Famers that was six deep at every position except third base. Ziegler explained that only three third basemen had been inducted into the Hall. That weekend, Nixon went to Camp David and spent Sunday making selections with his son-in-law David Eisenhower, the namesake of the compound. Eisenhower knew baseball and had worked briefly for the Washington Senators. "We sat down together and began to study the record books for the purpose of compiling a list of stars," Nixon wrote, "which would stand up under the scrutiny such a selection would receive from the sports writers and baseball fans throughout the country." With pads of yellow legal paper in front of him, Nixon decided to create a prewar and postwar all-star team for each league. "I found it impossible to limit the team to 9 men," he explained. He also figured it would be wise to go no further back than 1925, the year he started following baseball, and to stop with the 1970 season, so he could have a little distance in his evaluations.

Nixon found putting the prewar teams together a relatively easy task. He sat down with a yellow pad of legal paper and considered the names of some of the most accomplished men to play the game at each position on the diamond. He considered fewer names at each position than he did on the postwar teams. In fact, on his American League roster he often wrote just one name and never reconsidered his selections. He selected more than one pitcher, however, and included a listing for reserve players to allow for some additional names. He named John McGraw as manager for the National League prewar team, but later replaced him with Branch Rickey.

Nixon's notes show he had a more difficult time selecting the postwar teams. He had three and sometimes four players under consideration for each position. He had to resort to diagramming a baseball diamond for each league and placing the name of each player at his respective spot on the field. He later added a second catcher for each team and moved a few players from main selections to the reserves and vice versa.[25]

Nixon and Eisenhower did most of the work that weekend at Camp David—it rained, keeping him indoors—but the president continued to make revisions even after returning to Washington on Monday. He dictated an article that would accompany his selections. In an example of Nixon's mental detail and organization, the article was almost an exact copy of the first tape transcript, with the rearrangement of only a few phrases. Nixon also met again with Haldeman. Their conversation covered a number of political matters, but also baseball. The president told his chief of staff that he wanted to know the statistics and records that Jackie Robinson set at Pasadena City College, at UCLA, and in both the minor and major leagues of professional baseball. Haldeman wrote "Fast" in his notes. Later that day he gave the president his findings: the legendary baseball player had not competed in the Olympics as they had thought—they obviously had confused him with his older brother Mack, who had won a silver medal in the two-hundred-meter dash at the 1936 Berlin Games. Jackie Robinson, however, was the only athlete to have earned four varsity letters at UCLA in one year. That day Haldeman shared the research the White House staff had done on Robinson's college statistics. Haldeman's voice held a tone of wonder and respect as he made his report. Nixon too appreciated Robinson's athletic skills: "He has to probably be the best all-time athlete; all-around athlete of any baseball player in history. Nobody could have that. Track. He could have made the track team, football, basketball, baseball team in any college in America." He paused momentarily after "football" and "basketball," which gave his words more emphasis. Haldeman noted in his diary: "The P [is] all cranked up about his baseball all-time great story."[26]

On Tuesday, June 27, Nixon spent a third day working on his selections. He had decided to mention several players as having the best skills, such as base running and fielding. His early notes mention: Ferguson Jenkins, "quiet—already achieved 5 straight 20 win seasons"; Pete Rose, "hustle"; Richie Allen, "great natural talent"; and Larry Doby, "career shortened due to prejudice." He also considered designating future stars of the game, which would have included Reggie Jackson, Reggie Smith, Bobby Murcer, Vida Blue, Jim Palmer, and Don Wilson, among others. He apparently thought better of this idea, because his dictated comments make no mention of these players or of this category. He also continued to consider the selection of a prewar relief pitcher in the National League. Ziegler informed him that relievers "were less the vogue in pre-World War II baseball days, since starting pitchers were expected to play the whole game just like the other players." He recommended that Nixon consider Hugh Casey, a right-handed pitcher for the Brooklyn Dodgers, or Mace Brown, also right-handed, but of the Pittsburgh Pirates. "Casey is the better-known pitcher, but Brown falls more strictly into the pre-World War II relief category." Haldeman watched Nixon's actions with a certain amount of amusement. "The P got into quite a thing about his baseball piece," he recorded. "He's spending an incredible amount of time today on the whole thing. Working out all the little details. Kind of fascinating and not just a little amusing."[27]

As Nixon finished, Ziegler arranged to get maximum publicity for the selections. Haldeman recorded Nixon telling him "to get major play" in media with the list. The White House staff delivered with impressive results. The list was distributed through the Associated Press on June 30 under the president's byline for publication in the Sunday papers on July 2. Nixon did, however, remember who suggested the endeavor in the first place and insisted on doing a short, exclusive interview with Evans before the release. "As it was," he explained, "it was one of the most enjoyable things I've done." The president also gave Evans credit for the idea in the text that accompanied the selections.[28] Appendix C shows those selections. After looking at the finished list, Ziegler told David and Julie Eisenhower, "I never cease to be amazed at the President's knowledge of both the color and detail of the sports world."[29]

Nixon also provided the Associated Press with seven pages of text explaining and elaborating on his selections. His remarks included personal observations and experiences designed to show his firsthand knowledge and expertise in the sport. In one example, he wrote: "I was in Yankee Stadium for the first game of the World Series in 1963 when Sandy Koufax broke the World Series record when he struck out 15 Yankees. On that day no pitcher in baseball history could have surpassed him."[30]

The president admitted some of these experiences affected his selections. He included Arky Vaughan on his prewar National League team because they had gone to high school together. Dick Groat found his way onto the league's postwar team because he had roomed with Nixon's younger brother, Ed, at Duke University. In the American League, Bobo Newsom ended up on the prewar team, and Harmon Killebrew on the postwar team, in part for sentimental reasons. Nixon, however, argued that both made important but underappreciated contributions to their teams that merited their inclusion. Newsom spent most of his career playing for mediocre teams, which obscured his talent, while Killebrew's strong hitting made up for his weak fielding skills.[31]

The First Fan added some personal observations of the greatest performances he had witnessed. Ted Williams was his best hitter. For glove work, he wrote that Brooks Robinson was the best in the infield, while Joe DiMaggio "made all the difficult plays look easy" in the outfield. For base running and pitching, he named Maury Wills and Sandy Koufax respectively. He named Jackie Robinson as the "best all-round athlete" and Lou Gehrig as the "most courageous player," calling him, in an interesting choice of words, "baseball's Mr. Profile in Courage."[32]

The radio interview that Nixon conducted with Evans was particularly revealing about the man. The two discussed his selection of Lou Gehrig as the most courageous player. After making some comments about the New York Yankees legend, Nixon began to discuss what was to him the other great feat of courage in baseball—Red Schoendienst's battle with tuberculosis. A second baseman with the Milwaukee Braves, Schoendienst missed the 1959 season as he fought the disease. He managed to recover and played two more seasons, one with the Braves and the other with the St. Louis Cardinals. "That meant a great deal to me because my older brother died of tuberculosis," Nixon explained. "That left a mark on my memory and our family." He was most impressed that Schoendienst recovered enough so that he could play at the professional level again. That achievement ranked second only to Gehrig according to Nixon.[33]

In making his choices, Nixon admitted that some sports fans might take exception with him for leaving one of their favorites off his list. He called picking and choosing between great players "one of the hardest assignments I have ever undertaken." In his concluding sentence, he declared, "If some smart reporter asks me to name an all-star football team[,] the answer will be a flat—NO!"[34]

The all-star picks earned Nixon significant and positive publicity, although there was a good deal of variety in coverage among cities that had Major League Baseball teams. The president's political hometown newspaper, the *Los Angeles Times*, ran the full article on the front page of the sports section below the fold, using the president's byline. The *San Francisco Examiner*, the *Washington Sunday Star*, the Baltimore *Sun*, the *Kansas City Star*, and the *New York Times* also ran front-page sports section stories under Nixon's byline. The New York paper added photos of nine selectees as well as an insert box of the all-star roster. Neither the *Chicago Sun-Times* nor the *Boston Globe* ran the story on the front page of their sports sections, but both committed major amounts of inside space to the article. The *Chicago Sun-Times* devoted a full page, while the *Globe* used roughly three-fourths of a page and illustrated the piece with photos of Nixon and Eisenhower, along with those of Koufax, Wills, DiMaggio, and Jackie Robinson.[35]

A number of other baseball-city newspapers, many smaller in size, ran a condensed version of the story inside their sports sections. Most of these versions attributed the story to the Associated Press, including the premier publication for baseball enthusiasts, the *Sporting News*.[36] A few editors made some odd decisions. The *Detroit Free Press* and the *Pittsburgh Post-Gazette* waited a day before running the story, while the *Atlanta Journal and Constitution* ran the story on Sunday and then the *Atlanta Constitution* ran the story again on Monday.[37]

A number of prominent publications chose not to print any of Nixon's selections.[38] The most significant was *Sports Illustrated*, which called the president's list one of the "super alltime all-star publicity ploys."[39]

Nixon's essay also got a significant play in a number of publications in non-baseball cities. Perhaps the best coverage of the entire endeavor came in Indiana. The *Indianapolis Star* published the essay under Nixon's byline with photographs of seventeen of his selectees and another of Nixon throwing out the first pitch at the All-Star Game. All of this was on the front page of the paper above the masthead.[40]

The chosen players responded publicly and privately with gratitude, which gave Nixon even more publicity for his endeavor. "I'm tickled to death to be named with all those great players," Ted Williams said in an Associated Press story. "He knows more about baseball than some of the people in the game," Henry "Hank" Aaron remarked. He then added, "All I can say is that I'm quite honored." Harmon Killebrew, Henry Greenberg, and Robin Roberts wrote to the White House, thanking Nixon for their selections. "It is especially refreshing to a retired athlete to try to explain to his friends how this can be," Roberts commented. He then added a recollection of meeting Little Leaguer David Eisenhower and autographing his glove. Jackie Robinson's reaction was more mixed. "I'm honored that he thought of me that way," he told reporters immediately after learning of his selection as "best all-round athlete." A week later, however, *Sports Illustrated* found a more cynical Robinson questioning the president's expertise: "I mean, how many games has

Nixon actually seen?" Another Dodger, Walter Alston, selected as the postwar National League manager, simply said, "I'd be the last one in the world to argue with the President of the United States."[41]

Many of the families of deceased players privately expressed their thanks to Nixon. The widow of Robert Rolfe called her husband's selection a "wonderful addition" to his baseball honors. The daughter of Herb Pennock thanked Nixon for including her father and excluding her father-in-law, Hall of Famer Eddie Collins. The omission gave her an advantage in a continuing debate with her husband over the talents of their fathers. White House staff members made sure Nixon saw this letter. He playfully wrote back, leveling the playing field in the Collins household by saying he had made a mistake in leaving the elder Collins off his list. Joe Medwick wrote to thank the president for naming not only him, but also his former teammate Arky Vaughan, calling him "a great team man."[42] Nixon enjoyed these private correspondences and decided to build on them. He had the White House staff produce a special pamphlet, and he sent a copy to every one of his selectees, or their next-of-kin.[43]

The entire undertaking of picking the greatest players of all time is a bit of a fallacy. The disputes that these type of undertakings generate, however, only served to give the president more publicity. Objections fell into three groups. One collection of sportswriters criticized the merits of the endeavor. "It is impossible and a waste of time to compare players of one era with another in any sport," wrote the sports editor of New Hampshire's *Concord Monitor.* "As time changes, so does the game or sport." A columnist for the *Boston Herald Traveler and Record American* agreed, saying the exercise was "frivolous." A second group of reporters focused their attention on the creation of four all-star teams, rather than one. "If a segment of the electorate has been slighted, it's not much of a segment," the sports editor of Albany's *Knickerbocker News-Union Star* wryly observed. The final group chose to disagree with individual selections. These comments were inevitable. "Nobody can name all-stars who will be unanimous choices," Harold Kaese, a columnist for the *Boston Globe,* stated. With that in mind, Kaese went on to offer a number of alterations to the president's teams. Most of the objections focused on the selection of Nellie Fox, Bobo Newsom, Satchel Paige, and Hack Wilson over Joe Medwick, an omission that appears to have bothered sportswriters more than Medwick.[44]

The criticisms of *New York Times* sports columnist Red Smith had the widest circulation. Smith had despised Nixon since Eisenhower had selected him to be his running mate in 1952. "He was absolutely untrustworthy, a sleazy liar," Smith said of the then vice president. The biographer of the sports reporter notes that "nothing ever shook Smith from that view." When Nixon lived in New York in the mid-1960s, Smith made sure he never had to meet the man at sporting-related events. "I just made haste to get out of the way," he said. Smith was also offended when people told him that Nixon had an expert knowledge of sport, assuming that "a sportswriter, because he is a sportswriter, regards enthusiasm for football or a grasp of the infield fly rule as a qualification for public office."[45] The historical all-star team gave Smith a chance to cut Nixon down to size. He attacked the president's writing as poor, wordy, and "cliché-ridden." Then he offered two contradictory objections. First, he questioned the merit of the entire effort, and then he went on to challenge a number of Nixon's selections, implying that the endeavor was worthwhile after all. Smith's column appeared in a number of papers, under headlines like The President Strikes Out" or "Nixon Flunked Badly in Picking His Stars."[46]

Smith was influential, but the president had his defenders in the press. The sports editor of the *Birmingham News* remarked, "Richard Milhous Nixon finally convinced me Sunday he's a baseball fan." His picks were "excellent." Kaese of the *Boston Globe* and Arthur Daley of the *New York Times* offered more subdued praise. Both men differed with Nixon on some selections, but approved of his overall effort. The president's picks were "quite acceptable," Kaese observed, and Daley said he "did a reasonably good job." Sports columnist Bob Broeg of the *Sporting News* approved of the president's decision to go no further back than 1925. No one could or should try to pass judgment on players they never saw in action. All sportswriters, Broeg observed, should heed Nixon's example.[47]

Another measure of the attention the selections brought the president were the spin-offs and parodies that appeared in the press in various parts of the country. Tom Dowling, a sports columnist for the Washington *Evening Star*, satirized Nixon's choices with his own presidential all-star team, often adopting some of the language Nixon used. Abraham Lincoln appeared at first base, and other infielders included Harry "The Hat" Truman—"you need a scrappy little hustler on any all-star team"—and Ted "Boom Boom"

Roosevelt. A weak hitter, Roosevelt made the team for his infield chatter. "Boom Boom psyched out the opposition. Deception is one of the keys to presidential greatness and Ted had that quality." His starting pitcher was "Big" Lyn Johnson. He called that selection "the toughest challenge I have ever faced," because presidents "can pitch—fast balls, spit balls, bean balls, sinkers, sliders, curve balls, spit balls, bean balls, you name it. These guys can all move the stuff around pretty good." He picked Johnson, because he "struck out the whole Senate in a single afternoon with his famous Gulf of Tonkin pitch."[48]

Even ball players got into the act. Figuring turnabout was fair play, a reporter for the *Philadelphia Daily News* asked the Philadelphia Phillies to choose the best president. "I've been in the game 15 years," one player replied, "and nobody's ever asked me that question." Some responses were smart and sassy: "Who's on the $1000 bill?" Others chose to be serious. "I've got to go with Nixon," another player responded. "He's getting us out of Vietnam." For whatever reason, Nixon and Lincoln tied at two votes apiece.[49]

The parodies and even the criticisms of the president's selections worked to his advantage. Disagreements about the merits of one player over another were less divisive than other issues in the election, like the Vietnam War. More importantly, continued attention on the presidential baseball team furthered the larger campaign goal of "humanizing" Nixon. Differences over player selections or even on the merits of the entire endeavor were unlikely to cost the reelection campaign many votes and continued to present traits and interests of the president to which the public could relate. There were, of course, many voters who were never going to vote for Nixon, and the all-star selections mattered little to them.

8

The Election of 1972: The Second Half

Nixon and his lieutenants realized the man had captured lightening in a bottle. Actually Nixon knew long before they did that sport would work for them politically and that personality was an important consideration in the contest. He also realized the limits of sport as a political tool, and ordered his subordinates to end its use. He, however, was far from finished with sport. Far from it. In fact, along the way, he even provided a little social and policy leadership in the world of sport.

The Nixon campaign began planning more and more sports-related events that fall. Athletes for the Re-election of the President had over 550 members, including the likes of golfer Arnold Palmer, race driver Mario Andretti; Olympic gymnast Cathy Rigby; football players Johnny Unitas, Fran Tarkenton, and Merlin Olsen; hockey star Gordie Howe; and baseball players Johnny Bench and Don Newcombe. There was nothing new to this phenomenon in Nixon's political career. In 1960 prominent athletes in the Nixon campaign had included Jackie Robinson and Frank Gifford; and in 1968, it was Wilt Chamberlain of the Los Angeles Lakers. The campaign and White House staff showed some initial reluctance in the use sport, but they became quite enthusiastic after the success of the presidential all-star baseball team. On July 12, representatives of the Committee for the Re-election of the President were trying to get Nixon to make a brief stop at a Los Angeles Rams practice session. The White House staff arranged for Nixon to have several different meetings with athletes visiting the executive mansion. In communications with one another, Nixon's men were explicit: they were arranging these meetings because these sport celebrities supported Nixon's reelection. In the case of Nixon's meetings with former heavyweight boxing champion Floyd Patterson and retired Chicago Bears running back Gale Sayers, it was because they were African Americans. The documents in the case of Sayers are explicit on this matter. "PURPOSE To publicize Sayers'—a black athlete—support of the President and to show the President's interest to welcome blacks to the reelection drive." The press office was supposed to issue a press release aimed at the black media as a follow-up procedure, but Sayers missed a connecting flight and never arrived.

The most successful of these photo opportunity meetings was when Nixon welcomed Babe Ruth's widow, former New York Giants great Bobby Thomson, and legendary Brooklyn Dodgers pitcher Ralph Branca to the Oval Office. The two players became tied together in baseball history when Thomson hit a home run off Branca in a famous 1951 game to win the National League championship. White House documents make it clear that the meeting was arranged because all three supported Nixon's reelection. The president agreed to the meeting, but wanted Lou Gehrig's widow, whose political views were unknown, added. Efforts to track her down were to no avail, and the meeting went ahead as scheduled with the original three.[1]

Still, there were some setbacks. Nixon was disappointed to learn that eighty-three NFL players had endorsed McGovern. Worst of all, fifteen of them were Redskins. When he saw this item in his daily news summaries, he wrote on the margin: "Blacks?"[2]

In addition to being an election year, 1972 was also the twenty-fifth anniversary of the desegregation of Major League Baseball. Plans were under way to honor Jackie Robinson at the second game of the World Series, and the baseball commissioner's office contacted the White House, hoping the president would attend. There was real interest in this idea among White House staff members, and the NBC television network got a waiver from the Federal Communications Commission on equal-time requirements for political candidates so the event could be televised.[3]

A long personal history between Nixon and Robinson complicated the planning for this appearance. The best known account of their relationship is the one Robinson offered in his posthumously published memoirs *I Never Had It Made.* Written after the baseball legend had parted ways with Nixon, his bitterness colors his version of events, and factual errors mar its reliability. The two first met at the 1952 Republican convention in a Chicago hotel lobby, not in 1960 in the politician's office, as Robinson claims in his book. Nixon impressed Robinson, noting that he had hit a home run earlier in the day against the Cubs and recalling, in detail, a sixty-six-yard pass reception Robinson made in the 1939 UCLA-Oregon football game when he played for the Bruin Bears. A mutual admiration society developed between the two. Nixon admired Robinson's athletic talent, while the ballplayer appreciated the politician's strong stand—by the standards of the 1950s—on civil rights. In a column he wrote for the *New York Post* after his retirement from baseball, Robinson said he would support Nixon in the 1960 election owing to his views on civil rights. "I am certain you know what a favorable column on Richard Nixon does in the *New York Post*," he wrote the then vice president. "I haven't had so much mail since I left baseball."[4]

Robinson was an enthusiastic supporter for Nixon in the 1960 presidential election despite his later claims to the contrary. His support for Nixon in his columns grew through the spring months. Robinson was an independent and had first supported Senator Hubert Humphrey of Minnesota for the Democratic nomination. When Humphrey's campaign faltered, he came out for Nixon, finding Senator John F. Kennedy, the Democratic front-runner, "a cold, calculating political machine" and his main rival and eventual running mate, Senator Lyndon Johnson of Texas, a "a proven segregationist." Under some pressure from the editors of the paper, he left his column with the *Post* to work on the Nixon campaign. Writing a column, though, was a side endeavor for Robinson. His main job was his position as vice president in charge of personnel relations for the Chock Full o'Nuts Corporation. Robinson, though, was committed to Nixon and took a leave of absence from the firm to focus on the election. He made public appearances on behalf of the candidate, speaking with evident sincerity. He became disillusioned while on the campaign trail. He found most of the Nixon campaigners ignorant on issues of race. His advice fell on deaf ears. Campaign managers ignored his suggestions and refused to schedule any appearances in Harlem.[5]

Race grew as an issue as the campaign progressed. In October a judge in Georgia sentenced the Reverend Dr. Martin Luther King Jr. to a four-month jail sentence on some trumped-up charges. The baseball legend became bitterly disappointed when Nixon refused to make a phone call to a judge to demand bail for the civil rights leader. Robinson had a ten-minute private meeting with campaign manager Robert Finch and the candidate, but failed to convince Nixon to do something, anything. Robinson left in tears. "Nixon doesn't deserve to win," he blurted out. While Nixon stood idle, John F. Kennedy called Coretta Scott King to offer his sympathy. His brother Robert called the judge. Robinson believed this inaction cost Nixon the election. After Nixon and Robinson parted company in the 1960s, some attributed their split to Nixon's inaction on the King arrest. While Robinson was disappointed, he continued to support Nixon even though he seriously considered leaving the campaign and was under considerable pressure from other black leaders to support Kennedy. "I clung to the hope that Nixon would follow through on the things he had indicated were important to him in that first meeting after the pressures of the campaign were over," he offered as an explanation for staying with the campaign despite his disenchantment. "I have always felt that blacks must be represented in both parties. I was fighting a last-ditch battle to keep the Republicans from becoming completely white." Robinson suffered for this support. James Wechsler, the editor of the *New York Post,* fired him the day of the election. Robinson did, however, keep his much more lucrative position with Chock Full o'Nuts.[6]

Despite his disappointment, Robinson continued to believe in Nixon. He attended a dinner in honor of the departing vice president in January 1961. He later wrote to Nixon, calling the event "one of the highlights of my life. What happened there convinced me more than ever that I supported the right man." The politician wrote Robinson a letter of thanks and gave him a plaque for his efforts in the campaign. The beverage industry business executive responded in kind, sending Nixon a twenty-four-pound bag of Chock Full o'Nuts coffee. In 1962, after Nixon lost the California governor's race and gave his "last press conference," Robinson wrote: "I hope that you will reconsider, Dick, because it is the great men people attack. You are good for politics, good for America." In late 1963, in a public feud with Malcolm X Robinson continued to defend his decision to campaign on behalf of Nixon. In an exchange of open letters that appeared in newspapers, the Muslim leader called Robinson a puppet of the white power structure. "Very few Negroes were dumb enough to follow your MISLEAD" on Nixon. "Just who are you playing ball for today, good friend." Robinson made no concessions on this matter. He was proud of his support for Nixon and would do it again.[7]

It was only in 1964 when the Nixon-Robinson relationship came to an end. The former ballplayer broke with his friend over what he considered a feckless commitment to the cause of civil rights. "I do not consider my decision to back Richard Nixon over John F. Kennedy for the Presidency in 1960 one of my finer ones. It was a sincere one, however, at the time," he explained in later years. Nixon had endorsed the candidacy of Barry Goldwater, just before the Arizona senator secured the presidential nomination of the Republican Party. Robinson had campaigned hard for New York governor Nelson A. Rockefeller in the primaries, going as far as calling Goldwater a "bigot" in public. After attending the Republican National Convention in San Francisco that nominated the Arizonan and became notorious for the vicious behavior of Goldwater delegates toward their opponents, Robinson declared, "I now believe I know how it felt to be a Jew in Hitler's Germany."[8] Nixon, on the other hand, hit the campaign trail on behalf of Goldwater.

In 1968, Robinson campaigned again for Rockefeller against Nixon. In a press conference with the governor, Robinson let his feelings towards his one-time friend fly out. "If Nixon is elected President, we as Negroes are in serious trouble; we would, in my opinion, be going backward." With Nixon's nomination, Robinson went to work for the campaign of Democrat Hubert Humphrey, the then vice president of the United States. Shortly after Nixon's inauguration, Robinson sent him an extremely formal letter, given their past. He asked Nixon to advance the cause of civil rights even though he had received little support from the black community. "For Mr. President, Black people cannot afford a racial conflict; White people cannot afford one. And it's a fact that America cannot afford one. If we are to survive as a nation, we must do it together. Black people will work for one America if we are given hope. Without hope, the present feeling of despair will lead to worse problems." Nixon ignored the letter.[9]

Shortly after the inauguration Robinson was part of a group of thirty black leaders that showed up unannounced at the White House, hoping that Nixon would make time to meet with them. Presidents of the United States, even newly inaugurated ones, are busy men, and after half an hour the group departed without a meeting. In his memoirs, Robinson would describe the president as "capable of deep personal goodwill and grace in one-to-one relationships and particularly if he believes you can be useful to his goals. His instincts are flawless when he bends himself to win you to his cause."[10]

Nixon's attachment to Robinson was a bit stronger. In a meeting with a number of generals and admirals who were members of racial minority groups, Nixon said he believed in finding "the best man for the job." He made references to Robinson as an athlete of great skill who had made the Dodgers better and said that approach would make other organizations like the military better. "When you're trying to find the best man, you got to look through your whole list of people, and nobody can be ruled out." To another group of Hispanic Republican leaders, Nixon explained that the United States was a meritocracy and Robinson's success was good for the United States. "I think the best decision Branch, Branch Rickey made bringing him up was when he comes, he must be the best. And he was the best." Nixon started rambling about Robinson's skills in different sports, and then caught himself. "But anyway, so much for that."[11]

Despite this respect, Nixon decided against attending a ceremony honoring Robinson, claiming that his schedule was too busy. On October 15, Robinson threw out the first pitch of the second game of the World Series, and the Oakland A's then defeated the Cincinnati Reds. According to White House documents, Nixon spent the day at Camp David, relaxing and watching professional football games.[12]

Nine days later Robinson was dead. The White House staff released a statement in which Nixon eulogized his one-time associate. The president still admired Robinson for the strong morality of his social leadership. In Nixon's view, Jackie Robinson had understood the social obligations that came with being a visible athlete and had met his obligations well. "His courage, his sense of brotherhood, and his brilliance on the playing field brought a new human dimension not only to the game of baseball but to every area of American life where black and white people work side by side. This Nation to which he gave so much in his lifetime will miss Jackie Robinson, but his example will continue to inspire us for years to come." In press accounts that followed, Nixon's statement and his designation of Robinson as the "best all-round athlete" often preceded those comments of key baseball and civil rights figures paying tribute to the fallen legend. Nixon decided not to attend the funeral services for Robinson; he had never been popular with the Robinson family, even in the best of times. Instead, he sent Robert Finch, counselor to the president, to the funeral as the head of a forty-man White House delegation.[13]

The president's refusal to attend the World Series coincided with his decision to throttle down on appearances associated with sport. On October 14, Henry Cashen sent Haldeman a proposal to have Nixon meet with Bob Lilly, a defensive lineman for the Dallas Cowboys. Lilly would be in Washington in two weeks when his team played the Redskins. Haldeman slashed a line through thc proposal and added the notation: "*NO* The President disapproved and said, 'No more athletes until after the election.'"[14]

Despite this sentiment, Nixon did initiate action on another subject, which would end up becoming one of his most significant contributions in sport-related matters, even though many dismissed his effort as election-year pandering. On October 4, Assistant Attorney General Thomas E. Kauper of the Antitrust Division in the Justice Department announced in a Senate hearing that Nixon favored legislation to prohibit professional sport leagues from imposing blackouts of home games. The initiative was aimed directly at the NFL, which had a policy of prohibiting the telecast of games within a seventy-five-mile radius of the home city. Kauper noted that the league had received antitrust exemption on television matters, and "the N.F.L. can surely be required to undertake certain activities in the public interest." He also expressed Nixon's interest in seeing Congress act on the matter before the end of the year.[15]

While taking on the NFL clearly had electoral advantages, Nixon also genuinely believed in the effort. "I am all for it," he told Attorney General Richard Kleindienst.[16]

There was also some real partisanship behind the initiative. Forcing the NFL to change its television policy was also a good way to kick Edward Bennett Williams, the owner of the Washington Redskins. "Pour it on Williams and do it publically and say you met with the President," he instructed Kleindienst. "Get the whole bunch, get the whole country riled up. That's my point." That was a political objective, though, and Nixon wanted to know they had a strong legal case. The attorney general said he did. "I don't care about winning it," Nixon said. He just wanted to hurt Williams, and he wanted it done during the current season. "Ask for an injunction, or something." Making the NFL available to the public was something he believed in personally. "Seriously, though, I feel this way." It was also a way to represent the average citizen. "Let's speak up for the folks. The folks should be able to see the God-damned games on television. The playoff games. Playoffs.

All playoff games should be available." He explained that he was not doing this for himself. He would be in Florida for the NFL playoffs and had special telecommunications equipment that would allow him to watch any game he wanted. The White House staff should note that the president was speaking for all Americans regardless of politics. "He is speaking," Nixon said, talking about himself in the third person, "for all the people in Washington that didn't vote for him." Ehrlichman and Kleindienst chuckled in response.[17]

Nixon kept pushing on this issue. The next day he told the attorney general to talk to NFL commissioner Pete Rozelle. "*Playoff games, playoff games,* just like the World Series, should be open to the public," he said with emphasis. Even though he believed that the airwaves were a public common and that the government had a role to play in policy formation, he also wanted to get political advantage out of the initiative. "Let me say that I want us to get some publicity out of this. I just don't want to do this to accomplish it. You know that." At the same time, he believed this move was in the best interest of the NFL and would head off Congress passing legislation that required the league to televise all its games. "If you can get the playoff games, believe me, it will be the greatest achievement we have ever done."[18]

The initial reaction from the sports world was negative. Commissioner Pete Rozelle refused to change the league policy, expressing the fear that the initiative would turn professional football into a studio sport and kill stadium attendance. Sports columnist Arthur Daley of the *New York Times* was even harsher: "This is a gimmick used by countless cheap little politicians over the years in an effort to wheedle votes. It ill befits the President of the United States to descend to the same low level, especially when it doesn't appear that he needs it." Nixon was playing to sentiment among the American people, who failed to recognize that football was a business. "Through some peculiar process of ratiocination, the American public seems to believe that it has a God-given right to see all sports events on home television for free." Daley considered this a phenomenon unique to sport. "No one demands that Macy's or Bloomingdale's or Brooks Brothers or Bonwit Teller give away their products for free. Why should the same be demanded of football and other sports?"[19]

Reactions such as these had been worrying members of the White House staff even before the election ended. "You can argue, of course, that in a short time, more people oppose a blackout than favor it, but it seems to me that there was no need to get the President into the controversy," Herb Klein warned Haldeman. "I would hope that we do not get any further into this controversy since we have nothing to gain—and we do have something to lose."[20]

Nixon, however, had a better feel for the issue than Klein, Daley, and even Rozelle. In mid-December he directed Attorney General Richard Kleindienst to meet with the commissioner again to see if the league would consider modifying its policy if a game sold out forty-eight hours before kickoff. On the morning of December 20, Rozelle informed Kleindienst that the NFL would not comply with this request. The commissioner had sound reason for refusing the administration. Professional football in the United States was a monopoly, and the league often acted in ways designed to exploit the consumer. Television was no different. Speculation from those that knew Rozelle is that the Nixon offer was not as good as what he thought Congress might offer; and that he genuinely feared playing playoff games in empty stadiums. In a statement the attorney general released a few hours later, he announced that the administration "would strongly urge the new Congress to re-examine the entire antitrust exemption statue and seek legislation that is more in keeping with the public interest." The next day the editorial board of the *New York Times* repudiated Daley's position, noting that the public airways belonged to the people. The NFL players' union also supported the effort.[21] Nixon's position had more than a little merit, particularly for those who believed in open markets.

Nixon could have done more on the issue, but it lay dormant until the end of the summer as the league started preparing for a new season, but there was genuine anger over the issue. "We did not pull this problem out of thin air. This is a result of complaints being made by the public," Senator John Pastore of Rhode Island explained. On August 23, a subcommittee of the House Commerce Committee recommended legislation prohibiting local blackouts. Rozelle told the press that the league would not change its policy even though there was a good chance that Congress might pass the legislation prohibiting blackouts. On September 6, the Senate did just that with a vote of 76–6. Only a week later, in a speedy move for Congress, the House of Representatives voted along similar lines, 336–37. Conceding defeat, the NFL changed its policy that same day, allowing home games to be televised if the stadium sold out seventy-two hours in advance of the contest.[22] Nixon signed the bill nonetheless. A study done the year he resigned from office showed that the president had advocated a policy that was in the best interests of the NFL. A close examination of attendance showed that Rozelle's concerns were misplaced. Factors other than television broadcasts, such as weather, performance of the home team, and the caliber of the opponent, determined attendance numbers. Television actually helped, giving the teams more revenue and increasing visibility. Art Modell, owner of the Cleveland Browns, observed that "without television, I'd be out of business. It has literally made the game by giving it exposure."[23]

Despite the enormous success Nixon had that summer and fall in using sport to service his political interests, he did not like all that he saw that year. Disaster visited the international Olympic movement not once, but twice. The first episode was tragic, the next merely disappointing. Nixon and his administration attempted to respond to these reversals, offering social leadership in appropriate portions and context.

The first crisis was the hostage incident at the Olympic Games in Munich. Around 4 a.m. on September 5, a group of eight Palestinian terrorists broke into the apartments of the Israeli team at the Olympic Village, capturing nine coaches and athletes and killing two others in the assault. Nixon was in San Clemente at the time of the attack and quickly called Prime Minister Golda Meir of Israel to offer his support and sympathy. He offered the "total cooperation" of the US government in obtaining the release of the hostages. At her request, he sent a note to the IOC asking them to suspend the Games until the Israelis were released. The Games went on until IOC President Avery Brundage suspended the events scheduled for late that afternoon and evening. This delay would later be the subject of harsh criticism. After his phone call with Meir, Nixon talked with the reporters who had accompanied him to California, to express his personal outrage. The Germans directed the response to the crisis. Tense negotiations between the police and a terrorist spokesman went on for most of the day. The Palestinians demanded the release of 234 men in Israeli prisons, as well as the leaders of the Baader-Meinhof Gang being held in West Germany, and three jets for their escape to Egypt. Since Meir's government refused to negotiate with terrorists, the police decided to make a rescue attempt. The incident ended in a gun battle at Munich's Fürstenfeldbrück Airport during the late evening and early morning hours of September 5–6. German police sharpshooters opened fire on the Palestinians after they moved away from the helicopters that had brought them to the tarmac. The police were off-target, and after a firefight that lasted a little over an hour, they tried to close in on the terrorists. The Israelis were still tied up in the helicopters and before the Germans could rescue them, the Palestinians threw a grenade into one ship and shot the hostages in the other. All nine died. The police captured three of the terrorists. The others died in the gunfight.[24]

Nixon's contribution after the hostage incident came to its bloody conclusion was to lead the nation in mourning. "The heart of America goes out to you," he told Meir in a message he sent on September 6. "This tragic and senseless act is a perversion of all the hopes and aspirations of mankind which the Olympic Games symbolize." One of the Israeli athletes killed at the airport, David Berger, held dual US/Israeli citizenship, and his parents lived in Cleveland, Ohio. Nixon called late in the afternoon and expressed his sympathies to Berger's father. Two television networks—ABC and NBC—used Nixon's statement in their news coverage of the event, but Haldeman noticed that CBS refused. "It is absolutely unsettling," he told the president. The fact that CBS used comments from McGovern was a different matter. "It makes a statement," he observed. Nixon refused, however, to support an effort to cancel the Games as some Jewish-American groups and the editors of the *New York Times* wanted. Eight months later Nixon agreed to a request from Bowie Kuhn that he serve as an honorary chairman for an organization that was building a memorial to the athletes.[25]

The US results at the Olympics were not particularly good either. "We came out way behind on gold. That's for sure," Chuck Colson observed in the Oval Office. Nixon was not a real fan of most Olympic sports. He had attended one day of the track events at the 1932 Los Angeles Olympics, but like most Americans he became interested in the various sports of the Summer Games about a week before they started. Although not a big basketball fan, he was particularly angry about the officiating in the game between the USA and the USSR. "We got screwed," he told Haldeman. His chief of staff was angry as well. "I think that was a damn good move; the American team not to accept the silver."

"You're damn right," Nixon replied. "That would mean they were accepting a bad call."

Despite their agreement, Haldeman sensed that the issue was a sports topic that Nixon should avoid. "I think you're better off not to be on record as complaining about officiating or the judging." Nixon appears to have taken this advice. Despite his personal anger at the injustice done to the US basketball team, there was little he could do to rectify the matter, and he let it go.[26]

The president was almost done with the Olympics, but not quite. On the same day that Nixon achieved a decisive electoral landslide victory over McGovern—winning 60.7 percent of the popular vote and forty-nine states, *including* his opponent's home state, to give him the third-best showing in American history up to that time—another Olympic disaster occurred that would involve the administration much more closely than the events in Munich. Despite the initial euphoria that followed the IOC decision, the Denver Olympics soon became entangled in Colorado state politics. Much of the early opposition came not from liberal political activists, but from small businessmen and high-income-earning residents of affluent communities that were near the proposed host sites of Olympic events. They were less than excited about the disruptions and damage that large crowds would bring to their properties. There were also political activists in the state opposed to growth, and they worried that the Winter Games would have a detrimental effect on the environment and culture of the state. The individuals most responsible for bringing the Olympics to Denver were developers, businessmen, and politicians who disagreed with these views. These civic leaders believed that growth would bring greater economic prosperity to the state. The Denver Olympic Committee, with a membership of developers and other advocates of business expansion, began to lose favor with the people of the state. The wisdom of having the Games in Denver seemed self-evident to them, and most public presentations were aimed at like-minded business groups. There was no dialogue with the residents and landowners near the proposed event areas, which turned out to be a problem.[27]

As the Denver Olympic Committee (DOC) started to face these issues, many people, including members of the International Olympic Committee, began to have reservations about the honesty of the Denver committee's members. The official bid that Denver made to the IOC claimed there would be one hundred thousand hotel beds. Problem was there was only be thirty-five thousand in the area. Photographs of the city in the literature were misleading. The photographer used a telephoto lens to compress the scene and make it appear that the mountains for the ski events were right on the edge of the city. Denver representatives airbrushed snow into another photograph of the planned cross-country ski venue to hide the fact that it rarely received enough precipitation. Lieutenant Governor John Vanderhoof remarked, "The DOC had to meet all the IOC criteria and they were pressed for time so they lied a bit." The members of the International Olympic Committee were so tired of the misrepresentations and distortions that they voted unanimously at the committee meeting in January 1972 to take the Games away from Denver. A fast and furious lobbying effort that included phone calls from Nixon got the IOC to reverse itself the next day.[28]

A number of logistical and planning problems also made many observers question the committee's competence. Bob Murri, owner of the Loveland Basin ski area, learned from his car radio that his resort would host one of the medal events. Estimated costs had increased two and half times over the original estimate. Many Colorado taxpayers began to worry that they would be left to pay for cost overruns. "Financial abuse," said state representative Richard Lamm, an opponent of the Olympic movement, "was originally and remains now as our principal question and objection." Reassurances from the DOC that the state would only pay just over 10 percent of the expenses sounded hollow as the committee kept its meetings closed.[29]

A backlash developed, and opponents of growth formed Citizens for Colorado's Future (CCF). They circulated petitions and began collecting signatures to put an amendment to the state constitution on the November ballot that would prevent state funds from being used to finance the Winter Games. In the spring of 1972 the group got more than seventy-seven thousand eligible voters to sign these forms, the most signatures ever collected for a statewide referendum at that point in Colorado history.[30]

Clumsy efforts in support of the Olympics only added to the backlash. These actions ranged from putting literature into the pay envelopes of city employees to launching personal attacks against Olympic opponents. The two major Denver papers refused to run columns by their own writers that raised questions about the Olympic proponents. A Denver television station made news when it refused to provide equal time to the CCF, in violation of Federal Communications Commission regulations, until the organization filed formal charges that put the station's license at risk. "It is almost as if the Olympic contingent had some sort of death wish as far as the Games are concerned," the sports editor of the *Post* noted before the election. John Parr, coordinator of the CCF, agreed. The preference of Olympic supporters to talk about national honor and prestige rather than addressing taxpayer concerns about paying for the Games helped his cause immensely. "The people wanted concrete answers, not patriotism," he said on election night. That evening as Nixon stormed into office with one of the largest landslides in American political history, Colorado and Denver voters rejected the Olympics.[31]

As the International Olympic Committee began looking for a new host city, the Nixon administration tried to determine what actions it should take. White House officials talked with influential leaders in the athletic community. National prestige had always been the main factor in Nixon's interest in having the Olympics in the United States during the American Bicentennial. Needless to say, there was some concern in the executive mansion that losing the Winter Games would be a major blow to these celebrations and the public reputation of the country. "No strong arguments have been put forth that a United States city must sponsor the 1976 Winter Games, nor have any strong arguments been made that without the 1976 winter games our overall Bicentennial plans would be diminished," deputy assistant to the president for domestic affairs Ken Cole assured Nixon, apparently unaware of his boss's previous views on this topic. "To get involved in the Winter Olympic decision-making process would necessitate a Federal role in an effort heretofore handled entirely by the United States Olympic Committee and possibly set a bad precedent for future Olympic events," he stated, unaware of the effort the administration had made on behalf of Los Angeles. Despite his support for the Summer Games, Nixon had apparently learned from his mistakes and took Cole's advice; there is no evidence that the administration took any action to support efforts to keep the Winter Olympics in the United States, and the IOC decided the international gathering should take place in Innsbruck, Austria.[32]

When it came to future Olympic bids, the Nixon administration was far more restrained. In 1974, Los Angeles and Lake Placid, New York, were the American cities trying to win the 1980 Games, and the administration made almost no effort to support these initiatives. Lake Placid did a careful job of preparing. A small community of ten thousand people, the town had hosted the 1932 winter Olympics and was systematic in securing the support of the public in a referendum, and financial underwriting from the state, before it started lobbying the IOC. The Lake Placid bid committee asked Nixon for an endorsement of their effort, and after the administration checked to make sure that the group had solid support, the president agreed. He sent a short, formal letter to Lord Killanin, the new president of the IOC. There is no record, however, of any further support for the renewed Los Angeles effort.[33]

As the end of 1972 approached, Nixon returned to football. He predicted that the University of Southern California Trojans would win the Rose Bowl. "Nobody, not even, not even the Packers at their best, or the Redskins at their best could beat Southern Cal," he told Haldeman. "Ohio State is never sensational but it's always buh, buh, buh, buh, buh." That comment basically meant that the Buckeyes won games with small plays that incrementally added up, and yet, Nixon explained, that approach would not matter. "Southern Cal has the greatest personnel I have ever saw in college or professional football. Fast! Big! Everything!" He was right. The Trojans beat the Buckeyes, 42–17. It was the first of three consecutive USC–Ohio State matchups in the Rose Bowl, and USC went 2–1 in these games.[34]

The Olympics notwithstanding, Nixon could look at 1972 as a good year. He won reelection in a landslide due, in part, to his skilled use of the presidency's informal social and cultural leadership position shown in exercises like the selection a historic all-star baseball team. Sports fans are fond of arguing that a certain player is better than another, and often dream of seeing one legend play with or against another. When Nixon put together his all-star selections, he gave these fans a way to relate to him. This episode was one of many reasons for his landslide reelection. He also began to use the power and influence of his high position to shape events in the world of sport, but just a little. In the year and a half that followed, though, this state of affairs would undergo an almost complete reversal.

9

The Second Term, 1973–1974

The Watergate scandal destroyed Richard Nixon. Not even he would argue that point. A look at his interaction with sport during his second term shows in stark fashion the extent to which the crisis dominated his time. His interest in sport remained constant, but his dealings with this venue came close to disappearing altogether. Controlling the crisis, attempting to thwart the investigation into the misdeeds of his administration, came to consume more and more of his attention with each new day. With that point made, looking at his use of sport during this portion of his presidency shows how close he came to surviving it all.

The transition from 1972 to 1973 was an eventful one in the Nixon administration and in sport-related matters. Throughout the fall, Henry Kissinger had been negotiating with the North Vietnamese in an effort to end the war. In October, the North basically accepted the terms that Nixon had offered back in May when he announced the use of air power to stop the Easter Offensive. The South Vietnamese had balked at signing the agreement, fearing—correctly as things turned out—that the agreement was a false peace. Negotiations, threats, and some more bombings of the North eventually brought about an agreement that ended America's longest war.[1]

While the final elements of the settlement were being worked out, the Washington Redskins defeated the Dallas Cowboys 26–3 in the National Football Conference Championship Game held on December 31, 1972. Allen and Nixon talked about the contest a few days before it started. "They're the best team in football," the coach informed the president. "We are going to have to play over our heads to beat them." Allen thought the Redskins could do that. He explained that the president's visit to their practice session the year before was still having an impact. "What you gave us last year, they all feel that." The team really believed they had a bond with the District of Columbia that was different from what other teams in the league had with their host cities. "We are trying to use that, you see, for whatever it's worth." In a telephone conversation after the game, Allen claimed the Cowboys had surrendered. "They quit in the last quarter." He also saw tangible proof of the bond between the city and the team in the stadium. "The fans gave us a big lift playing at home." He could feel the ground trembling from the noise of the cheering crowd. "That stadium was just," Allen paused for a second, and then said with emphasis, "*weird*." Then he chuckled.[2]

The other conference championship game pitted the Miami Dolphins against the Pittsburgh Steelers in a contest that was much closer, 21–17. As a result, the Dolphins would meet the Redskins in the Super Bowl, putting Nixon in a difficult position. Would he cheer for the Miami team, as he had the year before, or would he back the hometown heroes? The day after the big win, Washington coach George Allen celebrated by giving his assistant coaches their first day off since the start of training camp, and he visited the White House with his wife, four children, and in-laws. After a chat in the Oval Office about football, Nixon and his guests went to the Rose Garden for picture taking, and the president ended the speculation. "I'm a part-time resident of Florida and I have a great deal of respect for Don Shula," he said, but "I root for the home town team."[3]

In addition to offering his support for the Redskins, Nixon also made a gracious gesture toward quarterback Billy Kilmer. He gave Allen a pin with the presidential seal and a letter addressed to Kilmer's thirteen-year-old daughter, Kathy, who had cerebral palsy and lived with her mother in California.[4]

What gave the act special meaning was the immediate history between Kilmer and Nixon. Back in December, the quarterback had been the subject of a front-page feature in the "Style" section of the *Washington Post.* The article depicted at length Kilmer's hard-drinking habits and made it clear that he was intoxicated during a good part of the interview, during which he claimed that Nixon's enthusiasm for the team was counterproductive and that he planned to ask Allen to do something about keeping the president away.[5]

These comments were an unexpected blow to Nixon. Had he not been the good fan, supporting his team even during their low moments? These remarks stung. The next day the president instructed Haldeman to talk with Allen and find out what was going on with Kilmer. Allen blamed the entire mess on the hostile Washington media, adding that Kilmer should not have given an interview while he was drinking. Several commentators dismissed the quarterback's comments with ridicule. An editorial in the *Wall Street Journal* observed that the team had an 11-1 record and had just won its first division title in twenty-seven years. "If only the President would clam up, the team would really be going places." Syndicated columnist Joseph Kraft wrote a piece about what various officials should get as Christmas gifts from the president. Kilmer's present should be a trade to the New England Patriots, who had just finished at the bottom of the standings with the worst record in the league.[6]

It was also clear that the gesture to Kilmer was not a publicity stunt. When Nixon told Colson that he planned to write the quarterback's daughter, the White House staffer said it would make a good story. Nixon said no. The letter was personal. Colson did not take Nixon seriously on this matter. The next day, he suggested again that they make the letter public. "It's his letter. It's private," Nixon countered. If it became public it would not be the doing of the administration. "It must be Kilmer's decision to put it out."[7]

Kilmer had other concerns on his mind at the moment. The Redskins were about to face a team of destiny, and no amount of presidential support was going to help them. The Miami Dolphins had not lost a game all season and were on the verge of finishing with a 17-0 record, the first undefeated campaign in NFL history. The Redskins might be his team, but Nixon was under no illusions. In a phone conversation with comedians Dan Rowan and Dick Martin, the hosts of the television program *Rowan & Martin's Laugh-In*, he conceded the obvious: "Just between you and me, that it's Miami—Miami would have to be given an edge, because they're younger and faster."[8]

Many critics, however, noted that the Dolphins had enjoyed a soft schedule, that Shula-coached teams had a habit of losing the big games—he had a 0-2 record in the Super Bowl—and that Washington had defeated Miami in a preseason contest. The Dolphins responded to these criticisms in the Super Bowl with a game in which they dominated the Redskins in every facet of play. Miami took a 14–0 lead in the first half and came close to shutting out Washington. The Dolphin defense prevented the Redskins offense from scoring at all. The only Washington touchdown came on a fluke play with 2:07 left in the game. The score resulted from a blocked Miami field goal attempt. After it bounced back, kicker Garo Yepremian tried to make a forward pass, but lost control of the ball. Washington's Mike Bass snatched it out of the air and ran forty-nine yards for the score. Despite this aggressive play, Washington could not score again, and Miami won the game, 14–7. "This is the greatest moment in my coaching life," Shula exclaimed afterward. "We dominated in every aspect of the game except for blocked field-goal recoveries."[9]

Dolphin fans and Florida sportswriters went wild with the victory and could not help taunting Nixon for his change in allegiance. In downtown Miami fans danced in the streets, waved white towels, and honked their cars horns as they drove around chanting, "Dolphins number one." The scene was similar in Key Biscayne. Dolphins supporters drove past the presidential compound blowing their horns. Some sports columnists took the opportunity to gloat at the president's expense.[10]

Nixon dealt with the defeat of his team with the tact that the situation and his office demanded. He sent a telegram to Shula after the game:

TODAYS VICTORY WAS A SMASHING CLIMAX TO A TRULY PERFECT SEASON. YOU AND ALL OF THE DOLPHINS HAVE MY HEARTIEST CONGRATULATIONS.

Nixon decided to wait until the next day to actually call Shula, which led to an awkward exchange between White House communications director Herbert Klein and the coach in the locker room after the game. Klein assumed Shula knew who he was and asked if he had received the message. "What do *you* do, Herb?," Shula asked suspiciously.

Klein's response was concise. "I work for the President."

League officials tried to have Shula take the phone call during a Monday morning press conference, but the White House operator refused to put the call through, saying Nixon wanted to talk to the coach privately. "This is all off the record, men," Shula joked with the reporters trying to listen in on the conversation. He later summarized the conversation that took place later in the day, saying Nixon knew what it was like to lose the big one and come back later for a victory. He also said that he discussed the relative strengths and ages of the offensive lines of the Dolphins and Redskins. "To me it's remarkable that he's as involved and interested as he is in football." Asked if Nixon talked about his support for Washington, Shula responded with a smile, "He didn't mention that."[11]

Nixon also contacted Allen and reiterated his support, thanking the coach for a wonderful season despite the outcome of the final game:

> THE REDSKINS PLAYED GALLANTLY FROM THE OPENING KICKOFF THIS FALL THRU THE FINAL SECONDS IN THE COLISEUM, BRINGING A NEW SENSE OF PRIDE TO THE ENTIRE WASHINGTON COMMUNITY.[12]

Nixon was the good, loyal fan to the bitter end.

Not all the news in football was bad. The St. Louis Cardinals of football—at the time, the city of St. Louis had two professional teams named the Cardinals, one in baseball and one in football—named a new coach, Don Coryell. "Say, did you notice incidentally that another Whittier coach got to the big time," Nixon remarked in the Oval Office. Coryell had replaced Allen as the head football coach at Whittier College. Nixon was more than a little proud that a small Quaker college had produced two NFL head coaches and a president of the United States.[13]

The same day that the Redskins won the NFC Championship game, a tragedy that hit the baseball world moved Nixon in a personal way—a very personal way. In 1972 an earthquake devastated the country of Nicaragua. Roberto Clemente, an outfielder with the Pittsburgh Pirates and arguably the best player ever to wear the team's uniform, quickly started organizing efforts in his native Puerto Rico to send humanitarian relief supplies to the Central American nation. Clemente believed, just as Nixon did, that he as an athlete had an obligation to use his status in society in a positive and constructive fashion. "If you have a chance to accomplish something that will make things better for people coming behind you, and you don't do that, you are wasting your time on this earth," he told a Houston, Texas, audience. Toward the end of his life, to use the words of his biographer David Maraniss, that "line had become his mantra."[14]

Nixon was a real Clemente fan. In a conversation with Secretary of State William P. Rogers about the 1971 World Series, Nixon was just plain awed at Clemente's performance: "Oh, *my* God! Unbelievable. Unbelievable, really."[15]

Not content to simply donate a check or put his name on some letterhead,

Clemente made appearances on local Puerto Rican television and radio asking for donations and served as the chairman of the nonprofit committee established to raise the funds needed to buy the supplies. He often put in fourteen-hour days working on behalf of the Nicaraguans, and he was able to encourage enough donations to send two cargo planes full of supplies. The ballplayer, however, began to hear reports that the Nicaraguan army was intercepting and pilfering the cargo for their own benefit. Clemente decided to accompany a third shipment, in order to make sure that the donations reached their intended beneficiaries. Despite the concerns of friends and his wife, Vera, that the small plane was overloaded, he was determined to go. The president of the charter company that Clemente had contracted assured him the plane was safe, and to prove his point volunteered to go on the trip as the copilot. The plane was to have departed early on January 31, but repeated mechanical problems kept delaying their departure. Finally in the late afternoon, the plane took off, but the engine caught fire almost immediately. The pilot tried to turn the plane around and return to the airport, but it dropped suddenly and then exploded a mile and a half from shore. Roberto Clemente, "The Great One," was dead. He was thirty-eight. His body was never recovered from the wreckage in the shark-infested waters.[16]

Nixon was stunned. He sat down and wrote out a statement that the White House staff released that same day. "Every sports fan admired and respected Roberto Clemente as one of the greatest baseball players of our time," he declared. Clemente was Nixon's type of athlete, a man of strong character who understood his social obligations. The death of any gifted and talented individual was awful, but to have died in such a noble endeavor made his loss even more poignant. "In the tragedy of his untimely death, we are reminded that he deserved even greater respect and admiration for his splendid qualities as a generous and kind human being," Nixon observed.[17]

Other politicians offered their own tributes, following in Nixon's wake, emphasizing Clemente's significance beyond baseball. The congressional delegation from Pennsylvania took the lead. "Mr. Speaker, how does one eulogize a giant," William Moorhead, a representative from Pittsburgh, asked at the start of his statement. Congressman John Heinz III called the ballplayer "a hero in every respect." Representative Wilmer Mizell of North Carolina, a former Pirates teammate, noted that Clemente was popular "not simply for the things he did, but for the kind of man he was."[18]

The death of Clemente had such significance that commentary appeared on the editorial pages—not sports pages—of papers across the country, and these journalists expressed sentiments similar to those of the president.[19] The editors of the Washington *Evening Star* argued: "Even in the land of heroes that big-league baseball represents, Roberto Clemente was special." They added, "It doesn't help very much, of course, to say he died on a mission of mercy. His death in any case is sad and brutally abrupt."[20]

Sports reporters also reflected on his personality and skill. "The side of Roberto that everybody missed was that he was a kind man," *Los Angeles Times* sportswriter Jim Murray observed. "For all the deadpan (he rarely smiled), bluster and complaints (he never talked, he yelled), he was always available."[21]

A grassroots movement quickly developed on Clemente's behalf to waive the mandatory five-year waiting period for induction into the Baseball Hall of Fame. This effort culminated on March 20 when Clemente received 93 percent of the vote in a special election for induction, making him the first Latin American player to be honored with membership.[22]

As far as Richard Nixon was concerned, such recognition was fine, but Roberto Clemente was more than just a ballplayer—talented though he may have been—and deserved some greater tribute. "The best memorial we can build to his memory is to contribute generously for the relief of those he was trying to help—the earthquake victims in Nicaragua," the president wrote.[23] Voicing such sentiment was one thing, but acting on it was another. Nixon's record in athletic matters up to that point would suggest that the fans and family of "The Great One" had little reason to expect any action, but this situation was different. The president saw Clemente as an athlete who had understood that he had a duty to inspire others as a good role model and had died performing his obligations to society. It was Nixon's duty to be the good fan and to support him in his efforts, even if his labors had come to a premature end.

The day of the crash, White House staff members called the offices of the Pittsburgh Pirates and asked that the team send a delegation to Washington to meet with the president. On January 3, pitchers Steve Blass and Dave Giusti along with team president Daniel Galbreath flew down and met with Nixon in the Oval Office. The meeting was a short one. "They were very nice," Nixon observed. The president did most of the talking and amazed

Blass with his detailed knowledge of Clemente's career and achievements on the baseball diamond. The president admitted that he had been stunned to learn about the level of volunteer and humanitarian work Clemente had done. "I had never known of it; I had never seen any of it!" Nixon clearly enjoyed talking baseball with the players, but he had asked them there to honor an impressive man. Nixon offered to help establish a memorial fund in Clemente's name that the team should run. The two players and, most importantly, Galbreath agreed. "It seems to me that there isn't any question—Clemente, based on what he was doing when he died, the memorial to him should be to help the cause he died for," the president observed. Nixon made several suggestions about the legal and administrative requirements. He proposed that the team use the money to build a baseball stadium in Managua or a school either of which, or maybe both, should be named after Clemente. The school was something the team should really consider, because it got the effort out of the world of sports and into something a bit more substantial. That same day, in an example of his genuine interest in such a project, Nixon sent a $1,000 personal check to the Nicaraguan embassy on behalf of Clemente.[24]

After the meeting, the three Pirates returned to Pittsburgh and held a press conference to report on their conversation with Nixon. "One thing that impressed me was the President's genuine interest in this project in terms of the sincere suggestions he made," Giusti said. Galbreath indicated that the team would administer funds in honor of Clemente. "It seems that the President's effort and $1,000 gift to the Nicaraguan embassy was the natural rallying point." The editors of the *Pittsburgh Post-Gazette* agreed, calling Nixon's donation "most appropriate." They observed, "The President's reaction to the tragedy typifies a broad response both in this country and in Roberto's native Puerto Ric[o] where many memorial plans are underway."[25]

After the meeting, Nixon told one of his staffers that he wanted to contact NFL Commissioner Pete Rozelle and have his league run a Clemente television ad during the Super Bowl instead of a public service for volunteers. "This is very important," he said. "I consider it enormously important." The next day the president was disappointed at the results. He told Haldeman and Ziegler that the meeting with the Pirates and the Clemente memorial efforts was not getting much coverage on national television. They disagreed. The meeting got significant play on both radio and local television. It is also worth noting that Nixon's efforts to honor Clemente and continue his work also got significant newspaper coverage across the country.[26]

Others took up the president's suggestion to continue the man's work. Before the end of the month, Moorhead and six other congressmen introduced House Resolution 3841, a bill to commission the Treasury Department to mint special commemorative coins honoring Clemente. The Pittsburgh Chamber of Commerce would pay for the expense of striking the medallions, and all proceeds would go to fund the Roberto Clemente Memorial Fund that the Pirates agreed to administer. The endowment would finance the construction of a long-term Clemente dream—a youth sports development facility in San Juan, Puerto Rico—and the sending of more relief supplies to Nicaragua. Moorhead added that the bill would not result in the expenditure of any US tax money. The bill sailed through both chambers of Congress with few complications or opposition and was on the president's desk three and a half months later, awaiting his signature.[27]

Nixon made baseball history as this legislation made its way through Congress. On April 6, he became the first president to throw out the first pitch of the season outside of Washington, DC. True to his word, he was at the California Angels–Kansas City Royals game. With the Senators gone, he hoped to start a new baseball tradition. "In a very real sense it has historical significance," he told Zeigler the day after the Senators left Washington. "Here the President for 71 years has thrown out the ball in the Washington ball park—it ain't going to happen next time and I am not going to let it happen—but I will throw out the ball and every president should in his home ball park and mine's going to be Angel Stadium."[28] He had considered making the Dodgers his home team—the first professional game he had seen in person had been a Brooklyn Dodgers game—but Orange County seemed a safer bet. "We ought to get a pretty good, pretty safe reception, don't you think?" he asked Haldeman. "Yes, sir," the chief of staff replied.[29]

After the Clemente legislation finished its way through Congress, Nixon welcomed a small group into the Oval Office for a two-part ceremony honoring the ballplayer on May 14. In the first phase of the event, he posthumously awarded the Pirates legend the Presidential Citizens Medal, the second-highest award the US government grants to civilians. Nixon had signed an executive order back in 1969 creating the award, but Clemente was the first person to receive the medal. "I would like to read the citation, because it is better than any speech I could make, I think, with regard to Roberto Clemente," Nixon said. The citation the president read stated:

> All who saw Roberto Clemente in action, whether on the diamond or on the front lines of charitable endeavor, are richer for the experience. He stands with that handful of men whose brilliance has transformed the game of baseball into a showcase of skill and spirit, giving universal delight and inspiration. More than that, his selfless dedication to helping those with two strikes against them in life blessed thousands and set an example for millions. As long as athletes and humanitarians are honored, Roberto Clemente's memory will live; as long as Citizens Medals are presented, each will mean a little more because this first one went to him.[30]

Vera Clemente then hugged Nixon. Never the most physically graceful man, the president understood the emotion of the moment, even if he looked a bit awkward holding the medal while hugging her back. After waiting for Clemente to regain her composure, the president presented the award to her on her husband's behalf. "Let me say our only regret is that he isn't here," he said immediately afterward.[31]

The second stage of the ceremony was the signing of Public Law 93-33 (87 Stat. 71), which authorized the striking of a gold commemorative coin and two hundred thousand duplicates for public sale. "It was a bill which received, as you might imagine, overwhelming and unanimous support in both the House and the Senate," the president remarked. With Moorhead, Scott, Mrs. Clemente, and Senator Richard Schweiker of Pennsylvania standing behind him and witnessing, Nixon affixed his signature to the required documentation. He then turned to his left where Vera Clemente was standing and gave her the first pen he used to sign the bill. Moorhead, the two Pennsylvania senators, and Resident Commissioner Jaime Benitez of Puerto Rico all made brief comments after the signing. Nixon closed by noting that the people of Managua, Nicaragua, and San Juan, Puerto Rico, would benefit directly from the program, but the Pittsburgh region would also profit from supporting such a noble endeavor. "I think that is the way Roberto Clemente would have wanted it."[32]

After this ceremony, Nixon's interaction with sport dropped off dramatically. The Watergate scandal quickly came to dominate his attentions and energies. Six weeks before the ceremony with the Clemente family, Nixon, in an effort to neutralize the investigations into the break-in at the headquarters of the Democratic National Committee and the cover-up that followed, gave a televised speech announcing the resignations of Haldeman, Ehrlichman, Kleindienst, and Dean. On Haldeman's recommendation, the president appointed Alexander Haig, now a full general with four stars, as the new White House chief of staff. These personnel changes brought new operating procedures to the executive mansion and made Nixon more vulnerable as the months progressed. As Stanley Kutler notes in his book on the Watergate affair, "The President's April 30 speech fueled charges of wider scandal and stimulated pressures for a wider investigation." The new attorney general, Elliot Richardson, appointed a special prosecutor, and the Senate Select Committee investigating Watergate began holding hearings in front of a national television audience.[33]

That summer brought good news and a welcome diversion. On May 28, C. A. Smith, owner of the San Diego Padres, was facing a series of legal and tax problems of his own, and he announced that he had sold the baseball team to a Washington, DC–based syndicate. The group, led by the same Joseph Danzansky who had tried to buy the Washington Senators, planned to move the team to Washington.[34] The nation's capital appeared to be back in the baseball business.

Nixon played a small role in support of that effort. Shortly after the election, he and Danzansky attended the same church service, where the president said he would support any initiative designed to bring professional baseball back to Washington. In early September, Danzansky took him up on his offer and asked, through Rose Mary Woods, if the president would write a letter on his behalf to help convince league owners to approve the sale and transfer. Nixon was more than willing. "With time rapidly approaching for the Chicago meeting of the National League club owners, I just want to cast my own vote in favor of returning major league baseball to the Nation's Capital," he told league president Charles Feeney. "You can be sure all of us in the Washington metropolitan area would enthusiastically welcome a National League team."[35]

The league took longer than expected to approve the sale. During this delay, a local California group interested in buying the team emerged, and the City of San Diego was threatening to sue since its twenty-year lease with the team still had another fifteen years to run. League owners had little interest in the California syndicate, since the lead investor had been involved in a bribery scandal that had sent the governor of Illinois to prison. On December 6, Smith, who was in a dire financial situation and wanted out of baseball, forced the league to act. Faced with only one alternative, the teams in the league approved the sale and transfer, contingent on Danzansky and his group, indemnifying them for any legal action brought by the City of San Diego.[36]

That same day Nixon sent a telegram to Danzansky, congratulating him for bringing baseball back to Washington:

> I AM SURE I SPEAK FOR ALL BASEBALL FANS IN THE WASHINGTON METROPOLITAN AREA IN EXPRESSING HEARTFELT THANKS FOR YOUR UNSTINTING EFFORTS WHICH PLAYED SUCH A MAJOR ROLE IN THE TRANSFER.[37]

The deal soon fell apart. The NL gave the Danzansky syndicate fifteen days to secure the necessary financial arrangements and insurance. Baseball commissioner Bowie Kuhn admitted that this deadline was "an exceedingly short tether." The City of San Diego fought back, making it clear that their threats of legal action were more than rhetoric. Members of Congress from the area raised questions about federal support for the move. "There is more at stake in the future of the San Diego Padres than whether there will be major league baseball in San Diego next year," the editors of the *San Diego Union* declared. "The transfer of the Padres franchise to Washington, D.C., is based on promises by members of Congress that the team can count on subsidies of federal funds. This raises the very serious question of whether taxpayers throughout the country have any obligation whatever to provide funds for a Washington baseball team." A sportswriter from the San Diego *Evening Tribune* questioned the priorities of Congress, given the energy crisis, air pollution, and the weak economy. "The rest of the country may not be able to drive, breathe or eat very well. But in Washington, congressmen will be able to watch baseball." On December 21, the Danzansky group failed to meet the financial requirements of the National League. Eight days later, Smith announced that he had sold the team to a California-based syndicate led by Ray Kroc, chief executive officer of the McDonald's restaurant chain. The Padres remained in San Diego.[38]

While the lords of the national pastime wrestled with the fate of the Padres, the Watergate crisis moved to the forefront of national attention during the second half of 1973 and then exploded in October. Congressional hearings revealed that Nixon had set up an audiotape recording system in the White House, secretly recording his conversations with aides and guests. Congress and Special Prosecutor Archibald Cox wanted to listen to these tapes, and they had Nixon served with subpoenas to turn over the tapes. At the same time, in a separate investigation, prosecutors in Baltimore were accumulating evidence against Vice President Spiro Agnew on extortion, bribery, and income tax evasion charges, stemming from his time as governor of Maryland. After several weeks of getting only tepid support from Nixon, Agnew decided to resign. On October 10, as part of an agreement with federal prosecutors, he sent a one-sentence letter to Secretary of State Henry Kissinger, the head of the cabinet, tending his resignation, and personally appeared in a federal courtroom to enter a plea of nolo contendere to income tax evasion charges. In refusing to back Agnew, however, Nixon undermined his own interests. Given his unpopularity and reservations about his skill and competence, the departure of Agnew from the national scene removed a major barrier to the impeachment of Richard M. Nixon.[39]

Nixon reacted swiftly in naming Agnew's successor: House Minority Leader Gerald R. Ford Jr. Although he had almost no national following, Ford would have little difficulty getting confirmed. On October 12, just two days after Agnew's resignation, Nixon announced his decision to the nation. Confirmation took a little longer, but after a 92–3 vote in the Senate and a tally of 387–35 in the House of Representatives, Ford took the oath of office on December 6.[40]

Nixon's selection of Ford set the stage for the US government to have a significant impact on the administration of sport in the United States. Despite Nixon's limited interest in Olympic sports, the performance of the US team at the Munich games had been so disappointing that it demanded the attention of Nixon and his administration. The president's work to address this matter is one of the few times he tried to provide any policy leadership in the area of sports, but it came after earlier refusals to act and eventually became a victim of the Watergate scandal. In Germany, the United States finished second to the Soviet Union in the medal tally, 94–99. American athletes had a close showing only due to a greater number of silver and bronze medalists. The United States won only thirty-three gold medals, to the fifty-six of Soviet athletes. The United States also did poorly in sports that it had dominated in previous Olympics. The track and field team had its weakest medal showing in Olympic history, and the basketball team failed to win the Olympic tournament for the first time ever after a controversial loss to the Soviet Union.[41] In many tangible ways, the United States had lost the competition to the Soviets.

This outcome was too much to bear. The National Collegiate Athletic Association, frustrated with Amateur Athletic Union actions that often involved only NCAA athletes, voted on October 25 to withdraw from the United States Olympic Committee (USOC).[42]

Roughly two months after the games in Germany ended, the *New York Times* brought the root causes of the defeat to the forefront of public attention when it published a long article in its sports section about the composition of the USOC. The thrust of the piece was that the bloated, faction-ridden umbrella organization was responsible for the team's poor performance. The USOC had 714 members and often allowed the institutional interests of component organizations, rather than the needs of the athletes and advancement of the individual sports, to determine membership on key subcommittees. "We're like the old woman in the shoe," Arthur G. Lentz, executive director of the committee, admitted to a reporter from the paper. "We have so many children we don't know what to do." An even larger problem was the feud between the National Collegiate Athletic Association and the Amateur Athletic Union over control of amateur federations in several sports. These organizational problems were having a detrimental influence on US participation in international athletic events. The *Times* noted that UCLA basketball head coach John Wooden was never a contender for the Olympics coaching assignment despite having won seventy consecutive games and eight NCAA national championships. Wooden, in fact, recognized only seventeen of the forty-nine members of the US Olympic basketball committee. In an editorial that appeared in the paper the next day, the editors demanded action. "Now, rather than the eve of the 1976 Montreal Olympics, is the time to start reforming the outmoded and inept management of American participation in this world sporting event."[43]

The administration was familiar with the problems that plagued amateur athletics in the country, but had deliberately chosen to avoid involving itself in the matter. In 1969, George Frenn, one of the best shot putters in the United States and a Nixon supporter in the 1968 election, sent a telegram to the White House alerting the president to the jurisdictional disputes between the various IOC member organizations. Internal feuds absorbed most of the time and interest of the individuals leading these groups, and as a result, they had little time to provide US athletes with adequate supplies, coaches, and training facilities necessary for international competition. Frenn asked Nixon to use his prestige and influence as president to force the warring amateur athletic associations to reach some type of settlement. John Ehrlichman gave Charles Wilkinson the responsibility of responding to this note. His letter to Frenn was polite but vague: "Your concern in improving the conditions in the sport is shared by President Nixon." Wilkinson also informed Frenn that no one from the administration would attend a meeting he was trying to organize to address the disputes in amateur athletics: "Organizations with a vital interest in your sport would not be represented at the meeting." He, however, gave Frenn reason to hope that Nixon eventually might resolve the internal conflict within the USOC: "The Administration is carefully studying the situation in the hope that some means can be found to resolve the current jurisdictional disputes." The White House staff understood the issues Frenn was trying to resolve. Tod Hullin advised Ehrlichman that the administration should proceed with caution. He supported the idea of getting involved, but this was not going to be an easy issue. "This problem—NCAA vs. AAU—is a 'can of worms' and does not lend itself to compromise. In essence, you're looking for a nice way of abolishing the AAU." In the end, Nixon's lieutenants decided to do nothing. Frenn continued to send letters and notes to the White House, but lower and lower-ranking staff members signed the response letters.[44]

Frenn finally went public with his complaints after a poor American showing in a US-Soviet track meet in Leningrad that was televised live to most of Europe. In an interview with *Los Angeles Times* sports columnist Charles Maher, the shot putter blamed the AAU and the USOC. He complained that while in the Soviet Union, the American team stayed in housing that was almost unlivable. "The water that came out of the bathtub smelled. Can you believe that? You'd mix it with soap and it would turn black." American athletes were served beef that was salted for preservation rather than refrigerated. He lost almost twenty pounds during the meet. "If we had a really well-run program, we wouldn't have gone to Russia under those conditions. We would have sent a man over ahead of time to inspect the accommodations." What made this treatment even more galling were the luxurious accommodations the United States provided to Soviet athletes during events in the United States. "You look at the way we treat those guys when they come over here. Like when they stayed at USC, they got steaks and fruit and the whole bit. The President doesn't eat that good." He added that the amateur athletic associations never provided them with enough resources to train properly. He wanted the federal government to intervene, at least to the degree of forcing the private organizations that administered the amateur athletic movement in the United States to resolve their differences. "You know, when you compete against a Communist country, you're not just competing against athletes. You're competing against a government." He also told Maher about his previous efforts to get Nixon involved in the matter. "But he's a football fan," Frenn observed. "I'm not trying to put football down. But what the hell? There's an Olympic program, you know, and our national prestige hinges on how we do in the Olympics, not in football." Despite his public complaints, Frenn's letters to the White House still received pro forma responses.[45]

There was a great deal of animosity among athletic administrators following Munich. A week after the NCAA left the US Olympic movement, John B. Kelly Jr., president of the AAU, delivered a speech in Philadelphia in which he took direct aim at Walter Byers, the executive director of the NCAA, describing his conduct as an "intrinsic evil." The NCAA, for its part, issued a thirty-one-page booklet on the organizational dispute between itself and the AAU. "The basic issue is the self assumed and continued monopolistic control that the Amateur Athletic Union has claimed and tried to maintain over various amateur sports in the United States mainly through the U.S. Olympic organization."[46]

The poor US performance at Munich, the NCAA's decision to leave the USOC, and the continuing coverage of the *New York Times* had more influence than Frenn. An internal debate within the administration started on how to resolve these problems. On December 1, James A. Lovell, a member of the White House staff but better known as the commander of the failed Apollo 13 mission to the moon, informed Ehrlichman that he and Carson Conrad, executive director of the President's Council on Physical Fitness, wanted to meet with him to discuss the Olympic problem. "We share the widespread conviction that our present Olympic administrative structure is incapable of assuring proper American representation in future Olympic games. In fact, a further rapid decline in our international athletic fortunes seems inevitable, if this structure is not soon changed." The problems the United States faced were primarily of its own making. "Although our team unquestionably suffered from incompetent and biased officiating, this was exaggerated by television commentators. Most of our major failures resulted from mismanagement and internal bickering." Lovell noted that there was widespread interest in the issue and that members of Congress were talking about restructuring the entire nature of athletic competition in the United States. Since the USOC had a federal charter, the government could easily mandate changes that would solve the organizational problems in international athletics, after a commission recommended such limited legislation. "It is essential that this concern be steered in a direction which will help to resolve, rather than compound, our Olympic problems. The public is clamoring for leadership, and the time to act will never be better."[47]

To that end, the NCAA had left the USOC set up its own organization, the Committee for a Better Olympics, to lobby for change. Cecil Coleman, the athletic director at the University of Illinois, wrote Nixon asking him to create a presidential commission to resolve the Olympic problem.[48] He followed up with letters to individual members of Congress.[49]

Everyone on both sides of the issue wanted action. Both the NCAA and the AAU wanted a resolution to come at the expense of the other organization. Kelly wrote members of Congress, asking them to resolve the dispute. "We turn," he stated, "to you and the rest of Congress for implementations of a solution to these problems." He made it clear, however, that the problem was the NCAA. The Kheel Commission, a congressionally appointed binding arbitrator, had issued a solution to this crisis in 1968, and the NCAA had refused to abide by its ruling. The NCAA, on the other hand, declared "the AAU and its cronyism technique of maintaining control requires a new Olympic structure."[50]

The administration was clearly inclined to adopt Lovell's position as its own, but others on the White House staff spent a good deal of time debating the issue as the Watergate crisis came to dominate the attention of various senior administration officials. Haldeman, still chief of staff at the time, agreed with Lovell and had one of his subordinates, Frederic V. Malek, draw up plans for a presidential commission on the Olympics. Tod Hullin quickly objected. "Before we go forth with this proposal," he told Ehrlichman, "I think we should assess the advantages and disadvantages of Presidential commissions." He worried that a commission would be an expensive undertaking, and it could commit Nixon to an unwise course of action that would be difficult to repudiate. Hullin did admit, however, that if the commission made acceptable recommendations, "the problem is solved and in a p.r. sense the President comes off smelling like a rose." He thought such a scenario unlikely. Instead, he recommended that the president appoint a special consultant to examine the amateur athletic organizations and prepare a private paper for Nixon. Hullin nominated Wilkinson for this assignment.[51]

Nixon decided to act. On February 23, 1973, he met with Wilkinson and asked him to serve as the chair of the commission. "Do you believe in the Olympics?" the president asked.

"Yes, sir," the former coach replied. Despite the direct answer, Wilkinson was ambiguous in his feelings. He did not really want the assignment.

"I don't know if it is a winner or a loser," Nixon explained. "For me there are no winners. I don't give a damn. I am going to do it, because I believe in the Olympics."[52]

Despite Nixon's interest, a number of forces caused the administration to let the issue of a presidential Olympic initiative drift through the first half of 1973, and the Senate moved to fill the vacuum. In February, John Tunney, the California Democrat, introduced a bill to give the federal government the power to sanction participation in international sporting events, create a new sports foundation that would receive federal matching funds, and form a commission to study the organizational structure of the USOC and recommend reforms. The bill gained sponsors throughout the spring. On June 27 the Commerce Committee reported the bill out. As Dean, Haldeman, Ehrlichman, Jeb Stuart Magruder, the former deputy director of the Committee to Re-elect the President, and others testified in front of the Select Committee, the White House staff began trying to decide how to derail this legislation. William Timmons, the White House congressional liaison, and Ken Cole recommended that the President's Council on Physical Fitness and Sports be charged with studying the AAU-NCAA rivalry. "Amateur athletics is not a burning issue on the Hill right now," Cole argued, "so, hopefully, this initiative should be sufficient to shut off the bad legislation which otherwise will probably end up on the President's desk." This position, however, was a minority view among the White House domestic affairs staff. Most of his lieutenants who weighed in on the issue wanted Nixon to create a special board and charge it with making recommendations for the reform. Cole dissented. "The last thing we need is a new Presidential commission!" he argued. "The AAU-NCAA squabble is beneath the President's dignity, particularly at this time when he should be focusing on problems with a clear Presidential dimension."[53]

The biggest of these Oval Office–level concerns was Watergate. Nixon was in the middle of a ferocious battle for his political survival when he had to make a decision on the Olympic commission. At the same time, the crisis with Agnew was reaching a crescendo. On August 15, Jerry Jones, director of the White House Personnel Office, and Mike Harrigan, a consultant to the President's Council on Physical Fitness and Sports, sent two memos to Nixon that were a combined seven pages in length, arguing for the creation of a special presidential commission. "You will never get the President to focus on so many options, especially if they are stated in abbreviations," Kissinger advised when asked to sign off on the proposal.[54]

The Jones and Harrigan memos were in many ways the worst type of government document, lengthy in size but terse in language. Nevertheless, the two authors made their main point quickly: amateur athletics in the United States were fragmented and in disarray. "If these conditions continue, all experts consulted believe the U.S. will be embarrassed and beaten severely in the 1976 Games, or bi-centennial year." Even though the Olympics were a private, nongovernmental undertaking, Jones and Harrigan believed that resolving the troubles besetting amateur athletics was a legitimate issue for White House attention. "To suggest that Olympic sports problems are not of 'clear Presidential dimension' ignores the fact that international sports activity has been an important factor in initiating . . . and improving . . . international relations. When the teams and coaches dispatched as Ambassadors of goodwill are less than our best as a result of organizational mismanagement and conflict, U.S. image is damaged internationally." They also argued that the commission idea was good politics. "In addition, initiative by you at this time would place your name on the much-read sports pages and be consistent with your well documented interest in athletics." In light of the action in the Senate, the amateur sports groups would welcome this presidential initiative. Timmons and Cole's suggestion to get these various private organizations to work out their problems was a bad idea. "This approach would further ensure passage of the bad Senate Bill and never solve the problem since this approach has been tried before."[55]

The fate of the Olympic commission shows the degree to which the battle for control of the tapes came to dominate Nixon's attention and interest during his last year in office. In September Nixon approved the creation of a presidential commission, but nothing happened. The situation drifted again. As Stephen Ambrose notes, Nixon proposed a number of policy initiatives early in his second term. These ideas might have been designed primarily to help get him out of a difficult position, but "they bore his personal stamp, and they held great promise."[56] Nixon and his administration, however, had other, more pressing, concerns and let Olympic reform fade away.

The commission idea and the Olympic problems, however, refused to go gentle into the good night. One reason was that Harrigan continued to work on creating a presidential commission. He meet with Vice President Ford, whose background as a football player at the University of Michigan, gave him authority to speak on athletic issues. Despite his high title, Ford had few duties to perform and, as a result, could concentrate his attention on the matter. Furthermore, it was becoming increasingly likely that the Michigan politician would eventually become the next president of the United States. If Ford became interested in the matter now, there would be Oval Office–level interest in resolving the problem in the not so distant future. The meeting was an easy sell for Harrigan. Like Nixon, Ford believed that sports developed good character. "Athletes today, despite the times and all the terrible crises, are really the vanguard of our young leadership. I know that in terms of spiritual awareness they are way out in front," he wrote in an article for *Sports Illustrated.* He also believed sport was an important tool in the confrontation with the Soviet Union. "I don't know of a better advertisement for a nation's good health than a healthy athletic representation." He was explicit. He wanted to do anything, short of the US government taking over the US Olympic movement, to improve its performance in the next series of Olympiads.[57]

The threat of congressional action had not gone away, either. The Senate was still considering a bill to create a Federal Amateur Sports Board, which would be both bad policy and bad politics. "S-3500 is a disaster," Harrigan informed Ford. "It violates everything this Administration stands for and could easily become the precursor of a Federal regulatory body for sports."

Harrigan feared the proposed organization might actually hurt US standing in the international athletic community. "Such action would also be in clear violation of International Olympic Committee rules which prohibit domestic political control from determining who will govern amateur sports." The policies of the IOC had to be heeded on this matter, since it had to approve changes in administrative control. Lord Killanin had already publicly warned that this legislation violated the Olympic charter. Harrigan saw the danger in this proposed statute. "Unless the White House has an alternative (Commission) operating which will cause Congress to forego legislative action, at least in the House, at this time, I think the Bill will make it."[58] Other ideas that the Congress considered included creating a national sports foundation, which would be a partnership between the private and public sectors.[59]

Ford agreed with Harrigan. Ten months after he became president of the United States, he issued Executive Order 11868 creating the President's Commission on Olympic Sports. "The Federal Government has never attempted to direct amateur athletics in this country, nor should it," he stated in announcing the creation of the panel and limiting the recommendations it could make. The specific mission of the commission was to "determine what factors impede or prevent the United States from fielding its best amateur athletes for participation in the Olympic games." A total of twenty-one people served on the special committee, including Wilkinson. Harrigan served as the executive director. After an investigation that lasted a year and a half, the group issued a two-volume report just before Ford left office. This report led to the passage of the Amateur Sports Act of 1978, which amended the charter of the US Olympic Committee, converting it from an umbrella organization into a coordinating body for all Olympic-related athletic activity in the United States. The USOC, rather than suborganizations, would have the power to recognize the national governing bodies of the various Olympic sports.[60]

The bill that Nixon and Ford had done so much to initiate reached the White House after both of them had departed. The president in 1978, Jimmy Carter, apparently did not want to sign this legislation into law. He preferred an effort that focused on building up mass participation in athletics from which elite athletics would develop, but the momentum that the Nixon/Ford administrations and Congress had developed limited his options, and he signed the bill.[61]

The resolution of these sports administration issues lay in the future. The more immediate consequence of Ford joining the administration was that Nixon thought he could in a quid pro quo rid himself of Cox and the troubling investigation of the Watergate affair. On Saturday, October 20, the day after the subpoena deadline, Nixon fired Cox in what became known as the "Saturday Night Massacre." White House Press Secretary Ron Ziegler announced the dismissal just after 8 p.m. Nixon had set the timing of the announcement so that it would come after the deadlines of the Sunday papers to reduce press coverage, but the attempt failed and a firestorm followed. Editorials in a number of prominent papers began calling for the president to resign. The intensity of the criticisms that followed soon forced Nixon to relent and appoint a new prosecutor: Leon Jaworski. A graduate of the Baylor University Law School, Jaworski was a former president of the American Bar Association and a southern Democrat who had actively supported Nixon's reelection.[62]

The Watergate affair was for Nixon a fight for his political survival, but he was still a powerful force in American politics. The president remained his own best weapon. Even after the Saturday Night Massacre, he could win over the crowds that gathered to hear him. References to sport were few and far between, but when he did make these comments they still worked. In November, he journeyed through the South, an area where he still had strong support. His first appearance was at Walt Disney World in Orlando, Florida, for a meeting of the Associated Press Managing Editors Association. Nixon's answers appear to have been candid, but one comment came to haunt him for the rest of his life when he told the public, "I am not a crook."[63]

In Georgia he recovered. He spoke at a ceremony to mark the centennial of the law school at Mercer University that was also doubling as a ninetieth birthday party for former congressman Carl Vinson. The former legislator had two nicknames: "the Swamp Fox," which he shared with Francis Marion, a war hero from the American Revolution, and "Mr. Defense," which was far more relevant to this gathering. "This is Atlanta Falcon territory," Nixon told the crowd. "I followed the Falcons, and I guess you could call them the comeback team of 1973. They lost their first three and they have won their last six, and I have been thinking I ought to have a talk with [head coach] Norm Van Brocklin . . . " Laughter and applause from the audience drowned out the rest of the sentence. It was one of several that the president received that afternoon.[64]

At the end of his speech he announced that in honor of Vinson's fifty years in the House of Representatives, including twenty years as chairman of the Naval Affairs Committee and its successor, the Armed Services Committee, the next *Nimitz*-class aircraft carrier would be named the USS *Carl Vinson*. The former congressman then came forward and stood with Nixon for a long standing ovation. Vinson, in an emotional speech, expressed his gratitude to Nixon for coming. "No tribute could be more touching to me than that which is paid to me today by the presence of our distinguished President, Richard Nixon." He told the crowd how Lyndon Johnson had promised to hold a ninetieth birthday party for him at his Texas ranch, but the Texan's death earlier in the year had ended those plans. "Thank you, Mr. President, for redeeming Lyndon Johnson's promise made five years ago by giving an old friend a presidential send-off into the tenth decade of life."[65]

The appearance in Georgia was everything Nixon could have wanted. He was even gracious to his political opponents, which drew positive coverage. He had a few personal remarks for Governor Jimmy Carter and Senator Herman Talmadge, both of whom were harsh critics, and as he left campus he waved to students protesting his presence. A reporter for the *Atlanta Constitution*, a paper that had already called on the president to resign, observed, "The reception seemed to support claims of presidential aides that the adverse reaction has been from organized, partisan sources, and did not represent grassroots thinking."[66]

Later in the month, the president's lawyers delivered several tapes to US District Judge John Sirica, complying essentially with the subpoena that Cox had obtained. When the prosecutors requested additional tapes, Haig informed Jaworski that Nixon would provide no more material. He also refused to comply with a subpoena from the Senate Select Committee investigating Watergate. On April 11, the House Judiciary Committee issued a subpoena as part of its impeachment inquiry. In this case, Nixon could not ignore the summons; the House was carrying out a duty that the Constitution clearly authorized. On April 18, Jaworski obtained another subpoena for additional tapes. On April 29, Nixon announced that he was making transcripts of the desired conversation available. The material and language shocked the nation. Despite some heavy-handed editing, the president of the United States came across as cold-blooded, cynical, vindictive, angry, and two-faced. The transcripts indicated that the White House staff had deleted a number of expletives that Nixon thought might hurt him politically. The removal of these comments allowed the public to fill in the blanks with their own imagination. The result was the erroneous idea that Nixon swore heavily and used obscenities on a regular basis. While his language was rough, it was hardly obscene. Nevertheless, the damage had been done. Nixon had stripped the public of its belief in the sanctity of the presidency. Now editorials demanding his resignation or impeachment appeared even in publications like the *Los Angeles Times* and the *Omaha World-Herald* that had been long-time supporters.[67]

The transcripts proved unsatisfactory to both the House Judiciary Committee and the special prosecutor. In a conversation with Haig, Jaworski tried to make a deal. He offered to end his efforts to obtain the tapes if Nixon would turn over eighteen of the sixty-two tapes he wanted to hear. Nixon refused. He would not make any of the tapes available; there would be no deal. On May 20, Judge Sirica ordered Nixon to comply with the subpoena. The president's lawyers promptly appealed, setting in motion *United States v. Nixon*, a case that the Supreme Court would eventually decide.[68]

Despite the trend moving against him, Nixon continued to perform some of the ceremonial duties in the athletic arena associated with his office, albeit under constrained conditions. A member of the White House staff had suggested that he attend the opening day game of the Atlanta Braves. At the end of the 1973, Henry "Hank" Aaron tied one of the most hallowed records in baseball, Babe Ruth's career home run total. The staff member also proposed that Nixon go to the game with Babe Ruth's widow. The suggestion was a good one; there would have been little question of his reception. Few would have booed him on that day in her company. No one followed up on the suggestion. The person who received the memo did not know who Mrs. Ruth was or the context of the opening day games.[69]

On April 8, without Nixon in attendance, Aaron broke the record. The president called during the middle of the game, but was disconnected as a team official tried to transfer the call to the Braves dugout. He called again and this time got through. Aaron and Nixon talked for a few minutes, and the president invited him to visit the White House. "I suppose with all that he was going through, he welcomed the chance to talk with a ballplayer for a few minutes," Aaron remarked. "If I'd known he was such a baseball fan, I might have voted differently."[70]

A month later Nixon gave one last speech, in which he used sport to reach out to those listening. In May 1974, the president flew to Oklahoma to give the commencement speech at Oklahoma State University. A crowd of six thousand gave Nixon a warm and friendly welcome after the *Spirit of '76*—the renamed Air Force One—landed at Vance Air Force Base in Enid, Oklahoma. The president could still draw a crowd, and his audience of thirty thousand was the largest group to attend a commencement ceremony in the school's eighty-three-year history. People in the crowd stood and cheered when he arrived at the school's football stadium. "I am somewhat of a sports fan, and as some of you probably know, the university that is best known from Oklahoma in football is not the Cowboys, but the Sooners," he said. "On the other hand, I am aware of the whole realm of sports, and I am aware of the fact that, except for my wife's alma mater, the University of Southern California, the university in all the United States that has won more national championships across the board is OSU. So congratulations." A reporter for the Oklahoma City *Daily Oklahoman* noted that with that remark, "He played skillfully on the crowd."[71]

In fact, journalists were more than a little surprised at the warm greeting the president received in Oklahoma, and they made numerous comments about his reception. They found the response so surprising because conventional thinking held that the Watergate affair had bled Nixon of his popularity and political support. According to one correspondent, when Nixon was introduced, the crowd in the football stadium "responded almost as loudly as if it was watching a Cowboy touchdown." He also got a strong ovation when he urged the nation to move on from Watergate and to address the real issues that were plaguing the country. Reporters from the Oklahoma dailies covering the trip observed that many members of the White House press corps accompanying Nixon were stunned at the positive reception offered to the president.[72]

Then, in July, just as the Judiciary Committee began debate on the impeachment articles, Nixon led the nation in mourning one last time, after the death of Jay "Dizzy" Dean, a pitcher for the St. Louis Cardinals in the 1930s. A member of the Baseball Hall of Fame, he died in a Las Vegas hospital from heart failure after a severe heart attack. In a statement that the White House released, Nixon stated, "To my generation of Americans, Dizzy Dean will always be remembered as the blazing young fastballer who led the Gashouse

Gang of St. Louis to the pinnacle of baseball glory. To the young, Dizzy will also be remembered as the sportscaster who brought an extra touch of excitement and color to every game he covered. Dizzy Dean was indeed a man for all generations." In a letter to the baseball legend's widow, the president was even more gracious. "Dizzy Dean was an exceptional man and an exceptional American. As an ardent baseball fan I shared the admiration millions of Americans had for him as a professional athlete."[73]

Nixon's tribute was hardly an isolated one. For a moment that summer, the country stopped and took a moment from the Watergate crisis to praise, honor, and remember the pitcher turned sportscaster. "Dizzy died the other day at the age of 11 or 12. The little boy in all of us died with him," wrote Jim Murray of the *Los Angeles Times.* He went on to reflect how much Dean's upbeat, cheerful, and carefree personality helped the nation during the difficult days of the Great Depression. Senator Barry Goldwater agreed and entered the article into the *Congressional Record.* Democrats and Republican members of Congress from Dean's home state of Mississippi, where he lived in retirement, from Missouri where he played ball, and from a number of other states reflected on his status in American society. "Dizzy Dean was an institution," one said.[74]

Nixon lasted three more weeks. On the morning of July 24, the Supreme Court in a 8–0 decision ruled in favor of the special prosecutor in *United States v. Nixon.* The president's legal team had argued that "executive privilege" protected Nixon from having to turn over the records of his administration. The justices agreed with him, but only to a degree and not enough. For the first time in US history, the court gave official sanction to the doctrine of "executive privilege." Other residents of the White House had made this argument, and now the justices agreed with the concept, giving it constitutional sanction, but the justices also said this protection did not make the chief executive immune from criminal proceedings. The claims of any president had to be measured against the interests of justice. Nixon would have to turn over the tapes to Jaworski and his staff. That evening the Judiciary Committee began debating the various articles of impeachment in proceedings that were aired live on television. Three days later, on July 27, the committee adopted Article I, citing Nixon with obstruction of justice, by a vote of 27–11. Article II, asserting that the president had abused his power, passed 28–10 on July 29. On July 30, the committee voted 21–17 to approve Article

III, charging Nixon with contempt of Congress. Articles IV and V, charging him with waging an illegal war in Cambodia and income tax evasion, failed by the same vote of 26–12.[75] Several Republican had crossed lines party lines to vote for the first three articles of impeachment and several Democrats had done likewise on the last two, but overall the vote was more partisan than is generally recognized. If this pattern had held, Nixon might have been impeached by the full House of Representatives, but probably would have survived a trial in the Senate.

Such a possibility vanished on August 5 when the transcript of the June 23, 1972, conversation between Nixon and Haldeman became public. On the tape, Nixon instructs Haldeman to have the Central Intelligence Agency intervene in the Watergate investigation and warn the Federal Bureau of Investigations that the inquiry might lead to "the whole Bay of Pigs thing." Nixon said, "The CIA should call in the FBI and say, 'Don't go further into this case[,] period.'" After the details of the tape became public, all but one of the Republicans who had voted against impeachment said they had would now vote for Article I when the full House of Representatives took up the matter.[76]

Nixon foresaw as much. Before the judiciary finished voting on the articles of impeachment, he decided to resign. He knew what was on the tapes. The only question that remained was how much longer he could last in office. The answer: three and half days. On August 7, Nixon met with a trio of Republican leaders, Senator Barry Goldwater of Arizona, Senate Minority Leader Hugh Scott of Pennsylvania, and House Minority Leader John Rhodes of Arizona. The three were waiting for Nixon when he arrived at the Oval Office. The president, reflecting the stress and strain he was under, began reminiscing about past campaigns and how long-time political allies had abandoned him. Goldwater was the spokesman for the group, and was blunt: "Things are bad." Nixon asked how many votes he had in the Senate. "Ten at most," Goldwater replied. "Maybe less. Some aren't firm." Scott was a little more optimistic, saying there might be as many as fifteen. Nixon had less than half of the thirty-four that he needed to survive. Goldwater added that he was one of the undecided. Rhodes refused to give any advice when Nixon asked what options he had.

Nixon, however, had already decided. He informed his family and Kissinger that he was going to resign. The next morning he met with Vice President Ford and told him. At 9:01 p.m. that evening, in a speech that 110 million people watched on television and another 40 million listened to on radio—half the nation—Richard Nixon announced that he would leave office the next day.[77]

Nixon still inspired strong feelings. His speech took sixteen minutes to deliver, but television commentary lasted until after midnight. The next day Bowie Kuhn, commissioner of baseball, wrote Nixon: "I feel, and most strongly, that our country is marvelously blessed to have you now as its President. I know that the responsibilities are heavy indeed but there is not the slightest question in my mind that you will carry them out with consummate wisdom and skill."[78]

Later that day, Gerald R. Ford Jr., a member of the University of Michigan football teams that won the national championship in 1932 and 1933, took the oath of office. In his inaugural address, he declared, "Our long national nightmare is over."[79]

Conclusion

Some concluding remarks are in order as this book comes to an end. Sport is a chapter in the story of Richard Nixon. While it is difficult to understand Nixon, he let a lot of his guard down when he interacted with the world of sport.

It is also important to remember that Nixon was a politician of the first order. In the wake of the Watergate scandal, many people felt betrayed and deceived. Many of Nixon's opponents questioned the legitimacy of his victory in 1972, suggesting that the illegal initiatives of administration and campaign invalidated the outcome of that contest. If nothing else, this book shows that contention to be what it is: false. Nixon's popularity was real and genuine.

Nevertheless, the scandal consumed Nixon long before he left office. The crisis was so pervasive that it dominated the administration even in endeavors such as sport. Nixon's activities dropped dramatically in this area as he found himself in the greatest political battle of his life. With that point made, he had the power to charm crowds almost until the very end, and his administration initiated some important efforts to reform amateur athletics in the United States that would be sustained by the two men that followed him.

How significant is Watergate in the Nixon presidency? There was more to his tenure in the White House than this scandal. Nixon partisans and supporters have substantive reasons for admiring him. It is worth pointing out that this study is based on the assumption that there is more to Nixon than Watergate, but it also shows that despite the merits of his other contributions, Watergate is his strongest legacy no matter how much we might wish otherwise.

This crisis was only one during this era. Nixon was elected because of splits among the Democrats. He quickly set out to try and turn the Republicans into the party of the majority. The resistance among the Democrats was intense, which was understandable. Too much was at stake for it to be otherwise.

The social transformations that were taking place during the late 1960s and the early 1970s were traumatic to be sure, but they also require a certain amount of detachment. Despite the sound and fury of the era, more things stayed the same than changed. Certain changes, though, were taking place in political culture, and this reorientation was in response to those changes. Interest-group politics rose in importance during this era, with an emphasis on rights-oriented liberalism that saw salvation through the judiciary and the bureaucracy. Single-interest constituencies attached themselves to the Democratic Party, and their identity politics alienated many of that organization's traditional supporters. With issues like free agency in both baseball and football, the legal challenge of Curt Flood, and the television policies of the National Football League, Nixon had an opportunity to use sport to challenge the orientation of these groups to the Democrats with an emphasis on the open competition of the marketplace that played well with conservatives while at the same time appealing to the personal liberties that attracted many liberals. The problem was that judicial solutions to social problems did not sit well with Nixon and Republican voters. These transformations of society—and sport—were hardly inevitable. Curt Flood's fate makes that clear.

On a larger scale, this study shows that the trend to break the 1960s into several periods is superficial. As this argument goes the middle part were the "good" years; a period of excess followed in the later part of the decade, which led to a Nixon epilogue that was a conservative backlash to the excess of the 1960s. The problem with this take on the 1960s is that it exaggerates almost everything that happened. Although there was change, it was never revolutionary. Basic ideals held and what turmoil did take place rarely entered into large areas of society, like sport.

The purpose of this book, however, is not to study Watergate or any other political crisis. These pages try to answer the second half of one simple question: why did the American people despise and love Nixon? This examination of Nixon's interaction with the world of sport goes a long way toward finding an answer. He used sport to promote himself and garner positive publicity, which is never a bad thing for a politician. It is also important to consider the psychological rhetoric that he used. To Nixon, sport showed the importance of hard work and personal resiliency. Competition was the way to bring about personal and social improvement. It was also important—and this mattered to Nixon on a profound basis—because it allowed the individual to be part of a cause larger than one's self. It showed the importance of will over material resources. To Nixon this attitude was America at its core. There were conventional norms in America, and if one accepted them and played by the established rules, appropriate rewards would follow. This message played very well with the public.

Critics, though, might take a different view. It is easy to argue that Nixon had a dark personality made on the field of play. As many coaches state—including Nixon favorite Vince Lombardi—winning is the only result that matters. As a result, determination to excel can easily mutate into brutal toughness and a ruthless pursuit of victory. Sport encourages conflict, and it clearly rewards the "haves" at the expense of the "have nots."

When it comes to Nixon, the confounding thing is that both views are correct. Nixon was his own best weapon, and his own worst enemy. In the end, he was a one-man Greek tragedy. Although Nixon was gifted with great abilities, those same attributes were the seeds of his own downfall.

Such factors were as important to his popularity as were the programs and policies that his administration pursued. When it came to matters involving sport, Nixon was content to let the relevant policy communities be. He designed his tangible efforts to shape sport as a way to neutralize the efforts of his political opponents. He was more interested in shaping the values of American society than in focusing on policy options like some nerdy wonk.

This approach made sense. The average American can only rarely correctly explain the policies of a presidential administration, but most have general opinions about their president. The resident of the White House is expected to do more than be the chief executive of the US government. The office is bigger than its formal powers. The public expects the president to be a national symbol like the flag. Unlike the case in other nations, there are few ties that bind the American people together. As a nation of immigrants, Americans have no common religion, racial background, or cultural heritage. Defining what make the Americans a people is a tricky business and often depends on an intangible set of ideas and values. As a result, factors that bind the nation together are extremely important. Nixon's interest in sport made him understandable to the American people and added to their sense of community. Oftentimes, such feelings worked to his political advantage. But even for those Americans who were not political supporters, he seemed to be a cultural reference point that they could use in defining American society. His use of sport added to this unique function and for a while made him an extremely good president, but only for a while.

One final point. Politics is more than the study of a small group of political leaders and activists—elites by another name. It can be that, but at its best it is far more than that. Politics is a study of how a society works out its interests, and these often conflict with one another. Politics is something else as well—and Nixon understood this fact: politics is about the symbols and values of a whole society. In the end, nothing could be broader or more inclusive.

Aftermath

Henry Aaron played two more seasons in professional baseball with the Milwaukee Brewers after breaking the record for most runs in a career. When he left the game he had set a new record of 755. He was inducted into the Baseball Hall of Fame in 1982, his first year of eligibility. He works as an executive with the Atlanta Braves and holds another position with Turner Broadcasting.[1]

George Allen coached the Redskins until 1977. He coached the Chicago Blitz and Arizona Wranglers of the United States Football League in 1983 and 1984. In 1990 he took over the football program at Long Beach State University and guided the 49ers to a winning record. He died on New Year's Eve of 1990, five weeks after the season ended. He never had a losing season as a head coach. He was inducted into the Football Hall of Fame in 2002.[2]

Spiro Agnew became an international business consultant, but faced continued legal problems from a Maryland taxpayers' suit. After writing his memoirs *Go Quietly . . . or Else* (1980), he avoided public life. Although bitter that Nixon had not done anything to help him, he attended the president's funeral. He died from leukemia in 1996. He was seventy-seven.[3]

Frank Broyles retired from coaching in 1976. During his nineteen years at Arkansas, the Razorbacks won seven Southwest Conference titles, made ten bowl appearances, and had a win-loss record of 144-58-5. The *Arkansas Democrat-Gazette* named him the most influential sports figure in Arkansas during the twentieth century. He continued to work at the school as athletic director and oversaw the school's move into the Southeastern Athletic Conference. During his tenure as athletic director, he was responsible for making the Razorbacks more competitive in sports other than football, but was also responsible for the decline of the school as a power in college football. He resigned as athletic director in 2007. He was elected to the College Football Hall of Fame in 1983. He died in 2017 at age ninety-two.[4]

Avery Brundage ended his tenure as president of the International Olympic Committee in 1972. His wife had died in 1971, and he married a second time in 1973, to Princess Marianne Reuss-Kostritz. He died at Barmisch-Partenkirchen, Germany, in 1975. He was eighty-seven.[5]

Kenneth Cole stayed on the White House staff until 1975. After leaving government service, he returned to a career in business, working for a paper company in New Jersey and then starting a venture capital firm. He died from a heart attack in 2001. He was sixty-three.[6]

Archibald Cox returned to Harvard University. After Watergate, he worked with Common Cause to defend the constitutionality of campaign finance reform laws. He died in 2004. He was ninety-two.[7]

Joseph Danzansky retired as president of Giant Foods in 1977. He died in 1979.[8]

Harry Dent pled guilty in 1974 to aiding an illegal fundraising campaign only because he believed he would not get a fair trial. The judge agreed, calling him "more of the victim than the perpetrator" and placed him on one-month unsupervised probation. He practiced law for a time and was an advisor to Presidents Ford and George Bush. He and his wife helped build churches and orphanages in Romania after the fall of communism. He died in 2007 at age seventy-seven.[9]

Bob Devaney retired from coaching after the 1972 season with an overall record of 136-30-11. He continued to serve as the athletic director at the University of Nebraska until 1993. He died in 1997. He was eighty-two.[10]

John Ehrlichman was convicted of perjury, and obstruction of justice in 1975. He spent eighteen months in prison. After his release, he became a writer and a sketch artist. He wrote three novels that are loosely based on his experiences in Washington: *The Company* (1976); *The China Card* (1986); *The Whole Truth* (1979). His bitterness, which he directed at Nixon, is apparent in his memoirs, *Witness to Power* (1982). Of this book, a historian noted, "Kissinger may have lied to suit his purposes and direct history; Ehrlichman seemed to lie for the hell of it." Married three times, he moved to Atlanta and became vice president of Law Environmental. He died in 1999. He was seventy-three.[11]

Curt Flood lived outside the United States for several years following the loss of his court case. He wrote memoirs about his experiences in baseball, *The Way It Is* (1971). "I'm no martyr," he told the *New York Times.* "All the martyrs in history are dead." In the early 1980s, he established a youth baseball league in Oakland, his home town. "Now my work is so rewarding. I'm so happy you couldn't believe it." In 1993, the Rawlings Corporation finally presented him with his 1969 Gold Glove Award. "A strange thing happened to me on the way to receive that Gold Glove," he joked. "I went to Denmark and I guess Rawlings decided not to go there to present it to me. I think was just a logistical situation." He died from cancer in 1997 at age fifty-nine.[12]

Gerald R. Ford served as president of the United States until 1977, having lost the 1976 presidential election to Jimmy Carter. Upon returning to private life, he moved to California and wrote his memoirs, *A Time to Heal: The Autobiography of Gerald R. Ford* (1979). In 1978 his wife went through a chemical dependency recovery program. In 1980, he declined to run for president and rejected Ronald Reagan's offer to be the vice presidential nominee of the Republican Party. He oversaw the establishment of the Gerald R. Ford Library in Ann Arbor, Michigan, and the Gerald R. Ford Museum in Grand Rapids, Michigan. He also helped his wife create the Betty Ford Center. In 1994 the University of Michigan retired his football jersey number. In 1999 President Bill Clinton awarded him the Presidential Medal of Freedom and the University of Michigan named its School of Public Policy after him. He died in 2006. He was ninety-three, making him the oldest former president in US history.[13]

George Frenn appeared on the cover of the July 6, 1970, issue of *Sports Illustrated*. He placed twenty-seventh out of thirty-two in the hammer throw at the Munich Olympics. In 1982 he carried the flag at the Gay Olympic Games. He later called the act "the biggest mistake of my life." Frenn was not a homosexual and was helping a friend who was an organizer of the event, but there was a good deal of controversy in his life afterward. "All it did was wreck my reputation." He taught science in California high schools for thirty-two years before retiring in 2002. He died in 2006.[14]

Frank Gifford was inducted into the Professional Football Hall of Fame in 1977. He worked on *Monday Night Football*, leaving after the 1997 season. He wrote *The Whole Ten Yards* (1993). He died in 2015. "Frank Gifford was the ultimate Giant," John Mara, president of the New York Giants, declared. Three months after his death, his family revealed that he had suffered from chronic traumatic encephalopathy, a degenerative brain disease caused by repeated trauma to the head.[15]

Alexander Haig returned to active duty with the US Army in 1974 as the supreme allied commander of North Atlantic Treaty Organization forces in Europe. He retired from active duty in 1979, and in 1981 President Ronald Reagan selected him to serve as secretary of state. He served briefly as president and chief operating officer of United Technologies Corporation before joining the Reagan administration. He briefly ran for the Republican presidential nomination in 1988. He served on the board of many corporations and nonprofit organizations. He wrote two memoirs: *Caveat: Realism, Reagan, and Foreign Policy* (1984) and *Inner Circles: How America Changed the World: A Memoir* (1992). He died in 2010.[16]

H. R. Haldeman served eighteen months in prison for his part in the Watergate conspiracy. After his incarceration, he returned to Southern California and worked as a real estate developer. He wrote *The Ends of Power* (1978) and *The Haldeman Diaries* (1994), which was published posthumously. He died from cancer died in 1993. He was sixty-seven.[17]

Woody Hayes coached at Ohio State until 1978. The school fired him after he punched a player from Clemson University during the Gator Bowl. His overall coaching record was 238-72-10. He was inducted into the College Football Hall of Fame in 1983. Ohio State gave him an honorary doctorate in 1986. He was seventy-four when he died in 1987. Nixon attended his funeral and eulogized him.[18]

Tod Hullin remained on the White House staff, working on domestic policy until 1976. He then became a deputy secretary of defense for public affairs. He turned to a career in business after 1977, working primarily in corporate public relations. During his time at Time Warner, he was considered the highest-paid public relations executive in corporate America.[19]

Leon Jaworski never stepped into a courtroom after the Watergate scandal ended. "You just don't argue another case after you've argued 'The United States versus Nixon' before the Supreme Court," he said. In 1977 he returned to Washington to serve as a special counsel to the House of Representatives during the influence-buying scandal known as "Koreagate." He died of a heart attack in 1982. He was seventy-eight.[20]

Billy Kilmer played with the Redskins until 1978. "I didn't have any withdrawal pains when I retired from the Redskins," he later said. "I was lucky to play as long as I did. I told myself." In the early 1980s, he served briefly as the commissioner of the American Football Association, a minor league sports business. He lives in retirement in Fort Lauderdale, Florida.[21]

Henry Kissinger became the fifty-sixth secretary of state in 1973. He won the Nobel Peace Prize that year as well. He held this position under Ford, resigning in 1977. In 1983, President Ronald Reagan selected him to chair the National Bipartisan Commission on Central America. He wrote three memoirs about his experiences in Washington: *White House Years* (1979); *Years of Upheaval* (1982); *Years of Renewal* (1999). He is chairman of Kissinger Associates, Inc., an international consulting firm.[22]

Herb Klein left the White House staff in 1973, returning to journalism. He worked for the broadcasting concern Metromedia and then became editor in chief of the Copley newspapers. He retired from Copley in 2003, but hosted a local San Diego television program on current events, recording the last show the day before he died. An alumnus of the University of Southern California, he was elected to the university's board of trustees in 1982 and remained on it until his death. He died from a heart attack in 2009 at age ninety-one.[23]

Bowie Kuhn served as commissioner of baseball until 1984. He failed to receive the required three-fourths majority of team owners for an additional term in office. His tenure as commissioner was the second-longest in baseball history. He wrote memoirs about his time as commissioner, *Hardball: The Education of a Baseball Commissioner* (1987). He returned to the legal profession and received unwanted publicity in 1990 when he attempted to evade personal liability when his law firm went bankrupt. With creditors coming after his personal assets, he sold his personal residences in New York and New Jersey and purchased a house in Florida, a state which has unlimited homestead exemptions, and declared bankruptcy. He died in in 2007. He was eighty.[24]

Tom Landry coached the Dallas Cowboys until 1988, when he was fired. He had a career coaching record of 270-178-6. He took the Cowboys to five Super Bowls, a record for one coach and the most by one team at the time. Those five appearances included Cowboys victories in Super Bowls VI and XII. He was inducted into the Professional Football Hall of Fame in 1990. That same year saw the publication of *Tom Landry: An Autobiography* (1990). He died in 2000 at age seventy-five.[25]

Marvin Miller retired as executive director of the Major League Baseball Players Association in 1983. He wrote his memoirs, *A Whole Different Ball Game* (1991). "I don't know of anyone who changed the game more than Marvin Miller," Robin Roberts, a Hall of Fame pitcher and early organizer of the players' union, remarked. He died in 2012. He was ninety-five.[26]

George Murphy lost his reelection bid in 1970 despite the incident at San Jose. For a time, he worked as a lobbyist in Washington. He retired, living in North Carolina and Florida. He died in 1992 from leukemia. He was eighty-nine.[27]

Lindsey Nelson wrote his memoirs, *Hello Everybody, I'm Lindsey Nelson* (1985). In 1988 the Baseball Hall of Fame gave him its Ford C. Frick Award, which goes to a broadcaster who has made major contributions to the game.

Two years later the Professional Football Hall of Fame gave him its Pete Rozelle Award, which has similar criteria. He is a member of six Halls of Fame: University of Tennessee Football, University of Tennessee Baseball, the Cotton Bowl, New York Mets, American Sportscasters, and Baseball. In 1993 his alma matter, the University of Tennessee, named its new baseball stadium after him. He died in 1995. He was seventy-six.[28]

Louie B. Nunn served as governor of Kentucky until 1971. A year later, he ran for the US Senate and lost. He tried to retake the governor's mansion later in the decade and failed. He practiced law in Lexington, Kentucky, and stayed active in state politics until he died from a heart attack in 2004. He was seventy-nine.[29]

Joe Paterno coached two more teams in 1973 and in 1994 that went undefeated, but never received any portion of the mythical championship. In an ironic twist, his 1982 squad with one loss won the title over an undefeated but once-tied SMU team. The 1986 team went undefeated and won the national championship. He was the first football coach to receive *Sports Illustrated*'s Sportsman-of-the-Year Award. "The purpose of college football is to serve education," he once said, "not the other way around." In 2011 he became the winningest coach in NCAA history. Days after his 409th victory, the Pennsylvania State University Board of Trustees fired him for his role in the child sex abuse scandal involving his former defensive coordinator Jerry Sandusky. Paterno died from lung cancer two months later in 2012 at age eight-five.[30]

Shirley Povich officially retired from the *Washington Post* in 1974, but he continued to write for the paper until the very end. In retirement, he taught journalism at American University and was inducted into the writers wing of the Baseball Hall of Fame in 1976. He was the first sportswriter to receive the Fourth Estate Award from the National Press Club. "For a lot of years, he carried the paper and that's no exaggeration," former *Post* executive editor Ben Bradley said of Povich's career. Povich died in 1998. He filed his last column the day before he died. He was ninety-two.[31]

Darrell Royal oversaw the desegregation of the Texas Longhorn football team in the early 1970s. He retired from coaching in 1976 with a career record of 184-60-5. His teams won eleven Southwest Conference titles and appeared in sixteen bowl games. He remained at Texas as athletic director until 1980. He lived in retirement in the Austin, Texas, area until he died in 2012. He was eighty-eight.[32]

Raymond Shafer served only one term as governor of Pennsylvania, leaving office in 1971. That same year Nixon appointed him to chair the National Commission on Marihuana and Drug Abuse. The president rejected the commission's findings as too weak. From 1974 to 1977, Shafer served on the staff of Vice President Nelson Rockefeller. He practiced private law in Washington and Pennsylvania in the years that followed. He died in 2006 at age eighty-nine.[33]

Bob Short sold the Texas Rangers shortly after the team relocated to Texas. He ran for a seat in the US Senate from Minnesota in 1978 and lost. He died in 1982.[34]

Don Shula coached the Dolphins to another Super Bowl victory in 1974. He took the team to the championship game two more times with two different quarterbacks, in 1982 and 1984. In 1993 he broke the record for most career coaching victories in the NFL. When he retired after the 1995 season, he had a career record of 347-173-6. At that time, the Dolphins had the best winning percentage of any team in the league since the NFL-AFL merger. He joined the Football Hall of Fame in 1997 in his first year of eligibility. Since the end of his football career, he has represented a chain of steak restaurants that bear his name.[35]

Bart Starr ended his playing career in 1972 and became the quarterback coach for the Packers. In 1973, the team retired his number, making him one of only four Packers so honored. In 1974, he returned to the franchise as head coach and general manager. He held this position for nine seasons and compiled a record of 53-77-3 with one appearance in the playoffs. The team let him go after the end of the 1983 season. While he was coaching the Packers, the league inducted him into the NFL Hall of Fame. The religious organization Athletes in Action established the Bart Starr Award in 1988, which they give to NFL players that display outstanding character in the community.[36]

Charles Stuart left the White House staff in 1972 to begin a career in real estate development. He died from complications following brain surgery in 2007 at age sixty-nine. His first novel, *Bin Laden's Second Strike*, was posthumously published later that year.[37]

Tom Vandergriff continued to serve as mayor of Arlington, Texas, until 1977. He won election to the US House of Representatives in 1982, but lost reelection in 1984. The Texas Rangers inducted him into their Hall of Fame. He died in 2010 at age eighty-four.[38]

Carl Vinson became the first living American to have a US Navy ship named after him. On March 15, 1980, the USS *Carl Vinson* went into active duty at Newport News, Virginia. He died at age ninety-seven in 1981.[39]

Paul Warfield played with the Dolphins until 1974. He played one season in the World Football League before returning to the Cleveland Browns, where he had started his professional career. He was inducted into the Professional Football Hall of Fame in 1983, his first year of eligibility. He had a successful business career and was part of a group that bid and lost to own the second Cleveland Browns in 1998.[40]

Edward Bennett Williams ended up on the infamous Nixon enemies list. He turned down offers by Presidents Ford and Reagan to run the Central Intelligence Agency. He fired George Allen in 1978, but then lost control of the team to Jack Kent Cooke. He then bought the Baltimore Orioles of baseball. "I was president of the Redskins when they won the Super Bowl in 1983 and I was owner of the Orioles when they won the World Series that year. I don't think anyone has ever won a Super Bowl and World Series in the same season." He fought an eleven-year battle with cancer that he lost in 1988. He was sixty-eight.[41]

Ted Williams managed the Texas Rangers for their first season and then retired from baseball. He lived in Florida for many years, and made a living from the baseball paraphernalia business. In 1999, he was named to Major League Baseball's All-Century team at the All-Star Game. He threw out the first pitch at the game, and raised his cap to the crowd at Fenway Park, a gesture he refused to make while a player. He died in 2002. He was eighty-three.[42]

Ron Ziegler worked for Nixon in the immediate aftermath of Watergate. He then went on to a successful career in business. He joined the international engineering firm Syske and Hennessy as senior vice president and managing director of international services. He then became president of the National Association of Truck Stop Operators, a trade organization based in the Washington, DC, area. He then became the president and chief executive officer of the National Association of Chain Drug Stores, also based in the Washington area. He retired in 1998. He died from a heart attack in 2003 at age sixty-three.[43]

Richard Nixon began work at rehabilitating his name and reputation after his resignation. Sport was part of that effort. Emotionally, he found solace in the game of golf. He still loved baseball, though. In 1985 he mediated a dispute between the major leagues and the umpires' union over pay for the expanded playoff format that baseball adopted. Both sides accepted his solution of increasing pay 40 percent for an increased work load of 40 percent. He also advised Bowie Kuhn when the former commissioner of baseball was lobbying the International Olympic Committee to turn baseball into an Olympic sport. In 1992, on the twentieth anniversary of his historic baseball All-Star selections, he and his son-in-law, David Eisenhower, released another set of lists. This time they had six lists instead of four. He even became a fan of basketball and rooted for his alma matter, Duke University, during the early 1990s when it dominated college basketball. Following a loss to the University of Arizona, he was once again the good fan. He visited the Blue Devils' locker room and offered words of consolation to Christian Laettner after he had missed some crucial free throws. Following his death, several sportswriters reflected on his love of sport, and James Dodson wrote in *Golf Magazine*, "Nixon was one of us."[44]

Appendix A
Major League Baseball Centennial Greatest Players

Greatest Players of All Time

1B	Lou Gehrig
2B	Rogers Hornsby
SS	John "Honus" Wagner
3B	Harold "Pie" Traynor
C	Mickey Cochrane
OF	Babe Ruth
OF	Joe DiMaggio
OF	Ty Cobb
Pitcher (right-handed)	Walter Johnson
Pitcher (left-handed)	Robert "Lefty" Grove
Manager	John McGraw
Greatest Player Ever	Babe Ruth

Greatest Living Players

B	George Sisler and Stan Musial (tie)
2B	Charlie Gehringer
SS	Joe Cronin
3B	Harold "Pie" Traynor
C	Bill Dickey
OF	Ted Williams
OF	Joe DiMaggio

(*continued on the next page*)

Greatest Living Players

OF	Willie Mays
Pitcher (right-handed)	Bob Feller
Pitcher (left-handed)	Robert "Lefty" Grove
Manager	Casey Stengel
Greatest Living Player	Joe DiMaggio

Source: *New York Times*, July 22, 1969.

Appendix B

US Supreme Court List of Greatest Players in Baseball History

Ty Cobb
Babe Ruth
Tris Speaker
Walter Johnson
Henry Chadwick
Eddie Collins
Lou Gehrig
Grover Cleveland Alexander
Rogers Hornsby
Harry Hooper
Goose Goslin
Jackie Robinson
Honus Wagner
Joe McCarthy
John McGraw
Deacon Phillippe
Rube Marquard
Christy Mathewson
Tommy Leach
Big Ed Delahanty
Davy Jones
Germany Schaefer
King Kelly
Big Dan Brouthers
Wahoo Sam Crawford
Wee Willie Keeler
Big Ed Walsh
Jimmy Austin
Fred Snodgrass
Satchel Paige
Hugh Jennings
Fred Merkle
Iron Man McGinnity
Three-Finger Brown
Harry and Stan Coveleski
Connie Mack
Al Bridwell
Red Ruffing
Amos Rusie
Cy Young
Smokey Joe Wood
Chief Meyers
Chief Bender
Bill Klem
Hans Lobert
Johnny Evers
Joe Tinker
Roy Campanella

(*continued on the next page*)

Miller Huggins
Rube Bressler
Dazzy Vance
Edd Roush
Bill Wambsganss
Clark Griffith
Branch Rickey
Frank Chance
Cap Anson
Nap Lajoie
Sad Sam Jones
Bob O'Farrell
Lefty O'Doul
Bobby Veach
Willie Kamm
Heinie Groh
Lloyd and Paul Waner
Stuffy McInnis
Charles Comiskey
Roger Bresnahan
Bill Dickey
Zack Wheat
George Sisler
Charlie Gehringer
Eppa Rixey
Harry Heilmann
Fred Clarke
Dizzy Dean
Hank Greenberg
Pie Traynor
Rube Waddell
Bill Terry
Carl Hubbell
Old Hoss Radbourne
Moe Berg
Rabbit Maranville
Jimmie Foxx
Lefty Grove

Source: *Flood v Kuhn* [407 US 258], 32 L Ed 2d 728, 92 S Ct 2099.

Appendix C
Richard Nixon's 1972 Historic Baseball All-Star Selections

Prewar		Postwar	
		American League	
1B	Lou Gehrig	1B	Harmon Killebrew
2B	Charlie Gehringer	2B	Nellie Fox
3B	Red Rolfe	3B	Brooks Robinson
SS	Joe Cronin	SS	Lou Boudreau
OF	Babe Ruth	OF	Ted Williams
OF	Joe DiMaggio	OF	Mickey Mantle
OF	Al Simmons	OF	Frank Robinson
C	Mickey Cochrane	C	Yogi Berra
C	Bill Dickey	C	Elston Howard
P	Satchel Paige	P	Bob Lemon
P	Herb Pennock	P	Bob Feller
P	Lefty Grove	P	Early Wynn
P	Red Ruffing	P	Whitey Ford
P	Bobo Newsom	P	Dave McNally
		Reserves	
IF	Jimmie Foxx	IF	Bobby Richardson
IF	Hank Greenberg	IF	Luis Aparicio
IF	Luke Appling	OF	Al Kaline
OF	Goose Goslin	OF	Carl Yastrzemski
OF	Harry Heilmann	OF	Tony Oliva
P	Johnny Murphy	P	Hoyt Wilhelm

(*continued on the next page*)

Prewar		Postwar	
	Manager		
	Connie Mack		Casey Stengel
	National League		
1B	Bill Terry	1B	Stan Musial
2B	Rogers Hornsby	2B	Jackie Robinson
3B	Pie Traynor	3B	Eddie Mathews
SS	Arky Vaughan	SS	Ernie Banks
OF	Paul Waner	OF	Hank Aaron
OF	Mel Ott	OF	Willie Mays
OF	Hack Wilson	OF	Roberto Clemente
C	Ernie Lombardi	C	Roy Campanella
C	Gabby Hartnett	C	Johnny Bench
P	Carl Hubbell	P	Sandy Koufax
P	Dizzy Dean	P	Warren Spahn
P	Bucky Walters	P	Juan Marichal
P	Mort Cooper	P	Bob Gibson
P	Burleigh Grimes	P	Robin Roberts
	Reserves		
IF	Frankie Frisch	IF	Maury Wills
IF	Marty Marion	IF	Dick Groat
OF	Ducky Medwick	IF	Willie McCovey
OF	Chuck Klein	IF	Ken Boyer
OF	Edd Roush	OF	Duke Snider
P	Mace Brown	P	Roy Face
	Manager		
	Branch Rickey		Walter Alston

Source: Nixon manuscript, June 27, 1972, Folder RE2 Baseball-Softball 1/1/71, Box 3, Recreation-Sports Files, Subject Files, White House Central Files, Nixon Presidential Project, National Archives, College Park, MD.

Appendix D

Richard Nixon's 1992 Historic Baseball All-Star Selections

	American League		National League
	Yankee Era (1925–1959)		
1B	Lou Gehrig	1B	Johnny Mize
2B	Charlie Gehringer	2B	Jackie Robinson
3B	George Kell	3B	Eddie Matthews
SS	Phil Rizzuto	SS	Ernie Banks
OF	Babe Ruth	OF	Stan Musial
OF	Joe DiMaggio	OF	Willie Mays
OF	Ted Williams	OF	Mel Ott
DH	Jimmie Foxx	DH	Rogers Hornsby
C	Mickey Cochrane	C	Roy Campanella
P	Lefty Grove	P	Carl Hubbell
P	Bobo Newsom	P	Dizzy Dean
P	Bob Feller	P	Warren Spahn
P	Early Wynn	P	Robin Roberts
P	Satchel Paige	P	Elroy Face
	Manager		
	Casey Stengel		Branch Rickey
	The Expansion Era (1960 1991)		
1B	Harmon Killebrew	1B	Willie McCovey
2B	Bobby Grich	2B	Joe Morgan
3B	Brooks Robinson	3B	Mike Schmidt

(*continued on the next page*)

	American League		National League
SS	Luis Aparicio	SS	Maury Wills
OF	Carl Yastrzemski	OF	Hank Aaron
OF	Mickey Mantle	OF	Lou Brock
OF	Reggie Jackson	OF	Roberto Clemente
DH	Rod Carew	DH	Pete Rose
C	Thurmon Munson	C	Johnny Bench
P	Catfish Hunter	P	Sandy Koufax
P	Jim Palmer	P	Juan Marichal
P	Whitey Ford	P	Bob Gibson
P	Luis Tiant	P	Steve Carlton
P	Rollie Fingers	P	Tom Seaver
	Manager		
	Billy Martin		Walter Alston
	Currently Active Players (1992)		
1B	Don Mattingly	1B	Will Clark
2B	Roberto Alomar	2B	Ryne Sandberg
3B	George Brett	3B	Howard Johnson
SS	Cal Ripken Jr.	SS	Ozzie Smith
OF	Rickey Henderson	OF	Tony Gwynn
OF	Ken Griffey, Jr.	OF	Darryl Strawberry
OF	Kirby Puckett	OF	Andre Dawson
DH	Jose Canesco	DH	Bobby Bonilla
C	Carlton Fisk	C	Gary Carter
P	Nolan Ryan	P	Dwight Gooden
P	Jack Morris	P	Bret Saberhagen
P	Roger Clemens	P	David Cone
P	Rich Gossage	P	Rob Dibble
P	Dennis Eckersley	P	Lee Smith
	Manager		
	Tony La Russa		Tommy Lasorda

Source: *Los Angeles Times*, July 16, 1992.

Appendix E
Nixon and Sports Time Line

1969

January 20

Richard M. Nixon becomes president of the United States of America.

February 6

Vince Lombardi becomes the new executive vice president and head coach of the Washington Redskins football team, controlling the major aspects of team operations. *Washington Post* sports columnist Shirley Povich calls the selection of the new coach "Washington's greatest transfer of power since Jan. 20." At the press conference, announcing his arrival, Lombardi remarks, "If the President is a pro football fan, he ought to be out to our games here in his home city."

February 13

Ted Williams becomes the manager of the Washington Senators baseball club.

April 7

Nixon throws out the first ball of the season at a Washington Senators–New York Yankees game at Robert F. Kennedy Stadium. While trying to throw the ball, the president dropped the ball, committing the first error of the 1969 season. The Yankees won the game, 8–4.

May 3

Nixon attends the Kentucky Derby at Churchill Downs in Louisville, Kentucky. This is the first time that a sitting US president has attended the race. Majestic Prince wins the contest.

May 24

Nixon informs White House chief of staff H. R. "Bob" Haldeman that he wants to hold a dinner or reception for the players in the Baseball All-Star Game that Washington, DC, will host in July.

June 11

Nixon attends a Washington–Oakland A's game at RFK Stadium. Reggie Jackson, an outfielder for Oakland, hits two home runs that day, keeping him on pace to break the eight-year-old record of Roger Maris for most home runs in a season.

June 16

The president sends a telegram thanking Jackson for hitting the home runs while he was in the ballpark.

July 14

Nixon signs a baseball from the Hall of Fame that displays the signatures of nine other presidents. "This is the most famous autographed baseball," he remarks in an Oval Office ceremony.

July 21

As part of the centennial celebrations of professional baseball, Major League Baseball holds a dinner at the Sheraton Park Hotel in Washington and names the greatest players at various positions, presenting these individuals or their next of kin with gold trophies.

July 22

Nixon hosts a White House reception for members of the Baseball Hall of Fame, the widows of deceased members, various Major League Baseball officials, and the players in the All-Star Game. In ceremonies before the reception, Warren Giles, president of the National League, presents Nixon with a gold lifetime pass to National League games. Baseball Commissioner Bowie Kuhn gives the president a trophy, similar to the type presented the night before, naming him "Baseball's Number One Fan." Thunderstorms and heavy rain start during the reception, forcing the postponement of the game. Nixon leaves that evening to welcome home the astronauts of Apollo 11.

July 23

Vice President Spiro Agnew throws out the first ball at the All-Star Game.

July 24

Nixon meets with the crew of Apollo 11 aboard the USS *Hornet*. Flight commander Neil Armstrong apologizes for making the president miss the All-Star Game. Nixon is surprised he knew the game was rained out.

September 27

Rutgers defeats Princeton in the one-hundredth anniversary game of college football, 29–0.

October 1

The Washington Senators end their season with a 86-76 record. This is the first winning mark in the history of this expansion franchise.

October 4

Nixon attends a Miami Dolphins–Oakland Raiders game at the Orange Bowl in Miami, Florida. The final score is a 20–20 tie. This contest is the first and only time that a president of the United States attends an American Football League game.

October 6

Harry Dent, the White House liaison with Southern members of Congress, suggests to Haldeman that the president attend a football game in the South as a good way to get regional publicity, given the importance of the sport in the region.

October 20

The Associated Press names Ted Williams American League Manager of the Year.

November 15

The Moratorium, an antiwar protest rally of 250,000, gathers in Washington. Nixon spends the day watching the Ohio State–Purdue football game. Ohio State wins, 42–14.

November 16

President Nixon sits in the stands at Robert F. Kennedy Stadium and becomes the first US president to attend a regular season National Football League game while in office. Washington loses to the Dallas Cowboys, 41–28.

November 22

The University of Michigan football team defeats defending national champion and top-ranked Ohio State, 24–12. Nixon cuts a budget meeting short to watch the game and has a television put in an office so he can continue to watch the game during a dental appointment. In his diary, H. R. Haldeman calls it a "pretty funny day."

December 1

Nixon decides he will attend the Texas-Arkansas game, a contest between the first and second spots in the Associated Press poll of college football, setting up a climactic match between the schools in the last weekend of the regular season. He also decides to present a presidential plaque naming the winner of the game the number-one team in the centennial year of college football. Several hours later, he receives telegrams from John Hammerschmidt, a member of the US House of Representatives from Arkansas, and John Mooney, president of the Football Writers Association of America and sports editor of the *Salt Lake Tribune*, inviting him to watch the game in person.

December 2

The White House announces that the president will attend the Texas-Arkansas game and present a national championship trophy to the winner. Press accounts attribute the decision to the Mooney telegram.

December 5

Governor Raymond Shafer of Pennsylvania holds a press conference and sends a telegram to the White House protesting Nixon's decision to award the national title to the Texas-Arkansas winner. The Penn State Nittany Lions are also undefeated and have a longer winning streak than either team. Shafer claims it would be better to wait until after the bowl games are played to determine who is the number-one team in college football. In response to these protests, White House press secretary Ron Ziegler announces that Nixon will present a plaque to Penn State for having the longest winning streak in college football.

December 6

Nixon travels to Arkansas to watch the Texas-Arkansas game. Poor weather causes him to arrive just after kickoff. Arkansas takes a 7–0 lead into halftime. In a television appearance during the intermission, the president predicts that the Texas offense is strong enough to score once or twice. The Longhorns score twice in the fourth quarter and win, 15–14. After the game, Nixon goes to the Texas locker room and presents head coach Darrell Royal with a plaque that awards the 1969 national championship to the Longhorns. He also visits the Razorback dressing room and talks with the team before returning to Washington.

After the game, Paterno announces he will not accept Nixon's award. "It would seem a waste of his very valuable time to present a plaque for something we already have undisputed possession of—the nation's longest winning streak," the coach explained. "To accept any other plaque prior to the bowl games, which will determine the final number one team, would be a disservice to our squad, to Pennsylvania, to the East, which we represent and perhaps, most important, to Missouri, which may be the best football team in the country." (Penn State will play Missouri in the Orange Bowl on January 1.)

December 7

The National Football Foundation and Hall of Fame awards the MacArthur Bowl, its national championship trophy, to the Texas Longhorns.

December 8

United Press International awards its national title to the Texas Longhorns.

At a press conference that evening, Nixon jokes that he might have made a mistake in trying to play a role in determining the national championship.

December 9

In a speech at the National Football Foundation and Hall of Fame dinner, Nixon remarks that Penn State deserves a portion of the national title. He also states that Texas deserves to be number one, because the team refused to give up even though Arkansas had a strong lead. At the dinner, Royal promises Nixon that the Longhorns will win the Cotton Bowl and secure their claim to the national title.

December 10

Penn State receives its third straight Lambert Trophy, which goes to the best team in the East matching the previous mark for consecutive awards. "Any team that can tie the record of the Army juggernaut of 1944-45-46 has carved for itself an enduring place in the annals of football greatness," Nixon states in a telegram to Paterno. In accepting the award, Paterno says, "I couldn't feel better about receiving this trophy if it were presented on television by the President of the United States."

December 21

The Washington Redskins end their season with a 7-5-2 record. This mark is the first winning season for the team in fourteen years.

1970

January 1

The Texas Longhorns defeat Notre Dame in the Cotton Bowl, 21–17, ending the season with a perfect record. Penn State defeats Missouri in the Orange Bowl, 10–3, also ending their season with a perfect mark. Nixon calls Royal and congratulates him on the victory.

January 3

The Football Writers Association of America gives Texas its Grantland Rice Award, and with it the organization's national championship title. The Associated Press releases its final poll, with Texas ranked first and Penn State second, giving Texas the Associated Press national title.

March 2

Haldeman assigns Chuck Stuart, a member of his staff, responsibility for coordinating the efforts of the federal government to support the bid of Los Angeles to host the 1976 Olympic summer games.

April 6

David Eisenhower, Nixon's son-in-law, throws out the first ball of the 1970 season at a Senators–Detroit Tigers game at Robert F. Kennedy Stadium. The president arrives during the fifth inning of the game after the US Senate voted 51–45 to reject his nomination of Judge G. Harrold Carswell to the US Supreme Court. The Tigers win, 5–0.

May 12

The International Olympic Committee awards the 1976 summer games to Montreal and the winter games to Denver, Colorado.

July 14

After making appearances in Louisville, Kentucky, Nixon goes to Cincinnati, Ohio, and throws out the first ball of the Major League Baseball All-Star Game. Robert Taft Jr., a representative from Ohio in the US House of Representatives and a candidate for the US Senate, sits with him at the game. Four young girls make news when they approach Nixon in his seat and get his autograph. The National League wins in a 5–4 game. Carl Yastrzemski, an outfielder for the Boston Red Sox, is named the Most Valuable Player of the game.

September 3

Washington Redskins' head coach Vince Lombardi dies from cancer.

October 2

A plane carrying members of the Wichita State University football team, their coaches, and members of the school's athletic staff crashes in Colorado. Of the forty people on board the plane, thirty-one die.

October 3

Nixon sends Wichita State president Clark Ahlberg a telegram from Air Force One. "Our thoughts and prayers are with all of you at this sad hour," he states.

October 17

Nixon travels to Green Bay, Wisconsin, to speak at a testimonial dinner in honor of Green Bay Packers quarterback Bart Starr.

November 14

The plane carrying the football team of Marshall University crashes, killing thirty-seven.

November 17

Nixon sends a cable to Donald Dedmon, president of Marshall University. He offers his condolences on the crash: "Our thoughts are with those who grieve the loss of their loved ones. We pray that God may arm them with the strength and courage to bear the anguish of a misfortune that touches the hears of all their fellow citizens."

December 9

Nixon contributes a $500 check to a fund for survivors of the Wichita State plane crash.

1971

January 1

Nebraska defeats LSU in the Orange Bowl, 17–12. The Cornhuskers end their season with an undefeated record.

January 6

George Allen becomes the head coach of the Washington Redskins, ending the tenure of interim coach Bill Austin.

January 13

While giving a speech at the University of Nebraska, Nixon presents head football coach Bob Devaney with a presidential plaque certifying that the Cornhuskers are the 1970 national champions.

April 13

In a visit to the White House, Carl Yastrzemski of the Boston Red Sox gives Nixon the All-Star Game MVP trophy he won in 1970.

July 1

Roger Ailes, a Republican campaign strategist, writes Larry Higby, an administrative aide to White House chief of staff H. R. "Bob" Haldeman, and suggests that it might help Nixon's public image if the president takes some action to help the Washington Senators with their financial difficulties, to make their reported move out of Washington unnecessary.

July 30

Nixon travels to Canton, Ohio, home of the Professional Football Hall of Fame. That evening he gives the keynote speech at a banquet honoring seven new inductees into the Hall of Fame.

July 31

An interview Nixon gave the day before with sports commentator Frank Gifford of the ABC television network is aired during halftime of the NFL Hall of Fame game.

August 16

Senator William B. Spong Jr. of Virginia writes Nixon and asks him to meet with Shirley Povich, a sports columnist for the *Washington Post*, about blocking the move of the Washington Senators.

August 25

Martie Zad, sports editor of the *Washington Post*, writes to Nixon, asking the president to agree to a short meeting with himself and Povich in the hope that they can invoke the prestige of the presidency to prevent the relocation of the Washington Senators.

September 7

Herbert Klein, White House director of communications, writes Zad and informs him it would be "inappropriate" for the president to intervene in the financial affairs of a professional baseball team.

September 19

Nixon publicly states that it would be "heartbreaking" if the Washington Senators move to Dallas, Texas.

September 21

In a 10–2 vote, the American League approves the move of the Senators to Arlington, Texas, a suburb between Dallas and Fort Worth. White House press secretary Ron Ziegler announces that the president is "distressed" about the Senators' departure and will consider the California Angels his home team now.

September 30

The Senators play their last game in Washington and are forced to forfeit the game to the Yankees when fans storm onto the field trying to take souvenirs from the game.

November 21

The Washington Redskins lose to the Dallas Cowboys, 13–0. The crowd in Robert F. Kennedy Stadium boos the home team.

November 23

Nixon makes an unannounced visit to the Washington Redskins at their practice facilities at Redskins Park, Virginia. He tells the team to ignore those who booed. "A great majority of people in this town back the team," he remarks. "You have been good for this city."

That same day the Washington Senators, now located in Arlington, Texas, announce they are changing their name to the Texas Rangers.

In a phone conversation with Nixon, Allen tells the president that he has designed a play that he is going to use, but will tell the team that Nixon designed it for them. "Oh, boy. Well, okay," Nixon responds.

December 13

The Redskins defeat the Los Angeles Rams, 38–24, and make the playoffs for the first time since 1945.

December 26

The Washington Redskins lose in the playoffs to the San Francisco 49ers, 24–20. The Redskins lose thirteen yards using the play that Allen says the president designed. After the game, Nixon calls the coach and tells him that the entire city is proud of the team.

1972

January 3

Nixon calls Miami Dolphins' head coach Don Shula at 1:30 a.m. in Miami—10:30 p.m. in California, where Nixon is located at the moment. During the phone conversation, the president suggests that the Dolphins use a quick slant pass play in the Super Bowl. Their talk lasts roughly ten minutes.

January 4

Press coverage of the Nixon-Shula conversation gives the misleading impression that Nixon actually designed a play for the Dolphins.

January 16

The Dallas Cowboys defeat the Miami Dolphins in Super Bowl VI by the score of 24–3. The Dolphins use a quick slant pass on the eighth play of the game, which results in an incompletion. Nixon calls Dallas head coach Tom Landry after the game and compares the Cowboys to the dominant Green Bay Packer teams of the 1960s.

March 31

The Major League Baseball Players Association votes to go on strike on April 1. The union and the owners disagree on the length of time and the amount that the owners should contribute to the players pension fund. The Players Association announces its willingness to accept the arbitration of a prominent individual not associated with the sport.

April 1

Professional baseball players go on strike.

April 8

Nixon suggests that he and Vice President Spiro Agnew act as arbitrators in the strike. Haldeman raises the idea in a telephone call with Bowie Kuhn, commissioner of Major League baseball. Kuhn declines.

April 9

Nixon publicly offers the services of the Federal Mediation and Conciliation Service to end the strike.

April 11

The owners and players agree on the pension issues, but the strike continues as they disagree on when to start the season and whether the players should be paid for any makeup games.

April 13

The owners and players agree not to make up the games lost to the strike.

April 15

The baseball season begins.

April 18

Bowie Kuhn, commissioner of Major League Baseball, testifies before the US Senate District of Columbia Affairs Committee, stating that if Washington is to get another professional baseball team, it will have to be through the relocation of an existing franchise. He explains that the sport has overextended itself and that there are no plans to create any new expansion teams in the near future.

June 17

Four men working for the Committee to Re-Elect the President break into the Watergate office of the Democratic National Committee. The four are caught and arrested while planting listening devices.

June 19

In *Flood v Kuhn* with a 5–3 vote, the United States Supreme Court rules that the antitrust exemption that Major League Baseball enjoys is constitutional, but calls on Congress to repeal the sport's special status.

June 22

Nixon holds a press conference at the White House. Only one question is about Watergate. Nixon has no comment to make when asked about the court ruling on baseball. At the end of the conference, Cliff Evans, a reporter for RKO Radio, asks the president to name his favorite baseball players. Nixon names three and then stops. Evans follows up and asks him to select an all-time all-star team. The president agrees.

June 23

At 10:04 a.m., Nixon meets with his chief of staff, H. R. "Bob" Haldeman, and directs cover-up efforts to block the investigation of the Watergate break-in. A recording of this conversation becomes known as the "Smoking Gun Tape" and proves that the president is guilty of obstruction of justice.

Nixon has the White House staff, including Haldeman and press secretary Ron Ziegler, begin collecting statistical information on former baseball players for his all-star team.

Nixon signs the Educational Amendments Act into law. Title IX of this legislation prohibits discrimination on the basis of sex, which will lead to growth of women's sports in the 1970s and 1980s.

June 25

While at Camp David, Nixon works on his historic all-star list with the help of son-in-law David Eisenhower.

June 27

Nixon makes revisions to his baseball all-star roster and writes an article to accompany the list, in which he names the most talented players in various baseball skills.

July 2

Nixon's article and historic all-star baseball team rosters appears in the Sunday edition of newspapers all across the country. Instead of one team, he selected four different teams: a prewar and postwar team for both the American and National Leagues. The amount of space given to this endeavor varies greatly from publication to publication, but Nixon generally receives considerable positive coverage for the effort.

September 5–6

Terrorists from the Palestine Liberation Organization kill two Israeli Olympic team members and take another nine hostage at the Munich games. During the course of the twenty-three-hour crisis, all the terrorists and Israelis are killed. The Nixon White House sends a note to Germany on behalf of Israel, asking that the games be suspended during the incident. The president refuses suggestions coming from the American Jewish community that the United States recall its Olympic team and boycott the rest of the games.

October 3

Assistant Attorney General Thomas E. Kauper testifies before a Senate subcommittee and states that Nixon wants legislation to prohibit professional sports leagues from blacking out home coverage of home games.

October 10

White Staff members propose that Nixon attend ceremonies scheduled for the second game of the World Series, honoring Jackie Robinson and recognizing the twenty-fifth anniversary of the desegregation of Major League Baseball. The White House staff has already obtained a waiver from the Federal Communications Commission to the equal time rule for political candidates. Nixon rejects the proposal, saying his schedule is too full.

October 15

Robinson throws out the first ball of game two at Riverfront Stadium in Cincinnati. Nixon spends the day at Camp David, watching professional football games.

October 24

Jackie Robinson dies. In a public statement on Robinson's death, Nixon says: "His courage, his sense of brotherhood, and his brilliance on the playing field brought a new human dimension not only to the game of baseball but to every area of American life where black and while people work side by side."

October 27

Robert Finch, counselor to the president, leads a forty-man White House delegation to the Robinson funeral in New York.

November 7

Nixon defeats the Democratic presidential nominee, Senator George McGovern of South Dakota, in the general election. Nixon's victory is a landslide. He garners 47 million votes, or 60.7 percent of the vote, and wins every state except Massachusetts.

Voters in Colorado approve a referendum initiative that prohibits the state from spending public funds in support of the Denver Winter Olympic Games.

November 8

The Denver Olympic Organizing Committee informs the International Olympic Committee that it is no longer possible for the city to host the winter games.

December 3

In an interview published as a cover article in the "Style" section of the *Washington Post*, a heavily intoxicated Washington Redskins' quarterback Billy Kilmer claims that Nixon's enthusiasm for the team is counterproductive and that he plans to ask head coach George Allen to do something about keeping the president away from the team.

December 30

Attorney General Richard Kleindienst ends a series of meetings he had been holding with NFL commissioner Pete Rozelle about ending the league's policy of blacking out home games. Kleindienst publicly states the administration will seek legislation that will force the league to end this practice.

December 31

While delivering humanitarian relief to victims of an earthquake in Nicaragua, Roberto Clemente, an outfielder for the Pittsburgh Pirates, dies in a plane crash off the coast of San Juan, Puerto Rico.

That same day the Washington Redskins defeat the Dallas Cowboys, 26–3, in the National Football Conference Championship Game. The Miami Dolphins defeat the Pittsburgh Steelers, 21–17 in the American Football Conference Championship Game. The winning teams will meet in Super Bowl VII.

1973

January 1

Redskins' coach George Allen visits the White House, and Nixon promises him that he will root for the Redskins in Super Bowl VII against the Miami Dolphins. The president also gives Allen a pin with the presidential seal and a letter. Both items are for Billy Kilmer to give to his daughter Kathy, who has cerebral palsy.

January 2

In a public statement about Clemente, Nixon calls him "one of the greatest baseball players of our time." He also says: "In the tragedy of his untimely death, we are reminded that he deserved even greater respect and admiration for his splendid qualities as a generous and kind human being."

January 3

Nixon gives a $1,000 check in Clemente's memory to the Nicaraguan embassy. At the president's request, Daniel Galbreath, president of the Pittsburgh Pirates, and Pirate players Dave Giusti and Steve Blass meet with him about setting up a memorial fund in Clemente's honor to continue his work of aiding the survivors of the earthquake.

January 8

While in San Juan to represent the president at the swearing in of the new mayor, Anne Armstrong, counselor to the president, visits the Clemente family to pay the president's respects.

January 14

The Dolphins defeat the Redskins in Super Bowl VII by the score of 14–7. The Dolphins end their season with a perfect 17-0 record. Dolphin fans honk their car horns as they drive past the residential compound in Key Biscayne, Florida, where Nixon is staying.

January 15

Nixon calls Shula and congratulates the Dolphins for their victory.

January 20

Nixon is sworn in for a second term as president of the United States.

April 6

Nixon throws out the first pitch of the season at a California Angels game, making it the first time that a US president has performed this ceremonial activity in a city other than Washington, DC.

April 30

In an effort to end the investigations into the Watergate affair, Nixon gives a televised speech from the Oval Office and announces the resignation of Kleindienst, Haldeman, counselor to the president John Ehrlichman, and counsel to the president John Dean.

May 14

In an Oval Office ceremony, Nixon posthumously presents the first Presidential Citizens Medal to Roberto Clemente. Vera Clemente accepts the award on her husband's behalf. Nixon also signs House Resolution 3841 into law (Public Law 93-33 [87 Stat.71]), which authorizes the striking of a gold commemorative medal in Clemente's honor. Profits from the sale of two hundred thousand duplicate medallions will go to the Roberto Clemente Memorial Fund.

May 28

C. A. Smith, owner of the San Diego Padres, announces that he has sold the baseball team to a Washington, DC–based syndicated. The group, led by Joseph Danzansky, president of Giant Foods, an area food store chain, plans to move the team to Washington.

July 13

Alexander Butterfield, former administrative aide to H. R. Haldeman, reveals to congressional staff members that the White House has a hidden tape recording system.

July 16

Butterfield appears before the select congressional committee investigating Watergate and repeats his remarks in public.

August 29

Archibald Cox, the independent prosecutor investigating Watergate, subpoenas the White House tapes.

September 6

In a 76–6 vote, the US Senate moves to ban television blackouts of professional sport games that sell out seventy-two hours or more before the event.

September 7

At Danzansky's request, Nixon sends a letter to Charles Feeney, president of the National League of professional baseball, supporting the return of a major league team to Washington, DC.

September 10

The Communications Subcommittee of the Commerce Committee in the US House of Representatives approves a bill to ban television blackouts of professional sport games that sell out seventy-two hours or more before the event.

September 13

The NFL repeals its blackout policy. The US House of Representatives approves the Communications Subcommittee bill with a 336–37 vote.

October 20

Nixon fires Cox and the subpoena for the tapes expires. Attorney General Elliot Richardson and Deputy Attorney General William Ruckelshaus resign rather than carry out this order to remove Cox. This episode becomes known as the "Saturday Night Massacre."

December 6

In a unanimous vote, the National League tentatively approves the sale and relocation to Washington of the San Diego Padres, provided that the Danzansky syndicate meets certain financial requirements.

Nixon sends Danzansky a telegram, congratulating him on bringing professional baseball back to the nation's capital.

December 21

The Danzansky group fails to meet the financial requirements of the National League.

December 29

C. A. Smith announces he has sold the Padres to a California-based syndicate.

1974

April 8

Outfielder Henry Aaron of the Atlanta Braves hits his 715th career home run, breaking the record previously held by Babe Ruth. Nixon calls Aaron during the game to congratulate him, and the two talk during the bottom half of the sixth inning.

July 17

Baseball Hall of Fame pitcher Dizzy Dean dies. Nixon issues a public statement: "To my generation of Americans, Dizzy Dean will always be remembered as the blazing young fastballer who led the Gashouse Gang of St. Louis to the pinnacle of baseball glory."

July 24

The US Supreme Court rules 8–0 in *United States v. Nixon* that the president must turn over the subpoenaed tapes.

August 5

The subpoenaed tapes, including the "Smoking Gun" recording are made public.

August 7

Nixon meets with Republican leaders in Congress. Senator Barry Goldwater, Senator Hugh Scott, and Representative John Rhodes inform him that the House of Representatives will impeach him and that a near-unanimous Senate will vote to remove him from office. Even though he had decided to resign before this meeting, Nixon will publicly explain that this conference convinced him to leave office.

August 8

Nixon gives a televised speech, announcing he will resign the presidency. A total of 150 million people either watch the announcement on television or listen to it on radio.

August 9

Nixon resigns. Vice President Gerald R. Ford Jr. becomes the president of the United States.

NOTES

INTRODUCTION

1. Personal observation of the author.

2. Transcript of *ABC News Special: Nixon Funeral*, April 27, 1994, ABC News Transcript #145-1, Lexis-Nexis Academic Universe Database Web Site, http://www.lexis-nexis.com/universe.

3. Theodore H. White, *Breach of Faith: The Fall of Richard Nixon* (New York: Atheneum, 1975); Stanley I. Kutler, *The Wars of Watergate: The Last Crisis of Richard Nixon* (New York: W. W. Norton, 1990); Fred Emery, *Watergate: The Corruption of American Politics and the Fall of Richard Nixon* (New York: Times Books, 1994); Keith W. Olson, *Watergate: The Presidential Scandal That Shook America* (Lawrence: University Press of Kansas, 2003).

4. This study hopes to contribute to several different areas of Nixon studies. The first is biography. Some of the first studies came from psychobiographers, and they saw his family as a source of weakness and often see policies and actions that they object to as stemming from a maladjusted personality: David Abrahamsen, *Nixon vs. Nixon: An Emotional Tragedy* (New York: Farrar, Straus and Giroux, 1977); Fawn M. Brodie, *Richard Nixon: The Shaping of His Character* (New York: W. W. Norton, 1981). A three-man team of psychiatrists and historians found that Nixon was a narcissist and his need for applause was both a strength and weakness: Varnik Volkan, Norman Itzkowitz, and Andrew Dodd, *Richard Nixon: A Psychobiography* (New York: Columbia University Press, 1997).

Another group of biographers have advanced what this author likes to call the "Dole synthesis." At Nixon's funeral, Senator Robert Dole of Kansas said in an emotion-choked eulogy:

> I believe the second half of the 20th century will be known as the age of Nixon. Why was he the most durable public figure of our time? Not because he gave the most eloquent speeches, but because he provided the most effective leadership. Not because he won every battle, but because he always embodied the deepest feelings of the people he led. One of his biographers said that Richard Nixon was one of us. And so he was.

Excerpts from Dole eulogy were printed in: "Richard Nixon: 1913–1994: 'He Stood on Pinnacles That Dissolved into Precipice,'" *Los Angeles Times*, April 28, 1994. This proposition, as the senator clearly stated, came from the works that put Nixon into a cultural and political context. The writers of these books contend Nixon was a centrist who provided bipartisan leadership to a generation that worried about its place in society and that his domestic achievements were far more significant than commonly thought. Herbert S. Parmet sees a genuine leader in Nixon who succeeded through will and work and was determined to steer a middle course between liberalism and conservatism for the middle class. He ignores Watergate, and that is a major, major absence, and really tells only half the Nixon story: Herbert S. Parmet, *Nixon and His America* (Boston: Little, Brown, 1990). Drawing on his own reporting, Tom Wicker sees Nixon as representative of America's efforts to realistically use power: Tom Wicker, *One of Us: Richard Nixon and the American Dream* (New York: Random House, 1991). Joan Hoff's book was published after the funeral, but her findings were appearing in article and conference presentations and fit into the "Dole synthesis" comfortably. Hoff advances the "there-is-more-to-Nixon-than-Watergate" theme even more than Parmet—it is a major element in her study, and advances the domestic-achievement theme further with the argument that Nixon's domestic policies had a greater impact than those concerning world affairs. She was also one of the first historians to begin using White House documents: Joan Hoff, *Nixon Reconsidered* (New York: Basic Books, 1994). Her book and Stanley Kutler's previously cited *Wars of Watergate* are the two most authoritative accounts on the Nixon presidency. A number of books since the funeral have also advanced the key elements of the "Dole synthesis." They include: Chris Matthews, Melvin Small, David Greenberg, and Daniel Frick. In assessing these books, it is important to note that there is much to be said for this man-of-the-people interpretation. It goes a long, long way to explaining Nixon's success in politics, but he is hardly the first president who could have been portrayed along these lines: Andrew Jackson, Abraham Lincoln, Ulysses S. Grant, William McKinley, and Warren G. Harding come to mind. More importantly, what exactly does it mean to be a "man of the people"? The American people have always been a diverse lot, and it is difficult to imagine any one man representing such a complex group. Put another way, presidents with aristocratic backgrounds such as George Washington and both Roosevelts were as much of the people as Nixon.

In contrast to these interpretations of symbolism are the biographies of substance. One of the first post–White House biographies came from the seventh Earl of Longford. Lord Longford's emphasis is on world affairs, and he argues, quite plausibly, that Nixon's Quaker upbringing was the dominant influence in his life. Religion might have played this role in Nixon's life, but Longford's account minimizes the importance of Watergate, which makes his argument less than persuasive: Frank Pakenham Longford (Lord Longford), *Nixon: A Study in Extremes of Fortune* (London: Weidenfeld and Nicolson, 1980). For a time, the best and fullest study of the life of the thirty-seventh President was the three-volume Stephen E. Ambrose study. Although revelations since Ambrose's death have exposed him as an intellectual fraud, his account of Nixon's life is still quite dependable. Most of the liberties Ambrose took with the truth were in his books on Eisenhower and World War II. The fact that Nixon was alive and could contest any findings that Ambrose might make kept the historian honest. The biography focuses mainly on domestic politics and is a balanced account, despite the author's politics and an initial dislike for his subject. Ambrose argues that the Nixon family was a source of strength. He rose quickly in politics because he was a quick study, had real ability, and was willing to take on lot of hard work: Stephen Ambrose, *Nixon*, 3 vols. (New York: Simon and Schuster, 1987–1991). Roger Morris set out to write another multivolume biography of Nixon. A former National Security Council staff member, Morris had his phones tapped while he worked in the Nixon White House and resigned in protest over the invasion of Cambodia. He seems to be trying to have his revenge on Nixon with this project. His Nixon is an ambitious California provincial with few ideas about statecraft: Roger Morris, *Richard Milhous Nixon: The Rise of an American Politician* (New York: Holt, 1990).

Hal Bochin's book is a monograph rather than a biography. In this study, he examines Nixon's rhetoric, but it examines his entire career and argues that the politician's competitive nature led him to use debating tricks like counterattacks and selective truth telling to reach the top. Nixon was willing to take calculated risks in moving advancing his career: Hal Bochin, *Richard Nixon: Rhetorical Strategist* (New York: Greenwood Press, 1990).

The most sympathetic biography is Jonathan Aitken's study. A British politician and a sitting member of Parliament at the time he wrote the book, Aitken had Nixon's cooperation. The two were fairly close. The Englishman served as an advance man when the former president made his first trip to the United Kingdom after leaving office. Aitken and his wife stayed with the Nixons on their honeymoon in 1979. Most of the book is devoted to the prepresidential years. Aitken emphasizes Nixon's foreign policies, which were far more important than Watergate: Jonathan Aitken, *Nixon: A Life* (Washington, DC: Regnery Publishing, 1993).

Pulitzer Prize winner Irwin F. Gellman has offered two volumes that look at Nixon's political career. Nixon made a name for himself as a hard-working politician who outthought his opponents and had a better feel for postwar American life. Negative charges against him during this time were largely the work of partisan opponents and not sustainable by the facts: *The Contender: Richard Nixon: The Congressional Years, 1946–1952* (New York: Free Press, 1999). In *The President and the Apprentice: Eisenhower and Nixon, 1952–1961* (New Haven, CT: Yale University Press, 2015) he finds a good working relationship with Eisenhower, who was impressed with his ability and made genuine efforts to prepare him for the top job.

The most negative and critical portrayal comes in Anthony Summers, *The Arrogance of Power: The Secret World of Richard Nixon* (New York: Viking, 2000). In this book, which borders on the edge of tabloid journalism and at times crosses into this genre, Summers contends that a number of personal demons drove Nixon and ultimately did great damage to the nation. Summers's findings will strike most objective readers as sensationalistic and unreliable.

Reflecting a trend among scholarly monographs, journalist Richard Reeves emphasized domestic over foreign policies in his biography. He also emphasized the influence of his reporter colleagues a bit too much and covers only the first term:

Richard Reeves, *President Nixon: Alone in the White House* (New York: Simon and Schuster, 2001). Iwan W. Morgan's short biography pays close attention to Nixon's role in helping the Republican Party recover from 1964 and argues that his domestic policies had more enduring significance than his foreign policies. Morgan notes one of the difficulties in assessing Nixon's life: "He was *both* much better *and* much worse than the norm." Morgan also added, "He had exceptional ability, exceptional intelligence, and exceptional vision. Yet no other leading figure of postwar politics was as lacking in moral scruple as Nixon, lied as often as he did or matched his determination to win at any cost." Iwan W. Morgan, *Nixon* (London: Arnold, 2002), 194.

The Baron Black of Crossharbour, writing under his original name, produced an extremely complimentary book on Nixon. Lord Black is quite good at developing his subject's personality. He is also strong in world affairs. He defends Nixon's leadership in Vietnam, which has much merit when one puts that conflict into the larger strategic context of US interests in world affairs. On the other hand, Black's coverage of domestic polices and understanding of domestic politics is weak: Conrad Black, *Richard M. Nixon: A Life in Full* (New York, 2007).

Perhaps the most influential account of Nixon's life is not a book but the Oliver Stone film *Nixon*. While it is not a serious study of the man, any theatrical film is going to have a larger audience than any book of history. In an effort to gain traction with historians, Stone had the screenplay and many of the supporting documents published in book form: Eric Hamburg, ed., *Nixon: An Oliver Stone Film* (New York: Public Affairs, 2007).

More recent Nixon biographers have argued he was a one-man Greek tragedy. The very traits that made him successful were also those things that brought about his downfall: Evan Thomas, *Being Nixon: A Man Divided* (New York: Random House, 2015); Tim Weiner, *One Man against the World: The Tragedy of Richard Nixon* (New York: Henry Holt, 2015).

John A. Farrell's one-volume biography is the best and fullest account and is important in separating rhetoric and symbolism from substance. The Nixon family shaped Richard Nixon's life in profound ways. His mother and father were significant influences, but the death of his two brothers was a loss that he never got over. He pushed hard and was ruthless, but worked to advance the common good . . . mostly: John A. Farrell, *Richard Nixon: The Life* (New York: Doubleday, 2017).

The second historiographical field this book will contribute to will be that of Nixon and domestic politics. After reaching the White House in 1968 Nixon attempted to bring a political realignment with the elections of 1970 and 1972: Robert Mason, *Richard Nixon and the Quest for a New Majority* (Chapel Hill: University of North Carolina Press, 2004). He used sport in those efforts. John Morton Blum argues that the political debate of this time was how—but also whether—the federal government should address social inadequacies. Blum admits that the liberal Kennedy and Johnson administrations and the Congresses of those years were sloppy in writing and administering the law, which alienated the public. "Nixon did not have to invent his 'silent majority,' his Middle Americans. They were waiting for him." John Morton Blum, *Years of Discord: American Politics and Society, 1961–1974* (New York: W. W. Norton, 1991), 479. Gareth Davies argues that the Democrats suffered a self-inflicted wound when they embraced entitlements as a way of combating poverty: Gareth Davies, *From Opportunity to Entitlement: The Transformation and Decline of Great Society Liberalism* (Lawrence: University Press of Kansas, 1996). Ronald Radosh contends Nixon put together a coalition in 1972 that had the potential to be a new electoral majority, but it was not an achievement of his own. It was the mistakes of McGovern and the liberals that put it together for him: Ronald Radosh, *Divided They Fell: The Demise of the Democratic Party* (New York: Free Press, 1996). Donald T. Critchlow argues that the 1970s were key, but the Right nearly undid itself, although liberal failures allowed their movement to survive. Donald T. Critchlow, *The Conservative Ascendancy: How the GOP Right Made Political History* (Cambridge, MA: Harvard University Press, 2007). Dominic Sandbrook believes cultural issues, the Vietnam War, and Watergate led to the decline of big government liberalism in the 1970s. Dominic Sandbrook, *Mad as Hell: The Crisis of the 1970s and the Rise of the Populist Right* (New York: Alfred A. Knopf, 2011).

Others historians have argued that the transition of the 1960s and 1970s had more to do with what the New Right did correctly than what the Democrats did wrong. Lewis L. Gould gives much of the credit to Nixon and his lieutenants: Lewis L. Gould, *Grand Old Party: A History of the Republicans* (New York: Random House, 2003). In another impressively researched study, Rick Perlstein attributes many of the divisions in American society to Nixon and the divisive political tactics he used: Rick Perlstein, *Nixonland: The Rise of a President and the Fracturing of America* (New York: Scribner, 2008). This argument is interesting, but difficult to sustain on macro and micro levels. On a macro level, when one considers American history over the long term, events like the American Revolution—which was a civil war—the US Civil War, Reconstruction, and the persistence of immigrant communities that refused to assimilate during the nineteenth and early twentieth centuries, the schisms of the 1960s do not seem that foreign to the American experience and probably not even as significant as previous divisions. On a micro level, this study of Nixon and sports shows that while the president used some divisions to his advantage, he was honestly trying to bridge the divides.

These accounts beg an obvious question: if this was a period of political realignment, why then did the Democrats retake the White House and maintain majorities in both chambers of Congress well into the 1990s? A number of individuals have offered answers to that question. William G. Mayer's book on public opinion confirms many of the arguments advanced about Democratic mistakes. The economy and foreign policy reverses were also very important in changing voting patterns. He also notes that it took time for these events to weigh on the public and change their voting patterns: William G. Mayer, *The Changing American Mind: How and Why American Public Opinion Changed between 1960 and 1988* (Ann Arbor: University of Michigan Press, 1992). Michael Schaller and George Rising believe that Nixon set the stage for Reagan. While he came close to destroying the Republican party with the Watergate crisis, he also broke the Democrats' hold on power with his Southern strategy and made it possible for another Republican not associated with his abuse of power—which is to say Ronald Reagan—to forge a new coalition: Michael Schaller and George Rising, *The Republican Ascendancy: American Politics, 1968–2001* (Wheeling, IL: Harlan Davidson, 2002). Writing at the same time, Earl Black and Merle Black advanced a more qualified view. They argue that Nixon had the potential to bring about a realignment until Watergate "arrested" that movement and that it was Reagan rather than Nixon who brought the South into the Republican party. Earl Black and Merle Black, *The Rise of Southern Republicans* (Cambridge, MA: Harvard University Press, 2002), 211. Robert Lublin sees Nixon making advances in the South "by being more racially conservative than the racially liberal Democratic Party": Robert Lublin, *The Republican South: Democratization and Partisan Change* (Princeton, NJ: Princeton University Press, 2004), 141. Godfrey Hodgson and Melvin Small argue that the revelations about the involvement of White House officials in the Watergate scandal stopped congressional Democrats from switching parties and giving Republicans a majority: Godfrey Hodgson, *The World Turned Right Side Up: A History of the Conservative Ascendance in America* (Boston: Houghton Miffilin, 1996); Small, *The Presidency of Richard Nixon.* Jefferson Cowie argues that Nixon was better at ideas than at execution: Jefferson Cowie, "Nixon's Class Struggle: Romancing the New Right Worker, 1969–1973," *Labor History* 43, no. 3 (September 2002): 257–283. Robert Mason advanced the novel idea that Nixon was not that good an electoral strategist. He rarely pushed reform with much enthusiasm, and his ideas often found little traction with Republicans or voters in general: Robert Mason, *Richard Nixon and the Quest for a New Majority*; Robert Mason, "'I Was Going to Build a New Republican Party and a New Majority': Richard Nixon as Party Leader, 1969–73," *Journal of American Studies* 39, no. 3 (December 2005): 463–483.

This argument is new and has some substance. Nixon won a majority on his own only once. Even then, McGovern was a cooperative opponent who made some really bad decisions that lost him even his home state. Daniel Galvin disagrees. Creating a new political majority was a priority for Nixon, and even though association with the Republican brand name hurt his own political opportunities, he committed his prestige to efforts to enhance the party's reputation. He worked behind the scenes to build the party's organization in the South and made sure that it provided campaign resources to candidates: Daniel J. Galvin, *Presidential Party Building: Dwight D. Eisenhower to George W. Bush* (Princeton, NJ: Princeton University Press, 2010).

These positions are interesting, and while Mason has some good points, the ability to get on a national ticket once is impressive in and of itself. Five times is stunning. As this study will show, Nixon connected with the American people in powerful ways, and his political use of sport was one of them. This argument has been advanced to a degree in article format: Nicholas Evan Sarantakes, "Richard Nixon, Sportswriter:

The President, His Historical All-Star Baseball Team, and the Election of 1972," *Journal of Sport History* 27, no. 1 (Summer 1997): 192–202. This article was also republished on *ESPN.com*: Nicholas Evan Sarantakes, "Baseball: The Great Political Equalizer," *ESPN.com*, March 12, 2002, http://espn.go.com/page2/wash/s/2002/0312/1349955.html; and Nicholas Evan Sarantakes, "Nixon versus Paterno: College Football, and Presidential Politics," *Pennsylvania History* 73, no. 2 (Spring 2006): 236–260.

This examination of Nixon and sport will also be of interest to students of the biggest political crisis in the United States since the end of Reconstruction: Watergate. Parmet's *Richard Nixon and His America* and then later Hoff's *Nixon Reconsidered* were strong arguments that the focus on Watergate was misleading; there was more to Nixon than Watergate. Parmet makes this argument by basically stopping his coverage in 1972. Hoff makes her point even more directly with the title of her introduction: "Nixon Is More Than Watergate" and her conclusion: "Watergate Is More Than Nixon." Hoff, *Nixon Reconsidered*, 1, 8, 329.

Kutler rejected this argument. His book *The Wars of Watergate* proceeds on the foundation that Watergate and the abuse of powers that it represented was a central element of Nixon's administration: "no 'fair' history of the Nixon era can overlook the centrality of Watergate." He also added: "His achievements will get their due, as different generations weigh them, favorably or unfavorably, but they will probably will not rival Watergate for historical attention." One page later, he observed: "Richard Nixon's cannot be separated from Watergate." Kutler, *The Wars of Watergate*, 616–617. Olson shows that Watergate unified the nation in way that is rare in American history. Republicans and conservatives supported reasonable legal procedures—the establishment of the Watergate committee, the confirmation of the special prosecutor, and the release of the White House tapes—which ultimately led to his demise. On the day Nixon left office, "Americans demonstrated a consensus of opinion regarding a vital public issue that was unprecedented in the nation's peacetime history": Olson, *Watergate*, 148.

This study will be highly relevant to the growing scholarship on Nixon's image and his role in American memory. One of the first to explore this topic was Thomas J. Johnson. In a study of public opinion, Johnson conducted a survey of University of Washington alumni and determined that those who obtained their information on Nixon from media accounts published since 1974 have less negative views of Nixon than those who lived through the Watergate scandal. In this sense, the media was Nixon's ally, not his enemy. This point is relative, however. Johnson's respondents still had fairly negative views of the man: Thomas J. Johnson, *The Rehabilitation of Richard Nixon: The Media's Effect on Collective Memory* (New York: Garland, 1995). Michael Schudson's focus is specifically on Watergate. He argues that different groups and institutions remember Watergate as either a political scandal or a constitutional crisis and America has done a good job of remembering: Michael Schudson, *Watergate in American Memory: How We Remember, Forget and Reconstruct the Past* (New York: Basic Books, 1992). David Greenberg argues Nixon "was the dominant politician of the age of image consciousness." Greenberg also adds "that the "images overlapped, mingled, coexisted." Because of Nixon and his actions, "Americans came to believe that politics revolves around the construction and manipulation of images—a shadow that Nixon still casts upon our age." Greenberg, *Nixon's Shadow: The History of an Image* (New York: W. W. Norton, 2003), xxvi, xxxi, xxxii. Daniel Frick, on the other hand, set out to directly examine Dole's thesis. Like Greenberg, he comes to the conclusion that the senator was basically correct in his assessment. "In saying that Nixon was a representative American, Bob Dole was absolutely correct. Arguably, no living politician can match the captivating force that Nixon exerted—and continues to exert on the culture of the United States." Frick, *Reinventing Richard Nixon: A Cultural History of an American Obsession* (Lawrence: University Press of Kansas, 2008), 7, 17.

These arguments are both interesting and frustrating. These authors raise important questions about Richard Nixon's meaning to American society, but they are not records of what he actually did during his life and career. Symbolism is nice, but substance is important too. These books are also based on the questionable idea that Nixon had no fixed identity, ideas, values, or beliefs. The charge of being a flip-flopper can be devastating to a politician, and Nixon is not the first and certainly not the last to be hit with that accusation. With those considerations in mind, this allegation is misleading. A smart individual can and should reassess their positions when they receive new information or when the context changes. More to the point, Herbert S. Parmet argues that there has been one and only one Nixon: "There have been, first of all, no truly 'new' Nixons. There has been one coherent, consistent Nixon, one whose commitment to what he called 'practical liberalism' was unwavering throughout the second half of the twentieth century. Just as consistent was his closeness to the culture of conservative populism, one that saw an idealized vision of capitalism and the demands of entrepreneurialism": Parmet, *Nixon and His America*, ix.

Although this study does use sport to explore Nixon's image making, it rejects the assumptions that underlie the Greenberg and Frick studies. When Nixon was interacting with the world of sport, he was not a Republican or a Democrat, conservative or liberal, he was just Richard Milhous Nixon. Did the president appear different to different groups, yes. No question. Did Nixon have political enemies, yes, but that is the case for all politicians. Every time an individual takes a stand on a political issue or implements a policy, they alienate those on the other side. To be more blunt: every politician has enemies and will appear different to supporters than they do it their opponents. Nixon engendered strong and passionate views among the public, but not that much compared to Abraham Lincoln.

The final Nixon historiography that this book contributes to is the one that focuses on his policies. Writers have given Nixon's foreign policy agenda far more attention. In many ways the positive assessments—and there have been many—of Nixon administration foreign policy have done little to bolster his reputation, since the president must share the stage with Henry Kissinger. Accounts on domestic affairs are small in number but have given the thirty-seventh president high marks. Joan Hoff turned Nixon studies upside down when she argued that Nixon left a stronger legacy in domestic policy than in foreign affairs: Hoff, *Nixon Reconsidered*. Since her book appeared in print, historians writing on domestic affairs have generally advanced that view. Another common theme running through these works is the pervasive presence and influence of political gain. In the Nixon administration partisan politics, polls, and popularity ratings were important factors in the decision-making process despite claims to the contrary from its alumni. Allen J. Matusow is very negative in his assessment of economic policy, which he sees as dependent on domestic politics: Allen J. Matusow, *Nixon's Economy: Booms, Busts, Dollars, and Votes* (Lawrence: University Press of Kansas, 1998). For the most part, though, the studies on domestic affairs have argued that Nixon left behind a much richer social agenda than was recognized at the time and that it has had far greater endurance than his foreign policies. Melvin Small, *The Presidency of Richard Nixon* (Lawrence: University Press of Kansas, 1999); Dean J. Kotlowski, *Nixon's Civil Rights: Politics, Principle, and Policy* (Cambridge, MA: Harvard University Press, 2002); and J. Brooks Flippen, *Nixon and the Environment* (Albuquerque: University of New Mexico Press, 2000). For a complex assessment of this man, which is in many ways appropriate, see Kevin L. Yuill, *Richard Nixon and the Rise of Affirmative Action: The Pursuit of Racial Equality in an Era of Limits* (Lanham, MD: Rowman and Littlefield, 2006).

A number of new studies make use of the White House tapes to explore new topics and questions about old views. Kevin McMahon, *Nixon's Court: His Challenge to Judicial Liberalism and Its Consequences* (Chicago: University Press of Chicago, 2011), sets out to explore why Nixon with the appointment of four justices to the Supreme Court of the United States failed to transform the judiciary into a bastion of conservative thinking. McMahon argues that Nixon's strong rhetoric on the topic is misleading. He never set out to make the judiciary conservative; he was actually appointing judges with an eye toward electoral politics, hoping to break the New Deal coalition and establish the Republicans as the party of the majority. His approach worked, and he, not Ronald Reagan, recruited "Reagan Democrats" to the Republican Party. Laura Kalman, *The Long Reach of the Sixties: LBJ, Nixon, and the Making of the Contemporary Supreme Court* (New York: Oxford University Press, 2017), agrees with McMahon that the nomination process became critical to presidential politics. This approach forced the Senate to take a more combative role, particularly as both presidents appointed men with minimal qualifications and ethically suspect backgrounds. The combative and ugly confirmation efforts that have taken place since then are the result of this approach. Stephen Hess, *The Professor and the President: Daniel Patrick Moynihan in the Nixon White House* (Washington, DC: Brookings Institute Press, 2015), shows that politics were not so polarized that Nixon could not have a liberal Democrat on his staff and that Moynihan maintained influence because of his respect for the president's intellect. John M. Logsdon, *After Apollo? Richard Nixon and the American Space Program* (New York: Palgrave Macmillan,

2015), shows that the Nixon White House decided to downplay the space program, reducing the daring, heroic focus on getting men into space, which led to large cuts in the National Aeronautics and Space Administration's budget. Busing was one of the contentious issues of the 1970s, and Matthew F. Delmont shows in *Why Busing Failed: Race, Media, and the National Resistance to School Desegregation* (Berkeley: University of California Press, 2016) that busing was an issue that opponents created to oppose desegregation without having to resort to racist language. Nixon turned to antibusing early in 1972 to neutralize the political threat that Governor George Wallace of Alabama posed to his political support in the South. Meg Jacobs, *Panic at the Pump: The Energy Crisis and the Transformation of American Politics in the 1970s* (New York: Hill and Wang, 2016) shows that Watergate limited Nixon's ability to respond with the crisis and that the feeling of frustration many Americans felt helped lead to the rise of the political right.

The fact that domestic politics plays a prominent role is understandable when one considers that Nixon was trying to bring about a realignment in party affiliation. Partisan considerations appear in this work, but the evidence in old White House files pertaining to sports suggests that it was the staff more than Nixon that let these considerations shape their options.

When it comes to sports history, there are four main historiographical fields. All of them overlap to some degree, but they are hardly equal. Many scholars focus on social history. This approach is far and away the most popular approach to the topic among sports historians. The main issues that these scholars explore are race, ethnicity, gender, and class. A second group of historians examines sport as a manifestation of culture. A third group looks at sport as a business enterprise. The role of the media is a small, but important, subfield of the business history approach. A subtopic running throughout this book is the relationship Nixon had with the sports media. Politics is a fourth and much smaller area of interest. Studies of the Olympics have dominated this approach. For an example, see Nicholas Evan Sarantakes, "Moscow versus Los Angeles: The Cold War Comes to the Olympic Selection Process," *Cold War History* 9, no. 1 (February 2009): 135–157. Only a few writers have looked at sport and domestic politics, which is what this study sets out to do. In 1983 historian Robert M. Collins wrote an essay in which he contended that athletics served psychic, political, and moral functions for Nixon. This composition is suggestive, but Collins lacked access to the documents that would have sustained his argument. Robert M. Collins, "Richard M. Nixon: The Psychic, Political, and Moral Uses of Sport," *Journal of Sport History* 10, no. 2 (Summer 1983): 77–84. This account will move in new directions such as the social and cultural influence Nixon had, or refused to take, in the world of sport, as well as the social obligations Nixon believed the fan and athlete had to one another and how these values shaped his actions while in office. Only two writers have examined the relationship of presidents to sport. Journalist Don Van Natta Jr. examines the relationship the chief executives have had with the game of golf in *First Off the Tee: Presidential Hackers, Duffers, and Cheaters from Taft to Bush*

(New York: Public Affairs, 2003), 225–248. Historian John Sayle Watterson, in an even broader study of presidential interaction with sport, argues that an examination of this relationship reflects presidential character. The material in this account certainly supports that conclusion, but will examine at greater length issues involving Nixon that Watterson never considered. John Sayle Watterson, *The Games Presidents Play: Sports and the Presidency* (Baltimore: Johns Hopkins University Press, 2006), 229–244.

5. For a study of film, see Mark Feeney, *Nixon at the Movies; A Book about Belief* (Chicago: University of Chicago Press, 2004).

6. Nixon conversation with Batson, Crutchfield, Eaton, Fetzer, Gilmore, Israel, Kluge, Mechem, Michaels, Murphy, Paine, Poor, Quaal, Reinsch, Shaw, Shaw, Slaughter, Snyder, Sonderling, Vadeboncoeur, Waters, Weber, Wells, Chapin, Klein, Ziegler, Flanigan, Ehrlichman, Romney, Colson, Moore, Snyder, Whitehead, and Burch, June 22, 1972, conversation number 103-4, CAB 103, Nixon Presidential Library, https://nixonlibrary.gov.

7. Stephen Ambrose, *Nixon*, vol. 1: *The Education of a Politician, 1913–1962* (New York: Simon and Schuster, 1987), 456.

8. The political science literature on voter behavior is vast. Long story made short—people vote for candidates for a variety of reasons. Some of it is policy, but other factors such as partisanship, family, peers, media coverage, and demographics (race, religion, gender, social economic status) all shape voting decisions. In the 1970s partisanship was waning, and this era saw the rise of "candidate-centered" politics. Voters sometimes looked at the policies of the candidates; others looked at the past performance of individuals in previous positions and made their decisions based on their job performance. The personal characteristics of the candidates—"trust" and "character" to name just two—also play a role in this decision-making process. To delve into this issue at greater length, see the following: Angus Campbell, Philip E. Converse, Warren E. Miller, and Donald Stokes, *The American Voter* (New York: Wiley, 1960), was a study of the elections of the 1960s that found that partisanship and assessments of personality were more significant factors in voting decisions than policy—even if policy mattered. Michael S. Lewis-Beck, William G. Jacoby, Helmut Norpoth, and Herbert F. Weisberg reproduced this study for the elections of 1996 and 2000, using the same chapter titles and saw the same basic patters as Campbell, Converse, Miller, and Stokes: Michael S. Lewis-Beck, William G. Jacoby, Helmut Norpoth, and Herbert F. Weisberg, *The American Voter Revisited* (Ann Arbor: University of Michigan Press, 2008). Other important studies include Stephen J. Wayne, *The Road to the White House: The Politics of Presidential Elections* (New York: St. Martin's Press, 1980). This book has been updated a number of times, and readers interested in more recent developments—like the role of the internet—should see newer editions. Other important studies include Morris P. Fiorina, *Retrospective Voting in American National Elections* (New Haven, CT: Yale University Press, 1981); Samuel L. Popkin, *The Reasoning Voter: Communication and Persuasion in Presidential Cam-*

paigns (Chicago: University of Chicago Press, 1991); Martin P. Wattenberg, *The Rise of Candidate-Centered Politics: Presidential Elections of the 1980s* (Cambridge, MA: Harvard University Press, 1991); Martin P. Wattenberg, *The Decline of American Political Parties, 1952–1996*, 5th ed. (Cambridge, MA: Harvard University Press, 1998); Larry Bartels, "Partisanship and Voting Behavior, 1952–1996," *American Journal of Political Science* 44, no. 1 (January 2000): 35–50. Christopher Wlezien and Robert S. Erikson show that elections matter in changing minds as well: Christopher Wlezien and Robert S. Erikson, "The Timeline of Presidential Election Campaigns," *Journal of Politics* 64, no. 4 (November 2002): 969–993. There are many different subfields in this literature with different arguments that are worth exploring at greater length, but for now what is clear is that Nixon's political success was not just because he was right on policy issues. Personality mattered.

CHAPTER 1. WELCOME TO WASHINGTON

1. David Brady, "'I Will Demand a Commitment To Excellence' New Chief Says," and Shirley Povich, "This Morning," *Washington Post*, February 7, 1969.

2. "Williams Views Senators' Job as a 'Challenge': Early Pennant Not Considered Likely," *Washington Post*, February 15, 1969.

3. Ted Williams with John Underwood, *My Turn at Bat: The Story of My Life* (New York: Simon and Schuster, 1988), 240–242; Frederic J. Frommer, *You Gotta Have Heart: A History of Washington Baseball from 1859 to the 2012 National League East Champions* (Lanham, MD: Taylor Trade Publishing, 2013), 124.

4. "Williams Views Senators' Job as a 'Challenge'"; Williams, *My Turn at Bat*, 240–242.

5. Nixon to Williams, March 3, 1969, Folder [EX] RE 2 Baseball-Softball Being 6/30/69, Box 3, Recreation-Sports Files, Subject Files, White House Central Files.

6. Bob Addie, "Forzano Follow-Up," *Washington Post*, February 15, 1969.

7. Charles C. Alexander, *Our Game: An American Baseball History* (New York: Henry Holt, 1991), 246–270; Mark Mulvoy, "Baseball Booms Again," *Sports Illustrated*, August 4, 1969, 15.

8. Alexander, *Our Game*, 246–270; Mulvoy, "Baseball Booms Again," 15; Nixon conversation with Charles B. Wilkinson, February 23, 1973, conversation number 413-1, EOB 413, Nixon Presidential Library, https://nixonlibrary.gov.

9. Alexander, *Our Game*, 246–270; Mulvoy, "Baseball Booms Again," 15; "The Last of the Ninth," *Washington Post*, April 7, 1969.

10. Mulvoy, "Baseball Booms Again," 15; Nixon statement, February 19, 1969, Folder [EX] RE 2 Baseball-Softball Begin 6/30/69, Box 3, Recreation-Sports Files, Subject Files, White House Central Files, Nixon Presidential Project, National Archives, College Park, MD [hereafter NPP, NACP].

11. "Nixon Invited by Reds to April 9 Centennial," *New York Times*, February 23, 1969; Chapin to Dale, February 18, 1969, Folder [GEN] RE 2 Baseball-Softball, Box 3, Recreation-Sports Files, Subject Files, White House Central Files, NPP, NACP.

12. "The Last of the Ninth"; Merrell Whittlesey, "Yanks Dance at Nixon's and Nat's Inaugural Ball," *Sporting News*, April 19, 1969, 9; Bowie Kuhn, *Hardball: The Education of a Baseball Commissioner* (New York: Times Books, 1987), 56.

13. Dave Brady, "Not All Errors on Diamond," *Washington Post*, April 8, 1969; Tom Wicker, "In the Nation: Mr. Nixon Sits It Out," and Edwin L. Dale Jr., "Nixon Opens Baseball Season: 2 Errors," *New York Times*, April 8, 1969.

14. George Minot Jr., "Nats Lose Opener to Yanks, 8–4," *Washington Post*, April 8, 1969; Brady, "Not All Errors on Diamond"; Wicker, "In the Nation"; Kuhn, *Hardball*, 56; Stephen J. Walker, *A Whole New Ballgame: The 1969 Washington Senators* (Clifton, VA: Pocol Press, 2009), 36.

15. Wicker, "In the Nation."

16. "President Autographs Ball," *New York Times*, July 15, 1969; Nixon to Mantle, March 17, 1969, Folder [EX] RE 2 Baseball-Softball Begin 6/30/69, Box 3, Recreation-Sports Files, Subject Files, White House Central Files, NPP, NACP.

17. Williams and Indiana University basketball coach Bobby Knight debated who were the greatest Americans in their lifetimes during a plane trip to Russia in 1991. Bob Knight with Bob Hammel, *Knight: My Story* (New York: Thomas Dunne Books, 2002), 3–4; Alexander, *Our Game*, 270–271; Walker, *Whole New Ballgame*, 56, 96; Edwin L. Dale Jr., "Nixon Opens Baseball Season: 2 Errors," *New York Times*, April 8, 1969; George Minot Jr., "Senators Sign Ramost to $21,000 Contract," *Washington Post*, March 21, 1970; Mulvoy, "Baseball Booms Again," 15; Haldeman, *Haldeman Diaries*, July 9, 1969.

18. Alexander, *Our Game*, 270–271; Mulvoy, "Baseball Booms Again," 15; George Minot Jr., "Nixon Sees Senators Lose in 13th," *Washington Post*, June 12, 1969; Haldeman, *Haldeman Diary*, July 9, 1969.

19. "Nixon Cites Home Runs by Jackson," *Washington Post*, June 19, 1969; Nixon to Jackson, June 16, 1969, Folder [EX] RE 2 Baseball Softball Begin 6/30/69, Box 3, Recreation-Sports Files, Subject Files, White House Central Files, NPP, NACP.

20. Mrs. Gary A. Weese Sr. to Nixon, July 15, 1969, Folder [EX] RE 2 7/1/69–9/30/69, Box 3, Recreation-Sports Files, Subject Files, White House Central Files, NPP, NACP.

21. Hughes to Chapin, June 13, 1969, Folder [EX] RE 2 Baseball-Softball Begin 6/30/69, Box 3, Recreation-Sports Files, Subject Files, White House Central Files, NPP, NACP.

22. Bob Adair, "95th Derby: A Prince or A Knight?," Louisville *Courier-Journal*, May 3, 1969, and James S. Tunnell, "Nixon Mixes Politics With a Visit to Derby," Louisville *Courier-Journal*, May 4, 1969; "Nixon Had the Winner Picked Out," Lexington *Sunday Herald-Leader*, May 4, 1969.

23. John Finley, "Cares Tossed to Winds at Derby," and Bill Peterson, "People-Watching 2nd Only To Sport of Kings at Derby," Louisville *Courier-Journal*, May 4, 1969; and Tunnell, "Nixon Mixes Politics with a Visit to Derby."

24. Peterson, "People-Watching 2nd Only To Sport of Kings at Debby."

25. Tunnell, "Nixon Mixes Politics with a Visit to Derby"; David Reed, "Trainer Longden Says He'll Know What's Next for the Prince," Lexington *Sunday Herald-Leader*, May 4, 1969.

26. Peterson, "People-Watching 2nd Only To Sport of Kings at Derby"; "Nixon Had the Winner Picked Out." .

27. "A Strike Gets Nixon Endorsement," *New York Times*, September 18, 1971; "Lanes Offer Relaxation for Chief Executive," *Washington Post*, July 21, 1970; President to Ziegler, June 16, 1969, Folder [EX] RE 5 Bowling-Billiards-Pool, Box 4, Recreation-Sports Files, Subject Files, White House Central Files, NPP, NACP.

28. "How the Presidents Rate," *Sporting News*, June 12, 1997; "Fan No. 1," *Newsweek*, December 22, 1969, 70; Don Van Natta Jr., *First Off the Tee: Presidential Hackers, Duffers, and Cheaters from Taft to Bush* (New York: Public Affairs, 2003), 226, 230, 232, 235; Shirley Povich, "To Whom It May Concern," *Washington Post*, July 12, 1970.

29. Van Natta, *First Off the Tee*, 235, 241; Brennan to the President, December 9, 1971, Folder [EX] RE 11 Golf 1/l/71, Box 7, Recreation-Sports Files, Subject Files, White House Central Files, NPP, NACP.

30. Nixon conversation with Sayers, Brown, and Jones, October 17, 1972, conversation number 801-16, Oval 801, Nixon Presidential Library, https://nixonlibrary.gov.

31. Adler to Garment, August 29, 1969, Folder [EX] RE 11 Golf Begin 9/30/69, Box 7, Recreation-Sports Files, Subject Files, White House Central Files, NPP, NACP.

32. Mary Wiegers, "Nixon's Gift: 'It's a Surfboard, Daddy,'" *New York Times*, June 16, 1969; Peter Wood, "Sharks and Swimmers: An Uneasy Coexistence," *New York Times*, August 9, 1970; Eileen Shanahan, "Nixon Invites World to Visit U.S. for Bicentennial," *New York Times*, July 5, 1972.

33. Nixon conversation with Haldeman and Ziegler, April 14, 1971, conversation number 479-7, Oval 479, http://www.nixontapes.org.

34. "Remarks at the International Exhibition 'Man and His World' in Montreal Canada," June 27, 1969; "Remarks at the Baseball All-Star Reception," July 22, 1969, *Public Papers of the Presidents of the United States: Richard Nixon, 1969–1974* (Washington, DC: Office of the Federal Register, 1970–1975) [hereafter *PPP*], 487, 539 .

35. Haldeman, *Haldeman Diaries*, May 24, June 2, 1969; Haldeman notes, May 26, 1969, Folder April–June 1972 [May 9, 1972–June 30, 1972] Part II (2), Box 40, Papers of H. R. Haldeman, Staff Member and Office Files, White House Special Files; Ruwe to Haldeman, June 18, 1969, Folder [EX] RE 2 Baseball-Softball Begin 6/30/69, Box 3, Recreation-Sports Files, Subject Files, White House Central Files, NPP, NACP.

36. Leonard Koppett, "Sport Honors Base Ruth as 'Greatest Player Ever,'" *New York Times*, July 22, 1969; Ruwe to Haldeman, July 18, 1969; Ruwe to Winchester, July 9, 1969, Folder [EX] RE 2 7/1/69–9/30/69, Box 3, Recreation-Sports Files, Subject Files, White House Central Files, NPP, NACP.

37. Koppett, "Sport Honors Base Ruth as 'Greatest Player Ever.'"

38. Mulvoy, "Baseball Booms Again," 15; Kuhn, *Hardball*, 59.

39. Mulvoy, "Baseball Booms Again," 15; Kuhn, *Hardball*, 58; "Bank Business

Good, Casey Tells Nixon," Baltimore *Evening Sun*, July 23, 1969; Merrell Whittlesey, "Nixon an All-Star, Too—In East Room," *Sporting News*, August 2, 1969, 4; "Remarks at the Baseball All-Star Reception," July 22, 1969, *PPP*, 538–541.

40. "Remarks at the Baseball All-Star Reception," 538–541; Tom FitzGerald, "Who Called the Play? Nixon Was the One," *San Francisco Chronicle*, April 26, 1994. Not every sportswriter appreciated these comments. John Jeansonne of *Newsday* noted: "This caused more than a few newspaper people to cringe, since Nixon's leanings, after all, were clearly toward partisan fandome rather than journalism." John Jeansonne, "The Sports Fan," *Newsday*, April 24, 1994.

41. "Remarks at the Baseball All-Star Reception," *PPP*, 538–541.

42. "Remarks at the Baseball All-Star Reception," *PPP*, 538–541.

43. "Remarks at the Baseball All-Star Reception," *PPP*, 538–541.

44. Leonard Koppett, "Nixon Hails Baseball Stars," *New York Times*, July 23, 1969; Milton Richman, "President's Needle Hits Target," Washington *Evening Star*, July 23, 1969; Whittlesey, "Nixon an All-Star, Too—In East Room," 4; Kuhn, *Hardball*, 58; Doug Brown, "Nixon Big Winner with Baseball Guests," Baltimore *Evening Sun*, July 23, 1969; Peter Finney, "Would-Be Sportswriter, Nixon Had It Covered," New Orleans *Times-Picayune*, April 27, 1994.

45. Koppett, "Nixon Hails Baseball Stars"; Richman, "President's Needle Hits Target"; Whittlesey, "Nixon an All-Star, Too—In East Room," 4; Brown, "Nixon Big Winner with Baseball Guests."

46. Finney, "Would-Be Sportswriter, Nixon Had It Covered."

47. Brown, "Nixon Big Winner with Baseball Guests."

48. Morris Siegel, "A Groovy Scene at White House," and Milton Richman, "President's Needle Hits Target," Washington *Evening Star*, July 23, 1969; "Bank Business Good, Casey Tells Nixon," Baltimore *Evening Sun*, July 23, 1969; "Pregame Party Isn't Called Off Although the Grounds Are Wet," *New York Times*, July 23, 1969; Wauhillau La Hay, "'I Never Dreamed<3.s>So Many Famous People,'" *Washington Daily News*, July 23, 1969.

49. Siegel, "A Groovy Scene at White House." Siegel was referring to an incident that took place during the first inauguration of Andrew Jackson. After the general took the oath of office, a huge herd barged into the White House to attend a scheduled reception. This gathering of people from diverse social, racial, and ethnic groups nearly turned into a rioting mob. Every room in the residence, was full and many individuals charged the waiters when they attempted to bring out punch and liquor. The guests smashed china and glassware, and many with mud-clogged shoes stood on silk-covered chairs to get a look at their new president. Jackson was nearly crushed to death at one point. The crowd broke up only after the White House service staff started serving drinks outside the building. The strategy worked, although much of the mob exited through the windows. Robert V. Remini, *Andrew Jackson and the Course of American Freedom, 1822–1832* (New York: Harper and Row, 1981), 177–178.

50. Siegel, "A Groovy Scene at White House."

51. Kuhn, *Hardball*, 59; Merrell Whittlesey, "President Makes a Baseball Date," Washington *Evening Star*, July 23, 1969; Joseph Durso, "All-Star Game Put Off by Rain for First Time and Is Rescheduled for Today: 3-Hour Downpour Drenches Field," *New York Times*, July 23, 1969; George Minot Jr., "All-Stars Play Today after First Rainout," *Washington Post*, July 23, 1969; Klein to Nixon, August 13, 1969, Folder [EX] RE 2 7/1/69–9/30/69, Box 3, Recreation-Sports Files, Subject Files, White House Central Files, NPP, NACP.

52. Kuhn, *Hardball*, 59; Merrell Whittlesey, "Postponement Dims All-Star Game," Washington *Evening Star*, July 23, 1969; Whittlesey, "President Makes a Baseball Date"; Anne Christmas, "Old Friends Amid a Flood," Washington *Evening Star*, July 23, 1969; Durso, "All-Star Game Put Off by Rain for First Time and Is Rescheduled for Today"; Bob Addie, "100 Years of Rainfall," *Washington Post*, July 23, 1969; Minot, "All-Stars Play Today after First Rainout"; Klein to Nixon, August 13, 1969, Folder [EX] RE 2 7/1/69–9/30/69, Box 3, Recreation-Sports Files, Subject Files, White House Central Files, NPP, NACP.

53. Kuhn, *Hardball*, 59; Whittlesey, "President Makes a Baseball Date"; Koppett, "Nixon Hails Baseball Stars"; Durso, "All-Star Game Put Off by Rain for First Time and Is Rescheduled for Today"; Mary Wiegers, "The Birthday Party That Struck Out," "Nixon Hails Baseball Heroes, Shows Knowledge of Game," and "President Honored as No. 1 Fan," *Washington Post*, July 23, 1969; Klein to Nixon, August 13, 1969, Folder [EX] RE 2 7/1/69–9/30/69, Box 3, Recreation-Sports Files, Subject Files, White House Central Files, NPP, NACP.

54. Morris Siegel, "NL Bids for Recognition," Washington *Evening Star*, July 24, 1969; "Writers Make Nixon an Honorary Member," *New York Times*, July 24, 1969.

55. Haldeman, *Haldeman Diaries*, July 22, 1969; Leonard Kopett, "Agnew Pitches Twice in Relief," *New York Times*, July 24, 1969; Mulvoy, "Baseball Booms Again," 16.

56. Kuhn, *Hardball*, 60; Mulvoy, "Baseball Booms Again," 16; Jerome Holtzman, *The Commissioners: Baseball's Midlife Crisis* (New York: Total Sports, 1998), 142.

57. Mulvoy, "Baseball Booms Again," 16; "Nixon's the One," *Sporting News*, August 9, 1969.

58. "Remarks to Apollo 11 Astronauts Aboard the U.S.S. *Hornet* Following Completion of their Lunar Mission," July 24, 1969, *PPP*, 541–542.

59. "Remarks to Apollo 11 Astronauts Aboard the U.S.S. *Hornet* Following Completion of their Lunar Mission," 541–542.

60. "Remarks to Apollo 11 Astronauts Aboard the U.S.S. *Hornet* Following Completion of their Lunar Mission," 541–542.

61. "Tuesday, Wednesday Sports Summary," *Washington Post*, October 3, 1969.

62. "Tuesday, Wednesday Sports Summary"; "Williams Wins by 11 Votes," *Washington Post*, October 3, 1969, and Shirley Povich, "Ted Williams Voted Manager of the Year, of Course," *Washington Post*, October 21, 1969; emphasis in the original of Williams, *My Turn at Bat*, 243–247; Nixon to Williams, October 21, 1969, Folder [EX]

RE 2 10/1/69, Box 3, Recreation-Sports Files, Subject Files, White House Central Files, NPP, NACP.

63. Alexander, *Our Game*, 251, 255, 265.

64. Alexander, *Our Game*, 274–275.

65. "No. 1 Fan Salutes Mets with White House Call," *New York Times*, October 17, 1969.

66. Hugh Sidey, "Parting Shots," *Life*, January 30, 1970, 66; President to Ehrlichman, June 16, 1969, Folder [EX] RE Recreation-Sports Begin 9/30/69, Box 1, Recreation-Sports Files, Subject Files, White House Central Files, NPP, NACP.

CHAPTER 2. THE SECOND CENTENNIAL: THE TEXAS-ARKANSAS GAME AND OTHER FOOTBALL-RELATED MATTERS

1. Herbert S. Parmet, *Richard Nixon and His America* (Boston: Little, Brown, 1990), 65; Nixon conversation with Sayers, Brown, and Jones, October 17, 1972, conversation number 801-16, Oval 801, Nixon Presidential Library, https://nixonlibrary.gov.

2. Frank Martinez, "12,000 Jam Nixon Rally," *Orange County Register,* January 3, 1969; Phil Hana, "Nixon in Anaheim: 'This Is Your Life,'" *Los Angeles Herald-Examiner,* January 3, 1969.

3. Michael O'Brien, *Vince: A Personal Biography of Vince Lombardi* (New York: Morrow, 1987), 364–365; Nixon letter quoted in David Maraniss, *When Pride Still Mattered: A Life of Vince Lombardi* (New York: Simon and Schuster, 1999), 478.

4. Dave Brady, "'I Will Demand A Commitment To Excellence,' New Chief Says," *Washington Post*, February 7, 1969; Mollenhoff to Ehrlichman, September 9, 1969, Folder [EX] RE 10 Football Begin 9/30/69, Box 5, Recreation-Sports Files, Subject Files, White House Central Files, Nixon Presidential Project, National Archives, College Park, MD [hereafter NPP, NACP].

5. News summary, no date, News Summaries June 1969, Box 30, Annotated News Summaries, President's Office Files, White House Special Files, NPP, NACP.

6. "Lists of White House 'Enemies' and Memorandums Relating to Those Named," *New York Times*, June 28, 1973; "Namath Stays in the Pocket," *New York Times*, June 29, 1973; Mark Kriegel, *Namath: A Biography* (New York: Viking, 2005), 350.

7. "Football Fans"; page one photo with no title, and Jim O'Brien, "Crowd Reaction Spurred Miami to Tie with Raiders," *Miami News*, October 6, 1969; Bill Braucher, "Dolphins Tie Raiders, 20–20," *Miami Herald*, October 5, 1969. The AFL played its first season in 1960 and merged with the NFL in 1970. There is no record in the daily logs at the Eisenhower, Kennedy, and Johnson Presidential Libraries that any of these three attended an AFL game.

8. Williams to Nixon, November 12, 1969 Folder [EX] RE 10 Football 10/1/69, Box 5, Recreation-Sports Files, Subject Files, White House Central Files, NPP, NACP.

9. Stephen E. Ambrose, *Nixon*, vol. 2: *The Triumph of a Politician, 1962–1972*

(New York: Simon and Schuster, 1989), 301; Parmet, *Nixon and His America*, 574; Melvin Small, *Johnson, Nixon, and the Doves* (New Brunswick, NJ: Rutgers University Press, 1988), 177, 182–183.

10. Small, *Johnson, Nixon, and the Doves*, 177, 182–183

11. Ambrose, *Triumph of a Politician*, 309–310; Small, *Johnson, Nixon, and the Doves*, 190.

12. Parmet, *Nixon and His America*, 584.

13. Ambrose, *Triumph of a Politician*, 309–310; Small, *Johnson, Nixon, and the Doves*, 190; Parmet, *Nixon and His America*, 584; Helen Thomas, *Front Row at the White House: My Life and Times* (New York: Scribner, 1999), 313; Tom Dowling, *Coach: A Season with Lombardi* (New York: W. W. Norton, 1970), 242–243.

14. Ambrose, *Triumph of a Politician*, 309–310; Small, *Johnson, Nixon, and the Doves*, 190; Parmet, *Nixon and His America*, 584; Thomas, *Front Row at the White House*, 313; Dowling, *Coach*, 242–243; Shirley Povich, "This Morning: Nixon Watches a War," *Washington Post*, November 17, 1969; William N. Wallace, "Cowboys Subdue Redskins, 41–28, as Hill Stars," *New York Times*, October 16, 1969.

15. "Remarks to NASA Personnel at the Kennedy Space Center," November 14, 1969, *Public Papers of the Presidents of the United States: Richard Nixon, 1969–1974* (Washington, DC: Office of the Federal Register, 1970–1975) [hereafter *PPP*], *1969*, 9136.

16. There is no record of any statements on college football in the *Public Papers of the President*, the index to the *New York Times*, or the sports-recreation records of the White House central files. Chapin to Case, February 27, 1969, Folder [GEN] RE 10 Football Begin 9/30/69, Box 6; Chapin to Ruwe, June 12, 1969; Wilkinson to Chapin, July 7, 1969; Wilkinson to Rossides, July 22, 1969; Wilkinson to Chapin, August 19, 1969; notation on Chapin to Cole, September 2, 1969; Chapin to Nixon, September 8, 1969; Chapin to Wilkinson, September 15, 1969; Wilkinson to Chapin, September 16, 1969; Bull to Chapin, September 17, 1969; Chapin to Nixon, September 17, 1969; Bull to Nixon, September 19, 1969, Folder [GEN] RE 10 Football Begin 9/30/69, Box 5, Recreation-Sports Files, Subject Files, White House Central Files, NPP, NACP; Lincoln A. Werden, "Rutgers Trounces Princeton, 29–0, in Centennial Game," *New York Times*, September 28, 1969.

17. Roy Reed, "In the South, Football Is a Religio-Social Pastime," *New York Times*, October 6, 1969.

18. Dent to Dwight Chapin and Bob Haldeman, October 6, 1969, Folder [EX] RE Football 10/11/69, Box 5, Recreation-Sports Files, Subject Files, White House Central Files, NPP, NACP.

19. Ambrose, *Triumph of a Politician*, 89–90, 118, 155, 365–66.

20. Dan Jenkins, "Kunte Would Have Agreed, Ara," *Sports Illustrated*, December 22, 1969, 28, 30; Terry Frei, *Horns, Hogs, and Nixon Coming: Texas vs. Arkansas in Dixie's Last Stand* (New York: Simon and Schuster, 2002), 71.

21. H. R. Haldeman, *The Haldeman Diaries: Inside the Nixon White House—The*

Complete Multimedia Collection (Santa Monica, CA: Sony Electronic Publishing, 1994), CD-ROM, December 31, 1969.

22. The dominance of these two schools would have a lingering influence in college and professional football well into the 1990s. A number of future head coaches, such as Fred Akers, Barry Switzer, Jimmy Johnson, and Ken Hatfield, learned how to coach at Arkansas under the tutelage of Frank Broyles. Akers went on to become the head coach at the University of Wyoming, the University of Texas, and Purdue University. Switzer won a national title as head coach of the University of Oklahoma, and a Super Bowl as head coach of the Dallas Cowboys. Johnson was head coach of Oklahoma State University and went to the University of Miami, where he won a national title. He also won two Super Bowls as head coach of the Dallas Cowboys, and later became the coach of the Miami Dolphins. Hatfield was the head coach at the Air Force Academy, University of Arkansas, Clemson University, and Rice University. Although Akers and Hatfield never won a national title, both had better winning percentages in the Southwest Conference than Broyles. Frank Broyles with Jim Bailey, *Hog Wild: The Autobiography of Frank Broyles* (Memphis, TN: Memphis State University Press, 1979), 133–155.

23. Roy Edwards, "No Clouds in Hog Heaven," and "Spiritual Guidance," *Dallas Morning News*, December 3, 1969; Ed Fowler, "'Champion Thrives on Pressure' Says Royal," *Austin American*, December 4, 1969; "Arkansas Fans Go Hog Wild," *Arkansas Democrat*, December 3, 1969; "Countdown Finds Tension Mounting," *Arkansas Democrat*, December 5, 1969; untitled photograph on front page of the sports section, *Houston Post*, December 4, 1969; Dan Jenkins, "Texas by an Eyelash," *Sports Illustrated*, December 15, 1969, 23; John Mooney, "Sports Mirror," *Salt Lake Tribune*, December 6, 1969. A casual examination of the sport sections during the first week of December in the following papers makes clear the intense hold the game had on both states: "Tickets Scarce," and Jimmy Banks, "Color It Red and Rowdy," *Dallas Morning News*, December 2, 1969; Jack Gallagher, "Merchants Trumpet Porker Message," *Houston Post*, December 4, 1969; Bob Galt, "Pressure Mounts for Big One," *Dallas Times Herald*, December 4, 1969; Charles Carder, "Texas 'Street' Paved with Confidence," *Houston Chronicle*, December 3, 1969; David Scott, "Heavy Rain Fails to Dampen Spirit of Longhorn Band," *Austin Statesman*, December 5, 1969; Lou Maysel, "The Ozarks at High Noon: 'Horn-Hog Battle for No. 1," *Austin Statesman*, December 6, 1969; "No Ticket at Any Price," *San Antonio Light*, December 4, 1969; "Texas, Porker Game Now a 'Happening,'" *San Antonio Light*, December 4, 1969; Bob Ostrum, "For the Record," *San Antonio Light*, December 5, 1969; Bob Ostrum, "Texas, Hogs Ready for 'Shootout': Showdown for All the Marbles," *San Antonio Light*, December 6, 1969; John Woodruff, "5,000 Hog-Callers Rally; Lynn Davis Yell Victorious," *Arkansas Gazette*, December 4, 1969; Collins Hemingway, "THE Week Passes Rapidly for Frank," *Arkansas Gazette*, December 5, 1969; Leroy Donald, "Everything Day Finally Arrives," *Arkansas Gazette*, December 6, 1969; Orville Henry, "Just Stand Back and Let Them

Play It," *Arkansas Gazette*, December 6, 1969; Dan Cook, "Epic Battle Looms for Hogs, Steers," *San Antonio Express and News*, December 6, 1969; and Jim Trinkle, "Cotton's Ready," *Fort Worth Star-Telegram*, December 4, 1969. Even national media outlets took notice of this frenzy: Kenneth Delinger, "Fayetteville Hog-Wild over Its Game," *Washington Post*, December 4, 1969; Kenneth Delinger, "It's Battle Royal in Arkansas," *Washington Post*, December 6, 1969.

24. "Longhorn Day Set Saturday," *Austin American*, December 2, 1969; "Longhorn Avenue," *Austin American*, December 3, 1969.

25. "Battlefield Commission," *Dallas Morning News*, December 4, 1969; "Governor of Texas Makes It an Order to 'Hook 'em Horns,'" *Arkansas Gazette*, December 4, 1969.

26. "Keeping 'The Game' in Perspective," *Austin American*, December 2, 1969; "Longhorn Day Set Saturday"; "Over 25,000 Fans at Longhorn Rally," *Austin American*, December 4, 1969; Dan Jenkins, "Texas by an Eyelash," *Sports Illustrated*, December 15, 1969, 24.

27. "Congress Takes Sides," *Austin American*, December 4, 1969.

28. Jenkins, "Texas by an Eyelash," 23.

29. Jack Gallagher, "Texas-Hog Game Even Bigger Than Johnny Cash," *Houston Post*, December 4, 1969; Dave Campbell, "Frank Has Cool Amid Confusion," *Austin American*, December 4, 1969; "Countdown Finds Tension Mounting."

30. Haldeman makes this point clearly in his diary: "Great combination of circumstances to make this possible as final game of season is between number one and number two teams, on national TV." Haldeman, *Haldeman Diaries*, December 6, 1969.

31. J. Neal Blanton in *Game of the Century* speculates that Nixon attended the game as part of an effort to attract voters in the South in general and build support in both Texas and Arkansas, states he lost in 1968. White House documents show that this view is only half right. Nixon took a number of congressmen and senators from Texas and Arkansas with him, which Blanton claims was a reason for the trip since it gave the president an opportunity to chat and improve relations with a number of important legislators. In this case, Blanton has accorded a simple perk too much significance; it is difficult to believe that Nixon actually took a trip so he could give other politicians a ride. Finally, he makes an intriguing argument that Nixon used the trip to provide the nation with some psychological reassurance during a trying moment of social unrest. There are, however, no documents in the sports-recreation files of the Nixon White House to support this interpretation. Blanton, *Game of the Century: Texas vs Arkansas, December 1, 1969* (Austin, TX: Pemberton, 1970), 37–39; Terry Frei documents the rumors that Nixon would attend the game when it was rescheduled, but it is careful not to accept this contention at face value. Frei, *Horns, Hogs, and Nixon Coming*, 13–15, 167–169; In his memoirs—which Frei did not have access to when he was writing his book—Arledge states that the announcement that Nixon was going to Arkansas forced him to back out on a trip to Hawaii with his

wife, which was an effort on their part to save their marriage. He would hardly have committed to this effort if he had known in advance that Nixon was going to the game. As things turned out, Arledge went to Arkansas, and he and his wife divorced. Roone Arledge, *Roone: A Memoir* (New York: HarperCollins, 2003), 106; Orville Henry, "Behind Those December Dates," *Arkansas Gazette,* December 2, 1969; Merriman Smith, "A Bench Warmer at Whittier, Nixon Is No. 1 Fan Saturday," *Arkansas Gazette,* December 3, 1969; Chapin to Keough, Wilkinson, Bull, and Brown, December 1, 1969, Folder [EX] RE Football 10/11/69, Box 5, Recreation-Sports Files, Subject Files, White House Central Files, NPP, NACP.

32. The date stamp on the Mooney telegram is 3:18 p.m., and 6:33 p.m. on the Hammerschmidt cable. The time on the Chapin memo is 12:45 p.m. John Mooney to Nixon, December 1, 1969; John Paul Hammerschmidt to Nixon, December 1, 1969, Folder [EX] RE Football 10/11/69, Box 5, Recreation-Sports Files, Subject Files, White House Central Files, NPP, NACP. For a story crediting Nixon's trip to one of the telegrams see "Nixon to Attend Game, Hopes to Present Plaque," *Austin American,* December 3, 1969, or "Nixon Accepts Invite to Attend Grid Game," *Salt Lake Tribune,* December 3, 1969.

33. Joe Paterno with Bernard Asbell, *Paterno by the Book* (New York: Random House, 1990), 145–146; Frei, *Horns, Hogs, and Nixon Coming,* 13–15; Nixon to J. Dallas Shirley, December 4, 1969; Chapin to Keough, Wilkinson, Bull, and Brown, December 1, 1969, Folder [EX] RE Football 10/11/69, Box 5, Recreation-Sports Files, Subject Files, White House Central Files, NPP, NACP.

34. "A World for Mr. Nixon," *Arkansas Gazette,* December 3, 1969; Roy Edwards, "No Clouds in Hog Heaven," *Dallas Morning News,* December 3, 1969; Maurice Moore, "No Politics in Trip, Says Aide to Nixon," *Arkansas Democrat,* December 5, 1969; emphasis in the original: "Welcome, Mr. Nixon, but<3.s>," *Arkansas Democrat,* December 5, 1969; Kyle Griffin, "It's Hog-Calling Week—All The Way To Austin," Memphis *Commercial Appeal,* December 3, 1969.

35. Maurice Moore, "Fayetteville Area Security Is Tight for Visit of Nixon," *Arkansas Democrat,* December 4, 1969.

36. White House documents indicate that several other politicians who were in the presidential party at the game did not travel to Fayetteville with Nixon. Schedule, December 6, 1969, Folder [EX] RE Football 10/11/69, Box 5, Recreation-Sports Files, Subject Files, White House Central Files, NPP, NACP; Moore, "Fayetteville Area Security Is Tight for Visit of Nixon"; "Guard Clears Fellow Traveler of Nixon," *Los Angeles Times,* December 7, 1969; Frei, *Horns, Hogs and Nixon Coming,* 198.

37. "Remarks during a Television Interview in Fayetteville, Arkansas," December 6, 1969, and "Remarks on Arrival at Ft. Smith, Arkansas, to Attend the Arkansas-Texas Football Game," December 6, 1969, *PPP,* 996–998, 995–996. For details on the crowd and a slightly different construction of Nixon's comments, see Maurice Moore, "President Receives a Warm Welcome from Chilled Crowd," *Arkansas Democrat,* December 7, 1969.

38. Moore, "President Receives a Warm Welcome from Chilled Crowd"; Martin Kirby, "Number 1 Fan Says Game Was 'Great,' Praises Razorbacks," *Arkansas Democrat*, December 7, 1969; "No. 1 Fan Roots for Both Sides in 'Great Game,'" *Arkansas Gazette*, December 7, 1969; Frei, *Horns, Hogs, and Nixon Coming*, 198.

39. Walter Robertson, "Longhorns Prove Their Mettle, 15–14," *Dallas Morning News*, December 7, 1969; Lou Maysel, "Street Engineers Desperate Gamble," *Austin American-Statesman*, December 7, 1969; Blanton, *Game of the Century*, 79.

40. Robertson, "Longhorns Prove Their Mettle, 15–14"; Maysel, "Street Engineers Desperate Gamble"; Blanton, *Game of the Century*, 79.

41. Memorandum for Ehrlichman, Chapin, Butterfield, Caulfield, and Taylor, December 5, 1969, Folder [EX] RE Football 10/11/69, Box 5, Recreation-Sports Files, Subject Files, White House Central Files, NPP, NACP; Jack Keady, "Every now 'n then," *Arkansas Democrat*, December 9, 1969; Frei, *Horns, Hogs, and Nixon Coming*, 247; someone at the *New York Times* was clearly hostile toward the Longhorns, since the paper used the derogatory name that Texas A&M Aggies use to refer to the school: James M. Naughton, "Nixon Gives Plaque to Texas U. Team as First in Nation," *New York Times*, December 7, 1941.

42. "Remarks during a Television Interview in Fayetteville, Arkansas," 996–998; Blanton, *Game of the Century*, 91; Frei, *Horns, Hogs, and Nixon Coming*, 214; Richard Horman, "Nixon Sees Top Football Game," *Washington Post*, December 7, 1969; John Mooney, "Sports Mirror," *Salt Lake Tribune*, December 7, 1969; "Videotape of Texas-Arkansas Football Game," December 6, 1969, ABC Television, Part I, WHCA #3552, Part II, WHCA # 3553, Audio Video Tape Recording Section, NPP, NACP.

43. "Remarks during a Television Interview in Fayetteville, Arkansas," 996–998; "Videotape of Texas-Arkansas Football Game."

44. "Remarks during a Television Interview in Fayetteville, Arkansas," 996–998; Blanton, *Game of the Century*, 91; Frei, *Horns, Hogs, and Nixon Coming*, 214; Horman, "Nixon Sees Top Football Game"; Mooney, "Sports Mirror"; "Videotape of Texas-Arkansas Football Game."

45. Robertson, "Longhorns Prove Their Mettle, 15–14"; Maysel, "Street Engineers Desperate Gamble"; Ken Denlinger, "Texas Stands Tall after 15–14 Victory; 14–Lead Not Enough for Arkansas Victory," *Washington Post*, December 7, 1969; Frei, *Horns, Hogs, and Nixon Coming*, 223.

46. Robertson, "Longhorns Prove Their Mettle, 15–14"; Maysel, "Street Engineers Desperate Gamble"; Denlinger, "Texas Stands Tall After 15–14 Victory."

47. Robertson, "Longhorns Prove Their Mettle, 15–14"; Maysel, "Street Engineers Desperate Gamble"; Denlinger, "Texas Stands Tall After 15–14 Victory."

48. Robertson, "Longhorns Prove Their Mettle, 15–14"; Maysel, "Street Engineers Desperate Gamble."

49. Robertson, "Longhorns Prove Their Mettle, 15–14"; Maysel, "Street Engineers Desperate Gamble"; Frei, *Horns, Hogs, and Nixon Coming*, 241.

50. Jack Keady, "Steers Win It, 15–14, with Late Comeback," *Arkansas Demo-*

crat, December 7, 1969; Robertson, "Longhorns Prove Their Mettle, 15–14"; Maysel, "Street Engineers Desperate Gamble."

51. "Remarks with Texas Coach Darrell Royal," December 6, 1969, *PPP,* 998; Ambrose, *Triumph of a Politician,* 285; John Maher and Kirk Bohls, *Long Live the Longhorns!: 100 Years of Texas Football* (New York: St. Martin's Press, 1992), 172; Lou Maysel, "Top O'Morn," *Austin American,* December 10, 1969.

52. Blanton, *Game of the Century,* 123; Gayln Wilkins, "The President Upstaged by a Guy Named Street," *Fort Worth Star-Telegram,* December 7, 1969; "Remarks with Texas Coach Darrell Royal," 998; "Videotape of Texas-Arkansas Football Game."

53. "Videotape of Texas-Arkansas Football Game"; Frei, *Horns, Hogs, and Nixon Coming,* 260–261.

54. Frei, *Horns, Hogs, and Nixon Coming,* 263–265; "Videotape of Texas-Arkansas Football Game"; "Remarks with Arkansas Coach Frank Broyles," December 6, 1969, *PPP,* 999; "President Nixon Addresses Defeated Razorbacks: 'They Know How to Win . . . And Lose,'" *Arkansas Democrat,* December 7, 1969; Kirby, "Number 1 Fan Says Game Was 'Great,' Praises Razorbacks"; Randy Roberts and James S. Olson, *Winning Is the Only Thing: Sports in America since 1945* (Baltimore: Johns Hopkins University Press, 1989), 113; Orville Henry and Jim Bailey, *The Razorbacks: A Story of Arkansas Football,* new ed. (Fayetteville: University of Arkansas Press, 1996), 250.

55. Henry and Bailey, *The Razorbacks,* 263–265; Kirby, "Number 1 Fan Says Game Was 'Great,' Praises Razorbacks"; Roberts and Olson, *Winning Is the Only Thing,* 113.

56. Henry and Bailey, *The Razorbacks,* 250, 263–265; Kirby, "Number 1 Fan Says Game Was 'Great,' Praises Razorbacks"; Roberts and Olson, *Winning Is the Only Thing,* 113.

57. Haldeman, *Haldeman Diaries,* December 6, 1969.

58. Papers that had front-page photos of Nixon in their December 7, 1969, issue included *Dallas Morning News, Houston Post, Los Angeles Times, New York Times, Fort Worth Star-Telegram,* and *Washington Post.* For the photo of Nixon in the stands, see: "WR and Nixon after THE Game's First TD," *Arkansas Gazette,* December 7, 1969. For the photo of Nixon in the Razorbacks' dressing room see the *Arkansas Democrat,* December 7, 1969. For coverage of Nixon at the game see the papers previously cited in this footnote and the December 7, 1969, issues of *Dallas Times Herald, Austin American-Statesman, Houston Chronicle, San Antonio Light,* and *San Antonio Express and News.*

59. Ed Fowler, "Tumor Discovered in Leg of UT Safety Steinmark," *Austin American,* December 11, 1969; "Steinmark Trust Fund Started for UT Grid Star," *Austin American-Statesman,* December 14, 1969; Blanton, *Game of the Century,* 137–138; Jimmy Banks, *The Darrell Royal Story,* rev. ed. (Austin, TX: Eakin Press, 1994), 135.

60. Press Summary, page 7, no date, Folder December 1969, Box 31, Annotated News Summaries, President's Office File, NPP, NACP; Ambrose, *Triumph of a Politician,* 256; Banks, *The Darrell Royal Story,* 140; "Cancer Kills Steinmark, Ex-Texas Star," *Washington Post,* June 8, 1971; 116 Cong. Rec. 2239–2240 (1970); 117 Cong. Rec.

18808 (1971); Freddie Steinmark, *I Play to Win* (Boston: Little, Brown, 1971), 208, 214, 238, 240; Frei, *Horns, Hogs, and Nixon Coming*, 280.

61. Nixon to Steinmark, December 18, 1968; "Telephone Call Recommendation," December 12, 1969, Folder [EX] RE Football 10/11/69, Box 5 Recreation-Sports Files, Subject Files, White House Central Files, NPP, NACP.

62. "Cancer Kills Steinmark, Ex-Texas Star"; 116 Cong. Rec. 2239–2240 (1970); 117 Cong. Rec. 18808 (1971); Steinmark, *I Play to Win*, 208, 214, 238, 240; Frei, *Horns, Hogs, and Nixon Coming*, 280.

63. Ambrose, *Triumph of a Politician*, 256; Banks, *The Darrell Royal Story*, 140; "Steinmark Buried in Denver, Eulogized as 'A Gentle Boy,'" *Washington Post*, June 11, 1971; "Cancer Claims Steinmark; Longhorns' Star Was 22," *Boston Globe*, June 7, 1971; "Cancer Kills Steinmark, Ex-Texas Star"; "Steinmark Loses Fight with Cancer," *Chicago Tribune*, June 7, 1971; "Ex-Texas Gridder Steinmark Dies of Cancer at 22," *Los Angeles Times*, June 7, 1971; 116 Cong. Rec. 2239–2240 (1970); 117 Cong. Rec. 18808 (1971); Frei, *Horns, Hogs, and Nixon Coming*, 280; Nixon and Haldeman Conversation, June 12, 1971, Conversation Number 518-5, Oval 518, http://www.nixontapes.org.

64. Sandy Padwe, "Laughter Didn't Hide Bitterness," *Philadelphia Inquirer*, December 1, 1969.

65. In an analysis of poll ranking between 1952 and 1983, Penn State finished tenth. Most of this success, however, came after 1967, when Paterno became head coach. John F. Rooney Jr., *The Recruiting Game: Toward a New System of Intercollegiate Sport*, 2nd ed. (Lincoln: University of Nebraska Press, 1987), 73.

66. George Paterno, *Joe Paterno: The Coach from Byzantium* (Champaign, IL: Sports Publishing, 1997), 55; Neil Amdur, "National Pollsters Ponder No. 1," Harrisburg *Patriot*, December 8, 1969; "Lion Fans Protest Texas Crowning," *Pittsburgh Press*, December 7, 1969; Shafer to Nixon, December 6, 1969; J. Bruce Whelihan to John Ehrlichman, December 6, 1969, Folder [EX] RE Football 10/11/69, Box 5, Recreation-Sports Files, Subject Files, White House Central Files, NPP, NACP.

67. Amdur, "National Pollsters Ponder No. 1"; "Pa. Governor Chides Nixon for Plans to Give Trophy," *Arkansas Gazette*, December 6, 1969; "Paterno Pockets Lambert Trophy," *Austin American*, December 11, 1969.

68. Carroll Kilpatrick, "Penn State Scores on Nixon Fumble," *Washington Post*, December 6, 1969; Henry and Bailey, *The Razorbacks*, 250; Robert B. Semple Jr., "Nixon Induced to Change Signals on No. 1 College Football Team," *New York Times*, December 6, 1969.

69. Carroll Kilpatrick, "Penn State Scores on Nixon Fumble," *Washington Post*, December 6, 1969; "Remarks with Texas Coach Darrell Royal," December 6, 1969, *PPP*, 998; Henry and Bailey, *The Razorbacks*, 250; Semple, "Nixon Induced to Change Signals on No. 1 College Football Team."

70. Semple, "Nixon Induced to Change Signals on No. 1 College Football Team"; emphasis in the original of Paterno, *By the Book*, 146–147.

71. Jimmy Banks, "More Kudos For Steers," *Dallas Morning News*, December 9, 1969.

72. "'Horns Still No. 1; Hogs 3rd," *Austin American*, December 9, 1969.

73. "MacArthur First Official Award to No. 1 Longhorns," *Austin American*, December 8, 1969.

74. "Paterno Mouths: UT Won't Be No. 1," *Austin American*, December 9, 1969; "No. 1 Honors Continue," *Dallas Morning News*, December 10, 1969: "Royal, Steers Mum over Ranking Uproar," *Austin American*, December 10, 1969.

75. Dan Jenkins, "Knute Would Have Agreed, Ara," 28, 31.

76. Paterno, *By the Book*, 144–145; Billy Joe Cannon, "That Chance to Prove Who's No. 1," *Philadelphia Inquirer*, December 10, 1969; Fred Faour, "Longhorns No. 1 in Last Grid Poll," *Houston Chronicle*, January 4, 1970; Sam Blair, "Having Fun with No. 1," *Dallas Morning News*, December 9, 1969; David Bloom, "The Game You Can't Top No. 1 vs. No. 2 Not Easy to Split Out," Memphis *Commercial Appeal*, December 3, 1969; Jack Keady, "Every Now 'n Then," *Arkansas Democrat*, December 9, 1969; Jenkins, "Knute Would Have Agreed, Ara," 28, 30.

77. Ambrose dismissed this comment as an example of Nixon's horrid sense of humor. Haldeman's notes, however, indicate that everything, including the football comment, went over well. Haldeman, *Haldeman Diaries*, December 8, 1969; Ambrose, *Triumph of a Politician*, 320; Haldeman Press Conference Analysis, December 8, 1969; Haldeman Notes, December 8, 1969, Folder July–Dec 1969 Part II [Oct–Dec 1969], Box 40, Papers of H. R. Haldeman, Staff Member and Office Files, NPP, NACP; "The President's News Conference of December 8, 1969," *PPP*, 1013.

78. "President Praises Penn State," *Austin American*, December 11, 1969.

79. "Remarks at the National Football Foundation and Hall of Fame Dinner in New York City," December 9, 1969, *PPP*, 1014, 1017–1018; Robert Lipsyte, "Night at the Waldorf," *New York Times*, December 11, 1969.

80. Michael Oriard, *Bowled Over: Big Time College Football from the Sixties to the BCS Era* (Chapel Hill: University of North Carolina Press, 2009), 279–280; Ronald A. Smith, *Pay for Play: A History of Big-Time College Athletic Reform* (Urbana: University of Illinois Press, 2011), 7, 211–212; "Remarks during a Television Interview in Fayetteville, Arkansas," 996–998; "Remarks at the National Football Foundation and Hall of Fame Dinner in New York City," 1014–1018; Neil Amdur, "Football Foundation Gives Nixon Gold Medal Award," *New York Times*, December 10, 1969. For the historical precedent of White House intervention in college football, see: John J. Miller, *The Big Scrum: How Teddy Roosevelt Saved Football* (New York: HarperCollins, 2011).

81. "Remarks at the National Football Foundation and Hall of Fame Dinner in New York City," 1014, 1017–1018; Lipsyte, "Night at the Waldorf."

82. "Remarks at the National Football Foundation and Hall of Fame Dinner in New York City," 1014, 1017–18.

83. Ziegler to Thorpe, December 15, 1969, Folder [Gen] RE 10 Football 10/1/69—

12/31/69, Box 6, Recreation-Sports Files, Subject Files, White House Central Files, NPP, NACP.

84. Jack Hanley, "Nixon's Pick Stands Up," *San Jose Mercury*, January 4, 1970; Banks, *The Darrell Royal Story*, 140; Michael O'Brien, *No Ordinary Joe: The Biography of Joe Paterno* (Nashville, TN: Rutledge Hill Press, 1998), 84; Paterno, *By the Book*, 147; Nixon to Royal, January 26, 1970, Folder [EX] RE 10 Football 10/1/69, Recreation-Sports Files, Subject Files, White House Central Files, NPP, NACP.

85. O'Brien, *No Ordinary Joe*, 84; Paterno, *By the Book*, 147.

86. Ed Fowler, "Did UT Receive Aid from Above?," *Austin American*, January 2, 1970; Hanley, "Nixon's Pick Stands Up"; Banks, *The Darrell Royal Story*, 140; O'Brien, *No Ordinary Joe*, 84; Paterno, *By the Book*, 147.

87. O'Brien, *No Ordinary Joe*, 95–96. Paterno's memoirs have a different construction for this quote and many others; see Paterno, *By the Book*, 165–166; Nixon to Paterno, February 2, 1970, Folder [EX] RE 10 Football 10/1/69, Recreation-Sports Files, Subject Files, White House Central Files, NPP, NACP.

88. Robert B. Semple Jr. "Football Fan Named Nixon Spends Day Like Millions of Others," *New York Times*, January 2, 1970.

89. The entry in the Haldeman diary is listed as February 2, but the text makes it clear that the date is in error due to either a computer malfunction or a mistake on the part of those who converted the material in the journal to its electronic format. Haldeman, *Haldeman Diaries*.

90. News Summary, January 7, 1972; Kehrli to Colson, January 8, 1972, Folder [Jan. 4–8, 1972], Box 37, Annotated News Summaries, President's Office Files, White House Special Files, NPP, NACP.

91. Nixon conversation with Kissinger, January 1, 1972, conversation number 17-132, WHT 17, Nixon Presidential Library, https://nixonlibrary.gov. For conversations about avoiding conflicts with other sporting events see: Nixon conversation with Ehrlichman, October 20, 1972, conversation number 371-7, EOB 371, Nixon Presidential Library, https://nixonlibary.gov, and Nixon conversation with Haldeman and Connally, October 17, 1972, conversation number 802-1, Oval 802, Nixon Presidential Library, https://nixonlibrary.gov.

CHAPTER 3. THE OLYMPICS AND THE ALL-STAR GAME

1. Washington Senators Official Program & Scorecard, no date [1970].

2. "Remarks at the International Exhibition 'Man and His World' in Montreal Canada," June 27, 1969, *Public Papers of the Presidents of the United States: Richard Nixon, 1969–1974* (Washington, DC: Office of the Federal Register, 1970–1975) [hereafter *PPP*], 487; "Remarks at the Baseball All-Star Reception," July 22, 1969, *PPP*, 539; Dick Young, "Call y Nixon Cheers Lenny," *Kansas City Times*, January 12, 1970; Nixon to Garagiola, January 23, 1970, Folder [EX] RE 10 Football 10/1/69, Box 5, Recreation-Sports Files, Subject Files, White House Central Files, Nixon Presidential

Project, National Archives, College Park, MD [hereafter NPP, NACP]; Herbert S. Parmet, *Richard Nixon and His America* (Boston: Little, Brown, 1990), 65.

3. Stephen E. Ambrose, *Nixon*, vol. 2: *The Triumph of a Politician, 1962–1972* (New York: Simon and Schuster, 1989), 296, 315–317, 330–337; "Eisenhower, Bosman, Lolich Share Pitching Assignments," and "Taking a Lesson," *Washington Post*, April 5, 1970; H. R. Haldeman, *The Haldeman Diaries: Inside the Nixon White House—The Complete Multimedia Collection* (Santa Monica, CA: Sony Electronic Publishing, 1994), CD-ROM, April 3, 1970; Chapin to Haldeman, April 1, 1970; Bull to Chapin, April 3, 1970; Chapin to Haldeman, April 3, 1970, Folder [EX] RE 2 10/1/69, Box 3, Recreation-Sports Files, Subject Files, White House Central Files, NPP, NACP.

4. George Minot Jr., "Senators Lose Another Opener, 5–0," *Washington Post*, April 7, 1970; Merrell Whittlesey, "Rain, Cold and Lolich Foul Up Nats' Takeoff," *Sporting News*, April 18, 1970, 9; Haldeman, *Haldeman Diaries*, April 6, 1970.

5. "Status of Los Angeles' Bid for 1976 Olympic Games," no date, enclosure to Rood to Haldeman, January 13, 1970, Folder 1976 Olympic Games, Box 170, Alpha Subject Files, Papers of H. R. Haldeman, Staff Member and Office Files, White House Special Files, NPP, NACP.

6. Kilroy to Dent, January 9, 1970, Folder [EX] RE 14 Olympic Games, Box 8, Recreation-Sports Files, Subject Files, White House Central Files; Rood to Haldeman, January 13, 1970, Folder 1976 Olympic Games, Box 170, Alpha Subject Files, Papers of H. R. Haldeman, Staff Member and Office Files, White House Special Files, NPP, NACP; and enclosure "Status of Los Angeles' Bid for 1976 Olympic Games."

7. Kilroy to Dent, January 9, 1970, Folder [EX] RE 14 Olympic Games, Box 8, Recreation-Sports Files, Subject Files, White House Central Files; Rood to Haldeman, January 13, 1970; and enclosure "Status of Los Angeles' Bid for 1976 Olympic Games."

8. Rood to Haldeman, February 6, 1970; Kilroy to Sonnenfeldt, February 4, 1970, Folder 1976 Olympic Games, Box 170, Alpha Subject Files, Papers of H. R. Haldeman, Staff Member and Office Files, White House Special Files, NPP, NACP.

9. Wilkinson to Ehrlichman, February 3, 1970, Folder [EX] RE 14 Olympic Games, Box 8, Recreation-Sports Files, Subject Files, White House Central Files, NPP, NACP.

10. Sonnenfeldt to Higby, February 13, 1970, Folder 1976 Olympic Games, Box 170, Alpha Subject Files, Papers of H. R. Haldeman, Staff Member and Office Files, White House Special Files, NPP, NACP.

11. Higby to Haldeman, February 27, 1970; Haldeman to Stuart, March 2, 1970, Folder 1976 Olympic Games, Box 170, Alpha Subject Files, Papers of H. R. Haldeman, Staff Member and Office Files, White House Special Files, NPP, NACP; Charles Stuart, *Never Trust A Local: Inside the Nixon White House* (New York: Algora Publishing, 2005), 159.

12. Haldeman to Kissinger, March 4, 1970, Folder 1976 Olympic Games, Box 170, Alpha Subject Files, Papers of H. R. Haldeman, Staff Member and Office Files, White House Special Files, NPP, NACP.

13. Stuart, *Never Trust A Local,* 159; Nixon to IOC members, no date, Folder Games of the XXI Olympiad 1976 Bid Los Angeles, Calif. (1970–1971), Box 194, Papers of Avery Brundage, University of Illinois at Urbana-Champaign.

14. Stuart Memorandum for File, March 20, 1970; Haig to Eliot, March 25, 1970; Haldeman to Stuart, March 17, 1970; Stuart to Haldeman, April 29, 1970, Folder 1976 Olympic Games, Box 170, Alpha Subject Files, Papers of H. R. Haldeman, Staff Member and Office Files, White House Special Files, NPP, NACP.

15. Kilroy to Brundage, December 10, 1969; Brundage to Kilroy, December 17, 1969; "Status and Needs of the Los Angeles 1976 Olympic Committee versus the Bid of Moscow for the XXIst Summer Olympiad," no date, Folder Games of the XXI Olympiad 1976 Bid Los Angeles, Calif. (1968–1969); Kilroy to Brundage, January 2, 1970; Brundage to Kilroy, July 10, 1970; W. H. Nicholas to Brundage, June 30, 1970; Brundage to Nicholas, July 3, 1970, Folder Games of the XXI Olympiad 1976 Bid Los Angeles, Calif. (1970–1971), Box 194, Papers of Avery Brundage, University of Illinois at Urbana-Champaign

16. Stuart to Haldeman, April 29, 1970; Stuart to Haldeman, March 18, 1970; Trent to Higby, March 3, 1970, Folder 1976 Olympic Games, Box 170, Alpha Subject Files, Papers of H. R. Haldeman, Staff Member and Office Files, White House Special Files; Ehrlichman to Kissinger, February 6, 1970; Haig to Kissinger, February 16, 1970; Kissinger to Ehrlichman, February 22, 1970, Folder [EX] RE 14 Olympic Games, Box 8, Recreation-Sports Files, Subject Files, White House Central Files, NPP, NACP.

17. Stuart to Haldeman, April 29, 1970; Stuart to Haldeman, March 18, 1970; Trent to Higby, March 3, 1970, Folder 1976 Olympic Games, Box 170, Alpha Subject Files, Papers of H. R. Haldeman, Staff Member and Office Files, White House Special Files; Ehrlichman to Kissinger, February 6, 1970; Haig to Kissinger, February 16, 1970; Kissinger to Ehrlichman, February 22, 1970, Folder [EX] RE 14 Olympic Games, Box 8, Recreation-Sports Files, Subject Files, White House Central Files, NPP, NACP.

18. Stuart to Haldeman, April 29, 1970; Stuart to Haldeman, March 18, 1970; Trent to Higby, March 3, 1970, Folder 1976 Olympic Games, Box 170, Alpha Subject Files, Papers of H. R. Haldeman, Staff Member and Office Files, White House Special Files; Ehrlichman to Kissinger, February 6, 1970; Haig to Kissinger, February 16, 1970; Kissinger to Ehrlichman, February 22, 1970, Folder [EX] RE 14 Olympic Games, Box 8, Recreation-Sports Files, Subject Files, White House Central Files, NPP, NACP.

19. Stuart to Haldeman, March 18, 1970; Stuart to Haldeman, April 29, 1970, Folder 1976 Olympic Games, Box 170, Alpha Subject Files, Papers of H. R. Haldeman, Staff Member and Office Files, White House Special Files; Eliot to Kissinger, May 14, 1970, Folder [EX] RE 14 Olympic Games, Box 8, Recreation-Sports Files, Subject Files, White House Central Files, NPP, NACP.

20. Stuart to Haldeman, April 29, 1970, Folder 1976 Olympic Games, Box 170, Alpha Subject Files, Papers of H. R. Haldeman, Staff Member and Office Files, White House Special Files, NPP, NACP; Allen Guttmann, *The Games Must Go On: Avery Brundage and the Olympic Movement* (New York: Columbia University Press, 1984).

21. Kilroy to Sonnenfeldt, February 4, 1970; Stuart to Haldeman, April 29, 1970, Folder 1976 Olympic Games, Box 170, Alpha Subject Files, Papers of H. R. Haldeman, Staff Member and Office Files, White House Special Files, NPP, NACP.

22. Michael Katz, "Moscow Beaten on Second Ballot," *New York Times*, May 13, 1970.

23. Stuart to Haldeman, March 18, 1970; Stuart to Haldeman, April 29, 1970, Folder 1976 Olympic Games, Box 170, Alpha Subject Files, Papers of H. R. Haldeman, Staff Member and Office Files, White House Special Files; Eliot to Kissinger, May 14, 1970, Folder [EX] RE 14 Olympic Games, Box 8, Recreation-Sports Files, Subject Files, White House Central Files, NPP, NACP; Katz, "Moscow Beaten on Second Ballot"; Arthur Daley, "Surprise Package," *New York Times*, May 15, 1970; Stuart, *Never Trust A Local*, 160.

24. Fernand Landry and Magdeleine Yerlès, *International Olympic Committee—One Hundred Years: The Idea—The Presidents—The Achievements*, vol. 3: *The Presidencies of Lord Killanin (1972–1980) and of Juan Antonio Samaranch (1980–)* (Lausanne, Switzerland: International Olympic Committee, 1994), 80–84; Lord Killanin, *My Olympic Years* (London: Secker and Warburg, 1983), 4–5, 9; Minutes of the 69th Session of the International Olympic Committee, May 12–16, 1970, 12–14, International Olympic Committee Historical Archives, Samaranch Olympic Studies Centre, Olympic Museum, Lausanne, Switzerland.

25. Stuart to Haldeman, March 18, 1970; Stuart to Haldeman, April 29, 1970, Folder 1976 Olympic Games, Box 170, Alpha Subject Files, Papers of H. R. Haldeman, Staff Member and Office Files, White House Special Files; Eliot to Kissinger, May 14, 1970, Folder [EX] RE 14 Olympic Games, Box 8, Recreation-Sports Files, Subject Files, White House Central Files, NPP, NACP; Katz, "Moscow Beaten on Second Ballot"; Daley, "Surprise Package."

26. Katz, "Moscow Beaten on Second Ballot."

27. Ambrose, *Triumph of a Politician*, 333–357; Parmet, *Nixon and His America*, 10–12.

28. Ambrose, *Triumph of a Politician*, 333–357; Parmet, *Nixon and His America*, 10–12.

29. Haldeman, *Haldeman Diaries*, April 3, 1970.

30. Quoted in Ambrose, *Triumph of a Politician*, 374.

31. Haldeman, *Haldeman Diaries*, July 6, 1970; Kuhn to Bull, June 3, 1970; Sloan to Bull, June 22, 1970, Folder [EX] RE 2 10/1/69, Box 3, Recreation-Sports Files, Subject Files, White House Central Files, NPP, NACP.

32. Haldeman, *Haldeman Diaries*, July 6, 1970; Kuhn to Bull, June 3, 1970; Sloan to Bull, June 22, 1970; Chapin's initials are on an otherwise unsigned "Memorandum for the File," July 7, 1970, Folder [EX] RE 2 10/1/69, Box 3, Recreation-Sports Files, Subject Files, White House Central Files, NPP, NACP.

33. "A Kentucky Welcome," *Lexington Herald*, July 15, 1970; Bill Billiter, "Nixon Visit Boosts 'New Federalism,'" and Kenneth E. Loomis, "A Kentucky Hurrah," *Lou-*

isville Courier-Journal, July 15, 1970; Glen Carpenter, "Nixon, Nunn in 'Euphoric' Mood during Visit in Louisville," *Lexington Leader*, July 15, 1970; Dick Kirschten, "Enthusiastic Welcome by Kentuckians Draws Happy Response from President: Top Aides Also Arrive for Meeting," *Louisville Times*, July 14, 1970.

34. Billiter, "Nixon Visit Boosts 'New Federalism'"; Loomis, "A Kentucky Hurrah"; Kirschten, "Enthusiastic Welcome by Kentuckians Draws Happy Response from President."

35. The governors attending the conference were Albert P. Brewer of Alabama, Lester G. Maddox of Georgia, Louie B. Nunn of Kentucky, Marvin Mandel of Maryland, John Bell Williams of Mississippi, Robert W. Scott of North Carolina, James A. Rhodes of Ohio, Raymond P. Shafer of Pennsylvania, Robert E. McNair of South Carolina, Buford Ellington of Tennessee, Linwood Holton of Virginia, and Arch A. Moore Jr. of West Virginia. Bill Powell, "Nixon Hears Governors Tell Views on Use of U.S. Funds at Conference in Louisville," *Lexington Herald*, July 15, 1970; Billiter, "Nixon Visit Boosts 'New Federalism.'"

36. James M. Naughton, "President Seeks Aid of Governors," *New York Times*, July 15, 1970; Bill Billiter, "Nixon Visit Boosts 'New Federalism'," *Louisville Courier-Journal*, July 15, 1970; Carpenter, "Nixon, Nunn in 'Euphoric' Mood during Visit In Louisville"; Powell, "Nixon Hears Governors Tell Views on Use of U.S. Funds at Conference in Louisville."

37. "Nixon No 'One-Bounce Thrower,'" Cincinnati *Enquirer*, July 15, 1970.

38. "Nixon No 'One-Bounce Thrower'"; Joseph Duro, "National League Wins All-Star Game, 5–4," *New York Times*, July 15, 1970; "Videotaped Excerpts of the President at the 1970 All-Star Game," July 14, 1970, WHCA #3791, Audio Video Tape Recording Section, NPP, NACP.

39. Lindsey Nelson, *Hello Everybody, I'm Lindsey Nelson* (New York: Beech Tree Books, 1985), 325–326.

40. Transcription by the author of "Videotaped Excerpts of the President at the 1970 All-Star Game"; Shirley Povich, "This Morning," *Washington Post*, July 16, 1970.

41. Nelson, *Hello Everybody*, 326; transcription by the author of "Videotaped Excerpts of the President at the 1970 All-Star Game."

42. "Nixon No 'One-Bounce Thrower"; handwritten note to Nixon, no date [July 14, 1970], Folder [EX] RE 2 10/1/69, Box 3, Recreation-Sports Files, Subject Files, White House Central Files; "Videotaped Excerpts of the President at the 1970 All-Star Game."

43. Shirley Povich, "This Morning"; Morris Siegel, "Rose's Steamroller Job Hardly Out of Character," Washington *Evening Star*, July 15, 1970; Duro, "National League Wins All-Star Game, 5–4"; Siegel, "Rose's Steamroller Job Hardley Out of Character"; John Eradi, "#3 Cinergy/Riverfront Moment: July 14, 1970: Rose Crashes into Fosse in Dramatic All-Star Finish," Cincinnati *Enquirer*, September 22, 2002.

44. Ron Kroichick, "Bowled Over: A Collision with Pete Rose in the 1970 All-Star Game Changed Ray Fosse's career," *San Francisco Chronicle*, July 10, 1999.

45. Povich, "This Morning"; Carl Sell, "Hodges Strategems Preserve Hex over AL," Washington *Evening Star*, July 15, 1970; Duro, "National League Wins All-Star Game, 5–4."

46. George Embrey, "President Takes Taft to All-Star Game," *Columbus Evening Dispatch*, July 15, 1970; "Weaver Wishes Nixon Had Sat Nearer AL," Washington *Evening Star*, July 15, 1970; "Nixon Has a Ball at All-Star Game," Cincinnati *Enquirer*, July 15, 1970; Bob Addie, "All-Star Game Scoreless in Sixth Inning," *Washington Post*, July 15, 1970; Duro, "National League Wins All-Star Game, 5–4"; Stan Isle, "Vagabond Hickman—All-Star Hero," Stan Isle, "Rose's Grid-Style Block Brings Praise, Brickbats," and "All-Star Items," *Sporting News*, July 25, 1970, 5 and 8.

47. 116 Cong. Rec. 24569 (1970).

48. Haldeman, *Haldeman Diaries*, July 14, 1970.

49. Bull to Kuhn, May 8, 1974; Bull, "Open Door Hour Presentation by Carl Yastrezemski [*sic*]," Folder [EX] RE 2 Baseball-Softball 1/1/71, Box 3, Recreation-Sports Files, Subject Files, White House Central Files, NPP, NACP.

50. Bob Addie, "It's the Image" *Washington Post*, July 15, 1970; Addie, "All-Star Game Scoreless in Sixth Inning"; Haldeman, *Haldeman Diaries*, July 15, 1970. For coverage of the game from newspapers, see: Sell, "Hodges Strategems Preserve Hex over AL"; "Nixon to Take Nation's Pulse with Top-Level Visits to States," *Arizona Republic*, July 15, 1970; "Nixon Sat Near Winner," *Kansas City Times*, July 15, 1970; Bill Bryson, "National Success: 8 Straight!," *Des Moines Register*, July 15, 1970; Frank Cormier, "Boosts GOP Aspirants at All-Star Game," Mitchell *Daily Republic*, July 15, 1970; "Nixon Gives Taft a Boost on Visit to All-Star Game," *Fairbanks Daily News-Miner*, July 15, 1970; "Huge Crowd Loves the Nixon Pitch," and Vito Stellino, "Another Rose for NL—5–4 Win in 12," *Honolulu Advertiser*, July 15, 1970; Max Greenwald, "George Crowe Back in Picture," and "Bloomin' Rose 'Bumps' in Winner: N.L. by 5–4 in 12 with Hickman Hit," *Indianapolis Star*, July 15, 1970; "National Stars Rally in Twelfth for 5–4 Win over Americans: Pete Rose Scores Clincher on Hickman's Clutch Blow" and "Nixon Tells Game Plan," *Idaho Statesman*, July 15, 1970; "National Leaguers Grit Teeth, Bump Americans in 12 Innings," *Bismarck Tribune*, July 15, 1970; John G. Griffin, "NL Stars Extend Winning Streak to Eight," *Wyoming State Tribune*, July 15, 1970; Trev Laudeman, "Rose Proves You've Gotta 'Hit' to Win: His Collision Decides Game; Yaz's Batting Draws Plaudits," *Louisville Times*, July 15, 1970.

CHAPTER 4. THE MIDTERM ELECTIONS OF 1970

1. "President's Phone Call Perks Up Lombardi," *Washington Post*, August 14, 1970; Michael O'Brien, *Vince: A Personal Biography of Vince Lombardi* (New York: Morrow, 1987), 375; "Statement on the Death of Football Coach Vincent T. Lombardi," September 3, 1970, *Public Papers of the Presidents of the United States: Richard Nixon, 1969–1974* (Washington, DC: Office of the Federal Register, 1970–1975) [hereafter *PPP*], 698–699; John A. Farrell, *Richard Nixon: The Life* (New York: Doubleday, 2017), 410.

2. "Vince Lombardi Dead at 57, Funeral Monday in New York: Lombardi, Redskin Boss Dead at 57," *Washington Post*, September 4, 1970; O'Brien, *Vince*, 375; "Statement on the Death of Football Coach Vincent T. Lombardi," 698–699. For other news coverage of Lombardi's death, see: William N. Wallace, "Vince Lombardi, Football Coach Dies: Vince Lombardi, Pro Football Coach, Is Dead at 57," *New York Times*, September 4, 1970; Bob Verdi, "Shaped Packers' Dynasty: Coach Vince Lombardi Dies Vince Lombardi, Famed Football Coach, Dies at 57," *Chicago Tribune*, September 4, 1970; George Frazier, "Vince Lombardi Lived for Football," *Boston Globe*, September 4, 1970.

For tributes from sports columnists, see: John Crittenden, Vince Lombardi: Love and Fear," *Miami News*, September 3, 1970; Sid Hartman, "Sid Hartman," *Minneapolis Tribune*, September 4, 1970; Bill Shefski, "His Legacy Lives On," *Philadelphia Daily News*, September 4, 1970; Bill McGrotha, "He Came Quietly," *Tallahassee Democrat*, September 4, 1970; Frank Dolson, "Vince Made Men as Well as Teams," *Philadelphia Inquirer*, September 4, 1970; Bob Maisel, "The Morning After," Baltimore *Sun*, September 4, 1970; Bob Broeg, "Lombardi: A Man of Contradictions and Simplicity," *St. Louis Post-Dispatch*, September 4, 1970; Bob Addie, "Lombardi: A Patriot," *Washington Post*, September 4, 1970; Shirley Povich, "Even at Top, Lombardi Looked Up," *Washington Post*, September 4, 1970.

Emphasis in the original editorial board tribute: "Vincent Lombardi," *Washington Post*, September 4, 1970. For editorial tributes from the other papers, see: "The Living Lombardi Legend," *Green Bay Press-Gazette*, September 3, 1970; "Head Coach Vince Lombardi," *Pittsburgh Post-Gazette*, September 4, 1970; "Vince Lombardi," *Philadelphia Daily News*, September 4, 1970; "Lombardi Knew the Game," *Kansas City Times*, September 5, 1970.

3. "Statement on the Death of Football Coach Vincent T. Lombardi," 698–699; O'Brien, *Vince*, 375; "Vince Lombardi Dead at 57; Funeral Monday in New York," *Washington Post*, September 4, 1970; "President Leads a Nation of Mourners," *Washington Post*, September 4, 1970; David Anderson, "Cardinal Celebrates Funeral Mass for Lombardi," *New York Times*, September 8, 1970; Dave Brady, "Lombardi Buried after Last Tribute," *Washington Post*, September 8, 1970; "Nixon Attends Services Here," *Washington Post*, September 8, 1970.

4. The states were Alaska, California, Connecticut, Florida, Illinois, Indiana, Maryland, Missouri, Nevada, New Jersey, New Mexico, North Dakota, Ohio, Tennessee, Texas, Utah, and Wyoming. Howard to Chapin, August 10, 1970, Folder [EX] RE 10 Football 10/1/69, Box 5, Recreation-Sports Files, Subject Files, White House Central Files, Nixon Presidential Project, National Archives, College Park, MD [hereafter NPP, NACP].

5. Chapin to Sloan, August 26, 1970; Sloan to Wilkinson, August 28, 1970; Wilkinson to Sloan, September 9, 1970, Folder [EX] RE 10 Football 10/1/69, Box 5, Recreation-Sports Files, Subject Files, White House Central Files, NPP, NACP.

6. H. R. Haldeman, *The Haldeman Diaries: Inside the Nixon White House—The*

Complete Multimedia Collection (Santa Monica, CA: Sony Electronic Publishing, 1994), CD-ROM, October 28, 1970; Dent to Chapin, October 6, 1970, Folder [EX] RE 10 Football 10/1/69, Box 5, Recreation-Sports Files, Subject Files, White House Central Files, NPP, NACP.

7. Klein to Nixon, December 7, 1970, Folder [EX] RE 10 Football 10/1/69, Box 5, Recreation-Sports Files, Subject Files, White House Central Files, NPP, NACP.

8. Klein to Nixon, December 7, 1970.

9. Emphasis in Stephen E. Ambrose, *Nixon*, vol. 2: *The Triumph of a Politician, 1962–1972* (New York: Simon and Schuster, 1989), 375–377; "Address in the Alfred M. Landon Lecture Series at Kansas State University," September 16, 1970, *PPP*, 757–758.

10. "Bart Starr—Citizen and Quarterback," *Green Bay Press-Gazette*, October 18, 1970.

11. "Nixon's Visit," *Milwaukee Journal*, October 17, 1970; James Bartlet, "Nixon Visit Gives 'Insiders' a Day," *Green Bay Press-Gazette*, October 18, 1970; "Politics Upstaging Starr," *Milwaukee Sentinel*, October 17, 1970.

12. The candidates were Lieutenant Governor Jack Olson for governor, John Erickson for the Senate and John Byrnes for reelection to the House of Representatives for a fourteenth term. Nixon added Byrnes to a prepared statement endorsing the other two candidates that was distributed to the press: James Bartlet, "Nixon Gets in Plugs as Hecklers Chant" and "Crowds Wait at Airport for Glimpse of Nixon," and Bob Woessner, "Green Bay Takes a Look at Mr. President," *Green Bay Press-Gazette*, October 18, 1970; "Remarks on Arrival at Green Bay, Wisconsin," October 17, 1970, *PPP*, 873.

13. "Remarks at a Testimonial Reception in Honor of Green Bay Packers Quarterback Bart Starr," October 17, 1970, *PPP*, 873–876; John P. Doyle, "Nixon Calls Starr No. 1 American; Bart: I'm Luckiest," *Green Bay Press-Gazette*, October 18, 1970.

14. "Remarks at a Testimonial Reception in Honor of Green Bay Packers Quarterback Bart Starr," 873–876.

15. "Remarks at a Testimonial Reception in Honor of Green Bay Packers Quarterback Bart Starr," 873–876.

16. "Remarks at a Testimonial Reception in Honor of Green Bay Packers Quarterback Bart Starr," 873–876.

17. Doyle, "Nixon Calls Starr No. 1 American."

18. Doyle, "Nixon Calls Starr No. 1 American."

19. "Welcome, Mr. President," *Green Bay Press-Gazette*, October 17, 1970; "2 'Quarterbacks' Shine: Crowd Loves Bart, Dick" *Green Bay Press-Gazette*, October 18, 1970; Bob Woessner, "Writer Gets the Best of Nixon Pen Exchange," *Green Bay Press-Gazette*, October 18, 1970; "Nixon Plugs State Ticket" and "6,000 Cheer Starr, Nixon," *Milwaukee Journal*, October 18, 1970; "Nixon Visit to Honor Starr May Save GOP Campaign," *Milwaukee Sentinel*, October 19, 1970.

20. "Welcome, Mr. President"; "2 'Quarterbacks' Shine"; Woessner, "Writer Gets

the Best of Nixon Pen Exchange"; "Nixon Plugs State Ticket"; "6,000 Cheer Starr, Nixon"; "Nixon Visit to Honor Starr May Save GOP Campaign."

21. "Remarks in the Ohio State House, Columbus, Ohio," October 19, 1970, *PPP*, 878; "President Nixon Speaks in Columbus, Urges Ohioans to Elect Taft, Cloud: Thousands Greet Him," *Columbus Evening Dispatch*, October 19, 1970; Haldeman, *Haldeman Diaries*, October 19, 1970; John Lombardo, *A Fire to Win: The Life and Times of Woody Hayes* (New York: Thomas Dunne Books, 2005), 159.

22. Paul Horning, "Nixon Phones Bucks, Hayes Lauds Defense," *Columbus Evening Dispatch*, November 15, 1970; "Nixon Congratulates DeMo, Woody for a Great Game," *Indianapolis Star*, November 15, 1970.

23. "Remarks in Kansas City, Missouri," October 19, 1970, *PPP*, 932–933; Ray Morgan, "Nixon to 13,000 in Arena," *Kansas City Times*, October 20, 1970.

24. "Remarks in Dundalk, Maryland," October 24, 1970; "Remarks in Rochester, Minnesota," October 29, 1970; "Remarks in Phoenix, Arizona," October 31, 1970, *PPP*, 932–933, 892, 1005, 1033.

25. "Remarks in Dallas," October 28, 1970, *PPP*, 981–982; "GOP's Team Tops, Nixon Tells Dallas," *Dallas Times Herald*, October 29, 1970; Carl Freund, "Nixon Pays a Surprise Visit" and "President Fumbles Ball in Tooting SMU Horn," *Dallas Morning News*, October 29, 1970; Jim Vachule, "Nixon Beats Drum for Bush, Eggers" and "Nixon Bobbles the Ball in Referring to SMU Team," *Fort Worth Star-Telegram*, October 29, 1970; Haldeman, *Haldeman Diaries*, October 28, 1970.

26. "Remarks in Omaha, Nebraska," October 29, 1970, *PPP*, 1011–1012; Dick Herman, "Rock Throwers, Fire Mar Nixon's Visit Home," *Lincoln Evening Journal*, October 30, 1970; David Tishendorf, "Pro-Nixon Crowd Doesn't Mind Chilly Floor," *Omaha World-Herald*, October 30, 1970; Haldeman, *Haldeman Diaries*, October 29, 1970.

27. Sydney Kossen, "Hundreds to Picket in San Jose," *San Francisco Examiner*, October 29, 1970; "Tight Police Security for Nixon Rally," *San Jose Mercury*, October 29, 1970; Earl C. Behrens, "Crowd Pelts Nixon's Car after a Rally in San Jose," *San Francisco Chronicle*, October 30, 1970; "Remarks in San Jose, California," October 29, 1970, *PPP*, 1020.

28. William Safire questions the accuracy of a *Newsweek* story attributing the comment to Nixon. Accounts in the October 30, 1970, issue of the *San Francisco Examiner* and *San Francisco Chronicle* include reports from journalists on the scene who heard him make the same comment. Behrens, "Crowd Pelts Nixon's Car after a Rally in San Jose"; Sydney Kossen, "Nixon Pledges Sharp Reply to Mob Violence," *San Francisco Examiner*, October 30, 1970; Haldeman, *Haldeman Diaries*, October 30, 1970; Richard M. Nixon, *RN: The Memoirs of Richard Nixon* (New York: Grosset & Dunlap, 1978), 492; William Safire, *Before the Fall: An Inside View of the Pre-Watergate White House* (Garden City, NY: Doubleday, 1975), 327–333 In his memoirs, Jeb Stuart Magruder uses language suggesting skepticism about the accuracy of reports that the president goaded the crowd from the hood of his car. The *San Francisco Chronicle*

ran a front-page photo in its October 30 issue of Nixon giving the double victory sign to the crowd from atop the limousine. Jeb Stuart Magruder, *An American Life: One Man's Road to Watergate* (New York: Atheneum, 1974), 128–129; "Presidential Gesture," *San Francisco Chronicle*, October 30, 1970; Kossen, "Nixon Pledges Sharp Reply to Mob Violence."

29. Behrens, "Crowd Pelts Nixon's Car after a Rally in San Jose"; "Mob Surprised Nixon," *San Francisco Chronicle*, October 31, 1970; Tom Harris and Jim Larimore, "Young Militants Hurl Epithets at President," *San Jose Mercury*, October 30, 1970; Haldeman, *Haldeman Diaries*, October 29, 1970.

30. "Statement about Disorders at San Jose, California," October 29, 1970; "Telegram to the President of the Student Body of San Jose State College," October 31, 1970; "Letter to the Publisher of the San Jose Mercury News," October 31, 1970, *PPP*, 1027–28, 1038, 1039; Haldeman, *Haldeman Diaries*, October 29, 1970; Magruder, *An American Life*, 128–129; Safire, *Before the Fall*, 327–333.

31. Harry Farrell, "City Violence Deplored by Both Parties," *San Jose Mercury*, October 31, 1970; "An Editorial," San Jose *Sunday Mercury News*, November 1, 1970.

32. Haldeman, *Haldeman Diaries*, October 30, 1970; Magruder, *An American Life*, 128–129; Safire, *Before the Fall*, 327–333.

33. Haldeman, *Haldeman Diaries*, October 30, 1970; Farrell, "City Violence Deplored by Both Parties"; "Mob Surprised Nixon"; "Murphy Is Very Upset at Violence," *San Francisco Examiner*, October 31, 1970.

34. Paul Dean, "Security for Visit Tightest Seen Here," *Arizona Republic*, November 1, 1970; Kathleen Hall Jamieson, *Packaging the Presidency: A History and Criticism of Presidential Campaign Advertising* (New York: Oxford University Press, 1984), 276–277.

35. "Grid Team Plane Crashes; 40 Aboard Feared Victims," *Wichita Eagle and Beacon*, October 3, 1970; "Last Hopes Dashed as Memorials Begin," *Wichita Eagle and Beacon*, October 4, 1970; "WSU Players Fly Home after Long Night in Utah," *Wichita Eagle*, October 5, 1970; "Nixon Aids Wichita State," *New York Times*, December 10, 1970; Nixon to Ahlberg, October 3, 1970, [EX] RE 10 Football 10/1/69, Recreation-Sports Files, Subject Files, White House Central Files, NPP, NACP.

36. "75 on Football Team Plane Die in West Virginia Crash," *New York Times*, November 15, 1970; Nixon to Dedmon, November 17, 1970, [EX] RE 10 Football 10/1/69, Recreation-Sports Files, Subject Files, White House Central Files, NPP, NACP.

37. The Senate candidates who won included Robert Taft, Ohio; Win Prouty, Vermont; Hugh Scott, Pennsylvania; William Brock, Tennessee; Glenn Beall, Maryland; Roman Hruska, Nebraska; and Paul Fannin, Arizona. The Senate candidates who lost included Nelson Gross, New Jersey; John Erickson, Wisconsin; Tom Kleppe, North Dakota; John Danforth, Missouri; Richard Roudebush, Indiana; William Cramer, Florida; George Bush, Texas; Ralph Smith, Illinois; Clark MacGregor, Minnesota; George Murphy, California; Andy Carter, New Mexico; William Raggio, Nevada; and Laurence Burton, Utah. The gubernatorial candidates who won included Ronald

Reagan, California; Jack Williams, Arizona; and Winfield Dunn, Tennessee. The gubernatorial candidates who lost included Deane Davis, Vermont; Ray Boderick, Pennsylvania; Jack Olson, Wisconsin; Roger Cloud, Ohio; Kent Frizzell, Kansas; Stanley Blair, Maryland; Claude Kirk, Florida; Paul Eggers, Texas; Douglas Hearn, Minnesota; Norbert Tiemann, Nebraska; Pete Domenici, New Mexico; and Ed Fike, Nevada. The House candidates who won included Bob Stafford, Vermont; Johnny Byrnes, Wisconsin; Jimmy Quillen, Tennessee; Wilmer Mizell, North Carolina; Earl Ruth, North Carolina; Charles Jonas, North Carolina; James Broyhill, North Carolina; Larry Hogan, Maryland; Bill Young, Florida; Harold Collier, Illinois; Phil Crane, Illinois; Bob McClory, Illinois; and Manny Lujan, New Mexico. The House candidates who lost included Ann Uccello, Connecticut; William Dowd, New Jersey; Bob McCarney, North Dakota; Frank Everett, North Carolina; Herbert Howell, North Carolina; Jack Hawke, North Carolina; Clifton Barnham, North Carolina; Frederick Weber, North Carolina; Luke Atkinson, North Carolina; Ross Adair, Indiana; Phyllis Schlafly, Illinois; and Ed Foreman, New Mexico. "Political Pros Reject G.O.P. Claim of Election Gain" and "Nixon: What Were His Real Conclusions on the '70 Campaign?," *New York Times*, November 15, 1970; Benjamin J. Guthrie, *Statistics of the Congressional Elections of November 3, 1970* (Washington, DC: US Government Printing Office, 1971).

38. Ron Calhoun, "Did Nixon Inspire More Votes for Bush?," *Dallas Times Herald*, October 29, 1970; Allen J. Matusow, *Nixon's Economy: Booms, Busts, Dollars, and Votes* (Lawrence: University Press of Kansas, 1998), 83; Ambrose, *Triumph of a Politician*, 396–397.

39. Haldeman, *Haldeman Diaries*, January 1, 1971.

40. Price to Nixon, November 13, 1970, quoted in Ambrose, *Triumph of a Politician*, 397.

41. Haldeman, *Haldeman Diaries*, January 5, 1971.

42. Buchanan to Haldeman and Price, January 5, 1971, Folder [EX] RE 10 Football 1/1/71–12/20/72, Box 5, Recreation-Sports Files, Subject Files, White House Central Files, NPP, NACP.

43. "Remarks to a Student-Faculty Convocation at the University of Nebraska," January 14,1971, *PPP*, 1971, 29–35.

44. Conde Sargent, "More Than Anything, I Was Pleased," *Omaha World-Herald*, January 15, 1971.

45. "Remarks to a Student-Faculty Convocation at the University of Nebraska," 29–35; Don Forsythe, "President's Trophy Presented," *Lincoln Evening Journal*, January 14, 1971; Fred J. Maroon, *The Nixon Years, 1969–1974: White House to Watergate* (New York: Abbeville Press, 1999), photo on 42.

46. "Remarks to a Student-Faculty Convocation at the University of Nebraska," 29–35.

47. "Remarks to a Student-Faculty Convocation at the University of Nebraska," 29–35; Don Pieper, "'Splendid Behavior' Lauded by Varner," *Omaha World-Herald*, January 15, 1971.

48. "Remarks to a Student-Faculty Convocation at the University of Nebraska," 29–35.

49. "No. 1 Coach Devaney No. 13 on Protocol List," *Omaha World-Herald*, January 15, 1971; Sargent, "More Than Anything, I was Pleased"; Pieper, "'Splendid Behavior' Lauded by Varner"; Haldeman, *Haldeman Diaries*, January 14, 1971.

50. Pieper, "'Splendid Behavior' Lauded by Varner."

51. "Mr. Nixon in Lincoln, Nebraska," *Washington Post*, January 18, 1971.

52. Haldeman, *Haldeman Diaries*, January 14, 1971.

53. Richard Reeves, *President Nixon: Alone in the White House* (New York: Simon and Schuster, 2001), 21–22, 25.

54. "The Head Coach Analogue," *Nation*, January 15, 1973, 66; James Reston, "Sports and Politics America," *New York Times*, September 12, 1969; Ira Berkow, *Red: A Biography of Red Smith* (New York: Times Books, 1986), 247.

55. "Remarks at the Dedication of Dwight David Eisenhower High School in Utica, Michigan," August 24, 1972, *PPP*, 806.

56. "Remarks to Members of the Washington Redskins Professional Football Team during a Practice Session at Redskins Park," November 23, 1971, *PPP*, 1135.

CHAPTER 5. THE FINAL DEATH OF THE WASHINGTON SENATORS

1. Thomas Boswell et al., *Redskins: A History of Washington's Team* (Washington, DC: Washington Post Books, 1997), v–vi.

2. Nixon to Williams, January 8, 1973, Folder [EX] RE 10 Football 1/1/73, Box 6, Recreation-Sports Files, Subject Files, White House Central Files, Nixon Presidential Project, National Archives, College Park, MD [hereafter NPP, NACP].

3. "Remarks at the Swearing In of Walter E. Washington as Mayor of the District of Columbia," February 22, 1973, *Public Papers of the Presidents of the United States: Richard Nixon, 1969–1974* (Washington, DC: Office of the Federal Register, 1970–1975) [hereafter *PPP*], 125–126. For other examples of this friendly banter about the plight of the Washington teams, see "Remarks at a Question-and-Answer Session with a 10-Member Panel of the Economic Club of Detroit," September 23, 1971, *PPP*, 966; "Toast of the President at a Dinner Honoring Labor Leaders," September 7, 1970, *PPP*, 709; "Remarks at the Republican Victory Dinner," May 7, 1969, *PPP*, 360; and "Remarks on Return from Meeting with President Thieu at Midway Island," June 10, 1969, *PPP*, 451.

4. John Matthew Smith, *The Sons of Westwood: John Wooden, UCLA, and the Dynasty That Changed College Basketball* (Urbana: University of Illinois Press, 2013), 169–170; Wilkinson to Sloan, October 15, 1969, Folder [EX] RE 1 Basketball, Box 1; Buchanan notation on Sloan to Buchanan, October 27, 1970; Nixon to Sharman, January 3, 1972, Folder [GEN] RE 1, Basketball 1/1/71; Sloan to Wilkinson, March 17, 1970, Folder [EX] RE 1 Basketball, Box 3, Recreation-Sports Files, Subject Files, White House Central Files, NPP, NACP.

5. Jerry Zgoda, "Nixon Chooses to See Wolves in His NBA Debut," *Minneapolis*

Star Tribune, March 1, 1992; comments after the President delivered his "Address to the Nation on Vietnam," April 26, 1972, Conversation number 715-6, Oval 715, http://www.nixontapes.org.

6. H. R. Haldeman, *The Haldeman Diaries: Inside the Nixon White House—The Complete Multimedia Collection* (Santa Monica, CA: Sony Electronic Publishing, 1994), CD-ROM, September 8, 1972; Katharine Graham, *Personal History* (New York: Knopf, 1997), 484.

7. David Quentin Voight, *American Baseball*, vol. 3, *From Postwar Expansion to the Electronic Age* (University Park: Pennsylvania State University Press, 1983), 112–115; Ron Fimrite, "Bad Case of the Short Shorts," *Sports Illustrated*, August 9, 1971, 21–25; Bowie Kuhn, *Hardball: The Education of a Baseball Commissioner* (New York: Times Books, 1987), 87; Marvin Miller, *A Whole Different Ball Game: The Sport and Business of Baseball* (Secaucus, NJ: Carrol Publishing, 1991), 178; Brad Snyder, *A Well-Paid Slave: Curt Flood's Fight for Free Agency in Professional Sports* (New York: Viking, 2006), 201, 216–217, 224, 231.

8. William Gildea, "No. 1 Fan Recalls Forgotten Athlete," *Washington Post*, March 31, 1970; "Post Man's Column on Nixon Rings Bell," *Washington Post*, April 1, 1970.

9. Fimrite, "Bad Case of the Short Shorts," 21–25; James Edward Miller, *The Baseball Business: Pursuing Pennants and Profits in Baltimore* (Chapel Hill: University of North Carolina Press, 1990), 177–178; Kuhn, *Hardball*, 87; George Minot Jr., "Senators Win on 2 Hits: Nixon Sees Howard's 25th," *Washington Post*, July 21, 1970; Washington Senators Official Program & Scorecard, [1970].

10. Nixon conversation with Haldeman, July 21, 1971, Conversation number 541-2, Oval 541, http://www.nixontapes.org.

11. Haldeman, *Haldeman Diaries*, March 14, 15, 1971; "Message on the Opening of the 1971 Baseball Season," April 5, 1971, *PPP*, 500–501. James N. Rowe was a POW with Pitzer and wrote *Five Years to Freedom* (Boston: Little, Brown, 1971) about their experiences in the custody of the Viet Cong.

12. Bull to Kuhn, May 8, 1974; Bull, "Open Door Hour Presentation by Carl Yastrezemski [*sic*]," Folder [EX] RE 2 Baseball-Softball 1/1/71, Box 3, Recreation-Sports Files, Subject Files, White House Central Files, NPP, NACP; Nixon conversation with H. R. Haldeman and Ronald L. Ziegler, April 13, 1971, Conversation number 478-11, Oval 478, http://www.nixontapes.org.

13. Personal observation of the author.

14. Larry Berman, *No Peace, No Honor: Nixon, Kissinger, and Betrayal in Vietnam* (New York: Free Press, 2001), 107–108; Stephen E. Ambrose, *Nixon*, vol. 2: *The Triumph of a Politician, 1962–1972* (New York: Simon and Schuster, 1989), 419–421.

15. Kuhn, *Hardball*, 94; Fimrite, "Bad Case of the Short Shorts," 21–25.

16. Kuhn, *Hardball*, 94–96.

17. Kuhn, *Hardball*, 96.

18. William B. Mead and Paul Dickson, *Baseball: The President's Game* (Washington, DC: Farragut Publishing, 1993), 107–108; Ailes to Higby, July 1, 1971; Spong to

Nixon, August 16, 1971; Zad to Nixon, August 25, 1971, Folder [GEN] RE 2 Baseball-Softball 1/1/71, Box 4, Recreation-Sports Files, Subject Files, White House Central Files, NPP, NACP.

19. Klein to Zad, September 7, 1971, Folder [GEN] RE 2 Baseball-Softball 1/1/71, Box 4, Recreation-Sports Files, Subject Files, White House Central Files, NPP, NACP.

20. Kuhn, *Hardball*, 97; Nixon-Haldeman-Ziegler conversation, September 20, 1971, Conversation Number 576-11, Oval 576, http://www.nixontapes.org.

21. Nixon-Haldeman-Ziegler conversation, September 20, 1971.

22. James Welsh, "Nixon Speaks Out: 'Keep Baseball Here,'" *Washington Evening Star*, September 20, 1971; Shelby Coffey, "Nixon Sees Baseball Void as 'Heartbreaking,'" *Washington Post*, September 21, 1971. There are different constructions of the Nixon statement in the two Washington dailies. The quotation here comes primarily from the *Evening Star*, which had a more informative article. Nixon-Haldeman-Ziegler conversation, September 20, 1971; Nixon photo session with Schaefer and George, September 20, 1971, Conversation Number 576-13, Oval 576, http://www.nixontapes.org.

23. Kuhn, *Hardball*, 97–98.

24. Kuhn, *Hardball*, 97–98; "Short Takes Senators to Texas," *Washington Post*, September 22, 1971.

25. Harry Gage, "'We've Made It Big in Baseball!'" *Dallas Times Herald*, September 22, 1971; Shirley Povich, "This Morning," *Washington Post*, September 22, 1971; Merrell Whittlesey, "Vote on Senators Tuesday," and Morris Siegel, "Kuhn Meets with Short, Danzansky," *Washington Evening Star*, September 17, 1971; Merrell Whittlesey, "The Future: Dim Hopes, Questions," and Morris Siegel, "Did Danzansky Have a Chance?" *Washington Evening Star*, September 22, 1971; Kuhn, *Hardball*, 97–98; Eric Nadel, *Texas Rangers: The Authorized History* (Dallas, TX: Taylor Publishing, 1997), 56; American League meeting minutes, September 21, 1971, attached to Fitzpatrick to Sisk and Horton, August 9, 1976, Folder 3, Box 1, Series IV, Papers of Bowie Kuhn, National Baseball Hall of Fame, Cooperstown, New York.

26. "D.C." notes, no date, and Arthur D. Little, Inc., "Comparative Statistics on Washington, D.C. and Ft. Worth–Dallas," September 1971, Folder 7, Box 13, Series VI: Hardball, Papers of Bowie Kuhn, National Baseball Hall of Fame, Cooperstown, New York.

27. Kuhn, *Hardball*, 98; "Short Takes Senators to Texas."

28. Merle Heryford, "Washington Is on the Trinity Now," and editorial, "Washington Is on the Trinity Now," *Dallas Morning News*, September 22, 1971; Randy Galloway, "A Hero's Welcome," *Dallas Morning News*, September 23, 1971, Merle Heryford, "Back in Saddle, Again," *Dallas Morning News*, September 23, 1971; Gage, "We've Made It Big in Baseball"; "A Big League Area," *Dallas Times Herald*, September 23, 1971; Galyn Wilkins, "Hizzoner Overcame Political Spitballs," *Fort Worth Star-Telegram*, September 23, 1971.

29. Sam Blair, "So, Back to Reality," *Dallas Morning News*, September 23, 1971;

Teague quoted in " . . . Texas Solons Pleased," *Dallas Times Herald*, September 22, 1971.

30. Tunney quote as it appeared in Shelby Coffey III, "'We're All Disappointed,' Mayor Says," *Washington Post*, September 22, 1971; Shelby Coffey III, "Congressional Wrath Boils," *Washington Post*, September 22, 1971; Smith column reprinted from the *New York Times* in Red Smith, "Senators' Move Invites Trouble," *Washington Post*, September 24, 1971; Gage, "We've Made It Big in Baseball"; Kuhn, *Hardball*, 100.

31. Harold McKinney, "Nixon to Get D-FW Invite," *Fort Worth Star-Telegram*, September 23, 1971; "Senators Go, Nixon for Angels," *Washington Evening Star*, September 22, 1971; Mike Shropshire, *Seasons in Hell: With Billy Martin, Whitey Herzog, and "The Worst Baseball Teams in History"—The 1973–1975 Texas Rangers* (New York: Donald I. Fine, 1996), 154.

32. Shirley Povich, "This Morning," *Washington Post*, November 25, 1971.

33. Nixon conversation with Mayor Walter E. Washington, Stephen B. Bull, Jerry V. Wilson, John D. Ehrlichman, and Egil G. ("Bud") Krogh Jr., October 13, 1971, Conversation number 590-3, Oval 590, http://www.nixontapes.org.

34. "Blue Meets the President," *Christian Science Monitor*, August 19, 1971; Albin Krebs, "Nixon Greets Blue," *New York Times*, August 18, 1971; Joseph Durso, "Orioles Win, 5–3 and Capture Pennant; Pirates Beat Giants, 2–1, to Go One Up," *New York Times*, October 6, 1971; Magruder to Butterfield and Chapin, July 20, 1971; Nixon to Blue, August 16, 1971, Folder [EX] RE 2 Baseball-Softball 1/1/71, Box 3, Recreation-Sports Files, Subject Files, White House Central Files, NPP, NACP.

35. Magruder to Butterfield and Chapin, July 20, 1971; Nixon to Blue, August 16, 1971; Chapin to Kuhn, September 23, 1971; Ziegler and Scali comments with emphasis in the original in Parker to Chapin, September 24, 1971; Parker to Haldeman, October 6, 1971; notations on two different Rhatican, "Recommended Telephone Calls" memos, both dated October 15, 1971, Folder [EX] RE 2 Baseball-Softball 1/1/71, Box 3, Recreation-Sports Files, Subject Files, White House Central Files, NPP, NACP; Nixon-Rogers conversation, October 17, 1971, Conversation Number 11-105, minute marker 58:00-102:30, WHT 011, http://www.nixontapes.org.

36. Leonard Koppett, "A Presidential Call—and Sayonara," *New York Times*, October 18, 1971; "Notes on People," *New York Times*, October 13, 1971; Haldeman, *Haldeman Diaries*, October 16, 1971; Magruder to Butterfield and Chapin, July 20, 1971; Nixon to Blue, August 16, 1971; Chapin to Kuhn, September 23, 1971; Parker to Haldeman, October 6, 1971; notations on two different Rhatican, "Recommended Telephone Calls" memos, both dated October 15, 1971, Folder [EX] RE 2 Baseball-Softball 1/1/71, Box 3, Recreation-Sports Files, Subject Files, White House Central Files, NPP, NACP.

37. Nixon conversation with Haldeman, October 7, 1971, Conversation number 285-16, EOB 285, http://www.nixontapes.org; Nixon conversation with Allen, October 8, 1972, Conversation number 31-24, WHT 31, Nixon Presidential Library, https://nixonlibrary.gov

38. Nixon conversation with Haldeman and Butterfield, September 17, 1971, Conversation number 574-3, Oval 574, http://www.nixontapes.org

39. Shav Glick, "Amazed Racers Recall Nixon's Car Knowledge," *Los Angeles Times*, April 28, 1994; "The 'White House 500'," *New York Times*, September 22, 1971; James F. Clarity, "Champagne Hits Spot—Barely," *New York Times*, September 23, 1971; Bull to Haldeman, March 16, 1971, Folder [EX] RE 5 Bowling-Billiards-Pool 1/l/71, Box 4; Clawson to Peterson, Haldeman, Flanigan, Colson and Scali, July 24, 1972, Folder [GEN] RE 5 Bowling-Billiards-Pool 1/1/7 1, Box 4; Haldeman to Magruder, January 9, 1970; Parter to Haldeman, December 23, 1971, Folder [EX] RE Recreation-Sports Begin 9/30/69, Box 1, Recreation-Sports Files, Subject Files, White House Central Files, NPP, NACP; Richard Reeves, *President Nixon: Alone in the White House* (New York: Simon and Schuster, 2001), 373–374.

40. Glick, "Auto Racing's Biggest Event."

41. Bull to Haldeman, March 16, 1971; Clawson to Peterson, Haldeman, Flanigan, Colson and Scali, July 24, 1972; Haldeman to Magruder, January 9, 1970; Parter to Haldeman, December 23, 1971; Reeves, *President Nixon*, 373–374.

42. Nixon conversation with Haldeman and Ziegler, November 18, 1971, Conversation number 576-6, Oval 576, http://www.nixontapes.org.

43. Nixon conversation with Haldeman and Ziegler, April 14, 1971, Conversation number 479-7, Oval 479, and Nixon conversation with Haldeman and Ziegler, November 18, 1971, Conversation number 576-6, Oval 576, http://www.nixontapes.org.

44. Nixon conversation with Haldeman, July 28, 1971, Conversation number 549-4, Oval 594, http://www.nixontapes.org.

45. John Strege, "Nixon Tables All the President's Men," *Orange County Register*, July 16, 1992; Bull to Haldeman, March 16, 1971; Clawson to Peterson, Haldeman, Flanigan, Colson and Scali, July 24, 1972; Haldeman to Magruder, January 9, 1970; Parter to Haldeman, December 23, 1971; Malek to Colson, November 18, 1971, Folder [EX] RE 11 Golf 1/1/71, Box 7, Recreation-Sports Files, Subject Files, White House Central Files, NPP, NACP.

46. Hugh Sidey, "Parting Shots," *Life*, January 30, 1970, 66.

47. Irwin F. Gellman, *The Contender: Richard Nixon: The Congressional Years, 1946*–1952 (New York: Free Press, 1999), 15.

48. Nixon conversation with Charles B. Wilkinson, February 23, 1973, Conversation number 413-1, EOB 413, Nixon Presidential Library, https://nixonlibrary.gov; John R. Wooden biography on a Wooden Classic website that has since been deleted (http://www.woodenclassic.com/bio/index-bio.html was the URL); Wilkinson to Sloan, October 15, 1969, Folder [EX] RE 1 Basketball, Box 1; Buchanan notation on Sloan to Buchanan, October 27, 1970; Nixon to Sharman, January 3, 1972, Folder [GEN] RE 1, Basketball 1/1/71; Sloan to Wilkinson, March 17, 1970, Folder [EX] RE 1 Basketball, Box 3, Recreation-Sports Files, Subject Files, White House Central Files, NPP, NACP.

CHAPTER 6. OF REDSKINS AND DOLPHINS

1. Melvin Small, *The Presidency of Richard Nixon* (Lawrence: University Press of Kansas, 1999), 215; William Gildea and Kenneth Turan, *The Future Is Now: George Allen—Pro Football's Most Controversial Coach* (Boston: Houghton Mifflin, 1972), 261; Jennifer Allen, *Fifth Quarter: The Scrimmage of a Football Coach's Daughter* (New York: Random House, 2000), 25, 100, 126.

2. "Lombardi Memorial Funds Starts," *Washington Post*, June 10, 1971; "The Sports Log," *Boston Globe*; Memorandum for the President, no date, Folder [EX] RE 10 football 1/1/71–12/20/72, Box 5, Recreation-Sports Files, Subject Files, White House Central Files, Nixon Presidential Project, National Archives, College Park, MD [hereafter NPP, NACP].

3. Joe Rice, "Nixon's Sports, Politics Captivate Area," *Akron Beacon Journal*, July 31, 1971; Cole to Chapin, April 8, 1971, Folder [EX] RE 10 football 1/1/71–12/20/72, Box 5, Recreation-Sports Files, Subject Files, White House Central Files, NPP, NACP.

4. George Embry, "Ohioans Hear Nixon Explain Peking Visit" and "Nixon Inaugurates Shrine Celebration," *Columbus Evening Dispatch*, July 31, 1971; Robert Burdock, "'Let's Be for Our Team,' Nixon Urges Americans," Cleveland *Plain Dealer*, July 31, 1971; Donn Gaynor, Doyle McGinley, and William Hershey, "Airport Throng Creates Monstrous Traffic Jam," *Akron Beacon Journal*, July 31, 1971; H. R. Haldeman, *The Haldeman Diaries: Inside the Nixon White House—The Complete Multimedia Collection* (Santa Monica, CA: Sony Electronic Publishing, 1994), CD-ROM, July 30, 1971; "Remarks on Arrival at Canton, Ohio," July 30, 1971, *Public Papers of the Presidents of the United States: Richard Nixon, 1969–1974* (Washington, DC: Office of the Federal Register, 1970–1975) [hereafter *PPP*], 833–834.

5. Stephen E. Ambrose, *Nixon*, vol. 2: *The Triumph of a Politician, 1962–1972* (New York: Simon and Schuster, 1989), 445, 453–454

6. George Embrey, "Ohioans Hear Nixon Explain Peking Visit," *Columbus Evening Dispatch*, July 31, 1971; Jack Patterson, "Nixon Called the Play . . . ," *Akron Beacon Journal*, July 31, 1971; Bob Addie, "Nixon Picks Brito for Hall of Fame," *Washington Post*, July 31, 1971; Arthur Daley, "The Nixon Nominee," *New York Times*, August 20, 1971. At the time this book was published, Brito was not a member of the Professional Football Hall of Fame.

7. Frank Gifford and Harry Waters, *The Whole Ten Yards* (New York: Random House, 1993), 26–27, 209; Arledge's comments are in Randy W. Roberts and James Olson, *Winning Is the Only Thing: Sports in America since 1945* (Baltimore: Johns Hopkins University Press, 1989), 113–114. For examples of Nixon making polite, idle conversation about sports, see: Nixon Conversation with George Bush, Conversation number 17-121, WHT 17, http://www.nixontapes.org; Nixon conversation with Hale Boggs, Gerald R. Ford, and Thomas P. "Tip" O'Neill Jr., January 18, 1972, Conversation number 18-102, WHT 18, Nixon Presidential Library, https://nixonlibrary.gov; Nixon conversation with H. R. Haldeman and John B. Connally, October 17,

1972, Conversation number 802-1, Oval 802, Nixon Presidential Library, https://nixonlibrary.gov.

8. Gifford and Waters, *The Whole Ten Yards*, 26–27, 209.

9. Gifford and Waters, *The Whole Ten Yards*, 26–27, 209; "Television Interview with ABC Sports Commentator Frank Gifford in Canton, Ohio," July 31, 1971, *PPP*, 838–839.

10. "Remarks at the Professional Football Hall of Fame Annual Banquet in Canton, Ohio," July 30, 1971, *PPP*, 834–838.

11. "Remarks at the Professional Football Hall of Fame Annual Banquet in Canton, Ohio," July 30, 1971, 834–838; "President Nixon Salutes New Members of Grid Hall of Fame," *Green Bay Press-Gazette*, July 31, 1971; Bob Addie, "Nixon Picks Brito for Hall of Fame," *Washington Post*, July 31, 1971; "Nixon Inaugurates Shrine Celebration," *Columbus Evening Dispatch*, July 31, 1971.

12. "Remarks at the Professional Football Hall of Fame Annual Banquet in Canton, Ohio," July 30, 1971, 837.

13. "President Nixon Salutes New Members of Grid Hall of Fame"; Addie, "Nixon Picks Brito for Hall of Fame"; "Nixon Inaugurates Shrine Celebration."

14. Haldeman, *Haldeman Diaries*, July 30, 1971; "Nixon Inaugurates Shrine Celebration"; "President Talks Football, Wins without 'Gipper,'" Cleveland *Plain Dealer*, July 31, 1971; Addie, "Nixon Picks Brito for Hall of Fame."

15. Joe Rice, "Nixon's Sports, Politics Captivate Area," *Akron Beacon Journal*, July 31, 1971; Cole to Chapin, April 8, 1971, Folder [EX] RE 10 football 1/1/71–12/20/72, Box 5, Recreation-Sports Files, Subject Files, White House Central Files, NPP, NACP.

16. Haldeman, *Haldeman Diaries*, July 31, 1971; Rice, "Nixon's Sports, Politics Captivate Area."

17. William N. Wallace, "Career of Bengals' Dyer Rated in Doubt after His Broken Neck," *New York Times*, October 5, 1971; "Dyer, Kenneth James," *Arizona Republic*, March 11, 2010; Jeff Ash, "Dyer, Who Broke Neck at Lambeau, Dies," *Green Bay Press-Gazette*, March 14, 2010; Nixon-Dyer phone conversation, October 13, 1971, Conversation number 11-81, WHT 011, http://www.nixontapes.org

18. Elton Casey, "McGee's Aid Request Gets Nixon's Cordial 'No,'" *Durham Morning Herald*, October 19, 1971; "Nixon Predicts 'Era of Pacific,'" *Seattle Post-Intelligencer*, September 27, 1971; Richard W. Larsen, "President Fields Tough Questions," *Seattle Times*, September 27, 1971.

19. Dave Brady, "Redskins Again Arrested by Busted Play, 13–0," and William Gildea, "Fans Shock Redskins," *Washington Post*, November 22, 1971; J. D. Bertha, "Phase 2," Washington *Evening Star*, November 24, 1971; Thomas Boswell et al., *Redskins: A History of Washington's Team* (Washington, DC: Washington Post Books, 1997), 85–89; Thom Loverro, *Washington Redskins: The Authorized History* (Dallas, TX: Taylor Publishing, 1996), 114.

20. Bertha, "Phase 2"; Paul Attner, "Nixon Visits Redskins, Predicts Victory" and

"Redskin Visitor Sees a Better Day," *Washington Post*, November 24, 1971. Other information comes from film of the visit in Haldeman, *Haldeman Diaries*, November 23, 1971; Bull to Nixon, November 22, 1971, Folder [EX] RE 10 football 1/1/71–12/20/72, Box 5, Recreation-Sports Files, Subject Files, White House Central Files; notes in Nixon's handwriting, November 23, 1971, Folder 7, Box 70, President's Speech File, President's Personal File, White House Special File, NPP, NACP.

21. The account used here is a combination of two different constructions of Nixon's remarks that appeared in Bertha, "Phase 2"; Attner, "Nixon Visits Redskins, Predicts Victory"; Attner, "Redskin Visitor Sees a Better Day." Other information comes from film of the visit in Haldeman, *Haldeman Diaries*, November 23, 1971; Bull to Nixon, November 22, 1971; notes in Nixon's handwriting, November 23, 1971.

22. "Remarks to the Members of the Washington Redskins Professional Football Team during a Practice Session at Redskins Park," November 23, 1971, *PPP*, 1134–1137. The Washington *Evening Star* and the *Washington Post* quote Nixon from this speech in their November 24, 1971, issues, but the construction of each varies a little from the remarks in the *Public Papers* volume. The account in *Papers* appears the more accurate and is used here because it include reversals, dependent clauses that modify nothing, and other miscues that are common in informal speech.

Nixon's comment referred to the events surrounding Pershing's removal of Major General William L. Sibert from command of the First Infantry Division in 1917. Pershing had been quite critical of Sibert for some time and found the pace of training in the division far too slow. The day after Pershing removed Sibert from command, he sent a memo to all his commanders warning them against having a pessimistic, defeatist attitude that could corrupt the morale of their unit. Such an attitude would be grounds for dismissal. Given Pershing's timing, he seemed to be implying that he had removed Sibert for such reasons. The cashiered general wanted the American Expeditionary Force to commission a court of inquiry that would either exonerate or court-martial him. Pershing later refused, saying the spirit in the division had little to do with his removal. Ed Cray, *General of the Army: George C. Marshall, Soldier and Statesman* (New York: W. W. Norton, 1990), 51–59; Meiron Harries and Susie Harries, *The Last Days of Innocence: America at War, 1917–1918* (New York: Random House, 1997), 214–215; Frank E. Vandiver, *Black Jack: The Life and Times of John J. Pershing* (College Station: Texas A&M University Press, 1977), 2:794–798, 839–840.

23. Gildea and Turan, *The Future Is Now*, 264–265; "Remarks to the Members of the Washington Redskins Professional Football Team during a Practice Session at Redskins Park," 1134–1137; notes in Nixon's handwriting, November 23, 1971.

24. Haldeman, *Haldeman Diaries*, November 23, 1971; the *Post* ran two stories, one on the front page of the paper and one on the first page of the sports section: Attner, "Nixon Visits Redskins, Predicts Victory," and Attner, "Redskin Visitor Sees a Better Day"; Bertha, "Phase 2."

25. "Boo unto Others," *Washington Post*, November 25, 1971; Nixon conversation

with Haldeman and Ziegler, November 23, 1971, Conversation number 623-24, Oval 623, http://www.nixontapes.org.

26. Nixon conversation with Allen, November 23, 1971, Conversation number 15-124, WHT 15, http://www.nixontapes.org.

27. Nixon conversation with Rogers, November 24, 1971, Conversation number 624-21, Oval 624, http://www.nixontapes.org.

28. Shirley Povich, "This Morning," *Washington Post*, November 25, 1971.

29. Allen, *Fifth Quarter*, 127; Dave Brady, "Kilmer Saves Victory as Jurgensen Is Injured," *Washington Post*, November 29; William Gildea, "George Allen Savors Biggest Victory: Redskins' Coach, Jefferson, Kilmer, Duncan Rewarded," *Washington Post*, December 14, 1971.

30. Brady, "Kilmer Saves Victory as Jurgensen Is Injured"; Gildea, "George Allen Savors Biggest Victory"; Haldeman, *Haldeman Diaries*, December 14, 1971; Richard Reeves, *President Nixon: Alone in the White House* (New York: Simon and Schuster, 2001), 405.

31. Nixon conversation with Haldeman, December 15, 1971, Conversation number 638-8, Oval 638, http://www.nixontapes.org.

32. Dave Brady, "Redskins Punchless in Playoff," and Kenneth Turan, "Redskins Future No Longer Is Now," *Washington Post*, December 27, 1971.

33. Turan, "Redskins Future No Longer Is Now"; Haldeman, *Haldeman Diaries*, December 27, 1971.

34. Turan, "Redskins Future No Longer Is Now"; Haldeman, *Haldeman Diaries*, December 27, 1971; Nixon to Burman, January 6, 1972, Folder [EX] RE 10 football 1/1/71–12/20/72, Box 5, Recreation-Sports Files, Subject Files, White House Central Files, NPP, NACP.

35. "49ers Make Reversal of Nixon Policy," *Washington Post*, December 28, 1971; Shirley Povich, "This Morning," *Washington Post*, January 6, 1972.

36. Jimmy Golen, "More Nixon Dirty Tricks Exposed," Associated Press Wire Story, provided to the author by Jimmy Golen, for which the author is quite grateful; Nixon conversation with Allen, November 23, 1971, Conversation number 15-124, WHT 15, http://www.nixontapes.org.

37. Bill Braucher, "Nixon Phones Congratulations, 'Strategy,'" *Miami Herald*, January 4, 1972, and Bill Braucher, "Shula Spends Birthday Viewing Cowboys' Films," *Miami Herald*, January 5, 1972; "Nixon Phones Shula, Hails Dolphin Play," *Washington Post*, December 29, 1971; "Super Expert Gives the Big Call to Shula," *Washington Post*, January 4, 1972; Reeves, *President Nixon*, 420.

38. Braucher, "Nixon Phones Congratulations, 'Strategy,'" and Braucher, "Shula Spends Birthday Viewing Cowboys' Films" ; Dave Anderson, "Coach Nixon Sends In a Play to the Miami Dolphins," *New York Times*, January 4, 1972; "Bombing Run," *Christian Science Monitor*, January 6, 1972; "Nixon's Game Plan," *Newsweek*, January 17, 1972, 52–53; Jack Saylor, "1:30 a.m.—Nixon, Shula," *Detroit Free Press*, January 4, 1972; "Nixon Phones Shula, Hails Dolphin Play," *Washington Post*, December 29, 1971;

"Super Expert Gives the Big Call to Shula," *Washington Post*, January 4, 1972; "President Gives Scouting Report," *Fort Worth Star-Telegram*, January 4, 1972; "Thank You, Mr. President," *Dallas Morning News*, January 5, 1972; Bob Hurt, "Here's Pointers For Coach Nixon," Oklahoma City *Daily Oklahoman*, January 5, 1972; Reeves, *President Nixon*, 420.

39. "Super Expert Gives the Big Call to Shula"; Povich, "This Morning," January 6, 1972.

40. "Now Put In Calls to Muskie, McGovern, Humphrey and Lindsay—," *Washington Post*, January 5, 1972; "Hello—Don Shula?" Washington *Evening Star*, January 5, 1972.

41. James Reston, "Coach Nixon's Game Plan," *New York Times*, January 5, 1972.

42. "Texas Governor Double-Reverses Nixon," *Miami Herald*, January 6, 1972; Bob St. John, "From Other Rooms," *Dallas Morning News*, January 6, 1972; "Thank You, Mr. President," *Dallas Morning News*, January 5, 1972; "Just Felt Roger No. 1," New Orleans *Times-Picayune*, January 12, 1972; Bob St. Johns, *Landry: The Legend and the Legacy* (Nashville, TN: Thomas Nelson, 2000), 300.

43. Blackie Sherrod, "Inside Dope," *Dallas Times Herald*, January 5, 1972.

44. Bill Guthrie, "Phone Put-On Puts Off Shula," *New Haven Journal-Courier*, January 14, 1972.

45. Abe Zaidan, "But, Mr. President . . . You Weren't That Clear," *Miami Herald*, January 11, 1972.

46. "Griese Nixes Nixon Play," *Dallas Morning News*, January 11, 1972; Bob Roesler, "Behind The Sports Scene," New Orleans *Times-Picayune*, January 16, 1972; Povich, "This Morning," January 6, 1972; Shirley Povich, "Staubach, Griese Must Finesse Today," *Washington Post*, January 16, 1972.

47. Shirley Povich, "Dolphins Go Down, Out," *Washington Post*, January 17, 1972; "Warfield Says Cowboys Closed Off Nixon's Down-and-In Pass," *New York Times*, January 17, 1972.

48. Larry McMillen, "Pokes Put Away Stigma, Frustration," New Orleans *Times-Picayune*, January 17, 1972; Steve Perkins, "Doomsday Demoralizing: Cowboys Scuttle Dolphins," *Dallas Times Herald*, January 17, 1972; Temple Pouncey, "Chips on Line," *Dallas Morning News*, January 17, 1972; Red Smith, "What Do They Do Now, Mr. President?," *New York Times*, January 17, 1972; Nixon to Staubach, January 19, 1972; Nixon to Don Shula, January 17, 1972; Nixon to Dorothy Shula, January 31, 1972, Folder [EX] RE 10 football 1/1/71–12/20/72, Box 5, Recreation-Sports Files, Subject Files, White House Central Files, NPP, NACP.

49. Nixon conversation with Boggs, Ford, and O'Neill, January 18, 1972, Conversation number 18-102, WHT 18, http://www.nixontapes.org.

50. "Thomas Speaks," *Dallas Morning News*, January 17, 1972; uncaptioned editorial cartoon, *Dallas Times Herald*, January 17, 1972; Dallas City Council resolution, no date, Folder [EX] RE 10 football 1/1/71–12/20/72, Box 5, Recreation-Sports Files, Subject Files, White House Central Files, NPP, NACP.

51. "Nixon's Dolphin Play Wins Bonehead Award," *Miami Herald*, January 11, 1972; "Boneheads Honor Footballer Nixon," *Dallas Morning News*, January 11, 1972; "Just Felt Roger No. 1," New Orleans *Times-Picayune*, January 12, 1972; ellipsis in original Nixon to Dallas Bonehead Club, January 13, 1972, Folder [EX] RE 10 football 1/1/71–12/20/72, Box 5, Recreation-Sports Files, Subject Files, White House Central Files, NPP, NACP.

CHAPTER 7. THE ELECTION OF 1972: THE FIRST HALF

1. Stephen E. Ambrose, *Nixon*, vol. 2: *The Triumph of a Politician, 1962–1972* (New York: Simon and Schuster, 1989), 497, 525–539; Larry Berman, *No Peace, No Honor: Nixon, Kissinger, and Betrayal in Vietnam* (New York: Free Press, 2001), 123–134; Stephen P. Randolph, *Powerful and Brutal Weapons: Nixon, Kissinger, and the Easter Offensive* (Cambridge, MA: Harvard University Press, 2007); Phil Haun and Colin Jackson, "Breaker of Armies: Air Power in the Easter Offensive and the Myth of Linebacker I and II in the Vietnam War," *International Security* 40, no. 3 (Winter 2015/16): 139–178.

2. Bowie Kuhn, *Hardball: The Education of a Baseball Commissioner* (New York: Times Books, 1987), 104–107; Marvin Miller, *A Whole Different Ball Game: The Sport and Business of Baseball* (Secaucus, NJ: Carrol Publishing, 1991), 203–213.

3. Kuhn, *Hardball*, 104–107; Miller, *A Whole Different Ball Game*, 203–213.

4. James B. Dworkin, *Owners versus Players: Baseball and Collective Bargaining* (Boston: Auburn House, 1981), 33–34; Lee Lowenfish, *The Imperfect Diamond: A History of Baseball's Labor Wars*, rev. ed. (New York: Da Capo Press, 1991), 215–217.

5. Miller, *A Whole Different Ball Game*, 205, 210; Kuhn, *Hardball*, 104–107; Leonard Koppett, "Nixon Offers Aid to Settle Strike," *New York Times*, April 10, 1972; Murray Chass, "Baseball Negotiators Near Pact; Latest Proposal Could Settle Strike Today," *New York Times*, April 13, 1972; Joseph Durso, "Baseball Strike Is Settled; Season to Open Tomorrow," *New York Times*, April 14, 1972.

6. Miller, *A Whole Different Ball Game*, 205, 210; H. R. Haldeman, *The Haldeman Diaries: Inside the Nixon White House—The Complete Multimedia Collection* (Santa Monica, CA: Sony Electronic Publishing, 1994), CD-ROM, April 8, 1972; Haldeman Notes, April 8, [1972], Folder 3, Box 4; Haldeman Notes, Papers of H. R. Haldeman, Staff Member and Office Files, White House Special Files, Nixon Presidential Project, National Archives, College Park, MD [hereafter NPP, NACP]; Koppett, "Nixon Offers Aid To Settle Strike"; Chass, "Baseball Negotiators Near Pact"; Durso, "Baseball Strike Is Settled."

7. Ambrose, *Triumph of a Politician*, 651.

8. Capitalization in the original. Kathleen Hall Jamieson, *Packaging the Presidency: A History and Criticism of Presidential Campaign Advertising* (New York: Oxford University Press, 1984), 277, 293–94, 300–02.

9. "The President's News Conference," June 22, 1972, *Public Papers of the Presidents of the United States: Richard Nixon, 1969–1974* (Washington, DC: Office of the Federal Register, 1970–1975) [hereafter *PPP*], 690, 695–696.

10. Kuhn, *Hardball*, 82–88; *Flood v Kuhn* [407 US 258], 32 L Ed 2d 728, 92 S Ct 2099; Miller, *A Whole Different Ball Game*, 198–199; Lowenfish, *Imperfect Diamond*, 208–213.

11. See Appendix B for the US Supreme Court's list of the greatest baseball players in history.

12. Bob Woodward and Scott Armstrong, *The Brethren: Inside the Supreme Court* (New York: Simon and Schuster, 1979), 224–226; *Flood v Kuhn*.

13. James Edward Miller, *The Baseball Business: Pursuing Pennants and Profits in Baltimore* (Chapel Hill: University of North Carolina Press, 1990), 180.

14. Kuhn, *Hardball*, 89.

15. "Nixon Lists All-Timers," *Washington Post*, June 23, 1972; Ziegler to Nixon, June 29, 1972, Folder RE2 Baseball-Softball 1/1/7, Box 3, Recreation-Sports Files, Subject Files, White House Central Files, NPP, NACP.

16. Richard M. Nixon, "Nixon Picks All-Time Baseball Teams: Nixon Picks Vaughan, Face, Groat and 77 Others for All-Time Baseball Teams," *New York Times*, July 2, 1972; Nixon manuscript, June 27, 1972, Folder RE2 Baseball-Softball 1/1/71, Box 3, Recreation-Sports Files, Subject Files, White House Central Files, NPP, NACP.

17. Stanley I. Kutler, *The Wars of Watergate: The Last Crisis of Richard Nixon* (New York: W. W. Norton, 1990), 534–535.

18. Welch Suggs, *A Place on the Team: The Triumph and Tragedy of Title IX* (Princeton, NJ: Princeton University Press, 2005), 21–23.

19. A fair amount of research shows that athletics is a money-losing operation for most colleges and universities. Football and men's basketball generate profits from some, but not all, schools. The fraction is roughly two-thirds. In all but a very few cases, this revenue is not enough to compensate for the fact that all other sports fail to turn a profit: Andrew Zimbalist, *Unpaid Professionals: Commercialism and Conflict in Big-Time College Sports* (Princeton, NJ: Princeton University Press, 1999); James L. Shulman and William G. Bowen, *The Game of Life: College Sports and Educational Values* (Princeton, NJ: Princeton University Press, 2001); James J. Duderstadt, *Intercollegiate Athletics and the American University* (Ann Arbor: University of Michigan Press, 2000); Charles T. Clotfelter, *Big-Time Sports in American Universities* (New York: Cambridge University Press, 2011); Rodney Fort and Jason Winfree, *15 Sports Myths and Why They're Wrong* (Stanford, CA: Stanford University Press, 2013); David Welch Suggs Jr., "Making Money—Or Not—On College Sports," *Data-Driven Decision Making in Intercollegiate Athletics: New Directions in Institutional Research*, no. 144 (Winter 2009): 19–32.

20. Ying Wushanley, *Playing Nice and Losing: The Struggle for Control of Women's Intercollegiate Athletics, 1960–2000* (Syracuse, NY: Syracuse University Press, 2004), 2, 158; Welch Suggs, *A Place on the Team: The Triumph and Tragedy of Title IX* (Princeton, NJ: Princeton University Press, 2005), 7.

21. Susan Ware, *Game, Set, Match: Billie Jean King and the Revolution in Women's Sports* (Chapel Hill: University of North Carolina Press, 2011), 47, 50; Suggs, *A Place on the Team*, 40–41.

22. Ware, *Game, Set, Match*, 47, 50; Suggs, *A Place on the Team*, 40–41.

23. Richard A. Swanson and Betty Spears, *History of Sport and Physical Education in the United States*, 4th ed. (Madison, WI: Brown and Benchmark, 1995), 324–327; Joan Hoff, *Nixon Reconsidered* (New York: Basic Books, 1994), 111.

24. Ware, *Game, Set, Match*, 48–51.

25. As a result of Nixon's decision to go no further back than 1925, legendary players such as Ty Cobb, Cy Young, Grover Cleveland Alexander, and "Shoeless" Joe Jackson never made his roster. Ziegler to Nixon, June 23, 1972, (twice); undated notes and diagrams on yellow legal paper, Folder 13 All-Star Baseball Teams, Box 5, Name/Subject File, President's Personal Files, White House Special Files; Nixon manuscript, June 27, 1972, Folder RE2 Baseball-Softball 1/1/71, Box 3, Recreation-Sports Files, Subject Files, White House Central Files, NPP, NACP. According to the makers of the movie *Kissinger and Nixon*, the president's old friend Bebe Rebozo helped him make these selections. White House daily logs, however, show that Rebozo had no contact with Nixon between the press conference and the public release of the finished roster. Daniel Petrie, dir., *Kissinger and Nixon*, script by Lionel Chetwynd, Daniel H. Blatt Productions, Dreyfuss/James Productions, Lionel Chetwynd Productions, Paragon Entertainment Corporation, 1995, film; June 23–July 2, 1972, daily presidential schedules in Haldeman, *Haldeman Diaries.*

26. Nixon and Clifford Evans conversation, June 30, 1972, Conversation number 744-16, Oval 744, Nixon Presidential Library, https://nixonlibrary.gov; Arnold Rampersad, *Jackie Robinson: A Biography* (New York: Knopf, 1997), 31; Haldeman Notes, June 26, 1972, Folder April–June 1972 [May 9, 1972—June 30, 1972] Part II (2)., Box 45, Papers of H. R. Haldeman, Staff Member and Office Files; Haldeman to Nixon, June 26, 1972; Nixon Tape Transcript, June 26, 1972, Folder 13 All-Star Baseball Teams, Box 5, Name/Subject File, President's Personal Files, White House Special Files, NPP, NACP; Haldeman, *Haldeman Diaries*, June 26, 1972; Nixon conversation with Haldeman, June 27, 1972, Conversation number 743-6, Oval 743, http://www.nixontapes.org.

27. Undated notes on yellow legal paper; Ziegler to Nixon, June 27, 1972; Nixon Tape Transcript, June 27, 1972, Folder 13 All-Star Baseball Teams, Box 5, Name/Subject File, President's Personal Files, White House Special Files; Ziegler to Eisenhower and Eisenhower, June 29, 1972, Folder RE2 Baseball-Softball 1/1/71, Box 3, Recreation-Sports Files, Subject Files, White House Central Files, NPP, NACP; Haldeman, *Haldeman Diaries*, June 27, 1972;

28. Haldeman Notes, June 26, 1972; Ziegler to Parker and Chapin, June 28, 1972, Folder RE2 Baseball Softball 1/1/71, Box 3, Recreation-Sports Files, Subject Files, White House Central Files, NPP, NACP; Haldeman, *Haldeman Diaries*, June 26, 1972; Nixon and Clifford Evans conversation, June 30, 1972, Conversation number 744-16, Oval 744, Nixon Presidential Library, https://nixonlibrary.gov.

29. Ziegler to Eisenhower and Eisenhower, June 29, 1972.

30. Ziegler to Eisenhower and Eisenhower, June 29, 1972.

31. Ziegler to Eisenhower and Eisenhower, June 29, 1972.

32. Ziegler to Eisenhower and Eisenhower, June 29, 1972.

33. Nixon and Clifford Evans conversation, June 30, 1972.

34. Ziegler to Eisenhower and Eisenhower, June 29, 1972.

35. Nixon bylines are as given: President Nixon, "Baseball Fan Nixon Picks All-Time All-Stars," *Los Angeles Times*, July 2, 1972; President Richard Nixon, "President Picks His Favorites," *San Francisco Examiner*, July 2, 1972; President Nixon, "Nixon Picks All-Star Baseball Teams," Baltimore *Sun*, July 2, 1972; "David Helps Nixon Pick His All-Time Baseball Team," *Kansas City Star*, July 2, 1972; and Nixon, "Nixon Picks All-Time Baseball Teams"; President Richard Nixon, "Nixon Selects His Baseball All-Star Teams," *Chicago Sun-Times*, July 2, 1972; President Richard Nixon, "Nixon, with an Assist, Picks His 'All-Time Baseball Team,'" *Boston Globe*, July 2, 1972; Richard Nixon, "Nixon's Latest All-Stars," Washington *Evening Star*, July 2, 1972; President Richard Nixon, "Some Surprises as Nixon Names His All-Time Baseball Favorites," *Los Angeles Herald-Examiner*, July 2, 1972.

36. Nixon bylines are as given: "Nixon the Fan Chooses Own All-Stars," *Sporting News*, July 15, 1972; "Nixon Picks All-Star Baseball Teams," *St. Louis Post Dispatch*, July 2, 1972; President Nixon, "President Nixon Picks His All-Time, All-Star Teams," *Philadelphia Inquirer*, July 2, 1972; Richard M. Nixon, "Pick the Stars, Mr. President,'" Cincinnati *Enquirer*, July 2, 1972; "2 Twins Named Nixon All-Stars," *Minneapolis Tribune*, July 2, 1972; "Nixon Gets Help with Selections," *Milwaukee Journal*, July 2, 1972; President Richard Nixon, "Nixon Selects All-Time Team," Cleveland *Plain Dealer*, July 2, 1972; Pres. Richard Nixon, "President Picks His All-Stars," *Dallas Times Herald*, July 2, 1972; President Richard Nixon, "Nation's No. 1 Fan Puts His Reputation on Line," New York *Daily News*, July 2, 1972; "Nixon All-Time Team," *Oakland Tribune*, July 2, 1972.

37. No Nixon bylines: "Nixon Cites 8 Pirate Greats," *Pittsburgh Post-Gazette*, July 3, 1972; "Jackie, Koufax . . . Nixon Picks All-Star Teams," *Detroit Free Press*, July 3, 1972; "Nixon's Picks: President Gives His All-Time Teams," *Atlanta Journal and Constitution*, July 2, 1972; "Nixon: 'Robinson Best Athlete,'" *Atlanta Constitution*, July 3, 1972.

38. *Dallas Morning News*, July 2, 1972; *Houston Post*, July 2, 1972; *Houston Chronicle*, July 2, 1972; *San Diego Union*, July 2, 1972; *Chicago Tribune*, July 2, 1972; *Orange County Register*, July 2, 1972; *Providence Journal*, July 2, 1972.

39. "Scorecard: Alltime Greats," *Sports Illustrated*, July 17, 1972, 10.

40. Nixon bylines are as given: Richard Nixon, "Nixon Picks His All-Time Baseball Teams," *Indianapolis Star*, July 2, 1972. For coverage in other non-baseball cities, see: Richard Nixon, "President Picks All-Time Baseball Teams," Charleston *Sunday Gazette-Mail*, July 2, 1972; Richard Nixon, "Nixon Selects All-Star Team," *Greenville News*, July 2, 1972; Richard M. Nixon, "I'm Glad You Asked Me That Question (I Think)," *Billings Gazette*, July 2, 1972; Richard Nixon, "Nation's No. 1 Baseball Fan Picks an All-Time Team," *Santa Fe New Mexican*, July 2, 1972; Richard Nixon,

"President Nixon Picks His Baseball All-Stars," *Albuquerque Journal*, July 2, 1972; President Nixon, "Nixon Selects All-Time Team," Long Beach *Independent Press-Telegram*, July 2, 1972; Richard Nixon, "President Nixon Names All-Time Baseball Favorites," *Colorado Springs Gazette-Telegraph*, July 2, 1972; Richard Nixon, "Nixon's All-Time Baseball Picks," *Akron Beacon-Journal*, July 2, 1972; Richard Nixon, "Nixon Picks All-Time Team," *San Antonio Express and News*, July 2, 1972; Richard Nixon, "Baseball Manager Nixon Picks His All-Time Team," *Orlando Sentinel*, July 2, 1972; President Richard Nixon, "Nixon Picks 4 'Top' Baseball Teams," *Youngstown Vindicator*, July 2, 1972.

41. Killebrew to Nixon, July 7, 1972; Greenberg to Nixon, October 18, 1972; Roberts to Nixon, July 3, 1972, Folder RE2 Baseball-Softball 1/1/71, Box 3, Recreation-Sports Files, Subject Files, White House Central Files, NPP, NACP; "Thanks, Mr. President," Cincinnati *Enquirer*, July 3, 1972; "Scorecard: Alltime Greats," *Sports Illustrated*, July 17, 1972, 10; Gordon S. White Jr. "Personalities: 'A Real Honor,'" *New York Times*, July 3, 1972; "Nixon Big Hit with His All-Star Players," *Philadelphia Inquirer*, July 3, 1972.

42. Isabel Rolfe to Nixon, October 9, 1972; Jane Collins to Nixon, July 4, 1972; Roland Elliott to Rose Mary Woods, July 7, 1972; Nixon to Jane Collins, July 17, 1972; Medwick to Nixon, December 6, 1972; Folder RE2 Baseball-Softball 1/1/71, Box 3, Recreation-Sports Files, Subject Files, White House Central Files, NPP, NACP.

43. Nixon to Ruth, Gehrig, Mantle, etc., September 29, 1972, Folder RE2 Baseball-Softball 1/1/71, Box 3, Recreation-Sports Files, Subject Files, White House Central Files, NPP, NACP.

44. Red Smith, "New, Slow Boy on the Baseball Beat," *New York Times*, July 3, 1972; Arthur Daley, "Minority Report on Some Selections," *New York Times*, July 6, 1972; Harold Kaese, "Why Lane, 73, Stays in the Game," *Boston Globe*, July 3, 1972; the comments from the other papers are in "Nixon Choices Thumbed Out," *Washington Post*, July 5, 1972.

45. Ira Berkow, *Red: A Biography of Red Smith* (New York: Times Books, 1986), 147, 204.

46. Smith, "New, Slow Boy on the Baseball Beat"; Red Smith, "A New Boy on the Baseball Beat," *Los Angeles Herald-Examiner*, July 3, 1972; Red Smith, "Nixon Called Out on All-Star Picks," Cleveland *Plain Dealer*, July 3, 1972; Red Smith, "The President Strikes Out," *Atlanta Constitution*, July 3, 1972; Red Smith, "Nixon Flunked Badly in Picking His Stars," *Detroit Free Press*, July 4, 1972; Red Smith, "President Nixon—Long Way to Go," *San Francisco Chronicle*, July 4, 1972; Red Smith, "'Cub' Nixon Marked Low," Cincinnati *Enquirer*, July 4, 1972; Red Smith, "View of Sports," *Youngstown Vindicator*, July 4, 1972.

47. Van Hoose, "Picks Prove Nixon a Real Baseball Fan," *Birmingham News*, July 3, 1972; Arthur Daley, "Minority Report on Some Selections," *New York Times*, July 6, 1972; Kaese, "Why Lane, 73, Stays in the Game"; Bob Broeg, "Broeg on Baseball," *Sporting News*, July 22, 1972.

48. Tom Dowling, "Writer Gets Inning, Picks Presidential Team," *Milwaukee Journal*, July 9, 1972.

49. "Presidential Race: Nixon 2, Taft 1," *St. Louis Post Dispatch*, July 6, 1972.

CHAPTER 8. THE ELECTION OF 1972: THE SECOND HALF

1. Memorandum for the President from Henry Cashen, Subject Meeting with Floyd Patterson, August 8, 1972, Folder [Ex] RE6 Boxing-Wrestling-Karate-Judo 1/1/71; Caldiero to Chapin, July 12, 1972; Robert J. Brown to Nixon, September 20, 1972, Bull to Haldeman, October 2, 1970, Folder [EX] RE10 Football 1/1/71–12/20/72, Box 5; Schedule Proposal from Henry Cashen, October 10, 1972; Cashen to Nixon, October 13, 1972, Folder RE2 Baseball-Softball 1/1/71, Box 3, Recreation-Sports Files, Subject Files, White House Central Files; Ruth Packard, "Final Report, Athletes for the Re-election of the President," November 14, 1972, Folder 6, Box 137, White House Social Events, President's Personal Files, White House Special Files, NPP, NACP; Wilt Chamberlain and David Shaw, *Wilt: Just Like Any Other 7-Foot Black Millionaire Who Lives Next Door* (New York: Macmillan, 1975), 237–244.

2. Richard Reeves, *President Nixon: Alone in the White House* (New York: Simon and Schuster, 2001), 467.

3. Joseph Reischler to Edward Blacksmith, Patrick O'Donnell to Charles Colson, Alvin Snyder to David Parker, October 10, 1972, Folder RE2 Baseball-Softball 1/1/71, Box 3, Recreation-Sports Files, Subject Files, White House Central Files, NPP, NACP.

4. Jackie Robinson, "Jackie Robinson," *New York Post*, December 30, 1959; "Jackie Robinson to Work for Nixon," *New York Post*, September 4, 1960; Robinson to Nixon, January 29, 1960; Memo by Harrison McCall, January 3, 1959, Folder Jackie Robinson (1 of 2), Box 649, Pre-Presidential Papers of Richard Nixon, National Archives Los Angeles Branch, Laguna Niguel, California [hereafter NALB]; Jackie Robinson as told to Alfred Duckett, *I Never Had It Made* (New York: Putnam, 1972), 147.

5. Arnold Rampersad, *Jackie Robinson: A Biography* (New York: Knopf, 1997), 342–352.

6. Robinson, *I Never Had It Made*, 152; Rampersad, *Jackie Robinson*, 342–352; William C. Rhoden, "Robinson's Battles Went Far beyond the Diamond," *New York Times*, April 13, 1987; Tom Wicker, *One of Us: Richard Nixon and the American Dream* (New York: Random House, 1991), 240.

7. Robinson to Nixon, November 12, 1962, Folder Jackie Robinson (2 of 2), Box 649, Pre-Presidential Papers of Richard Nixon, NALB; Robinson, *I Never Had It Made*, 147; David Falkner, *Great Time Coming: The Life of Jackie Robinson from Baseball to Birmingham* (New York: Simon and Schuster, 1995), 309; Rampersad, *Jackie Robinson*, 352.

8. Rampersad, *Jackie Robinson*, 385, 426, 429–30, 432; Robinson, *I Never Had It Made*, 147; Taylor Branch, *Pillar of Fire: America in the King Years, 1963–65* (New York: Simon and Schuster, 1998), 404.

9. Rampersad, *Jackie Robinson*, 385, 426, 429–30, 432; Robinson, *I Never Had It Made*, 147.

10. Rampersad, *Jackie Robinson*, 385, 426, 429–30, 432; Robinson, *I Never Had It Made*, 147.

11. Nixon meeting with Laird, Bryant, Hunton, and Gravely, September 24, 1971, Conversation number 578-8, Oval 578, http://www.nixontapes.org; Nixon meeting with Ramirez, Sanchez, Banuelos, Villarreal, Jova, Telles, Montejano, Rodriquez, Conde, Gallegos, Nunez, Cordova, Hidalgo, Armendariz, Marumoto, Clawson, Hanzlik, Colson, and Dole, October 27, 1972, Conversation number 109-1, CAB 109, Nixon Presidential Library, https://nixonlibrary.gov.

12. Alvin Snyder to David Parker, October 10, 1972, Folder RE2 Baseball-Softball 1/1/71, Box 3, Recreation-Sports Files, Subject Files, White House Central Files, NPP, NACP; October 15, 1972, daily presidential schedule, in Haldeman, *Haldeman Diaries.*

13. "Statement on the Death of Jackie Robinson," October 24, 1972, *PPP*, 1023; Phil Pepe, "A Heart Attack Kills Jackie Robinson at 51," *New York Daily News*, October 25, 1972; Philip Pepe, "A Last Sad Cheer for Jackie Robinson," and Red Foley, "They All Remembered Something of His Greatness," *New York Daily News*, October 28, 1972; "Nixon Joins Baseball World in Mourning Jackie Robinson," *Hartford Courant*, October 25, 1972; "'Hope of the People' Laid to Rest," *Hartford Courant*, October 28, 1972.

14. Cashen to Haldeman, October 14, 1972, Folder [EX] RE10 Football 1/1/71–12/20/72, Box 5 Recreation-Sports Files, Subject Files, White House Central Files, NPP, NACP. This memo accurately reflects the president's thinking. According to the White House tapes, when Alexander Butterfield and Stephen Bull took the issue directly to Nixon he said, "No, I, I, uh, think it's a mistake to [do] anymore football." He then added: "Baseball is the same." He was very clear. "No more athletics until after the election." Nixon conversation with Butterfield and Bull, October 18, 1972, Conversation number 803-13, Oval 803, Nixon Presidential Library, https://nixon library.gov.

15. "TV Blackout Ban Backed by Nixon," *New York Times*, October 4, 1972.

16. Nixon meeting with Kleindienst and Ehrlichman, December 18, 1972, Conversation number 381-18, EOB 381, Nixon Presidential Library, https://nixonlibrary.gov.

17. Nixon meeting with Kleindienst and Ehrlichman, December 18, 1972.

18. Nixon conversation with Kleindienst, December 19, 1972, Conversation number 34-136, WHT 34, Nixon Presidential Library, https://nixonlibrary.gov.

19. Arthur Daley, "The President Fumbles the Ball," *New York Times*, October 5, 13, 1972.

20. Klein to Haldeman, October 6, 1972, Folder [EX] RE10 Football 1/1/71–12/20/72, Box 5, Recreation-Sports Files, Subject Files, White House Central Files, NPP, NACP.

21. Dave Brady, "Pay TV Offers Haven for NFL," and Sandford J. Ungar, "Nixon Bid Spurned by NFL: Rozelle Refuses to Lift TV Curb on Playoffs," *Washington Post*,

December 21, 1972; Murray Chase, "Super Matchup: White House vs. N.F.L.," *New York Times*, December 21, 1972; " . . . Where It's Possible to See Redskins," *New York Times*, December 23, 1972; David George Surdam, *The Big Leagues Go to Washington: Congress and Sports Antitrust, 1951–1989* (Urbana: University of Illinois Press, 2015), 186–187; "NFL Nixed Nixon Bid on TV Blackouts," *ESPN.com*, February 11, 2012, http://www.espn.com/nfl/story/_/id/7565229/nfl-rejected-president-nixon-blackout-proposal-white-house-tapes-reveal.

22. "Sports News Briefs," *New York Times*, August 22, 1973; "TV Blackout Ban Seen Likely to End," *New York Times*, September 3, 1973; Joseph Durso, "Senate Votes 76–6 , to Restrict TV Blackouts of Sports Events," *New York Times*, September 7, 1972; William N. Wallace, "Congress Votes Bill to Limit TV Ban on Football Games," *New York Times*, September 14, 1973; Surdam, *Big Leagues Go to Washington*, 186–187; "NFL Nixed Nixon Bid on TV Blackouts."

23. Ira Horowitz, "Sports Broadcasting," in *Government and the Sports Business*, ed. Roger G. Noll (Washington, DC: Brookings Institution, 1974), 284–287.

24. Simon Reeve, *One Day in September: The Full Story of the 1972 Munich Olympics Massacre and the Israeli Revenge Operation "Wrath of God"* (New York: Faber and Faber, 2000), 1–124; George Jonas, *Vengeance: The True Story of an Israeli Counter-Terrorist Team* (New York: Simon and Schuster, 1984), 13–19; David Binder, "9 Israelis on Olympic Team Killed with 4 Arab Captors as Police Fight Band That Disrupted Munich Games: A 23-Hour Drama: 2 Others Are Slain in Their Quarters in Guerrilla Raid," *New York Times*, September 6, 1972; "Remarks to Reporters about the Assault on Israeli Athletes at the Olympic Games in Munich, Germany," September 5, 1972, *PPP*, 857.

25. "Message to Prime Minister Golda Meir of Israel about the Deaths of Israeli Athletes at the Olympic Games in Munich, Germany," September 6, 1972, *PPP*, 858; notations on "Recommended Telephone Call" Memo, September 6, 1972, Folder RE 14 Olympic Games 1/1/71 2 of 2, Box 8, Recreation-Sports Files, Subject Files, White House Central Files, NPP, NACP; Haldeman, *Haldeman Diaries*, April 7, 1973; "Munich, 1972 . . . ," *New York Times*, September 7, 1972; Nixon conversation with H. R. Haldeman and Ziegler, September 11, 1972, Conversation number 360-20/358-1, EOB 360, Nixon Presidential Library, https://nixonlibrary.gov.

26. Nixon conversation with Chris Schenkel, September 11, 1972, Conversation number 774-8, Oval 774, and Nixon conversation with Colson, September 12, 1972, Conversation number 775-6, Oval 775, and Nixon conversation with H. R. Haldeman and Ziegler, September 11, 1972, Conversation number 360-20/358-1, EOB 360, Nixon Presidential Library, https://nixonlibrary.gov.

27. Richard O'Reilly, "Growth, Funds Key Issues in Olympics Controversy," *Rocky Mountain News*, November 1, 1972; Joanne Ditmer, "'Yes' Really Is 'No' in Vote on Olympics," *Denver Post*, November 2, 1972; James Whiteside, *Colorado: A Sports History* (Niwot: University Press of Colorado, 1999), 146, 148, 151–153, 157.

28. Whiteside, *Colorado*, 156, 158. 170.

29. O'Reilly, "Growth, Funds Key Issues in Olympics Controversy"; Ditmer, "'Yes' Really Is 'No' in Vote on Olympics"; Whiteside, *Colorado*, 165–167, 171.

30. O'Reilly, "Growth, Funds Key Issues in Olympics Controversy."

31. "KBTV and CCF Reach Accord over Olympics," *Rocky Mountain News*, November 3, 1972; Richard O'Reilly, "Colorado Voters Reject 1976 Winter Olympics," *Rocky Mountain News*, November 8, 1972; Dick Lucas, "Big 'Negative' Vote May Save Olympics," *Denver Post*, November 5, 1972; Whiteside, *Colorado*, 173.

32. Cole to the President, November 21, 1972, Folder [EX] RE 14 Olympic Games 1/1/71 2 of 2, Box 8, Recreation-Sports Files, Subject Files, White House Central Files, NPP, NACP.

33. Fell to Nixon, December 4, 1973; Harrigan to Cole, January 22, 1974; Nixon to Killanin, February 13, 1974, Folder [EX] RE 14 Olympic Games 1/1/73, Box 8, Recreation-Sports Files, Subject Files, White House Central Files, NPP, NACP.

34. Nixon meeting with Haldeman, December 15, 1972, Conversation number 824-2, Oval 842, Nixon Presidential Library, https://nixonlibrary.gov.

CHAPTER 9. THE SECOND TERM, 1973–1974

1. Larry Berman, *No Peace, No Honor: Nixon, Kissinger, and Betrayal in Vietnam* (New York: Free Press, 2001), 131–240.

2. Nixon-Allen conversation, December 26, 1972, Conversation number 35-9, and Nixon-Allen conversation, December 31, 1972, Conversation number 35-41, WHT 035, Nixon Presidential Library, https://nixonlibrary.gov.

3. Quoted in David DuPree, "Allen Gives Staff Day Off, Celebrates with President," *Washington Post*, January 2, 1973; David Anderson, "Nixon Pledges Allegiance to Redskins," *New York Times*, January 2, 1973; Vito Stellino, "Nixon Reassures Allen He'll Root for Redskins," *Miami Herald*, January 2, 1973; "Nixon Will Root for Redskins," *Florida Times-Union*, January 2, 1973.

4. Anderson, "Nixon Pledges Allegiance to Redskins."

5. Sally Quinn, "BILLY KILMER: Some are born great Some achieve greatness and Some have greatness thrust upon 'em . . . Besides , You Only Go Around Once in Life," *Washington Post*, December 3, 1972.

6. DuPree, "Allen Gives Staff Day Off, Celebrates with President"; Joseph Kraft, "'Spirited' Suggestions for Mr. Nixon's Gift List," *Washington Post*, December 21, 1972 "Clam Up, Mr. President," *Wall Street Journal*, December 5, 1972; H. R. Haldeman, *The Haldeman Diaries: Inside the Nixon White House—The Complete Multimedia Collection* (Santa Monica, CA: Sony Electronic Publishing, 1994), CD-ROM, December 4, 1972; Kraft, "'Spirited' Suggestions for Mr. Nixon's Gift List."

7. Nixon conversation with Colson, January 1, 1973, Conversation number 392-14, EOB 392, and Nixon conversation with Colson, January 2, 1973, Conversation number 830-6, Oval 830, Nixon Presidential Library, https://nixonlibrary.gov.

8. Nixon–Rowan and Martin conversation, January 10, 1973, Conversation number 35-124, WHT 035, Nixon Presidential Library, https://nixonlibrary.gov.

9. Leonard Shapiro, "Nixon Finesses Shula Call," *Washington Post*, January 16, 1973; Bob Oates, "Who Said Nobody's Perfect? Dolphins Go 17–0," *Los Angeles Times*, January 15, 1973.

10. "No. 1 Fan Dismayed by Defeat" and "Fans Take to Streets," *New York Times*, January 15, 1973; Richard Harwood, "Miami Bursts Redskins' Bubble, 14–7," *Washington Post*, January 15, 1973; Darrell Eiland "'Has Peace Been Declared?,'" *Miami Herald*, January 15, 1973; Edwin Pope, "Redskins 3-Point Choice? Ho Ho Ho Ha Ha Ha," *Tallahassee Democrat*, January 15, 1973.

11. Nixon to Shula, January 14, 1974, Recreation-Sports Files, Subject Files, White House Central Files, Nixon Presidential Project, National Archives, College Park, MD [hereafter NPP, NACP]; Leonard Shapiro, "Nixon Finesses Shula Call," *The Washington Post*, January 16, 1973; "Nixon's Call to Shula Is Blacked Out," *The New York Times*, January 16, 1973; "It Was a Super Monday For Shula," *The Tampa Tribune*, January 16, 1973; emphasis in the original Shula quote in Jeff Prugh, "Shula: Our 17–0 Mark Says It All," *Los Angeles Times*, January 15, 1973; Haldeman, *Haldeman Diaries*, January 15, 1973.

12. Nixon to Allen, January 14, 1974, Folder [EX] RE 10 Football 1/1/73, Box 6, Recreation-Sports Files, Subject Files, White House Central Files, NPP, NACP.

13. Nixon conversation with Price and Ziegler, January 19, 1973, Conversation number 397-7, EOB 397, Nixon Presidential Library, https://nixonlibrary.gov.

14. David Maraniss, *Clemente: The Passion and Grace of Baseball's Last Hero* (New York: Simon and Schuster, 2006), 265.

15. Nixon-Rogers conversation, October 17, 1971, Conversation number 11-105, WHT 011, http://www.nixontapes.org.

16. Bruce Markusen, *Roberto Clemente: The Great One* (Champaign, IL: Sports Publishing, 1998), 310–314, 320–321.

17. "Statement about the Death of Roberto Clemente," January 2, 1973, *Public Papers of the Presidents of the United States: Richard Nixon, 1969–1974* (Washington, DC: Office of the Federal Register, 1970–1975) [hereafter *PPP*], 1; Bull to R[ose] M[ary] W[oods], January 2, 1973, Folder 9—Clemente, Roberto Statement, Box 7, Name/Subject File, President's Personal File, White House Special Files, NPP, NACP.

18. Moorhead Statement, January 6, 1973; Scott Statement, January 4, 1973; Heinz Statement, January 9, 1973; Stevenson Statement, January 11, 1973; Burton Statement, January 18, 1973; Mizell statement, January 22, 1973; Rodino statement, February 5, 1973, 119 Cong. Rec. part 1: 484, 333–334, 547, 808; part 2: 1699, 1790; part 3: 3395 (1973). Also see the statements of Senator Richard Schweiker of Pennsylvania, January 4, 1973; Representative William Cotter of Connecticut, January 18, 1973; Resident Commissioner Jaime Benitez of Puerto Rico, January 30, 1973; Representative James Burke of Massachusetts, February 5, 1973, 119 Cong. Rec. part 1: 349; part 2: 1742; part 3: 2563, 3371 (1973).

19. For editorial commentary on Clemente's death, see the following: "Sports Glory and Tragedy," *Newport News Daily Press*, January 2, 1973; "Roberto Clemente,

the Great One," *Pittsburgh Post-Gazette*, January 2, 1973; "Wealth Lies in the Heart," *Bennington Banner*, January 3, 1973; "Roberto: A Hero's Death," *Wilmington News Journal*, January 3, 1973; "Clemente: Heroism, Humanity," *Detroit Free Press*, January 3, 1973; "More than Just a Baseball Player," Louisville *Courier-Journal*, January 3, 1973; "A Star in the Game of Life, Too," *Philadelphia Inquirer*, January 3, 1973; "Roberto Clemente," *Ogden Standard-Examiner*, January 3, 1973; "Clemente Man of Excellence," *Orlando Sentinel*, January 3, 1973; "Clemente, the Quiet Superstar," *Kansas City Times*, January 3, 1973; "Class All the Way," *Lincoln Evening Journal*, January 3, 1973; "How Roberto Clemente Died," *Baltimore Sun*, January 3, 1973; "Clemente: 'Touch of Royalty,'" *Arizona Republic*, January 3, 1973; "Roberto Clemente," *Palm Beach Post*, January 4, 1973; "A Fallen Star," *Lansing State Journal*, January 4, 1973; "Exemplary Behavior," *Arizona Daily Star*, January 5, 1973; "Roberto Clemente," Cincinnati *Enquirer*, January 5, 1973; "Roberto Clemente," *Hartford Courant*, January 5, 1973; "Roberto Clemente," Newark *Star-Ledger*, January 5, 1973.

20. "Clemente Dies in Plane Crash," *Pittsburgh Post-Gazette*, January 2, 1973; "A Memorial for Clemente," *Washington Evening Star*, January 5, 1973.

21. Jim Murray, "Clemente: You Had to See Him to Disbelieve Him," *Los Angeles Times*, January 3, 1973. This column was syndicated in a number of other papers: Jim Murray, "Clemente Best 'Sick,'" *Lansing State Journal*, January 3, 1973; Jim Murray, "Roberto Clemente," *Honolulu Advertiser*, January 4, 1973; Jim Murray, "Clemente Was Quick Pitched," *Arizona Republic*, January 4, 1973; Jim Murray, "Robert Wasn't Born, He Was Mined," *Philadelphia Inquirer*, January 4, 1973; Jim Murray, "There Was Only One Clemente," *Des Moines Register*, January 4, 1973. For other tributes in sports pages: Bruce Keidan, "Roberto Clemente: Baseball's 'Magnificent Militant,'" *Philadelphia Inquirer*, January 2, 1973; Phil Musick, "The Great One: Most of All, He Was Human," *Pittsburgh Press*, January 4, 1973; Bill Schelthammer, "Eulogy to Roberto—Man With Golden Arm," *Wilmington Morning News*, January 3, 1973.

22. Markusen, *Clemente*, 325, 327.

23. "Statement about the Death of Roberto Clemente," January 2, 1973, *PPP*, 1.

24. "A $100,000 Grant Honors Clemente," *New York Times*, January 5, 1973; Milton Jaques, "Nixons Donate $1,000 to Start Clemente Fund," *Pittsburgh Post-Gazette*, January 4, 1973; Margie Carlin, "1,300 at Clemente Service Here," *Pittsburgh Press*, January 4, 1973; Nixon-Colson conversation, January 3, 1973, Conversation number 35-78, WHT 035, and Nixon-Blass-Giusti, January 3, 1972, Conversation number 832-4, Oval 832, Nixon Presidential Library, https://nixonlibrary.gov.

25. Carlin, "1,300 At Clemente Service Here"; "Memorials to Roberto Clemente," *Pittsburgh Post-Gazette*, January 5, 1972.

26. "Nixon Contributes to Clemente Fund," *Tallahassee Democrat*, January 4, 1973; "Nixon Donates $1,000," *Santa Fe New Mexican*, January 4, 1973; "President Donates $1,000 to Clemente Charities," *Wilmington Evening Journal*, January 4, 1973; "Nixon Donates to Clemente Cause," *Hattiesburg American*, January 4, 1973; "Clemente Memorial Fund Begins," *Lincoln Star*, January 4, 1973; "Nixon Honors Clemente," *Lan-*

sing State Journal, January 4, 1973; Jaques, "Nixons Donate $1,000 to Start Clemente Fund"; "Nixon Asks Quake Aid in Honor of Clemente," *New York Times*, January 3, 1973; "Fame He Craved Now Finds Clemente," *Boston Globe*, January 4, 1973.

27. The other sponsors were Heinz, Mizell, Thomas "Doc" Morgan of Pennsylvania, Frank Clark of Pennsylvania, John Dent of Pennsylvania, and Herman Badillo of New York. 119 Cong. Rec. part 2: 1770; part 8: 9522; part 11: 13933, 14083 (1973).

28. Nixon conversation with Ziegler, September 22, 1971, Conversation number 9-131, WHT 9, http://www.nixontapes.org.

29. Nixon conversation with Haldeman, March 17, 1973, Conversation number 882-12, Oval 882, Nixon Presidential Library, https://nixonlibrary.gov; Farrell, *Nixon*, 202.

30. "Remarks at a Ceremony Honoring Roberto Clemente," May 14, 1973, *PPP*, 529–531.

31. "Remarks at a Ceremony Honoring Roberto Clemente," 529–531; photo contact sheet, Roll E0797, 5-14-74 contact sheet book, White House Photographic Office, NPP, NACP. In 2003 President George W. Bush upgraded the award, presenting the Clemente family with the Presidential Medal of Freedom.

32. "Remarks at a Ceremony Honoring Roberto Clemente," 529–531; photo contact sheet, Roll E0797, 5-14-74 contact sheet book, White House Photographic Office, NPP, NACP.

33. Stanley I. Kutler, *The Wars of Watergate: The Last Crisis of Richard Nixon* (New York: W. W. Norton, 1990), 323–382; Stephen E. Ambrose, *Nixon*, vol. 3: *Ruin and Recovery, 1973–1990* (New York: Simon and Schuster, 1991), 132–164.

34. Sam Goldpaper, "Padres Are Sold to a Washington Group," *New York Times*, May 29, 1973; "C. Arnholt Smith and IRS Come to Terms Allowing Him to Continue His Business," *Wall Street Journal*, August 13, 1973; Al Delugach, "C. Arnholt Smith: Troubles Are Far from Over," *Los Angeles Times*, October 31, 1973.

35. Woods to the President, September 6, 1973; Nixon to Feeney, September 7, 1973, Folder [EX] RE 2 Baseball-Softball 1/1/73, Box 3, Recreation-Sports Files, Subject Files, White House Central Files, NPP, NACP.

36. Bowie Kuhn, *Hardball: The Education of a Baseball Commissioner* (New York: Times Books, 1987), 101–103; Joseph Durso, "Padres' Shift to Washington Granted; Wynn Goes to Dodgers for Osteen," *New York Times*, December 7, 1973.

37. Nixon to Danzansky, December 6, 1973, Folder [EX] RE 2 Baseball-Softball 1/1/73, Box 3, Recreation-Sports Files, Subject Files, White House Central Files, NPP, NACP.

38. Steve Bishoff, "Politicians Tromp over Local Fans," San Diego *Evening Tribune*, December 7, 1973; "Foul Ball," *San Diego Union*, December 8, 1973; see the comments of Clair W. Burgener, Lionel Van Deerlin, and William Ketchum in the *Congressional Record*, 119 Cong. Rec. part 25: 33059–33060, part 31: 40595–40596, 40897 (1973); Kuhn, *Hardball*, 101–103.

39. Kutler, *Wars of Watergate*, 389, 391–398. Major League Baseball returned to

Washington, DC, in 2005 when the Montreal Expos relocated and changed their name to the Washington Nationals.

40. Ambrose, *Ruin and Recovery*, 235–239; Kutler, *Wars of Watergate*, 421.

41. "Chaos, Tragedy Haunt Games," *New York Times*, September 12, 1972; Neil Amdur, "Olympic Group: Tower of Babel," *New York Times*, November 5, 1972.

42. Ramer to Ford, December 4, 1972, Folder 1973–1974 Olympics, Box 154, Paul Miltich Subject File, Vice-Presidential Papers, Gerald R. Ford Presidential Library.

43. Neil Amdur, "Olympic Group: Tower of Babel," *New York Times*, November 5, 1972; "Olympian Needs," *New York Times*, November 6, 1972.

44. Ehrlichman notations on Hullin to Ehrlichman, August 27, 1969; Wilkinson memo, August 19, 1969; Wilkinson to Frenn, September 4, 1969; Sloan to Frenn, February 16, 1970, Folder [GEN] RE 22 Track-Field Matters, Box 10, Recreation-Sports Files, Subject Files, White House Central Files, NPP, NACP.

45. Charles Maher, "What Say, Mr. Nixon?," *Los Angeles Times*, August 19, 1970; Melencamp to Frenn, October 29, 1970, Folder [GEN] RE 22 Track-Field Matters, Box 10, Recreation-Sports Files, Subject Files, White House Central Files, NPP, NACP.

46. "Remarks of AAU President John B. Kelly, Jr.," November 1, 1972, and "United States Olympic Crisis: The Problem That Won't Go Away," 29, November 24, 1972, Folder 1973–1974 Olympics, Box 154, Paul Miltich Subject File, Vice-Presidential Papers, Gerald R. Ford Presidential Library.

47. Lovell to Ehrlichman, December 1, 1972, Folder RE 14 Olympic Games 1/1/71 2 of 2, Box 8, Recreation-Sports Files, Subject Files, White House Central Files, NPP, NACP.

48. Thomas M. Hunt, "Countering the Soviet Threat in the Olympic Medals Race: The Amateur Sports Act of 1978 and American Athletics Policy Reform," *International Journal of the History of Sport* 24, no. 6 (June 2007): 800–801.

49. "Comments on a Presidential Commission to Examine the U.S. Olympic Effort," attached to Hullin to Ehrlichman, January 9, 1973, Folder RE 14 Olympic Games 1/1/73, Box 8, Recreation-Sports Files, Subject Files, White House Central Files, NPP, NACP; Coleman to Ford, November 9, 1972, Folder 1973–1974 Olympics, Box 154, Paul Miltich Subject File, Vice-Presidential Papers, Gerald R. Ford Presidential Library.

50. Kelly to Ford, December 1, 1972, Folder 1973–1974 Olympics, Box 154, Paul Miltich Subject File, Vice-Presidential Papers, Gerald R. Ford Presidential Library; "United States Olympic Crisis: The Problem That Won't Go Away," 29.

51. "Comments on a Presidential Commission to Examine the U.S. Olympic Effort."

52. Nixon conversation with Wilkinson, February 23, 1973, Conversation number 413-1, EOB 413, Nixon Presidential Library, https://nixonlibrary.gov.

53. Claiborne Pell of Rhode Island, Philip Hart of Michigan, Alan Cranston of California, and Tom Eagleton of Missouri joined Tunney as cosponsors of the bill.

119 Cong. Rec. part 5: 5267; 12: 15136; 16: 20831 (1973); Cole to Staff Secretary, July 20, 1973; Jones and Harrigan to the President, August 15, 1973, Folder RE 14 Olympic Games 1/1/73, Box 8, Recreation-Sports Files, Subject Files, White House Central Files, NPP, NACP.

54. Kissinger to Lehman, August 18, 1973, Folder RE 14 Olympic Games 1/1/73, Box 8, Recreation-Sports Files, Subject Files, White House Central Files, NPP, NACP; Jones and Harrigan to the President, August 15, 1973

55. Kissinger to Lehman, August 18, 1973; Jones and Harrigan to the President, August 15, 1973.

56. Ambrose, *Ruin and Recovery*, 202.

57. Gerald R. Ford with John Underwood, "In Defense of the Competitive Urge," *Sports Illustrated*, July 8, 1974, 17, 18, 23

58. Harrigan to the Vice President, May 22, 1974, Folder [EX] RE Recreation-Sports 1/1/73, Box 1, Recreation-Sports Files, Subject Files, White House Central Files, NPP, NACP.

59. Hunt, "Countering the Soviet Threat in the Olympic Medals Race," 802; Robert Fachet, "Despite Capital Ideas, Athletes Are Still in the Soup," *Washington Post*, March 26, 1974.

60. The members of the commission were chairman Gerald B. Zornow, chairman of the board, Eastman Kodak; Senator J. Glenn Beall Jr. of Maryland; Senator John C. Culver of Iowa; Olympic gold medalist Donna de Varona; cross country skier W. Michael Elliot; Barbara Ellen Forker, director of women's physical education at Iowa State University; Jerome H. Holland, director of the New York Stock Exchange; Lamar Hunt, owner of the Kansas City Chiefs football team; Olympic gold medalist Rafer Johnson; Congressman Jack Kemp of New York, a former professional football player; Captain Micki King, US Air Force, an Olympic gold medalist; James A. McCain, Kansas state commissioner of labor; Congressman Ralph H. Metcalfe of Illinois, a member of the US Olympic team in 1932 and 1936; Congressman Robert H. Michel of Illinois; Congressman Norman Y. Mineta of California; Howard K. Smith, ABC News; Senator Ted Stevens of Alaska; Olympic gold medalist William A. Toomey; Ernest M. Vandeweghe, US Olympic Basketball Committee; Willye White, woman's track coach, Chicago State University; and Charles "Bud" Wilkinson, former head football coach at the University of Oklahoma. "Statement on the Establishment of the President's Commission on Olympic Sports," June 19, 1975, *PPP*, 835–836; Philip Shabecoff, "Ford Chooses Olympic Unit: President Picks Panel for Olympic Athletics," *New York Times*, June 20, 1975; Neil Amdur, "U.S. Report Urges New Body to Direct Amateur Athletics," *New York Times*, January 13, 1977; "Athlete Aid Bill Gains," *New York Times*, May 9, 1978.

61. Hunt, "Countering the Soviet Threat in the Olympic Medals Race," 807–808.

62. Fred Emery, *Watergate: The Corruption of American Politics and the Fall of Richard Nixon* (New York, 1994), 400–401; Ambrose, *Ruin and Recovery*, 247–250; Kutler, *Wars of Watergate*, 404–407, 413, 426–427.

63. Ambrose, *Ruin and Recovery*, 269–276.

64. Nixon often spoke without a formal text, and the compilers of the *Public Papers* series appear to have made transcriptions of these remarks from recordings, which appears to be the case for this Georgia appearance. Reporters noted that it appeared Nixon was speaking extemporaneously. The speech in the *Public Papers* series includes the last part of the sentence, but journalists covering the appearance said the crowd reaction cut Nixon off. "Remarks at Ceremonies in Macon, Georgia, Marking the 100th Anniversary of the Walter F. George School of Law and the 90th Birthday of Carl Vinson," November 18, 1973, *PPP*, 966–967; Howell Raines, "'Football Bluff,'" *Atlanta Constitution*, November 19, 1973; David Nordan, "President Relaxed, in Good Humor," *Atlanta Journal*, November 9, 1973.

65. Howell Raines, "Nuclear Carrier to Be Named for Vinson," *Atlanta Constitution*, November 19, 1973; David Nordan, "Another First for Vinson in Long Career of Firsts," *Atlanta Journal*, November 9, 1973. On March 15, 1980, Vinson became the first individual in the history of the US Navy to witness the launching of a ship named in his or her honor.

66. Bob Fort, "Thousands Warmly Welcome Nixon at Robins and Mercer Ceremonies," *Atlanta Constitution*, November 19, 1973.

67. Kutler, *Wars of Watergate*, 445, 448–450; Ambrose, *Ruin and Recovery*, 291, 325–339.

68. Kutler, *Wars of Watergate*, 463, 467–468; Ambrose, *Ruin and Recovery*, 337, 343.

69. Scheduling Ideas, March 19, 1974, Folder [EX] RE 2 Baseball-Softball 1/1/73, Box 3, Recreation-Sports Files, Subject Files, White House Central Files, NPP, NACP.

70. Frank Hyland, "It's Over: Hammerin' Hank Stands All Alone at 715," *Atlanta Journal*, April 9, 1974; Henry Aaron with Lonnie Wheeler, *I Had a Hammer: The Hank Aaron Story* (New York: HarperCollins, 1991), 271–272.

71. "Remarks at Commencement Exercises at Oklahoma State University, Stillwater, Oklahoma," May 11, 1974, *PPP*, 427; Allan Cromley, "Nixon Brings Fight to State: President Visits 'God's Country' to Dispute Foes," Oklahoma City *Daily Oklahoman*, May 12, 1974.

72. Mike Flanagan, "32,000 Cheer Nixon in Patriotic OSU Talk," *Tulsa Daily World*, May 12, 1974; Cromley, "Nixon Brings Fight to State."

73. "Statement on the Death of Dizzy Dean," July 17, 1974, *PPP*, 594; Nixon to Dean, July 17, 1974, Folder [EX] RE 2 Baseball-Softball 1/1/73, Box 3, Recreation-Sports Files, Subject Files, White House Central Files, NPP, NACP.

74. "Dizzy Dean, Famed Pitcher Turned 'Commultator,' Dies: Free-Spirit Dizzy Dean Stilled," and "Dean Remembered, Kindly," *Washington Post*, July 18, 1974; Jim Murray, "He Never Grew Up," *Los Angeles Times*, July 19, 1974; see the comments of Barry Goldwater, Silvio Conte, Leonor Sullivan, Wilmer Mizell, and Thad Cochran, 120 Cong. Rec. part 19: 24711; part 18: 24167–24168, 23906, 23641, 23895 (1974).

For commentary from sports columnists, see: Ronnie Joyce, "Dizzy Dean Slud Home," *Pensacola News Journal*, July 18, 1974; Bob Broeg, "Nobody Could Stay Angry at Big-Hearted Diz," *St. Louis Post-Dispatch*, July 18, 1974; Ron Bennett, "A Real Sports Hero," *Reno Gazette-Journal*, July 18, 1974; David Condon, "There'll Never Be Another Like Dizzy," *Chicago Tribune*, July 18, 1974; Mickey Edwards, "Dizzy Dean: People Loved Him," *Hattiesburg American*, July 21, 1974.

For commentary from editorial boards, see: "Success Never Spoiled Ol' Diz," *Kansas City Times*, July 18, 1974; "Legend," *St. Louis Post-Dispatch*, July 18, 1974; "Dean: A True, Unique Character," *Decatur Review*, July 18, 1974; "Dizzy Dean," *Pittsburgh Press*, July 18,1974;

75. Kutler, *Wars of Watergate*, 513–514, 525–530.

76. Kutler, *Wars of Watergate*, 534–538.

77. Ambrose, *Ruin and Recovery*, 400, 426, 435–436, 445.

78. Ambrose, *Ruin and Recovery*, 400, 426, 435–436, 445; Kuhn to Nixon, August 9, 1974, Folder 7, Box 17, Series VII: Correspondence, Papers of Bowie Kuhn, National Baseball Hall of Fame, Cooperstown, New York.

79. Ambrose, *Ruin and Recovery*, 400, 426, 435-436, 445.

AFTERMATH

1. Howard Bryant, *The Last Hero: A Life of Henry Aaron* (New York: Random House, 2010), 462-526.

2. William Gildea, "Ex-Redskins Coach Allen Dies: Guided 'Over-the-Hill Gang to 1972 Super Bowl Appearance," *Washington Post*, January 1, 1991; "George Allen Dies: Coach, Dead at 72; Led Redskins to Super Bowl VII," *New York Times*, January 1, 1991; Thomas George, "Hall of Fame Induction Is Mostly Kelly's Show," *New York Times*, August 4, 2002.

3. Francis X. Clines, "Spiro T. Agnew, Point Man for Nixon Who Resigned Vice Presidency, Dies at 77," *New York Times*, September 19, 1999

4. Frank Litsky, "Frank Broyles, Coach Who Put Arkansas on the Map, Dies at 92," *New York Times*, August 15, 2017; Matt Jones, "Frank Broyles, Arkansas Icon, Dies at 92," *Arkansas Democrat-Gazette*, August 15, 2017.

5. "Avery Brundage of Olympics Dies," *New York Times*, May 9, 1975.

6. "Kenneth Reese Cole Jr., 63, Aide to Nixon," *New York Times*, August 23, 2001.

7. "Archibald Cox, 92, Is Dead; Helped Prosecute Watergate," *New York Times*, May 30, 2004.

8. Jerry Knight, "Danzansky Relinquishes Presidency at Giant; Succeeded by Israel Cohen," *Washington Post*, September 6, 1977; William H. Jones, "Tireless Civic Work Typified Businessman; Danzansky: Consumerism Mattered," *Washington Post*, November 14, 1979.

9. David Stout, "Harry Dent, 77, an Architect of Nixon 'Southern Strategy,'" *New York Times*, October 2, 2007.

10. Frank Litsky, "Bob Devane, 82, Nebraska Coach, Dies," *New York Times*, May 10, 1997.

11. David Stout, "John D. Ehrlichman, Nixon Aide Jailed for Watergate, Dies at

73," *New York Times*, February 16, 1999; Martin Weil, "Key Nixon Adviser John D. Ehrlichman Dies at 73," *Washington Post*, February 16, 1999; John D. Ehrlichman, *Witness to Power: The Nixon Years* (New York: Simon and Schuster, 1982); Richard Reeves, *President Nixon: Alone in the White House* (New York: Simon and Schuster, 2001), 666.

12. Joseph Durso, "Curt Flood Finds His Niche," *New York Times*, May 26, 1981; "Flood Recaptures a Golden Moment at Awards Dinner," *Palm Beach Post*, November 19, 1993; Joseph Durso, "Curt Flood Is Dead at 59: Outfielder Defied Baseball," *New York Times*, January 21, 1997.

13. Marjorie Hunter, "Dignitaries Praise Ford At Museum Dedication," *New York Times*, September 19, 1981; Donnie Radcliffe, "Betty Ford, after the Battle: Helping Others Learn from Her Experiences," *Washington Post*, April 24, 1983; DeNeen Brown, "Eight Who Let Freedom Ring," *Washington Post*, August 12, 1999; James M. Naughton and Adam Clymer, "President Gerald R. Ford, Who Led U.S. Out of Watergate Era, Dies at 93," *New York Times*, December 28, 2006; Jeffrey Brainard, "Gerald Ford Offered Academe Olive Branches, but Little Money," *Chronicle of Higher Education* 53, no. 18 (January 5, 2007): A23; Ted Janes, "Wolverines Honor Their Legends (Again)," *Detroit Free Press*, November 28, 2015.

14. Bill Syken, "Catching up with . . . George Frenn, Hammer Thrower, July 6, 1970," *Sports Illustrated*, September 16, 2002, 20; "George Frenn," *Sacramento Bee*, July 11, 2006.

15. Richard Goldstein and Bruce Weber, "Frank Gifford, 84, Dies; His Celebrity Helped Push N.F.L. into Spotlight," *New York Times*, August 10, 2015; Ken Belson, "Gifford's Family Reveals He Had Brain Disease," *New York Times*, November 26, 2015.

16. Tim Weiner, "Alexander M. Haig Jr. Dies at 85; Was Forceful aide to 2 Presidents," *New York Times*, February 21, 2010.

17. J. Y. Smith, "H. R. Haldeman Dies; Was Nixon Chief of Staff; Watergate Role Led to 18 Months in Prison," *Washington Post*, November 13, 1993; Lloyd Grove, "Every Trick's in the Book; Haldeman Diaries Put a Wrinkle in the Rehabilitation," *Washington Post*, May 18, 1994.

18. Robert McG. Thomas Jr., "Woody Hayes, Fiery Coach, Is Dead," *New York Times*, March 13, 1987; "Sports People; 3 in Football Hall of Fame," *New York Times*, February 9, 1983; John Switzer, "Hayes Eulogized as Renaissance Man," *Columbus Dispatch*, March 18, 1997; Linda Kay, "Nixon on Hayes: 'Not an Ordindary Man,'" *Chicago Tribune*, March 18, 1987.

19. "Tod Hullin Is Named Public Affairs Chief of Seagram U.S. Unit," *Wall Street Journal*, September 15, 1988.

20. Martin Weil, "Leon Jaworski, Key Prosecutor, Dies of Apparent Heart Attack at Age 77," *Washington Post*, December 10, 1982.

21. William N. Wallace, "Kilmer Sees a Future in Summer Football," *New York Times*, May 31, 1981; Paul Attner, "Kilmer Resigns Position as AFA Commissioner,"

Washington Post, August 30, 1981; Sam Blair, "Life after Football Still Fun and Games for Kilmer," *Chicago Tribune*, September 13, 1987.

22. Marilyn Berger, "Burger Swears In Kissinger: Refugee from Nazis Vows 'Structures of Peace,'" *Washington Post*, September 23, 1973; Murray Marder, "Kissinger, Tho Get Nobel Peace Prize," *Washington Post*, October 17, 1973; Leslie H. Gelb, "Kissinger Means Business," *New York Times*, April 20, 1986.

23. Carol J. Williams, "Herbert G. Kelin, 1918–2009: Veteran Journalist Was Nixon Press Secretary," *Los Angeles Times*, July 3, 2009; Adam Clymer, "Herbert G. Klein, 91, Aide in the Nixon White House," *New York Times*, July 4, 2009.

24. Joe Holley, "Bowie Kuhn; Commissioner Modernized Baseball," *Washington Post*, March 15, 2007; Richard Goldstein, "Bowie Kuhn, 80, Former Baseball Commissioner, Dies," *New York Times*, March 16, 2007.

25. Thomas George, "Tom Landry Is Dead at 75; Innovative Coach of Cowboys," *New York Times*, February 13, 2000; Tom Landry with Gregg Lewis, *Tom Landry: An Autobiography* (Grand Rapids, MI: Zondervan Books, 1990).

26. Richard Goldstein, "The Bargainer Who Remade the Old Ball Game," *New York Times*, November 28, 2012.

27. Kenneth Reich, "George Murphy, 89; Actor-Dancer Who Served 1 Term in U.S. Senate," *Los Angeles Times*, May 5, 1992.

28. "Hall of Fame Sportscaster Lindsey Nelson Dies at 76," *Washington Post*, June 12, 1995; Furman Bisher, "Nelson's Voice One of Honesty," *Atlanta Journal*, January 14, 1995; Matthew Silverman, *New York Mets: The Complete Illustrated History* (Minneapolis: MBI Publishing, 2011).

29. Charles Wolfe, "Former Gov. Louie B. Nunn dead at 79," *Lexington Herald-Leader*, January 30, 1994.

30. Richard Goldstein, "Joe Paterno, 1926–2012: Unequaled Coach and Face of Penn State, Felled by Scandal," *New York Times*, January 23, 2012; Ron Musselman, "Joseph Vincent Paterno; Dec. 21, 1926–Jan. 22, 2012; For Penn State's 'Joepa,' a Storied but Scarred Legacy," *Pittsburgh Post-Gazette*, January 23, 2012; "Paterno's Life Strikes a Balance: Penn State Coach Emphasizes Academics as Well as Football," *Chicago Tribune*, December 22, 1996.

31. Leonard Shapiro, "Post Sports Columnist Shirley Povich Dies," *Washington Post*, June 5, 1998.

32. Berry Tramel, "Darrell Royal: 1924–2012; Former OU Quarterback Never Forgot His Sooner-State Roots; Hollis Native; Coaching Icon Not Embraced in the State Where He Was Born," Oklahoma City *Daily Oklahoman*, November 8, 2012; Richard Goldstein, "Darrell Royal, Innovative Coach at Texas, Dies at 88," *New York Times*, November 8, 2012.

33. Sean D. Hamill, "Raymond P. Shafer, 89, Governor of Pennsylvania," *New York Times*, December 14, 2006; Tracie Mauriello, "Raymond P. Shafer, March 5, 1917–December 12, 2006," *Pittsburgh Post Gazette*, December 13, 2006.

34. Wolfgang Saxon, "Robert E. Short, Businessman Dies," *New York Times*, November 22, 1982.

35. Dave Anderson, "Shula's Backup QB Success," *New York Times*, November 4, 1993; Leonard Shapiro, "Dolphins' Shula Calls It a Career, Coach 'At Peace' after Ending 33-Year Tenure with 347 Victories," *Washington Post*, January 6, 1996; Thomas George, "Pro Football: Four Football Heroes Finish Game at Canton," *New York Times*, July 27, 1997; Jeff Ostrowski, "For Shulas, Running Restaurants Win-Win," *Palm Beach Post*, July 15, 2013.

36. "Packers Pick Bart Starr," *Chicago Tribune*, December 25, 1974; "Packers' Starr, Gregg Lead Entry to Pro Hall," *New York Times*, July 24, 1977; "Packers Dismiss Starr as Coach," *New York Times*, December 20, 1983; Jason Wilde, "Reggie Gets His Day Too: The Late Reggie White Will Have His Number Retired, the Fifth Packer to Be So Honored," *Wisconsin State Journal*, September 18, 2005.

37. Philip Rucker, "St. Charles Developer Charles E. Stuart Dies," *Washington Post*, August 23, 2007; Charles E. Stuart, *Bin Laden's Second Strike* (Charleston, SC: BookSurge Publishing, 2007).

38. Joe Simnacher and Elizabeth Zavala, "Former Arlington Mayor Tom Vandergriff Dies at 84," *Dallas Morning News*, December 30, 2010; Michael Mink, "Bart Starr, the Aptly Named Football Champ," *Investor's Business Daily*, February 2, 2011.

39. Marjorie Hunter, "Carl Vinson, 97, Ex-Congressman Was in House 50 Years, Dies," *New York Times*, June 2, 1981.

40. "5 Inducted at Pro Football Hall of Fame," *New York Times*, July 31, 1983; Richard Sandomir, "Lerner Wins Browns for $530 Million," *New York Times*, September 9, 1998.

41. Marc Fisher, "Legal Titan Edward Bennett Williams Dies; Famed D.C. Lawyer-Politician Owned Redskins, Ten Orioles," and Richard Justice, "Williams Practiced a Relentless Drive to Win," *Washington Post*, August 14, 1988.

42. Jack Curry, "Williams and Fenway: They Still Click," *New York Times*, July 14, 1999; Richard Goldstein and Robert McG. Thomas, "Ted Williams, Red Sox Slugger and Last to Hit .400, Dies at 83," *New York Times*, July 6, 2002.

43. Todd S. Purdum, "Ronald L. Ziegler, Press Secretary to President Nixon Is Deat at 63," *New York Times*, February 12, 2003.

44. "Umpires Will Get More Pay," *Boston Globe*, October 29, 1985; Mal Florence, "At Least Laettner Didn't Say of Shot, 'That Is Not a Brick,'" *Los Angeles Times*, October 20, 1992; Mark Landsbaum, "A League of His Own," *Los Angeles Times*, July 16, 1992; Gordon Edes, "A President Who Was a Real Fan," *Chicago Tribune*, May 1, 1994; James Dodson, "Nixon Was One of Us," *Golf Magazine*, October 1994, 20.

BIBLIOGRAPHIC ESSAY

When Richard Nixon was born in 1913, historians of that day did their job much as they had done for decades and centuries previous, by examining letters and diaries, attempting to decipher handwriting. Almost all of the information from the past was recorded on paper. Due to technological limitations, photographs were mainly posed; for all practical purposes they were nothing more than paintings made with celluloid.

Although it was popular in the 1990s to talk about the revolution that was taking place in information storage and retrieval, a much more profound transformation took place over the course of the entire twentieth century, changing not only the way information was stored, but also the types of data that could be recorded. The decade and a half before Nixon's birth saw the development of typewriters, motion pictures, audio recordings, and small portable cameras. These new technologies quickly became available to the public, and in the years that followed, people improved upon these inventions and created new devices. During his life, Nixon saw the advent and widespread use of radio, television, electric typewriters, photocopy machines, tape recorders, home movie and video cameras, FAX machines, computers, and the internet. Perhaps it is appropriate that tape recordings played such a pivotal role in the Nixon presidency. Woodrow Wilson, who was president when Nixon was born, probably never imagined that such a contraption could play a significant role in the presidency.

Historians have both profited from and ignored these changes in technology. With computers and photocopiers it is now possible to write and research at a much faster pace than was possible as recently as the late 1960s. Case in point, Stephen Ambrose stated in the acknowledgments section of *Education of a Politician* that photocopy machines reduced the research time for that biography by a factor of twenty from the amount of time it took him to write his first book.

While these devices have helped in scholarly production and professional activity, historians have turned a blind eye to the new forms of information that have resulted from these new technologies for a number of reasons. One major consideration is applicability. Many of the new technologies came into being after the time period a historian studies, limiting the relevance of these new devices. Put simply, Theodore Roosevelt never gave a televised speech, so there is no reason for a historian of the Gilded Age to worry about video footage. Another reason is the speed required to process the material. Researchers can read the text of a State of the Union speech much faster than they can watch or listen to a recording of its presentation. Also, it is easier, depending on the archive, to access paper documents than photographs and films, and the text on paper normally contains more data than the images. Finally, there is the issue of access. Audiotape and videotape storage consumes more space and money than paper. Few institutions have such storage, and many of those that do, such as the various network news departments, limit outside access to their material.

Nevertheless, those who really want to study the full impact Richard Nixon had on American life must make an effort to garner information from sources other than those on paper. To that end, I have used compact discs, motion pictures, the White House tapes, and websites. The most important of the nonpaper technologies is the CD-ROM version of H. R. Haldeman's diary. The journal of Nixon's White House chief of staff was also published in traditional book format, but the paper version contains only 40 percent of his words. On a daily basis and in a matter-of-fact fashion, Haldeman made handwritten entries in his diary—before switching to audiotapes—in which he recorded events both positive and negative, flattering and disparaging to Nixon and the administration. In addition to his journal, the CD-ROM includes home movies Haldeman took—including the president's visit to the Redskins' practice—photographs, and the president's daily schedule. These items, combined with the search capabilities of a CD-ROM, make the electronic version of *The Haldeman Diaries* the single most important source on the Nixon presidency—even more than the tapes.

Anyone studying a postwar president should consult the *Public Papers of the Presidents.* This series started during the administration of Harry S. Truman and is a compilation of speeches, interviews, and public statements of each president arranged by year. Each volume is compiled shortly thereafter, usually less than twelve months later. This series was of fundamental importance in the writing of this book. Nixon made most of his speeches from an outline, and the compilers of this series were far better at recording his remarks accurately than most of the journalists covering the events. Since obtaining film recordings of his speeches is difficult, this series is the primary source on his public appearances and speeches, but it is not absolute. Some of his remarks are missing, including Nixon's all-time baseball all-star team and his interview with Lindsey Nelson at the 1970 All-Star Game in Cincinnati. The other limitation of this series is that a key element in Nixon's speeches was the tone and cadence of his voice. These elements were critical parts of his presentation, and it is simply impossible to present them in a transcript. Fortunately, the Nixon White House staff videotaped many of his appearances on television. Given the emphasis Nixon and his administration placed on public relations, the fact that they made these recordings is far from surprising. These tapes, along with their more famous audio cousins, were in the audiovisual section of the Nixon Presidential Project at the National Archives complex in College Park, Maryland, when I consulted them and have now been moved to the Nixon Library in Yorba Linda, California. These videos capture many of the nonverbal elements that gave a Nixon speech its force. In addition, these videos were the only record I could find of the interview Nixon gave with Nelson in Cincinnati. Watching the telecast of the Texas-Arkansas game was fun. Even though the game was thirty years old and I knew who was going to win, I found myself whooping and cheering when the Longhorns—I am a Texas graduate—made an impressive play; that is, until other patrons at the National Archives started looking at me.

I also listed to the infamous White House tapes. In a major change in accessibility, all the recordings—except a few hundred hours that contain discussions of matters involving personal privacy—are available online. I spent about six weeks listening and transcribing. I had a number of reactions to the tapes. I was entertained, impressed, disappointed, saddened, confused, and confounded. Most of all, I marveled at the opportunity to be in the meetings, to listen to history being made. It was one of the highlights of my career as a historian. The tapes have a number of shortcomings. There is no way to tell if there are facial expressions or hand gestures that change the nature of the conversations, some rooms were not good for acoustics, and the hidden microphones often picked up and magnified small sounds like pens on paper, creaking chairs, and flashbulbs of photographers that often overwhelmed the voices. The finding aids that Luke Nichter, Rick Moss, and others created offered me guidance in understanding who was in the room. The first time I used the tapes was when they were available only in College Park, and I quickly realized that I did not know the voices of most of Nixon's subordinates—or sometimes what they were talking about.

Things have changed significantly since I made that first research trip. The finding aids, which did not exist when I started this project, are crucial in navigating the long silences and static on the recordings and also in letting the listener know who is in the room. The aids are in and of themselves massive, but once I mastered them I could listen to the conversations I wanted. With all that said, even now these recordings are not easy to use.

The investment and frustration in learning the organization of this system is worthwhile. The tapes are fascinating. They allow the average American to listen to White House–level decision-making in real time. It is decades later, but the conversations are still powerful stuff and an incredible tool for the historian. It is almost like time travel. They are also more accessible than one might think. Almost all of the White House Tapes are available for research, and available online at several different websites. The only exceptions are a few conversations that the National Archives withheld for matters of personal privacy. After listening to them, I finally understood the power of the tapes. It is something that historians can only wish existed for other administrations.

Even though I made an effort to use new sources of information, the core of this study comes from the traditional paper documents that were stored in the Nixon Presidential Project. The White House staff had a special recreation-sports file that is arranged topically by sport. This collection is the single largest source of information about athletic activities that the president took an interest in. The staff was interested mainly in finding ways to use sport to stage effective public relations events that would boost Nixon's popularity, but other topics appear in this collection, including ramifications of presidential trips to the ballpark or White House staff interest in using the prestige of his office to influence issues in the sporting world. The president's personal files, which were the documents Nixon saw and produced, contained useful items such as his handwritten drafts of his speeches, transcripts of dictabelt dictations, and notes in his hand for his legends of baseball all-star team. The papers of White House chief of staff H. R. Haldeman were particularly useful. Haldeman was Nixon's most trusted advisor, and he left an extensive paper trail. In fact, these records were so detailed they were key in bringing about his conviction on perjury charges. The contents of his files also document White House efforts in support of the Los Angeles bid to host the Olympics in 1976, which included bribing International Olympic Committee members.

Since I conducted my research, Nixon's papers have moved to California. The long legal battle Nixon and then his estate fought over control of these documents ended, and the Nixon Library became part of the presidential library system that the National Archives administers. As part of the settlement, White House files from the Nixon years ended up in this institution. These files were transferred one for one, and all the collections at the Nixon Library are the same as they were when they were in Maryland, or at least, that is the way things are supposed to have developed. Having made a number of moves over the course of my life, I know items get lost in transit and people make changes, sometimes inadvertently. I have seen this in personal moves, and know it has happened when collections are shipped from one archive to another. Rather than go to the Yorba Linda and check every one of my citations, or simply replace "National Archives" with "Nixon Library" in my footnotes and bibliography and hope no one notices, I have kept the original format. If there have been or will be changes, these citations should be a solid start for finding these items in their new homes.

Newspapers and magazines were another important source for this study, equal in significance to the documents stored at the Nixon Presidential Project. The *New York Times* and the *Washington Post* were the two papers that proved to be most useful. If these papers were biased against Richard Nixon, that sentiment did not reach into their sports departments. Both publications reported extensively, and largely in positive terms, about Nixon's interaction with the world of sport. As far-ranging as the coverage of these two single papers was, regional publications as a collective whole were of greater value. The president's initiatives in sports transpired across the country and took him to many different cities. When he visited, it was the news of the day. Local reporters, eagerly seizing the opportunity to cover a national story, devoted an extensive amount of space to all sorts of aspects related to the trip—interviews with advance men, descriptions of flights on Air Force One, explanations of the logistical details, and local reactions. I have attempted to use these newspapers to give color to this account, provide information not available in White House files, and show how the various sports public relations initiatives went over with the crowds.

In the late 1960s and early 1970s, most major American cities still had more than one newspaper, and the competition between these publications gives the researcher that much more information to draw upon. The titles in the sources' section are as they appeared at the time; the titles in note citations omit *The* in those that used it. The titles of some papers did not include the name of the city they served; in these cases I have added them. The article "the" was part of some paper's names, and was not for others. The guide for determining the proper listing was—with a few exceptions—the front page banner of the paper. On Sundays, many newspapers issued a combined edition with their metro competition and slapped both banners on the front page and left it to the reader to figure out the exact title. In those cases, the word "and" is used to connect the proper nouns without repeating the name of the city. The use of the word "Sunday" in the title of the large weekend issue has been ignored when it is the sole distinction from the name of the weekday editions, but has been included when it was part of a combined title. Finally, in a few instances, shorter versions of titles are used when the longer name was the temporary product of a merger or buy out. The most prominent example is that of the *Washington Post,* which during this era was technically the *Washington Post Times-Herald* after the Washington Post Company purchased a rival morning newspaper. These additional nouns were slowly phased out over time, and the paper is cited by its shorter, better known name.

The published literature on the presidency of Richard Nixon is extensive. The best guides to this material are the bibliographies in the back of Hoff, *Nixon Reconsidered,* and Small, *The Presidency of Richard Nixon.* Despite this abundance, no published work was of much consequence in this study. The documents in the archives and newspapers provided most of the information. Most memoirs of athletes and sportscasters had little in them about Nixon. Those who met or interviewed the president talked about their encounters in a few lines, or at most a paragraph or two. The memoir literature of administration officials was no different. Most of these individuals were writing after the Watergate scandal and focused on that scandal, oftentimes to the exclusion of all else. Most of them were trying to raise money to pay for their legal defenses or were trying to rehabilitate their reputations. The 1969 Texas-Arkansas game was not what the public wanted to read about or what the authors wanted to write about if they were going to make enough money to pay their legal bills. As a result, their books said little about the interest and success Nixon had with sporting events.

SOURCES

Archives

Gerald R. Ford Presidential Library, Ann Arbor, Michigan
- Vice Presidential Papers

National Baseball Hall of Fame, Cooperstown, New York
- Papers of Bowie Kuhn

Olympic Museum, Lausanne, Switzerland
- Samaranch Olympic Studies Centre
  - International Olympic Committee Historical Archives

University of Illinois at Urbana-Champaign, Urbana, Illinois
- Papers of Avery Brundage

US National Archives, College Park, Maryland
- Nixon Presidential Project
  - Audio Video Tape Recording Section
  - White House Central Files
    - White House Subject Files
      - Recreation-Sports Files
    - White House Special Files
      - President's Office Files
        - Annotated News Summaries
      - President's Personal Files
        - Name/Subject File
        - White House Social Events
      - Staff Member and Office Files
        - Papers of H.R. Haldeman
  - White House Photographic Office

US National Archives—Los Angeles Branch, Laguna Niguel, California
- Pre-Presidential Papers of Richard Nixon

Government Documents

Flood v Kuhn [407 US 258], 32 L Ed 2d 728, 92 S Ct 2099.

Guthrie, Benjamin J. *Statistics of the Congressional Elections of November 3, 1970* (Washington, DC: US Government Printing Office, 1971).

Public Papers of the Presidents of the United States: Gerald R. Ford, 1975, vol. 1: *January 1 to July 17* (Washington, DC: US Government Printing Office, 1977).

Public Papers of the Presidents of the United States: Richard Nixon, 1969-1974. (Washington, DC: US Government Printing Office, 1970-1975).

US Congress, *Congressional Record*, 1970, 1971, 1973, 1974 (Washington, DC).

Websites

Lexis-Nexis Academic Universe Database (http://www.lexis-nexis.com/universe). ABC News Transcripts
nixontapes.org (http://www.nixontapes.org).

CD-ROMS

H. R. Haldeman, *The Haldeman Diaries: Inside the Nixon White House—The Complete Multimedia Collection.* (Santa Monica, CA: Sony Electronic Publishing, 1994).

Films and Motion Pictures

Kissinger and Nixon. (1995). Directed by Daniel Petrie. Script by Lionel Chetwynd. Daniel H. Blatt Productions; Dreyfuss/James Productions; Lionel Chetwynd Productions; Paragon Entertainment Corporation, 1995.

Unpublished Sources

Jimmy Golen, "More Nixon Dirty Tricks Exposed," Associated Press Wire Story [no date].
Washington Senators Official Program & Scorecard [1970].

Newspapers and Magazines

Akron Beacon Journal
Albuquerque Journal
Arizona Republic
Arkansas Democrat
Arkansas Democrat-Gazette
Arkansas Gazette
Atlanta Constitution
Atlanta Journal
Atlanta Journal and Constitution
Austin American
Austin American-Statesman
Austin Statesman
Baltimore Evening Sun
Baltimore Sun
Billings Gazette
Birmingham News
Boston Globe
Cedar Rapids Gazette
Charleston Sunday Gazette-Mail

Chicago Sun-Times
Chicago Tribune
Christian Science Monitor
Chronicle of Higher Education
Cincinnati Enquirer
Cleveland Plain Dealer
Colorado Springs Gazette-Telegraph
Columbus Evening Dispatch
Dallas Morning News
Dallas Times Herald
Decatur Review
Denver Post
Des Moines Register
Detroit Free Press
Durham Morning Herald
Fairbanks Daily News-Miner
Florida Times-Union
Fort Worth Star-Telegram
Golf Magazine
Green Bay Press-Gazette
Greenville News
Harrisburg Patriot
Hartford Courant
Hattiesburg American
Honolulu Advertiser
Houston Chronicle
Houston Post
Indianapolis Star
Investor's Business Daily
Kansas City Star
Kansas City Times
Lexington Herald
Lexington Herald-Leader
Lexington Leader
Lexington Sunday Herald-Leader
Life
Lincoln Evening Journal
Long Beach Independent Press-Telegram
Louisville Courier-Journal
Louisville Times
Los Angeles Herald-Examiner
Los Angeles Times

Memphis Commercial Appeal
Miami Herald
Miami News
Milwaukee Journal
Milwaukee Sentinel
Minneapolis Tribune
Mitchell Daily Republic
Nation
Newark Star-Ledger
New Haven Journal-Courier
New Orleans Times-Picayune
Newsday
Newsweek
New York Daily News
New Yorker
New York Post
New York Times
Oakland Tribune
Oklahoma City Daily Oklahoman
Omaha World-Herald
Orange County Register
Oregonian
Orlando Sentinel
Palm Beach Post
Pensacola News Journal
Philadelphia Daily News
Philadelphia Inquirer
Pittsburgh Post-Gazette
Pittsburgh Press
Portland Oregonian
Reno Gazette-Journal
Rocky Mountain News
Sacramento Bee
Salt Lake Tribune
San Antonio Express and News
San Antonio Light
San Diego Evening Tribune
San Diego Union
San Francisco Chronicle
San Francisco Examiner
San Jose Mercury
San Jose Sunday Mercury News

Santa Fe New Mexican
Seattle Post-Intelligencer
Seattle Times
Sporting News
Sports Illustrated
St. Louis Post-Dispatch
Tallahassee Democrat
Tampa Tribune
Tulsa World
Wall Street Journal
Washington Daily News
Washington Evening Star
Washington Post
Weekly Standard
Wichita Eagle
Wichita Eagle and Beacon
Wisconsin State Journal
Youngstown Vindicator

Books and Articles

Aaron, Henry, with Lonnie Wheeler. *I Had a Hammer: The Hank Aaron Story.* New York: HarperCollins, 1991.

Abrahamsen, David. *Nixon vs. Nixon: An Emotional Tragedy.* New York: Farrar, Straus and Giroux, 1977.

Aitken, Jonathan. *Nixon: A Life.* Washington, DC: Regnery Publishing, 1993.

Alexander, Charles C. *Our Game: An American Baseball History.* New York: Henry Holt, 1991.

Allen, Jennifer. *Fifth Quarter: The Scrimmage of a Football Coach's Daughter.* New York: Random House, 2000.

Ambrose, Stephen E. *Nixon.* Vol. 1: *The Education of a Politician, 1913–1962.* New York: Simon and Schuster, 1987.

———. *Nixon.* Vol. 2: *The Triumph of a Politician, 1962–1972.* New York: Simon and Schuster, 1989.

———. *Nixon.* Vol. 3: *Ruin and Recovery, 1973–1990.* New York: Simon and Schuster, 1991.

Arledge, Roone. *Roone: A Memoir.* New York: HarperCollins, 2003.

Banks, Jimmy. *The Darrell Royal Story.* Rev. ed. Austin, TX: Eakin Press, 1994.

Bartels, Larry. "Partisanship and Voting Behavior, 1952–1996." *American Journal of Political Science* 44, no. 1 (January 2000): 35–50.

Berkow, Ira. *Red: A Biography of Red Smith.* New York: Times Books, 1986.

Berman, Larry. *No Peace, No Honor: Nixon, Kissinger, and Betrayal in Vietnam.* New York: Free Press, 2001.

Black, Conrad. *Richard M. Nixon: A Life in Full.* New York: Public Affairs, 2007

Black, Earl, and Merle Black, *The Rise of Southern Republicans.* Cambridge, MA: Harvard University Press, 2002.

Blanton, J. Neal. *Game of the Century: Texas vs. Arkansas, December 1, 1969.* Austin, TX: Pemberton, 1970.

Blum, John Morton. *Years of Discord: American Politics and Society, 1961–1974.* New York: W. W. Norton, 1991.

Bochin, Hal. *Richard Nixon: Rhetorical Strategist.* New York: Greenwood Press, 1990.

Boswell, Thomas, et al. *Redskins: A History of Washington's Team.* Washington, DC: Washington Post Books, 1997.

Branch, Taylor. *Pillar of Fire: America in the King Years, 1963–65.* New York: Simon and Schuster, 1998.

Brodie, Fawn M. *Richard Nixon: The Shaping of His Character.* New York: W. W. Norton, 1981.

Broyles, Frank, with Jim Bailey. *Hog Wild: The Autobiography of Frank Broyles.* Memphis, TN: Memphis State University Press, 1979.

Bryant, Howard. *The Last Hero: A Life of Henry Aaron.* New York: Random House, 2010.

Campbell, Angus, Philip E. Converse, Warren E. Miller, and Donald Stokes. *The American Voter.* New York: Wiley, 1960.

Chamberlain, Wilt, and David Shaw. *Wilt: Just Like Any Other 7-Foot Black Millionaire Who Lives Next Door.* New York: Macmillan, 1975.

Clotfelter, Charles T. *Big-Time Sports in American Universities.* New York: Cambridge University Press, 2011.

Collins, Robert M. "Richard M. Nixon: The Psychic, Political, and Moral Uses of Sport." *Journal of Sport History* 10, no. 2 (Summer 1983): 77–84.

Cowie, Jefferson. "Nixon's Class Struggle: Romancing the New Right Worker, 1969–1973." *Labor History* 43, no. 3 (September 2002): 257–283.

Cray, Ed. *General of the Army: George C. Marshall, Soldier and Statesman.* New York: W. W. Norton, 1990.

Critchlow, Donald T. *The Conservative Ascendancy: How the GOP Right Made Political History.* Cambridge, MA: Harvard University Press, 2007.

Davies, Gareth. *From Opportunity to Entitlement: The Transformation and Decline of Great Society Liberalism.* Lawrence: University Press of Kansas, 1996.

Delmont, Matthew F. *Why Busing Failed: Race, Media, and the National Resistance to School Desegregation.* Berkeley: University of California Press, 2016.

Dowling, Tom. *Coach: A Season with Lombardi.* New York: W. W. Norton, 1970.

Duderstadt, James J. *Intercollegiate Athletics and the American University.* Ann Arbor: University of Michigan Press, 2000.

Dworkin, James B. *Owners versus Players: Baseball and Collective Bargaining.* Boston: Auburn House, 1981.

Ehrlichman, John D. *Witness to Power: The Nixon Years.* New York: Simon and Schuster, 1982.
Emery, Fred. *Watergate: The Corruption of American Politics and the Fall of Richard Nixon.* New York: Times Books, 1994.
Falkner, David. *Great Time Coming: The Life of Jackie Robinson from Baseball to Birmingham.* New York: Simon and Schuster, 1995.
Farrell, John A. *Richard Nixon: The Life.* New York: Doubleday, 2017.
Feeney, Mark. *Nixon at the Movies: A Book about Belief.* Chicago: University of Chicago Press, 2004.
Fiorina, Morris P. *Retrospective Voting in American National Elections.* New Haven, CT: Yale University Press, 1981.
Flippen, J. Brooks. *Nixon and the Environment.* Albuquerque: University of New Mexico Press, 2000.
Fort, Rodney, and Jason Winfree. *15 Sports Myths and Why They're Wrong.* Stanford, CA: Stanford University Press, 2013.
Frei, Terry. *Horns, Hogs, and Nixon Coming: Texas vs. Arkansas in Dixie's Last Stand.* New York: Simon and Schuster, 2002.
Frick, Daniel. *Reinventing Richard Nixon: A Cultural History of an American Obsession.* Lawrence: University Press of Kansas, 2008.
Frommer, Frederic J. *You Gotta Have Heart: A History of Washington Baseball from 1859 to the 2012 National League East Champions.* Lanham, MD: Taylor Trade, 2013.
Galvin, Daniel J. *Presidential Party Building: Dwight D. Eisenhower to George W. Bush.* Princeton, NJ: Princeton University Press, 2010.
Gellman, Irwin F. *The Contender: Richard Nixon: The Congressional Years, 1946–*1952. New York: Free Press, 1999.
———. *The President and the Apprentice: Eisenhower and Nixon, 1952–1961.* New Haven, CT: Yale University Press, 2015.
Gifford, Frank, and Harry Waters. *The Whole Ten Yards.* New York: Random House, 1993.
Gildea, William, and Kenneth Turan. *The Future Is Now: George Allen—Pro Football's Most Controversial Coach.* Boston: Houghton Mifflin, 1972.
Gould, Lewis L. *Grand Old Party: A History of the Republicans.* New York: Random House, 2003.
Graham, Katharine. *Personal History.* New York: Knopf, 1997.
Greenberg, David. *Nixon's Shadow: The History of an Image.* New York: W. W. Norton, 2003.
Guttmann, Allen. *The Games Must Go On: Avery Brundage and the Olympic Movement.* New York: Columbia University Press, 1984.
Hamburg, Eric, ed. *Nixon: An Oliver Stone Film.* New York: Hyperion, 1995.
Harries, Meiron, and Susie Harries. *The Last Days of Innocence: America at War, 1917–1918.* New York: Random House, 1997.

Haun, Phil, and Colin Jackson. "Breaker of Armies: Air Power in the Easter Offensive and the Myth of Linebacker I and II in the Vietnam War." *International Security* 40, no. 3 (Winter 2015/16): 139–178.

Henry, Orville, and Jim Brady. *The Razorbacks: A Story of Arkansas Football.* New ed. Fayetteville: University of Arkansas Press, 1996.

Hess, Stephen. *The Professor and the President: Daniel Patrick Moynihan in the Nixon White House.* Washington, DC: Brookings Institute Press, 2015.

Hodgson, Godfrey. *The World Turned Right Side Up: A History of the Conservative Ascendance in America.* Boston: Houghton Mifflin, 1996.

Hoff, Joan. *Nixon Reconsidered.* New York: Basic Books, 1994.

Holtzman, Jerome. *The Commissioners: Baseball's Midlife Crisis.* New York: Total Sports, 1998.

Horowitz, Ira. "Sports Broadcasting." In *Government and the Sports Business*, edited by Roger G. Noll, 284–287. Washington, DC: Brookings Institution, 1974.

Hunt, Thomas M. "Countering the Soviet Threat in the Olympic Medals Race: The Amateur Sports Act of 1978 and American Athletics Policy Reform." *International Journal of the History of Sport* 24, no. 6 (June 2007): 796–818.

Jacobs, Meg. *Panic at the Pump: The Energy Crisis and the Transformation of American Politics in the 1970s.* New York: Hill and Wang, 2016.

Jamieson, Kathleen Hall. *Packaging the Presidency: A History and Criticism of Presidential Campaign Advertising.* New York: Oxford University Press, 1984.

Johnson, Thomas J. *The Rehabilitation of Richard Nixon: The Media's Effect on Collective Memory.* New York: Garland, 1995.

Jonas, George. *Vengeance: The True Story of an Israeli Counter-Terrorist Team.* New York: Simon and Schuster, 1984.

Kalman, Laura. *The Long Reach of the Sixties: LBJ, Nixon, and the Making of the Contemporary Supreme Court.* New York: Oxford University Press, 2017.

Killanin, Michael Morris, Baron. *My Olympic Years.* London: Secker and Warburg, 1983.

Killen, Andreas. *1973 Nervous Breakdown: Watergate, Warhol, and the Birth of Post-Sixties America.* New York, 2006.

Knight, Bob, with Bob Hammel. *Knight: My Story.* New York: Thomas Dunne Books, 2002.

Kotlowski, Dean J. *Nixon's Civil Rights: Politics, Principle, and Policy.* Cambridge, MA: Harvard University Press, 2002.

Kriegel, Mark. *Namath: A Biography.* New York: Viking, 2005.

Kuhn, Bowie. *Hardball: The Education of a Baseball Commissioner.* New York: Times Books, 1987.

Kutler, Stanley I. *The Wars of Watergate: The Last Crisis of Richard Nixon.* New York: W. W. Norton, 1990.

Landry, Fernand, and Magdeleine Yerlès. *International Olympic Committee—One Hundred Years: The Idea—The Presidents—The Achievements*, Vol. 3: *The Presi-*

dencies of Lord Killanin (1972–1980) and of Juan Antonio Samaranch (1980–). Lausanne, Switzerland: International Olympic Committee, 1994.

Landry, Tom, with Gregg Lewis. *Tom Landry: An Autobiography*. Grand Rapids, MI: Zondervan Books, 1990.

Lewis-Beck, Michael S., William G. Jacoby, Helmut Norpoth, and Herbert F. Weisberg. *The American Voter Revisited.* Ann Arbor: University of Michigan Press, 2008.

Logsdon, John M. *After Apollo? Richard Nixon and the American Space Program.* New York: Palgrave Macmillan, 2015.

Lombardo, John. *A Fire to Win: The Life and Times of Woody Hayes.* New York: Thomas Dunne Books, 2005.

Longford, Frank Pakenham, Earl of. *Nixon: A Study in Extremes of Fortune.* London: Weidenfeld and Nicolson, 1980.

Loverro, Thom. *Washington Redskins: The Authorized History.* Dallas, TX: Taylor Publishing, 1996.

Lowenfish, Lee. *The Imperfect Diamond: A History of Baseball's Labor Wars.* Rev. ed. New York: Da Capo Press, 1991.

Lublin, Robert. *The Republican South: Democratization and Partisan Change.* Princeton, NJ: Princeton University Press, 2004.

Mackenzie, G. Calvin, and Robert Weisbrot, *The Liberal Hour: Washington and the Politics of Change in the 1960s.* New York: Penguin Press, 2008.

Magruder, Jeb Stuart. *An American Life: One Man's Road to Watergate.* New York: Atheneum, 1974.

Maher, John, and Kirk Bohls. *Long Live the Longhorns!: 100 Years of Texas Football.* New York: St. Martin's Press, 1992.

Maraniss, David. *Clemente: The Passion and Grace of Baseball's Last Hero.* New York: Simon and Schuster, 2006.

———. *When Pride Still Mattered: A Life of Vince Lombardi.* New York: Simon and Schuster, 1999.

Markusen, Bruce. *Roberto Clemente: The Great One.* Champaign, IL: Sports Publishing, 1998.

Maroon, Fred J. *The Nixon Years, 1969–1974: White House to Watergate.* New York: Abbeville Press, 1999.

Mason, Robert. "'I was Going to Build a New Republican Party and a New Majority': Richard Nixon as Party Leader, 1969–73." *Journal of American Studies* 39, no. 3 (December 2005): 463–483.

———. *Richard Nixon and the Quest for a New Majority.* Chapel Hill: University of North Carolina Press, 2004.

Matthews, Christopher. *Kennedy and Nixon: The Rivalry That Shaped Postwar America.* New York: Simon and Schuster, 1996.

Matusow, Allen J. *Nixon's Economy: Booms, Busts, Dollars, and Votes.* Lawrence: University Press of Kansas, 1998.

Mayer, William G. *The Changing American Mind: How and Why American Public Opinion Changed between 1960 and 1988.* Ann Arbor: University of Michigan Press, 1992.

McMahon, Kevin. *Nixon's Court: His Challenge to Judicial Liberalism and Its Consequences.* Chicago: University of Chicago Press, 2011.

Mead, William B., and Paul Dickinson. *Baseball: The President's Game.* Washington, DC: Farragut Publishing, 1993.

Miller, James Edward. *The Baseball Business: Pursuing Pennants and Profits in Baltimore.* Chapel Hill: University of North Carolina Press, 1990.

Miller, John J. *The Big Scrum: How Teddy Roosevelt Saved Football.* New York: Harper Collins, 2011.

Miller, Marvin. *A Whole Different Ball Game: The Sport and Business of Baseball.* Secaucus, NJ: Carrol Publishing, 1991.

Miroff, Bruce. *The Liberals' Moment: The McGovern Insurgency and the Identity Crisis of the Democratic Party.* Lawrence: University Press of Kansas, 2007.

Morgan, Iwan W. *Nixon.* London: Arnold, 2002.

Morris, Roger. *Richard Milhous Nixon: The Rise of an American Politician.* New York: Holt, 1990.

Nadel, Eric. *Texas Rangers: The Authorized History.* Dallas, TX: Taylor Publishing, 1997.

Nelson, Lindsey. *Hello Everybody, I'm Lindsey Nelson.* New York: Beech Tree Books, 1985.

Nixon, Richard M. *RN: The Memoirs of Richard Nixon.* New York: Grosset & Dunlap, 1978.

O'Brien, Michael. *No Ordinary Joe: The Biography of Joe Paterno.* Nashville, TN: Rutledge Hill Press, 1998.

———. *Vince: A Personal Biography of Vince Lombardi.* New York: Morrow, 1987.

Olson, Keith W. *Watergate: The Presidential Scandal That Shook America.* Lawrence: University Press of Kansas, 2003.

Oriard, Michael. *Bowled Over: Big Time College Football from the Sixties to the BCS Era.* Chapel Hill: University of North Carolina Press, 2009.

Parmet, Herbert S. *Richard Nixon and His America.* Boston: Little, Brown, 1990.

Paterno, George. *Joe Paterno: The Coach from Byzantium.* Champaign, IL: Sports Publishing, 1997.

Paterno, Joe, with Bernard Asbell. *Paterno by the Book.* New York: Random House, 1990.

Perlstein, Rick. *Nixonland: The Rise of a President and the Fracturing of America.* New York: Scribner, 2008.

Petrie, Daniel, dir. *Kissinger and Nixon.* Script by Lionel Chetwynd. Daniel H. Blatt Productions; Dreyfuss/James Productions; Lionel Chetwynd Productions; Paragon Entertainment Corporation, 1995. Film.

Popkin, Samuel L. *The Reasoning Voter: Communication and Persuasion in Presidential Campaigns.* Chicago: University of Chicago Press, 1991.

Public Papers of the Presidents of the United States: Gerald R. Ford, 1975. Vol. 1: *January 1 to July 17.* Washington, DC: Office of the Federal Register, 1977.
Public Papers of the Presidents of the United States: Richard Nixon, 1969–1974. Washington, DC: Office of the Federal Register, 1970–1975.
Radosh, Ronald. *Divided They Fell: The Demise of the Democratic Party.* New York: Free Press, 1996.
Rampersad, Arnold. *Jackie Robinson: A Biography.* New York: Knopf, 1997.
Randolph, Stephen P. *Powerful and Brutal Weapons: Nixon, Kissinger, and the Easter Offensive.* Cambridge, MA: Harvard University Press, 2007.
Reeve, Simon. *One Day in September: The Full Story of the 1972 Munich Olympics Massacre and the Israeli Revenge Operation "Wrath of God."* New York: Faber and Faber, 2000.
Reeves, Richard. *President Nixon: Alone in the White House.* New York: Simon and Schuster, 2001.
Remini, Robert V. *Andrew Jackson and the Course of American Freedom, 1822–1832.* New York: Harper and Row, 1981.
Roberts, Randy W., and James Olson. *Winning Is the Only Thing: Sports in America since 1945.* Baltimore: Johns Hopkins University Press, 1989.
Robinson, Jackie, as told to Alfred Duckett. *I Never Had It Made.* New York: Putnam, 1972.
Rooney, John F., Jr. *The Recruiting Game: Toward a New System of Intercollegiate Sport.* 2nd ed. Lincoln: University of Nebraska Press, 1987.
Rowe, James N. *Five Years to Freedom.* Boston: Little, Brown, 1971.
Safire, William. *Before the Fall: An Inside View of the Pre-Watergate White House.* Garden City, NY: Doubleday, 1975.
Sandbrook, Dominic. *Mad as Hell: The Crisis of the 1970s and the Rise of the Populist Right.* New York: Alfred A. Knopf, 2011.
Sarantakes, Nicholas Evan. "Baseball: The Great Political Equalizer." ESPN.com. March 12, 2002. http://espn.go.com/page2/wash/s/2002/0312/1349955.html.
———. "Moscow versus Los Angeles: The Cold War Comes to the Olympic Selection Process." *Cold War History* 9, no. 1 (February 2009): 135–157.
———. "Nixon versus Paterno: College Football, and Presidential Politics." *Pennsylvania History* 73, no. 2 (Spring 2006): 236–260.
———. "Richard Nixon, Sportswriter: The President, His Historical All-Star Baseball Team, and the Election of 1972." *Journal of Sport History* 27, no. 1 (Summer, 1997): 192–202.
Schaller, Michael, and George Rising. *The Republican Ascendancy: American Politics, 1968–2001.* Wheeling, IL: Harlan Davidson, 2002.
Schudson, Michael. *Watergate in American Memory: How We Remember, Forget and Reconstruct the Past.* New York: Basic Books, 1992.
Shropshire, Mike. *Seasons in Hell: With Billy Martin, Whitey Herzog, and "the Worst*

Baseball Teams in History"—the 1973–1975 Texas Rangers. New York: Donald I. Fine, 1996.

Shulman, James L., and William G. Bowen. *The Game of Life: College Sports and Educational Values.* Princeton, NJ: Princeton University Press, 2001.

Silverman, Matthew. *New York Mets: The Complete Illustrated History.* Minneapolis, MN: MBI Publishing, 2011.

Small, Melvin. *Johnson, Nixon, and the Doves.* New Brunswick, NJ: Rutgers University Press, 1988.

———. *The Presidency of Richard Nixon.* Lawrence: University Press of Kansas, 1999.

Smith, John Matthew. *The Sons of Westwood: John Wooden, UCLA, and the Dynasty That Changed College Basketball.* Urbana: University of Illinois Press, 2013.

Smith, Ronald A. *Pay For Play: A History of Big-Time College Athletic Reform.* Urbana: University of Illinois Press, 2011.

Snyder, Brad. *A Well-Paid Slave: Curt Flood's Fight for Free Agency in Professional Sports.* New York: Viking, 2006.

Steigerwald, David. *The Sixties and the End of Modern America.* New York: St. Martin's Press, 1995.

Steinmark, Freddie. *I Play to Win.* Boston: Little, Brown, 1971.

St. Johns, Bob. *Landry: The Legend and the Legacy.* Nashville, TN: Thomas Nelson, 2000.

Stuart, Charles. *Bin Laden's Second Strike.* Charleston, SC: BookSurge Publishing, 2007.

———. *Never Trust A Local: Inside the Nixon White House.* New York: Algora Publishing, 2005.

Suggs, David Welch Jr. "Making Money—Or Not—On College Sports." *Data-Driven Decision Making in Intercollegiate Athletics: New Directions in Institutional Research,* no. 144 (Winter 2009): 19–32.

———. *A Place on the Team: The Triumph and Tragedy of Title IX.* Princeton, NJ: Princeton University Press, 2005.

Summers, Anthony. *The Arrogance of Power: The Secret World of Richard Nixon.* New York: Viking, 2000.

Surdam, David George. *The Big Leagues Go to Washington: Congress and Sports Antitrust, 1951–1989.* Urbana: University of Illinois Press, 2015.

Swanson, Richard A., and Betty Spears. *History of Sport and Physical Education in the United States.* 4th ed. Madison, WI: Brown and Benchmark, 1995.

Thomas, Evan. *Being Nixon: A Man Divided.* New York: Random House, 2015.

Thomas, Helen. *Front Row at the White House: My Life and Times.* New York: Scribner, 1999.

Vandiver, Frank E. *Black Jack: The Life and Times of John J. Pershing.* Vol. 2. College Station: Texas A&M University Press, 1977.

Van Natta, Don, Jr. *First Off the Tee: Presidential Hackers, Duffers, and Cheaters from Taft to Bush.* New York: Public Affairs, 2003.

Voight, David Quentin. *American Baseball.* Vol. 3: *From Postwar Expansion to the Electronic Age.* University Park: Pennsylvania State University Press, 1983.

Volkan, Varnik, Norman Itzkowitz, and Andrew Dodd. *Richard Nixon: A Psychobiography.* New York: Columbia University Press, 1997.

Walker, Stephen J. *A Whole New Ballgame: The 1969 Washington Senators.* Clifton, VA: Pocol Press, 2009.

Ware, Susan. *Game, Set, Match: Billie Jean King and the Revolution in Women's Sports.* Chapel Hill: University of North Carolina Press, 2011.

Wattenberg, Martin P. *The Decline of American Political Parties, 1952–1996.* 5th ed. Cambridge, MA: Harvard University Press, 1998.

———. *The Rise of Candidate-Centered Politics: Presidential Elections of the 1980s.* Cambridge, MA: Harvard University Press, 1991.

Watterson, John Sayle. *The Games Presidents Play: Sports and the Presidency.* Baltimore, MD: Johns Hopkins University Press, 2006.

Wayne, Stephen J. *The Road to the White House: The Politics of Presidential Elections.* New York: St. Martin's Press, 1980.

Weiner, Tim. *One Man against the World: The Tragedy of Richard Nixon.* New York: Henry Holt and Company, 2015.

White, Theodore H. *Breach of Faith: The Fall of Richard Nixon.* New York: Atheneum, 1975.

Whiteside, James. *Colorado: A Sports History.* Niwot: University Press of Colorado, 1999.

Wicker, Tom. *One of Us: Richard Nixon and the American Dream.* New York: Random House, 1991.

Williams, Ted, with John Underwood. *My Turn at Bat: The Story of My Life.* New York: Simon and Schuster, 1988.

Wlezien, Christopher, and Robert S. Erikson. "The Timeline of Presidential Election Campaigns." *Journal of Politics* 64, no. 4 (November 2002): 969–993.

Woodward, Bob, and Scott Armstrong. *The Brethren: Inside the Supreme Court.* New York: Simon and Schuster, 1979.

Wushanley, Ying. *Playing Nice and Losing: The Struggle for Control of Women's Intercollegiate Athletics, 1960–2000.* Syracuse, NY: Syracuse University Press, 2004.

Yuill, Kevin L. *Richard Nixon and the Rise of Affirmative Action: The Pursuit of Racial Equality in an Era of Limits.* Lanham, MD: Rowman and Littlefield Publishers, 2006.

Zimbalist, Andrew. *Unpaid Professionals: Commercialism and Conflict in Big-Time College Sports.* Princeton, NJ: Princeton University Press, 1999.

INDEX

Aaron, Henry "Hank"
  breaks career home run record, 203
  conversation with Nixon, 203
  reaction to Nixon's historic all-star team, 161
  retirement of, 212
Abrams, Creighton, 149
Addie, Bob, 5, 22, 73, 76
Agnew, Spiro, 20, 144
  and antiwar movement, 29
  death of, 212
  resignation of, 192
  retirement of, 212
Ailes, Roger, 116
Akers, Fred, 41, 269
Akron Beacon-Journal, 135
Alcindor, Lew, 110
Aldrin, Colonel Edwin "Buzz," 21
Alexander, Charles C., 22
Allen, George, 95, 138, 140
  conversations with Nixon, 139, 141, 142, 180–181
  death of, 212
  fabricates story that Nixon designed play for the Redskins, 141–142
  impact on Washington Redskins as coach, 136
  Nixon reaction, 142
  relationship with Nixon, 129–130
  retirement of, 212
  White House visit of, 181
Allen, Hank, 8
Allen, Jennifer, 130
Alston, Walter, 162
Ambrose, Stephen, 1, 2, 29, 78, 199
American Basketball Association, 110
  merger with National Basketball Association, 122
American League, 115, 116
Anderson, Dave, 145
Andretti, Mario, 12, 165
Arizona Republic (Phoenix, AZ), 87
Arkansas Democrat, 35, 36, 38, 43, 48
Arkansas Gazette, 36, 43
Arkansas, Razorbacks football team, University of
  and 1969 Texas game, 32–52
  success of, 32, 269
Arledge, Roone, 34, 132, 270–271
Armstrong, Neil, 21
Ashbrook, John, 148
Associated Press, 161
Atlanta Constitution, 161, 202
Atlanta Falcons, 201
Atlanta Journal and Constitution, 161
Austin American, 34, 40
Austin Straubel Field, 79–80
auto racing, 125–126

Baltimore Colts, 144
Baltimore Orioles, 17, 83, 112–113, 118
  in 1969 World Series, 23
  in 1971 World Series, 124–125
baseball, 109–110, 128, 175–176
  popularity of, 5–7, 20
  rule changes in, 6–7, 9, 68
Baseball Hall of Fame, 9, 71, 162, 186, 204, 212, 217, 218
Bass, Mike, 183
Bell, Upton, 144
Bellard, Emory, 41
Bench, Johnny, 69, 165

Benitez, Jaime, 189
Berger, David, 175
Berner, Dennis, 42
Birmingham News, 163
Blackmun, Harry A., 152
Blass, Steve, 125, 186–187
Blue, Vida, 124
Boggs, Hale, 146
Borman, Colonel Frank, 15
Boston Globe, 160–161, 163
Boston Herald Traveler and Record American, 162
Bow, Frank, 130, 131
bowling, 12, 126–127
Branca, Ralph, 166
Brennan, Jack, 73
Brito, Gene, 131–132
Broeg, Bob, 163
Brooklyn Dodgers, 23, 166, 188. *See also* Los Angeles Dodgers
Brown, Clarence J., 19
Brown, Doug, 17
Brown, Jim, 134
Brown, Larry, 141
Brown, Mace, 158
Brown County Veterans Memorial Arena, 80
Broyles, Frank, 33, 34, 35, 40, 42, 269
  death of, 213
  retirement of, 212–213
Brundage, Avery, 62, 63–64, 174
  death of, 213
  retirement, 213
Brundige, Bill, 141
Buchanan, Pat, 91, 110
Bull, Stephen, 136
Burger, Warren, 152
Burman, George, 141
  Nixon letter to, 141
Burning Tree Country Club, 13
Bush, George, 33, 36, 83
Byers, Walter, 30, 195
California, Berkley, University of, 154
California, Los Angeles, University of (UCLA), 167
  basketball team of, 110
  Robinson, Jackie, playing career at, 158
California Angels, 121, 189
Campanella, Roy, 19
Camp David, 12, 157
Candlestick Park, 141
Carl Vinson, USS, 202, 220
Carter, Jimmy, 200, 202, 214
Cashen, Frank, 17
Cashen, Henry, 171
Central Intelligence Agency, 153, 206
Chamberlain, Wilt, 110, 165
Chapin, Dwight
  Nixon and auto racing, 126
  Nixon's attendance at the 1969 Texas-Arkansas game and, 34
  Nixon's campaigning for the 1970 midterm elections and, 77
  Nixon's political setbacks in 1970 and, 56
  Nixon's recognition of collegiate football's centennial and, 30, 31
  Nixon's security at sporting events and, 10
  Nixon's visit to the 1970 All-Star Game and, 68
Chicago Bears, 13, 26, 166
Chicago Cubs, 23
Chicago Sun-Times, 160–161
Chicago Tribune, 20
Chicago White Sox, 123
Christian Science Monitor, 142
Chronicle of Higher Education, 155
Churchill Downs, 11, 12
Cincinnati Bengals, 135
Cincinnati Reds, 7, 69, 150, 170
Clemente, Roberto
  awarded posthumous Presidential Citizens Medal, 188–189

death of, 185
in 1971 World Series, 125
Nixon comments about playing abilities, 184
Nixon comments on death, 185, 186–187
Nixon honors, 186–189
Clemente, Vera, 185, 189
Cleveland Browns, 135, 140, 174
Cleveland Rams, 140
Cobb, Ty, 153
Cole, Kenneth, 197–198
death of, 213
retirement of, 213
Coleman, Cecil, 196
college football
centennial of, 30–31
and national championship, 35, 48–49, 52, 91
and news service polls, 31–32, 35, 45–46, 47–48, 49, 83
Collins, Eddie, 162
Collins, Mike, 21
Columbus Evening Dispatch, 131
Concord Monitor (Concord, NH), 162
Cooperstown, New York. *See* National Baseball Hall of Fame and Museum
Coryell, Don, 184
Cosell, Howard, 133
Cotton Bowl, 32, 44, 48, 49, 51, 218
Courier-Journal (Louisville, KY), 11
Cox, Archibald, 192, 202
retirement of, 213
Cox, Patricia, 131
wedding of, 131
Cronin, Joe, 116, 120

Daily Oklahoman (Oklahoma City, OK), 204
Dallas Bonehead Club, 147
Dallas Cowboys, 28, 136, 142, 171
Super Bowl VI and, 145–146
Dallas Morning News, 120, 121, 143, 146
Dallas Times Herald, 89, 120, 122, 146
Dale, Francis, 150
Daley, Arthur, 131, 163
Danzansky, Joseph
attempted purchase of San Diego Padres, 190–191
death of, 213
retirement of, 213
Dean, Jay "Dizzy," 18
death of, 204
Nixon comments on, 204–205
Dean, John W., III, 27
firing of as White House counsel, 190
Dent, Harry, 31–32, 35, 77
death of, 213
retirement of, 213
Des Moines Register, 26
Detroit Free-Press, 161
Detroit Tigers, 56, 111
Devaney, Bob
death of, 213
retirement of, 213
Devine, Bing, 17
DiMaggio, Joe, 15, 16–17, 19, 160, 161
Dirksen, Everett, 11
Dole, Robert, 251
"Dole synthesis," 251–252
Dowling, Tom, 163
Duke University, 135, 137
Dyer, Ken, 135

Education Amendments Act, 153–156
Nixon on, 156
Ehrlichman, John, 26–27, 62, 129, 194, 197
conviction of, 214
death of, 214
fired, 190
retirement of, 214

Eisenhower, David, 20, 56, 66, 68, 157, 159, 161, 221
  assists Nixon in historic all-star selections, 157
Eisenhower, Dwight D., 2, 77, 117, 163
Eisenhower, Julie, 20, 66, 159
Evans, Cliff, 159
  radio interview of Nixon, 160, 161
  suggests historic all-star team to Nixon, 153–154
Evening Star (Washington, DC), 17, 19, 116, 121, 163, 186
  editorial cartoons, 143
Evening Sun (Baltimore, MD), 17
Evening Tribune (San Diego, CA), 191
Ervin, Sam, 122
Exon, J. J., 92

Faulkner, Jack, 144
Federal Baseball Club v. National League, 152
Federal Bureau of Investigation, 153, 206
Feeney, Charles, 190
Finch, Robert, 77, 168, 170
Fleming, Bill, 41
Flood, Curt
  death of, 214
  retirement of, 214
  as Washington Senator, 112
Flood v. Kuhn, 112, 151–153
  Blackmun opinion, 152
  Nixon statement on, 151–152, 153
Ford, Frick, 17
Ford, Gerald R., Jr., 146
  appoints presidential commission on Olympic sport, 200
  and baseball, 122
  death of, 214
  nominated as vice president, 192
  Olympic policy and, 199–200
  presidency of, 122, 207, 214
  retirement of, 214
Fort Worth Star-Telegram, 121
Fosse, Ray, 71–72
Freehan, Bill, 69
Freen, George
  death of, 215
  writes Nixon on support for Olympic athletes, 193–194
Fulbright, J. William, 36, 42

Galbreath, Daniel, 186–187
Garagiola, Joe, 16, 124
Gehrig, Eleanor, 166
Gehrig, Henry Louis "Lou," 81, 153, 166
Gifford, Frank
  death of, 215
  and 1960 election, 165
  and Nixon interview, 132–133
Giles, Warren, 16
Giusti, Dave, 186–187
Goldwater, Barry, 169, 205, 206
Gonzalez, Aida, 12
Green Bay Packers, 79, 80, 81, 146
Green Bay Press-Gazette, 79, 81
Greenberg, Henry
  reaction to Nixon's historic all-star team, 161
Grove, Lefty, 16, 112
Guthrie, Bill, 145

Haig, General Alexander, 61, 114, 202
  becomes White House chief of staff, 190
  career of, 215
  death of, 215
Haldeman, H. R., 31, 36, 44, 49, 53, 56, 72–73, 84, 89, 90, 111, 129, 136, 140, 141, 150, 157, 159, 171, 179, 187, 188, 198
  and bowling, 127
  death of, 216
  discussion with Nixon about Jackie Robinson, 158
  fired as White House chief of staff, 190

historic all-star team selections, views on, 158
and Los Angeles Olympic bid, 57–64
and Munich Olympics, reaction to US-USSR basketball game, 175–176
on Nixon and baseball, 14, 72–73
on Nixon and football, 29–32, 89
on Nixon and sports, 67
on Nixon trips to Nebraska, 84, 93–94
on Nixon trip to 1969 Texas-Arkansas football game, 42–43
on Nixon trip to Professional Football Hall of Fame, 131, 134
and Nixon visit to Washington Redskins' practice session, 137, 138
and Olympics, 57–61, 63–64, 175–176
and race car event, 125–126
on San Jose riot, 85–86
"smoking gun" tape conversation and, 153
Hammerschmidt, John Paul, 34, 36, 37
Hardman, Cedrick, 141
Harraway, Charlie, 138
Harrigan, Mike, 198, 199, 200
Harris, Cliff, 146, 147
Hayes, Bob, 144
Hayes, Woody, 82–83, 95
career of, 216
death of, 216
Heinz, John, III, 185
Higby, Larry, 59–60
Hodges, Gil, 23, 69
Holtzman, Jerome, 20
Howard, Frank, 8
Howe, Gordie, 165
Houston Astros, 116
Houston Oilers, 132
Hughes, Lieutenant General James D. "Don," 10, 77
Hullin, Tod, 196–197
career of, 216

Indianapolis Star, 161

Jackson, Andrew, 18
Jackson, Reggie, 10, 16–17, 158
Jamieson, Kathleen Hall, 151
Jaworski, Leon, 202, 205
death of, 216
named special prosecutor, 201
Jefferson, Roy, 141, 145
Jefferson, Thomas, 18
Johnson, Lyndon, 144, 164, 167, 202
Johnson, Walter, 18, 131–132
Jurgesen, Sonny, 136, 137, 139

Kaese, Harold, 162
Kansas City Royals, 189
Kansas City Star, 160
Kansas State University, 78
Keady, Jack, 38, 48
Kennedy, John F., 167, 168–169
Kennedy, Robert F., 168
Killanin, Lord Michael Morris, 65, 179
Killebrew, Harmon, 72
Nixon on, 159
reaction to Nixon's historic all-star team, 161
Kilmer, Billy, 136, 138, 140–141
career of, 216
comments about Nixon to *Washington Post,* 181–182
daughter of, 181–182
Kilroy, John, 57, 59, 60, 64, 65
King, Coretta Scott, 168
King, Martin Luther, Jr., 167–168
Kissinger, Henry, 36, 53, 94, 180, 192, 198, 206, 214
career of, 216
and Olympics, 60–62
peace negotiations with North Vietnam, 180
Klein, Herb, 17, 117
conversation with Don Shula, 183

Klein, Herb, *continued*
 death of, 217
 on Nixon and sports, 77–78
Kleindienst, Richard
 antitrust action against the NFL, 171, 172, 173
 firing of as US attorney general, 190
Knickerbocker News-Union Star (Albany, NY), 162
Kraft, Joseph, 182
Kroc, Ray
 buys San Diego Padres, 191
Kuhn, Bowie, 70, 124, 152, 175, 191
 bankruptcy of, 217
 as baseball commissioner, 6, 14–16, 18–20, 68, 217
 death of, 217
 and legal issues of baseball, 122, 152–153
 letter to Nixon, 207
 and 1969 opening day, 7–8
 and 1972 players' strike, 149–150
 and Washington Senators' relocation, 115–120
 on Williams, Ted, 7
Kutler, Stanley, 190

Laird, Melvin, 80, 113
Landry, Tom, 144
 career of, 217
 conversation with Nixon, 146
 death of, 217
Lentz, Arthur G., 193
Lilly, Bob, 171
Lincoln, Abraham, 163, 164
Lombardi, Vince, 129, 130, 133, 210
 arrival in Washington, DC, 4–5
 death of, 75–77
 and Landry, Tom, 146
 and Nixon, 26
 as Washington Redskins' coach, 28
 wedding anniversary of, 134
 Williams, Edward Bennet on, 26
Los Angeles Dodgers, 188
Los Angeles Lakers, 110, 115, 165
Los Angeles Rams, 132, 140, 165
Los Angeles Times, 186, 194, 203, 205
Lovell, James A., 195, 196
Luther, Edwin R., 12

Malek, Frederic V., 196
Mansfield, Mike, 11
Mantle, Mickey, 9, 17, 153
Maris, Roger, 10
Marshall University, 88
Martin, Dick, 182
Mays, Willie, 15
McCall's, 151
McClellan, John, 36
McCloskey, Pete, 148
McGee, Mike, 135
McGovern, George, 151
McKay, Bob, 40
McLain, Denny, 111–112
Medwick, Joe, 162
Meir, Golda, 174
Miami Dolphins
 1972 AFC championship win, 181
 Nixon attends game, 27
 Nixon on, 182
 Super Bowl VII, 182–184
 undefeated season of, 182, 183
Miami Herald, 142–143, 144
Miami News, 27
Michigan, Wolverines football team, University of, 32, 207
Millan, Felix, 17
Miller, Marvin
 death of, 217
 1972 players strike and, 149–150
Mills, Wilbur, 33, 36
Milwaukee Bucks, 110
Milwaukee Journal, 79
Milwaukee Lakers, 115
Milwaukee Sentinel, 79

Minnesota Timberwolves, 110
Mississippi, Rebels football team, University of, 32
Mitchell, Bobby, 41
Mizell, Wilmer, 185
Mollenhoff, Clark, 26–27
Monday Night Football, 132, 140
Montgomery, Bill, 37, 39, 40
Moody, Orville, 13, 23–24, 34
Mooney, John, 33, 34
Moorhead, William, 185, 188, 189
Mullins, David, 35
Murphy, George
  death of, 218
Murray, Jim, 186, 205
Musial, Stan, 17, 153

Namath, Joe, 27
Nation, 95
National Baseball Hall of Fame and Museum, 9, 71, 162, 186, 204, 212, 217, 218
National Basketball Association, 20, 110, 115
  merger with American Basketball Association, 122
National Collegiate Athletic Association, administrative dispute with AAU, 194–198
National Football League, antitrust action against, 171–174
National League, 115, 190–191
Nebraska, Cornhuskers football team, University of, 90–95
Nelson, Lindsey, 124
  death of, 217–218
  interview of Nixon, 70–71
Newcombe, Don, 165
New Haven Journal-Courier, 145
New York Giants (baseball team), 166
New York Giants (football team), 27, 140, 146, 215
New York Knicks, 110
Newman, Wallace "Chief," 26, 133
  and Nixon, 95
Newsom, Bobo, 162
  Nixon on, 159
Newsweek, 142
New York Mets, 22–23
  Nixon phone call to locker room after World Series victory, 23–24
New York Post, 167, 168
New York Times, 7, 8, 17, 20, 53, 65, 95, 121, 131, 145, 160, 163, 171, 175, 191
  distorted reporting on Nixon-Shula conversation, 142, 143
  reporting on football in the South, 31, 38
New York Times editorials
  against Title IX, 155
  favoring Olympic reform, 193
  on NFL television broadcasting, 173
New York Yankees, 7, 8, 9, 81, 117, 153, 160
Nicholas, Bill, 57
Nixon, Edward, 159
Nixon, Julie. *See* Eisenhower, Julie
Nixon, Richard
  Allen, George, fabricates story that Nixon designed play for the Redskins and, 141–142
  and Apollo 11 astronauts, 21
  and baseball, 8–10
    1969 All-Star Game, 18–20
    1970 All-Star Game, 68–73
    White House reception, 14–21
  on baseball, 6, 14, 15–16
  and basketball, 109–110
  and bowling, 12, 126–127
  and Clemente, Roberto
    Nixon comments about playing abilities, 184
    Nixon comments on death of, 185, 186–187
    Nixon honors, 186–189

Nixon, Richard, *continued*
conversations with
Aaron, Henry, 203
Allen, George, 139, 141, 142, 180–181
Gilda, William, 112
Landry, Tom, 146
Shula, Don, 142, 183–184
crowd reactions to his presence, 7, 11, 27, 30, 37, 41–43, 66–67, 68–70, 72–73, 78, 81, 82, 84–86, 130–131, 201, 204
Dean, Jay "Dizzy," Nixon comments on death of, 204–205
death of, 221
distorted press coverage of, 142–145
Education Amendments Act, comments on, 156
and elections
1970 midterm, 79–90
1972 presidential, 148–176
Flood v. Kuhn, Nixon on, 151–152, 153
on football, 6, 30, 49–51, 89, 133–134
and golf, 12–13
historic baseball all-star team, 151–164
judicial nominations of, 55–57
impeachment articles against, 205–206
and Kentucky Derby trip, 10–12
Killebrew, Harmon, Nixon on, 159
letter to
Burman, 141
Staubach, Roger, 146
and media coverage of, 41–43, 53, 142–143
Miami Dolphins, Nixon on, 182
and Munich Olympics
terrorist attack, response to, 174–175
US-USSR basketball game, reaction to, 175–176
and National Football League, antitrust action against, 171–174
and Nebraska, University of, trip, 90–95
and "new Federalism" program, 69
on Newsom, Bobo, 159
at 1969 Texas-Arkansas football game, 36–43
Oklahoma State University, Nixon commencement address at, 204
and Olympics, 60–61, 175, 195
and Munich Olympics, reaction to US-USSR basketball game, 175–176
and phone calls after big wins, 23–24
and Professional Football Hall of Fame visit, 130–135
resignation of, 206
retirement of, 221
and rhetoric
conciliatory, 90–95
confrontational, 78, 85, 87
and Robinson, Jackie, 166–170
second term of, 180–207
sport, on importance of, 14, 15–16, 30, 49–51, 89, 126–127, 133–134
and sports, media coverage of, 11–12, 17–21, 38–39, 40–41, 43, 69–71, 72–74, 79, 81, 132–133, 138, 160–164
and Super Bowl VI, 142–147
and Super Bowl VII, 182, 183, 184
and table tennis, 14
and Washington Redskins, 136–141
and Washington Senators, 56–57, 112–113, 118
and water sports, 14
Williams, Ted, Nixon on, 153
and Yastrzemski, Carl, meeting, 113–114
North Vietnam, Easter offensive of, 148–149
Notre Dame, Fighting Irish football team, University of, 48, 49, 51, 77
Nunn, Louie B., 10, 11, 68, 69
death of, 218

Oakland Athletics, 10, 16, 119, 123–124, 170. *See also* Philadelphia Athletics
Oakland Raiders, Nixon attends game, 27
Ohio State University, Buckeyes football team, 29, 31–32, 44–45, 47, 48, 90, 95, 179, 215–216
  and Nixon, 82–83, 89
Oklahoma State University, Nixon commencement address at, 204
"Ole Miss," 32
Olsen, Merlin, 165
Olympics
  Berlin Summer Games (1936), 158
  Denver Winter Games (1976), 57, 58, 60, 62, 63, 66
    Colorado voters reject, 176–178
  International Olympic Committee, 174
    and bidding process by host cities, 57–66
    and bribing of members by Nixon administration, 63–64
  Lake Placid Winter Games (1932), 179
  Lake Placid Winter Games (1980)
    Nixon administration support for bid, 178–179
  Los Angeles hosting bids, 57–66, 179
  Munich Summer Games (1972)
    terrorist incident, 174–175
    US results at, 192–193
    US-USSR basketball game, 175–176
  Squaw Valley Winter Games (1960), 57
  United States Olympic Committee
    administrative reorganization of, 193–200
Omaha World-Herald, 203
O'Malley, Walter, 115
O'Neill, Thomas "Tip," 146
Orange Bowl, 27, 46, 47, 48, 51, 90, 94
Orange County Register (Santa Anna, CA), 26
Oriard, Michael, 50
Owens, Steve, 36

Paige, Satchel, 162
Palmer, Arnold, 165
Palmer, Jim, 70
Pan Am (Pan American World Airways), 62
Parmet, Herbert, 25–26
Pastore, John, 173
Paterno, Joe, 25, 49, 91
  career of, 218
  death of, 218
  on 1969 national title, 44–47, 51–52
Payson, Joan, 23
Percy, Charles, 11
Pershing, General of the Armies John J., 138
Peschel, Randy, 40
Philadelphia Athletics, 16. *See also* Oakland Athletics
Philadelphia Daily News, 164
Philadelphia Eagles, 139
Pickle, J. J. "Jake," 36
Pittsburgh Pirates, 124–125, 139, 184, 186–187
Pittsburgh Post-Gazette, 161, 187
Pitzer, Master Sergeant Daniel, 113
Ploetz, Greg, 41
Pompidou, George, 140
Povich, Shirley
  death of, 218
  on Lombardi, Vince, 4
  on 1970 All-Star Game, 70–72
  on Nixon attending Washington Redskins game, 29–30
  on Nixon play design for Miami Dolphins, 143, 145
  on Nixon play design for Washington Redskins, 141
  on Nixon visit to Washington Redskins' practice session, 139

Povich, Shirley, *continued*
on Super Bowl VI, 146
and Washington Senators' relocation, 117
on Washington Senators, relocation of, 122–123, 139
on Williams, Ted, 21–22
Price, Robert, 36
Purdue University, Boilermakers football team, 29

Ramos, Pedro, 112
Reeves, Dan, 143
Renfro, Mel, 146–147
Reston, James, 143
Rhodes, John, 206
Richardson, Elliot, 62, 190
Rigby, Cathy, 165
Robert F. Kennedy Memorial Stadium, 7, 9, 18–19, 57, 115, 119, 136
Roberts, Robin, reaction to Nixon's historic all-star team, 161
Robinson, Frank, 72
Robinson, Jackie, 153
death of, 170
and 1960 election, 165, 167–168
Nixon on, 153, 160, 170
playing career at UCLA, 158
reaction to Nixon's historic all-star team, 161–162
relationship with Nixon, 165–170
Robustell, Andy, 133
Rockefeller, Nelson A., 169
Rockefeller, Winthrop, 32, 36, 43
Rogers, William, 139
Rolfe, Robert, 162
Rood, Rodney, 57–60
Roosevelt, Theodore, 50, 163
Rose, Pete, 71–72, 158
Rose Bowl, 50, 82, 83, 85, 89, 179
Roush, Ed, 71
Rowan, Dan, 182
Rowan & Martin's Laugh-In, 182
Royal, Darrell, 33, 40, 41, 43, 44, 47, 49, 51, 52
career of, 218
death of, 219
Rozelle, Pete, 20, 131, 187
rejects compromise with Nixon administration on television broadcasting, 172–174
Ruth, Claire M., 17, 166
Ruth, George Herman "Babe," 15, 166, 203

Salt Lake Tribune, 33, 34
San Diego, legal action to keep Padres in San Diego, 191
San Diego Padres
move to Washington, 190–191
Nixon supports relocation of, 190
remain in San Diego, 191
San Diego Union, 191
San Francisco Examiner, 160
San Francisco 49ers, 140–141
Sayers, Gale, 13, 26, 166
Schenkel, Chris, 38, 42, 50
Schultz, George P., 13
Schweiker, Richard, 189
Scott, Hugh, 189, 206
Seaver, Tom, 70
Shafter, Raymond, 44, 46, 48, 51
death of, 219
Sherrod, Blackie, 144
Short, Bob, 8, 55, 56, 136
death of, 219
US Senate race of, 219
and Washington Senators
management of, 5, 111–113
relocation to Texas, 115–121
Williams, Ted, on, 4–5
Shula, Don
career of, 219
conversations with Nixon, 142, 183–184
distortions of, 142–145

Nixon on, 181
Super Bowl VII, 182–184
Sidey, Hugh, 128
Siegel, Morris, 17–18
Sirica, John, 202, 203
Sloan, Hugh, 77
Small, Melvin, 28
Smith, C. A., 123, 190
Smith, Preston, 33, 143–144
Smith, Red, 95, 121, 163
Smith, Ronald A., 50
Smith College, 66
Snead, Sam, 13
Sonnenfeldt, Helmut, 59–60
Southern California, Trojans football team, University of, 50, 47, 77, 128, 204
Nixon on awesomeness of, 179
Spong, William, Jr., 116, 122
Sport, 156
Sporting News, 20–21, 149, 161, 163
Sports Illustrated, 15, 32, 199
analysis of 1969 baseball season, 20
criticism of Nixon's 1972 all-star list, 162
Stanford University, 154
Stanford Indians football team, 83, 85, 89
Stargell, Willie, 125
Starr, Bart, 78–82, 219
Staubach, Roger, Nixon letter to, 146
Steinmark, Freddie, 43–44
Stengel, Casey, 18, 19
Stewart, Jackie, 126
Stewart, Terry, 42
St. Louis Cardinals (baseball team), 17, 124, 152, 204
St. Louis Cardinals (football team), 184
Stram, Hank, 55
Street, James, 37, 39, 40
Stuart, Charles, 60–65
death of, 219
Sun (Baltimore, MD), 160
Super Bowl IV, 55
Super Bowl VI , 145–146
Super Bowl VII, 182–184

table tennis, 14
Taft, Robert, Jr., 69, 72, 73, 102, 135
Taft, William Howard, 149
Tagge, Jerry, 94
Talmadge, Herman, 202
Tarkenton, Fran, 165
Teague, Olin, 121
Teamsters Union, 111
Tennessee, Volunteers football team, University of, 31–32, 77, 218
Texas, Longhorns football team, University of
awesomeness of, 32, 269
and 1969 Arkansas game, 32–52
Texas Rangers, 136
Thompson, Bobby, 166
Timmons, William, 197–199
Title IX, 154–156
Tittle, Y. A., 133
Tournament of Roses Association, 57
Trevino, Lee, 127
Truman, Harry, 163
Tunney, John, 87
introduces legislation on Olympic administrative reform, 197
on Washington Senators' departure, 122
TWA (Trans World Airlines), 62

Unitas, Johnny, 165
United States Olympic Committee, 57
reform of organizational structure, 192–200
United States v. Nixon, 203, 205

Vandergriff, Tom, 119–122
death of, 219

Vanderhoof, John, 177
Van Natta, Don, Jr., 13
Vaughan, Arky, 159, 162
Vietnam War, 114
  antiwar protests against, 28–29
Vinson, Carl
  aircraft carrier named after, 202, 220
  death of, 220
  Nixon attends ninetieth birthday party of, 201–202

Wall Street Journal, 151, 182
Walt Disney World, 201
Warfield, Paul, 145, 146–147
  retirement of, 220
Warren, Earl, 150
Washington, Martha, 18
Washington, Walter E., 109, 121, 123
Washington Post, 4, 5, 7, 8, 22, 29, 39, 72, 109, 111, 112, 116, 117, 121, 138, 141, 181
  distorted reporting on Nixon-Shula conversation, 143
  editorial cartoons, 143
Washington Post Company, 117
Washington Post editorials on
  death of Vince Lombardi, 76
  Nixon visit to Nebraska, 94
  Nixon visit to Washington Redskins' practice, 139
Washington Redskins, 79, 111
  booed at home, 136
  and Lombardi, Vince, 4, 28
  1971 playoff loss, 140–141
  1972 NFC championship victory, 180–181
  Nixon and Brito, Gene, 131–132
  Nixon attends game, 29–30
  Nixon visits practice session, 136–139
    impact of visit, 139–140
  players endorse McGovern, 166
  and Williams, Edward Bennett, 26–29
Washington Senators, 55, 131–132, 138, 157
  in 1969 season, 7–9, 14, 21–22
  relocation to Minnesota (first franchise), 111
  relocation to Texas (second franchise), 111–123
Watergate crisis, 52
  break in, 151
Weaver, Earl, 69, 125
Webb, Del, 117
Wechsler, James, 168
White House tapes, 14, 118, 192, 199, 202, 203, 205
  "smoking gun" tape, 153
Whitman College football team, 135–136
Whittier College, 26, 129, 184
Whittlesey, Merrell, 119
Wichita State University, 87–88
Wicker, Tom, 7, 8–9
Wilkinson, Charles, 30, 31, 34, 35, 43, 44, 77, 194
  on ABA-NBA rivalry, 110
  Nixon offers chair of Olympic commission, 197
  Olympic policy and, 59, 200
Wilkinson, Jay, 44
Williams, Dick, 124
Williams, Edward Bennett
  death of, 220
  and Nixon, 26–27, 111, 171
Williams, Ted, 18, 115
  death of, 221
  and Flood, Curt, 112
  Kuhn, Bowie, on, 7
  impact of, 22
  named manager of the year, 22
  and Nixon, 9
  on Nixon, 20, 161
  Nixon on, 19–20, 153, 159
  retirement of, 220
  Washington Post editorial on, 7
  and Washington Senators, 4–5, 7, 8, 112
Wills, Maury, 127, 160

Wilson, Hack, 162
Wilson, Woodrow, 18
Wooden, John, 110, 193
Woods, Rose Mary, 190
World Series
  1963, 159
  1969, 23
  1971, 124–125
  1972, 166, 170
Worster, Steve, 40
Wright, Jim, 36

X, Malcom, 168

Yankee Stadium, 159
Yastrzemski, Carl, 72
  and Nixon meeting, 73, 113–114
Yepremian, Garo, 183
Yorty, Sam, 66

Zad, Martie, 117
Zaidan, Abe, 144–145
Ziegler, Ron, 46–47, 127, 187, 188, 201
  death of, 221
  Nixon and bowling, 127
  Nixon and table tennis, 14
  Nixon and the California Angels, 121
  Nixon and the 1969 collegiate football national title dispute, 46–47, 51
  Nixon and the 1971 Washington Redskins, 139
  Nixon and the 1971 World Series, 124
  on presidential all-star team project, 158, 159
  research for Nixon's historic all-star team and, 156–157
  and "Saturday Night Massacre," 201
  and Washington Senators' relocation, 118